I0084182

John Maclean

History of the College of New Jersey

Vol. 1

John Maclean

History of the College of New Jersey
Vol. 1

ISBN/EAN: 9783337338794

Printed in Europe, USA, Canada, Australia, Japan

Cover: Foto ©ninafisch / pixelio.de

More available books at **www.hansebooks.com**

HISTORY

OF THE

COLLEGE OF NEW JERSEY,

FROM ITS ORIGIN IN 1746 TO THE COMMENCEMENT OF 1854.

BY

JOHN MACLEAN,
TENTH PRESIDENT OF THE COLLEGE.

VOLUME I.

PHILADELPHIA:
J. B. LIPPINCOTT & CO.
1877.

Entered, according to Act of Congress, in the year 1877, by

JOHN MACLEAN,

In the Office of the Librarian of Congress at Washington.

TO

JAMES LENOX, Esquire, LL.D.,

WHOSE MUNIFICENCE TO THE COLLEGE

DURING THE AUTHOR'S ADMINISTRATION

GIVES HIM A CLAIM TO THE GRATITUDE

OF ALL ITS FRIENDS,

THIS HISTORY OF THE COLLEGE OF NEW JERSEY

IS MOST RESPECTFULLY

DEDICATED.

PREFACE.

THE plan of this work will be seen at once by a glance at the table of contents.

In his letter to the Trustees resigning the office of President, the writer mentioned that it was his purpose to devote a portion of his time to the collecting of *materials* for a history of the College. Accordingly, the earlier portions of his manuscripts were labelled "materials for a history." But, learning that his former colleagues, and also the friends of the College generally, looked to him to set in order and to publish, as well as to collect, the requisite facts for a history of the institution, he determined to do what he could in this direction; and the following volumes are the result.

This statement will account, in a measure, for whatever lack there may be of a proper grouping of the incidents given in the narratives of the different administrations.

Several important matters, which at the first he intended to introduce into this work, have been omitted, for the reason that they have already been given to the public,—viz., sketches of the two literary societies of the College, and brief notices of the more distinguished graduates. The Histories of the Societies, by Professors Giger and Cameron, and the work of the Rev. Dr. Samuel D. Alexander, entitled "Princeton College during the Eighteenth Century," have happily relieved the writer from any obligation to attempt what these gentlemen have done so well; and it is earnestly hoped that Dr. Alexander's work may be so enlarged as to include at least the graduates of the first half of the *nineteenth* century.

In this work the writer has had in view two classes of readers: one being those friends of the College who wish to have a general

5

knowledge of the institution,—viz., of its origin, its design, its methods of instruction, and its success ; and the other consisting of those who desire to know more fully the various measures adopted from time to time to attain the ends sought; and a knowledge of which may be of special use to those whose duty it is to watch over the institution, and to whom a detail, to some extent, of the various doings of the Trustees and of the Faculty in times past may be of assistance in determining their own course of action. To many of the graduates, too, it may be a matter of interest to have an authentic account of the views and plans of the Trustees in different periods of the history of the College ; and for them numerous extracts are given from the Minutes of the Board and from other documents.

To meet these different views, the writer has adopted the plan of having the work printed with two different sets of type, in the smaller of which most of the extracts from minutes and public records will be printed. The rest of the work will be in larger type, and of itself will form a narrative suited to the class of readers first spoken of.

Another object aimed at in giving the official statements is to secure their preservation in case the volumes containing them should be lost or destroyed.

The citations from the College records are in some cases followed by an expression of the writer's own views in reference to the matters therein mentioned.

Had the writer's health permitted it, he would have devoted some time to a thorough revision of this work, omitting some parts and rewriting others, in the hope of thereby making the entire work more acceptable to the reader; but, his age and health forbidding this, it must go to the press as it is. He is not, however, without hope that, whatever may be its defects, he has clearly shown that it was the design of the founders of the College, and of their successors in office, to make the institution one devoted to the upbuilding of the Redeemer's kingdom, by promoting the advancement of piety and learning in happy union.

For reasons which will readily occur to the mind of the reader, this history is brought down only to the date of the writer's inauguration as President. It would give him sincere pleasure to bring into *full view* the valuable services rendered by all his colleagues, and especially by those associated with him in the instruction and government of the institution from the beginning of his presidency to its close; but the limit which he has assigned himself prevents this from being done. Doubtless some other annalist of the College will give such a record of the labors of those who contributed so greatly to its success from 1854 to 1868, during which period the number of undergraduates increased from two hundred and forty-seven to three hundred and fourteen, as was the case in 1860–61 ; and although these numbers, in consequence of the civil war, were reduced in 1861–2 to about two hundred and twenty, yet in 1868, the last year of the writer's connection with the College, they again reached two hundred and sixty-four, with a fair prospect of a still larger increase in the course of the ensuing year,—the number of *new* students for the College year of 1867–68 being one hundred and eleven, of whom one hundred and five entered College the first term of that year.

At different periods in the history of the College the curriculum has varied more or less, and greater prominence was given to one class of studies than to another; and in the period just referred to, the course of study, religious and secular, was considerably enlarged, and the requirements for admission to the first degree in the Arts kept pace with the progress of learning. With the exception of the French and German languages, the study of which was optional, all the branches of knowledge taught in the College were made parts of the regular course, which every student was required to pursue.

Of the condition of the College finances during the same period, viz., from 1854 to 1868, while the subject is yet fresh in his mind, the writer deems it due to some of his friends to say in this connection a few words.

Within the time here mentioned, and the year preceding, viz., the last year of Dr. Carnahan's administration, after paying all the ordinary and contingent expenses of the College, and those incurred in the rebuilding of Nassau Hall in 1855–56, *the actual increase* in the *funds* vested in *bonds, mortgages,* and *public*

securities, and mainly through the efforts of Professors Hope and
Atwater, was *not less* than two hundred and forty thousand
dollars. Of this sum, one hundred and fifteen thousand dollars were contributed for professorships, over fifty-five thousand
dollars for scholarships, about sixty-four thousand dollars for
general purposes, and six thousand dollars for prizes.

From a gift and a bequest by the late Dr. John N. Woodhull,
of Princeton, to found a professorship, the College became the
owner of all his houses and lots adjacent to the College grounds,
and extending on William Street from the road or path west
of Dickinson Hall to Washington Street, with the exception of
a small house and lot purchased by the College a year or two
before, and on Washington Street from the corner of William
and Washington Streets to Nassau, on the main street of Princeton, the corner house and lot on Nassau Street included; the
estimated value at that time being twenty thousand dollars.
Since then this property has greatly increased in value.

The house and lot on William Street, mentioned as having
been purchased by the College, cost between one and two
thousand dollars.

This increase in the real estate and in the other permanent
funds of the College is exclusive of the first ten thousand dollars given in 1865 by General N. N. Halsted for the erection of
the Astronomical Observatory, which was completed by him in
1872, at an expense of fifty thousand dollars; exclusive, too, of
the sum of five thousand five hundred dollars expended by the
College in the purchase of the site on which the Observatory
stands,—of which sum three thousand dollars were a bequest
by the Rev. Dr. C. Van Rensselaer towards the establishment of
an Observatory; exclusive also of the sixteen thousand dollars
given in 1866 by John C. Green, Esq., for the purchase of the
lots on which " Dickinson Hall" was built by him three or four
years after; and of the further gift of one hundred thousand
dollars in the spring of 1868 by the same gentleman. It is
also exclusive of the thirty-eight thousand dollars, over and
above the twelve thousand dollars insurance, expended in the
rebuilding and enlarging of " Nassau Hall" in 1855–56; of
which sum eighteen thousand dollars were gifts and twenty

thousand dollars the excess of the receipts above the ordinary expenses of the College from 1854 to 1860. The aggregate of the above sums is four hundred and thirty thousand dollars, of which more than four hundred thousand dollars were gifts or bequests. Besides the above, there were three bequests amounting to sixteen thousand dollars, which have been paid since 1868; and another bequest of thirty thousand dollars, a *vested legacy* (to found a professorship), not yet due, but the payment of which was made sure by the donor.

It was the intention of the donors that these several bequests should be made parts of a permanent endowment; and if they be added to the above they will make the increase in this class of funds from July, 1853, to July, 1868, not less than four hundred and seventy-six thousand dollars.

During this period the President's house and a house occupied by one of the Professors were also enlarged and improved, at an expense of several thousand dollars, which without any impropriety might have been added to the above amount. And within the same time two other friends of the College in their respective wills made provision for the endowment by each of them of a professorship, which at a future day will doubtless be established and the original bequests enlarged. In addition to the sums above mentioned as contributed to the *permanent* funds, nine thousand dollars were given towards the *current* expenses of the College, viz., five thousand dollars, in ten semi-annual instalments of five hundred dollars each, to aid in establishing a professorship of Mental and Moral Philosophy, fifteen hundred dollars for the professorship of Geology and Physical Geography, and twenty-five hundred dollars to meet a deficiency in the income of the College consequent on losses during the first year of the late civil war. Several thousand dollars were also given to an association formed for the purpose of aiding indigent and worthy young men, without respect to the particular professions to which they proposed to devote themselves. This fund has already rendered valuable assistance to as many as thirty students of the College.

To what extent the College was indebted to its then Treasurer, the late Governor Charles S. Olden, for the above-mentioned gifts of the late John C. Green, Esq., will appear from the following correspondence, begun on the 4th of August, 1866, very nearly two years before the end of the writer's administration. This difference of dates will account for one or two *seeming* discrepancies between the writer's statement and that of the Governor's in regard to the College finances.

Governor Olden's letter to Mr. Green:

"PRINCETON, August 4, 1866.

"JOHN C. GREEN, ESQ.:

"DEAR SIR,—In the age in which we live, whatever has a tendency to improve agriculture and manufactures and advance useful science is attracting the attention of the best men of the civilized world. The urgent necessity of thoroughly educating a large portion of the youth in those branches termed 'Applied Science' is apparent. This necessity has led to the establishment of many private schools and academies in which these subjects receive special attention, and it has led to the organization by most of the principal colleges of the country of departments in which these subjects are thoroughly taught. Several of the prominent colleges of New England have recently established such departments, and where already in existence they have been greatly enlarged. The college at Easton, Pennsylvania, has by the contributions of the citizens of that State organized a department of 'Applied Science.' So also has Rutgers College, at New Brunswick, in this State. And a college is started at Allentown [Bethlehem], Pennsylvania, through the munificence of Judge Packer, to be under Episcopal influence, in which these are to be prominently taught. This gives those institutions advantages over the College of New Jersey, and has already drawn away some of her students and deterred others from coming. The Faculty realizing this, and unwilling this time-honored institution should lose the position (so long occupied) among the foremost in the United States, drew a paper which was laid before the Trustees, setting forth what they thought should be taught in the department of 'Applied Science,' and what was needed to carry it into effect. A copy of this is enclosed herewith, and I have noted on it some changes that could, I think, be advantageously made.

"Your brother, the Chancellor, is one of the oldest and most influential Trustees, and always manifested great interest in the College. His attention had been for some time directed to this subject, and in conversation with him about a year ago he told me that on a recent visit to Princeton he had looked at the land owned by the College, with the view of ascertaining whether there was any eligible site for a building suitable for a scientific department. I gave him some information about lands adjoining the College property, which induced him to ask me to furnish him with some maps, etc., and ascertain the price for which the land referred to could be obtained, in order that he might fully understand the matter. Some time after, I did so, and told him that I had obtained a refusal of the property until the first of January next (now last). His official business was at this time very engrossing, and I forbore saying anything further to him on the subject until the expiration of the time for which I had the refusal of the property, when he informed me that he had not had leisure to give the subject the attention he desired, but would do so ere long. With some difficulty I got the time extended (for which I had the refusal) one month; but before I saw him again he was taken sick, and I have not since thought it proper to call his attention to it, as he had more requiring his supervision than the state of his health warranted. In our first conversation he intimated, as I understood him, that he believed you felt interested in Princeton College, and possibly, if satisfied that decided good could be effected, this subject might be considered by you favorably. I am emboldened by this allusion to you to lay this matter before you; and I have no doubt that, if known to him, my doing so would meet his approval. I send you herewith a copy of the map furnished the Chancellor, giving a sketch of the property now owned by the College, and of that which it is desirable to obtain in order to carry out the plan of a scientific department properly,—also the prices at which I had the refusal of the several parcels making up the plot.

"You are aware that the College of New Jersey is among the

oldest institutions of the kind in the United States, two only
(or at most three) being older, and yet it has had less outside
assistance by far than any of the other prominent ones. It has
struggled along, relying on its own resources almost entirely,
until within a few years, when several friends have come to its
aid.   In 1844, when I became particularly acquainted with its
financial condition, it had a charitable fund of about twelve
thousand dollars, and all the other funds belonging to it, after
paying its debts, did not exceed one hundred dollars.   Its
finances improved somewhat between this time and 1855, when
the main building of the College was burned.   It was insured
for twelve thousand dollars; about eighteen thousand were
contributed by sundry persons towards rebuilding it, and the
balance of the fifty thousand dollars which it cost to erect it
was supplied by the savings of the business of the College the
previous and the succeeding five years, during which its affairs
were quite prosperous.*

"A short time before this event, an effort had been commenced
to raise a sum by establishing scholarships, of one thousand
dollars each, to aid in educating destitute young men intended
for the ministry, and, in some cases, others.   This effort was
continued through several years, and was quite successful,
realizing over fifty thousand dollars.

"In the year 1862 it became apparent that the loss of the
Southern students in consequence of the rebellion, and the increased cost of living, required an increase of the Professors'
salaries; and, as the College could not get on with the means
then at command, an effort was in consequence made to secure what was termed an 'Endowment Fund.'   Over sixty-five
thousand dollars were subscribed and paid to the College, and
one professorship of thirty thousand dollars and one of thirty-
five thousand dollars were also established.   A professorship
of twenty-five thousand dollars had been formed some years
before by the united contributions of a number of individuals,
and there is a probability that another will be secured ere long.
The whole funds of the College now amount to about two hun-

---

* These six years were the first six years of Dr. Maclean's administration.

dred and forty thousand dollars,* which it is believed is securely invested at an interest averaging seven per cent. per annum. As at present situated, and with a continuance of the number of students in attendance the last three years, the income and the expenses of the College are about equal. There is little or nothing left at the close of each year with which to make improvements or to enlarge the operations of the institution. When the resources of the College are compared with those of other prominent colleges of the country, it is astonishing that it has been able to maintain its established reputation. While Harvard and Yale each have funds amounting to millions of dollars, and colleges of less note quadruple of those of Princeton, it has required all the talent of the Faculty and Trustees of Princeton College to maintain her reputation; and without further aid it will probably be impossible for them to do it much longer. For some reason, after the College of New Jersey was fairly in operation, it appears to have been taken for granted that it needed no further assistance. It received nothing, comparatively, until within a few years, while other colleges have been the recipients of munificent gifts. Other States have made liberal appropriations to their colleges. New Jersey, though solicited, has done nothing in aid of that which for many years was her only one. Individuals appear to have forgotten her altogether. Mr. James Lenox, of New York, is an exception, and had it not been for his liberality the College would have been seriously embarrassed. At a later period other friends of the institution have contributed liberally and made up what is the present fund. The great importance of the College, its influence for good to the country generally and the Presbyterian Church in particular, have not, I think, been duly considered.

*   *   *   *   *   *   *   *   *   *

* This sum does not include the notes of the late Captain Silas Holmes, of New York, amounting to thirty thousand dollars, given by him to found a professorship and five scholarships, the principal payable at the option of the donor, the interest at six *per cent.* payable on the 1st of January and the 1st of July in each year. Captain Holmes died before the date of this letter, and, as the payment of the principal was not *at that time* fully secured by bond and mortgage, Governor Olden did not reckon the notes of Captain Holmes as a part of the vested funds of the College.

"Princeton stands alone as having *for more than a century*
taught nothing in Theology but the purest doctrines, as understood by the Old School branch of the Presbyterian Church,
and, pursuing the same course unwaveringly, is at this time
doing more probably for the cause of sound principles and true
religion than any institution in the land; in evidence of which
it may be stated that two-thirds of all the students in College
during the last session were professors of religion, the greater
portion of whom became such after entering. The opportunity
afforded of making lasting impressions on the minds of youth
at a period when they are most impressible is nowhere more
fully understood or diligently improved than by the President
and Professors of this College. While errorists abound and
are zealous in disseminating heterodoxy over the land, the influence for good of the band of young men yearly passing out
from 'the College of New Jersey' is incalculable. We need
only look over the country and observe what men are giving
direction to public sentiment, to see how mighty the influence
exercised by it. In the pulpit her graduates are unsurpassed
for learning and piety. In the Senate of the United States (the
only men in that body whom no one ventured to approach with
business on the Sabbath were Frelinghuysen and Berrien, both
graduates of Princeton), in Congress, on the bench of the Supreme Court, in the State Courts (all the Chancellors of the
State under the present Constitution were graduates of this
College), and of eminent and influential men, there are more in
proportion to the number of graduates who are from Princeton
than from any other institution in this country. But I will not
enlarge further on the importance of the College. My object
is, principally, to inform you that those best able to judge think
that a department of 'Applied Science' is very much needed
to enable her to keep her standard of instruction equal to that
of other prominent institutions. Knowing that you are a Jer-
seyman, and believing you are interested in all that concerns
our native State, I do not doubt that you sympathize with those
who congratulate themselves on having at least one institution
in New Jersey of which they are proud. Should you feel sufficient interest in the matter to induce you to desire further in-

formation, I will cheerfully give it; or can you not make me a visit, and I could point out the localities and explain everything more fully here than elsewhere? If you should incline to come, let me know a few days before, as I should regret being absent. No one connected with the College knows that I am writing to you, and you can, if you desire it, be entirely private while here.

"Trusting that you will not consider me intrusive in addressing you, I am, very respectfully,

"Yours, etc.,

"CHAS. S. OLDEN."

Copies of two letters of the same date from John C. Green, Esq., to the Hon. Charles S. Olden:

"NEW YORK, December 24, 1870.

"HON. CHARLES S. OLDEN, Princeton, New Jersey:

"MY DEAR SIR,—I have your letter of the 23d instant, accompanying the final accounts of the cost of Dickinson Hall and the grounds pertaining thereto.

"Herewith I hand you my check on the National Bank of Commerce, in New York, payable to your order, for ten thousand and ninety-seven dollars and twenty-nine cents ($10,097.29), which is the balance represented in said accounts to be due to the College of New Jersey.

"It was my intention to leave the provisions of the Elizabeth Endowment absolutely to you and my brother, the Chancellor. I have not the deed at hand, and cannot, therefore, express an intelligent opinion on the point regarding which you ask my 'further directions.' I leave it to your own judgment, and whatever your decision may be I now confirm it.

"This letter is official. I write another of a personal character, which is due to the occasion, but which, for want of time, may not reach you by this mail.

"Very truly yours,

"JNO. C. GREEN."

"NEW YORK, December 24, 1870.

"HON. CHARLES S. OLDEN, Princeton:

"MY DEAR SIR,—I have already acknowledged the receipt of

your letter of the 23d instant, and complied with its business requirements. Now I propose to add what the occasion calls for besides.

"Your letter of August 4, 1866, now lies before me, and has just been reperused. This was the beginning of our correspondence on the subject of the affairs of the College of New Jersey, and the origin of all that I have done for the institution.

"My belief in the fulness of your knowledge, and confidence in your judgment and public spirit, led me to consider your opinions with more than ordinary care, and to examine anew the claims of the College to public aid. My brother Henry was absent in Europe. On his return, consultation with him confirmed my own favorable conclusions, and induced me to enter upon the work which has just been finished. Its subsequent conduct having been intrusted absolutely to my brother and yourself, no cause of anxiety was allowed to remain lest the money bestowed should be extravagantly or unwisely disbursed.

"The first proposed contract, which was not executed, strengthened my conviction that a restraining and controlling power was needed other than that of the official authorities. With the prosecution and completion of the undertaking I am fully satisfied, and beg you, my dear sir, to accept my hearty thanks for your ready acceptance of the trust, and for the fidelity, wisdom, and success with which it has been discharged.

"My pleasure is enhanced by the consideration that a tried and valued friend has crowned a life of honor and usefulness by rendering this (among other important services running through a long course of years) important aid to an eminent institution of learning which confers blessings on the State and the world.

"I remain, my dear sir, very faithfully, your friend,

"JNO. C. GREEN."

In preparing this history, the author has availed himself of all the sources of information within his reach, and, except through some inadvertence, he has not failed to refer to his authorities and to name the authors from whom he had occasion to cite either passages or facts. Among these, and *chiefly*, are:

The College Records.

The Minutes of the Synods of New York and of Philadelphia.

The Diary, in *manuscript*, of President Davies, during his visit to Great Britain in behalf of the College in 1753-4.

An Account of the College, published by order of the Trustees, in 1764.

Memoranda, by Mr. N. F. Randolph, of Princeton, respecting the charters, and the erection of Nassau Hall.

Governor Belcher's Correspondence, in *manuscript*.

Letters of the Rev. Charles Beatty to the Rev. Dr. Treat, of Abington, Pennsylvania, written from Scotland in 1767.

President Witherspoon's Address to the Inhabitants of Jamaica and other West India Islands in behalf of the College, and other papers in the fourth volume of his works, W. W. Woodward publisher.

President Green's Notes respecting the College, his Autobiography, and his Address before the Alumni Association of Nassau Hall.

"History of the College of New Jersey, from 1746 to 1783," by a *graduate* (Rev. Dr. William A. Dod), in 1844.

"Historical Sketch of the College of New Jersey," by Robert Edgar, a student of the College, 1859.

Dr. Samuel D. Alexander's "Princeton College."

Professor Cameron's "History of the American Whig Society."

Professor Giger's "History of the Cliosophic Society."

The "New York Gazette and Mercury."

The "Pennsylvania Gazette."

The "Pennsylvania Chronicle."

"Wood's Gazette," of Newark, New Jersey.

"Newark Daily Advertiser."

"New Jersey State Gazette."

Mr. Samuel Smith's "History of New Jersey."

Hon. William Smith's "History of New York."

Mr. William A. Whitehead's "East Jersey under the Proprietors."

Mr. Whitehead's "Contributions."

"Minutes of the Provincial Council."

Judge Field's "Provincial Courts."

Judge Elmer's "Constitution, etc., of New Jersey."

Dr. Hodge's "History of the Presbyterian Church."

Rev. Richard Webster's "History of the Presbyterian Church."

Dr. A. Alexander's "Log College."

"Transactions of the American Philosophical Society," vol. i.

Dr. Bellamy's Correspondence, in *manuscript*.

Dr. Sprague's "Annals."

President Quincy's "History of Harvard University."

"Life of Mrs. Quincy," by her daughter, Miss Quincy.

Charters and Catalogues of Yale College.

Professor Kingsley's sketches of the history of Yale College.

President Clap's "Defence of the Charter of Yale College," given in the appendix to the "History of the Dartmouth College Case."

President Porter's " Life of Professor Silliman, of Yale College."

" History of the College of William and Mary, of Virginia."

" History of Brown University," by Mr. R. A. Guild, the Librarian.

Judge Bradley's Discourse at the Centennial Anniversary of Rutgers College.

Dr. Stearns's " History of the First Presbyterian Church, Newark, New Jersey."

Dr. Hall's " History of the First Presbyterian Church, Trenton, New Jersey."

Dr. Davidson's " History of the First Presbyterian Church, New Brunswick, New Jersey."

Dr. Hatfield's " History of Elizabeth, New Jersey."

Dr. Gibbon's " Sermon on the Death of President Davies," London.

President Finley's " Sermon on the Death of President Davies."

Dr. Rodgers's " Sermon on the Death of Dr. Witherspoon."

Dr. E. S. Dwight's " Life of President Edwards."

Dr. Beasley's " Life of President S. S. Smith."

" Princeton Review."

" New York Medical Repository."

" The Presbyterian Magazine," of Philadelphia, edited by Dr. C. Van Rensselaer.

" Princeton Magazine," edited by William C. Alexander, LL.D.

Mr. Bancroft's " History of the United States."

Dr. Foote's " Sketches of Virginia" and " Sketches of North Carolina."

" Life of the Rev. Dr. Miller," by his son, the Rev. Samuel Miller, D.D.

" Life of the Rev. Dr. A. Alexander," by his son, the Rev. Dr. James W. Alexander.

" Life of James Madison, Fourth President of the United States," by William C. Rives, of Virginia, United States Senator.

Dr. Franklin's Life and Essays.

Bishop Johns's " Life of Bishop Meade, of Virginia."

Mrs. Lee's Life of her father, George Washington Parke Custis.

Judge Duer's " Life of Lord Stirling."

Dr. Carnahan's " Life of Dr. John Johnston, of Newburgh, New York," and some manuscripts · papers of his, including Dr. Carnahan's Sermon at Colonel Aaron Burr's funeral.

" The Forum and the Bar," by David Paul Brown, Esq.

Dr. Allibone's " Dictionary of Authors."

Dr. Morse's " American Gazetteer."

Messrs. Barber and Howe's " Historical Collections from New Jersey and Virginia."

Frank Moore's " Diary."

The Biographical Dictionaries of the Rev. Drs. Allen, Blake, and Lempriere.

Manuscript letters of Joseph Shippen, a student in the College of New Jersey in 1750–53.

Mr. Parton's account of Rittenhouse's orrery, in the " New York Ledger."

The readers of this history cannot fail to observe that the writer has freely expressed his opinions in reference to various measures adopted from time to time by the authorities of the

College touching its course of instruction and discipline, and with respect to its fiscal affairs. For these opinions he alone is responsible; and yet he cannot but indulge the hope that some of them at least will have the hearty approval of the friends of the College generally.

In collecting his materials the writer had but little aid, with the exception of that given him by one of his friends, who is unwilling that any mention should be made of his services, although to him the writer is more indebted in this matter than to all others. Still, the writer is under obligations to many of his friends for the constant encouragement they have given him to persevere in his arduous work,—how arduous none but those who have faithfully and laboriously engaged in like undertakings can fully appreciate; and it is a pleasure for him to add, that to his distinguished successor in the office of President of the College, Dr. McCosh, the writer is indebted for important suggestions as to the plan of the work, and for the deep interest which he has manifested in its preparation for the press.

To his friend the Rev. Dr. Duffield he is under peculiar obligations for making the requisite arrangements for the publication of this work, all pecuniary interest in which the writer has transferred to the Princeton Charitable Institution, for the aid of indigent and worthy youths engaged in seeking a liberal education.

To the publishers of the work, also, the writer must tender his thanks for the careful and satisfactory manner in which they have performed their part in issuing it from the press.

When he began to gather materials for a history of the College, the writer scarcely dared to hope that he should be spared to complete that undertaking; still, he cheerfully gave himself to it, under the impression that his labors in this line might be of service in the hands of another, in preparing a truthful account of the origin, design, and progress of the College. But in the kind providence of God he has been permitted to go beyond this, and to bring to its close a history of the College of New Jersey from its foundation in 1746 to the annual Commencement of 1854, a period of *one hundred and eight years;*

and it is his fervent prayer that this work may help to keep in perpetual remembrance the design of those truly good and great men who, in laying the foundations of the College, sought to erect an institution for the advancement of piety and sound learning, and one especially devoted to the upbuilding of the kingdom of our Lord and Saviour Jesus Christ.

CONTENTS.

21

CHAPTER X.

HISTORY

OF THE

COLLEGE OF NEW JERSEY.

CHAPTER I.

THE ORIGIN OF THE COLLEGE.

On the occasion of his inauguration as President of the College of New Jersey, on the 28th of June, 1854, the writer of this History gave a brief outline of its origin and design. In this outline the College was represented as "being in fact a continuation of the one over which the pious and learned Jonathan Dickinson presided," and as being established under the auspices of the Synod of New York; which Synod at that time embraced not only the Presbyterian churches in New York, but also the larger part of those in New Jersey.

A more thorough examination has served to confirm the view then taken as to the identity of the College, under the charter given in 1746, by the Honorable John Hamilton, President of his Majesty's Council; and under the one granted two years after, by his Excellency Jonathan Belcher, Esq., his Majesty's Governor of the Province of New Jersey. But the statement as to the Synod was not as exact as it might have been. The credit given to the Synod of New York belongs almost exclusively to certain leading members of that body, one of whom was the pastor of the only Presbyterian church in the city of New York, and the others pastors of Presbyterian churches in East Jersey.

Particular attention is due to both these matters, for the reason that they have been misapprehended by most of those who have undertaken to write or to speak of them. At the time application was first made to the civil authorities of New Jersey for a college charter, the state of things in the Presbyterian Church in this country was a very peculiar one, and the condition of the civil affairs of the Province was also peculiar. In any other circumstances than those which existed at the time the first charter was obtained, and for a few years after, it is hardly probable that a charter, in the name of the King, would have been granted by the Governors and Council of New Jersey for the erection of a college to be under the control of ministers and laymen of the Presbyterian Church. It will therefore not be amiss to recite the facts to which reference is here made, before entering upon a regular chronological detail of the events which properly constitute the history of the College.

The first efforts for the erection of a college in New Jersey have an intimate connection with the first schism in the Presbyterian Church. This schism began in 1741, with the separation of the Presbytery of New Brunswick from the Synod of Philadelphia. It was consummated in 1745, by the withdrawal of the Presbytery of New York from the same Synod, *then the only one;* and by the organization of a new Synod, "under the title of the Synod of New York," in the autumn of that year.

At its formation the Synod of New York consisted of the Presbyteries of New York, New Brunswick, and New Castle. There was another and older Presbytery of the name of New Castle, in the Synod of Philadelphia.

The Presbytery of New York was formed in 1738, by uniting the Presbyteries of Long Island and East Jersey, and the Presbytery of New Brunswick was also formed in 1738, upon the petition of some members of the Presbytery of New York, then just constituted, to be erected into a distinct Presbytery with some members of the Presbytery of Philadelphia. The Presbytery of New Castle, the second of that name, was formed in

1741, and it was composed of members who sympathized with their New Brunswick brethren, and who refused to remain any longer in Presbyteries connected with the Synod of Philadelphia, from which these brethren had been virtually cut off without any respect had to the usual forms of citation and trial. This Presbytery was first known as the Presbytery of Londonderry, but before the Synod of New York was organized it took the name of New Castle.

The schism above mentioned arose not from any different views in reference to the Calvinistic system of doctrine as set forth in the Westminster Confession of Faith, which had been adopted by the entire Synod, but chiefly from conflicting opinions with respect to the requisites for admission to the ministry, and in regard to the countenance which should be given to the religious excitements of that period, which prevailed to a greater or less extent in New England and in the middle Provinces. A majority of the old Synod insisted upon a regular training of candidates in studies usually pursued at colleges or universities, and they were unwilling to license and ordain preachers whose preliminary training had been defective, although they might be sound in the faith and give evidence of fervent piety. The majority also objected earnestly to all intrusion into their congregations, on the part of the revivalists, which some of the New Brunswick ministers and their friends openly advocated and practised.

These differences in opinion and practice were the occasion of many sharp and bitter controversies, which prepared the way for the rending asunder of the entire body.

The ministers and elders who organized the Synod of New York were all of one mind as to the desirableness of religious revivals, and as to the duty of doing all in their power to promote them; but they were not equally prudent in the use of the requisite means for attaining their object, nor were they all agreed as to the evidences of true conversion. As a body the Presbytery of New York was more conservative than the Presbytery of New Brunswick. And *while these two Presbyteries were yet in connection with the Synod of Philadelphia*, the leading men in them evidently differed in opinion as to the provision which should be made for the education of candidates for the holy ministry. The New Brunswick men, several of whom had been trained at the school established by the Rev. William Tennent, Sr., on the southwest bank of the Neshaminy, in Pennsylvania, and who had been greatly blessed of God in their labors as ministers of the gospel, were content with the comparatively meagre instruction in the arts and sciences given at that seminary of learning; and they deemed the different efforts made to establish a school of a higher order as aimed against their foster-mother and school of theology. In this school, now well known under the designation of the "Log College," more account was very properly made of personal piety and religious experience, in candidates for the ministry, than of a complete knowledge of both their preparatory and their professional studies. And it is equally true that at this school the great benefits of mental discipline and of a familiar acquaintance with the several branches of philosophy and of polite learning were not estimated at their full value.

The ministers of the New York Presbytery, most of whom were pastors of churches in East Jersey and residents in that part of the Province, were no less ardent friends of revivals than were their brethren of the Presbytery of New Brunswick. Nor were they less fully persuaded of the unspeakable importance of personal piety as an element of success in preaching the gospel. But they did not approve the course of their New Brunswick brethren in reference to intrusion, and in the matter of licensing candidates. They were also desirous that the best possible provision should be made for the preparatory and professional education of all candidates for the ministry. Before the schism they concurred with their brethren in the Synod of Philadelphia in the project of founding, for this very purpose, a school or seminary of learning. This is evident from the following record in the minutes of that body at their sessions in Philadelphia, May, 1739, six years before the schism of 1745: "An overture for erecting a school or seminary of learning being brought in by the Committee, the Synod *unanimously* approved the design of it; and in order to the accomplishing it did nominate Messrs. Pemberton, Dickinson, Cross, and Anderson, two of which, if they can be prevailed upon, to be sent home to Europe to prosecute this affair with proper directions. And in order to this, it is appointed that the Commission of the Synod, with correspondents from every Presbytery, meet at Philadelphia on the third Wednesday of August next. And if it should be found necessary that Mr. Pemberton should go to Boston, pursuant to this design, it is ordered that the Presbytery of New York supply his pulpit during his absence."

Messrs. Pemberton and Dickinson were members of the New York Presbytery, they were leading men in that body, they were present at the meeting of the Synod, they were members of the Committee which brought the overture before the Synod, they had the respect and confidence of all their brethren, both of the Old Side and of the New, as the two principal parties in the Synod of Philadelphia were then called. Had they not been in favor of the proposed measure, they would not have been the first persons named to take so active a part in carrying it into effect. Mr. Pemberton was a native of Boston, well known and highly esteemed by the ministers and people there, and perhaps the most influential person the Synod could have selected to solicit aid in that city.

This statement of the different views entertained by the leading men in the Presbyteries of New York and New Brunswick is confirmed by what is said in a letter, of May 30, 1746, addressed by the Synod of Philadelphia to President Clap, of Yale College, and which has reference to a proposed arrangement by which candidates for the ministry at the school established by the Synod of Philadelphia at New London, Pennsylvania, in 1744, might have certain privileges granted to them by Yale College. The writers of it say, "And by his [Mr. Whitefield's] interest, Mr. Gilbert Tennent grew hardy enough to tell our Synod that he would oppose their design of getting assistance to erect a college, wherever we should make application, and would maintain young men at his father's school in opposition to us."

This must have occurred at the meeting of the Synod of Philadelphia in 1739, and the language here attributed to Mr. Tennent was most probably used by him before the *above-*

mentioned overture was submitted to the Synod; for it appears
from the minutes of 1739, that, on *the morning* of the day on
which the design of the overture was approved in the afternoon,
the Rev. Gilbert Tennent protested in behalf of himself and of
such as would join with him, viz., William Tennent, Sr., William
Tennent, Jr., Samuel Blair, Eleazar Wales, Charles Tennent, *ministers*, Thomas Worthington, David Chambers, William McCrea,
John Weir, *elders*, against the act respecting the trial of candidates. This act required all candidates who had not studied at
a college or university to be examined by a committee of Synod
before being received under the care of any Presbytery and
placed on trial for license to preach the gospel. In the debate
on this subject it is highly probable that Mr. Tennent gave
utterance to his feelings in no very measured terms, under the
deep conviction that the resolution then under consideration
was aimed against his father's school and was designed to prevent his "training gracious men for the ministry." Words to
this effect are also given in the Synod's letter to President Clap
as having been uttered by Mr. Tennent in connection with his
protest. It is not likely, therefore, had Mr. Tennent and his
friends been present when the Synod expressed its approval of
the design of the overture respecting the erection of a school
to be under the care of the Synod, that they would have even
acquiesced in a resolution approving that design. If, upon
presenting their protest against the act in regard to candidates,
they retired and took no further part in the proceedings of the
Synod, which were then drawing to a close, and which were
closed that very day, we can readily understand how it was
that the design of the overture was *unanimously* approved, as
stated in the record.

No member of the New York Presbytery united with Mr.
Tennent and his friends in their protest at this meeting, or in
the one presented by them the following year, when the Synod
reaffirmed their act respecting the examination of candidates
by a committee of the Synod.

The plan of sending two of their number to Europe to
solicit funds to aid in the establishing of a school, was given
up by the Synod of Philadelphia; and the reason for giving it

up may be learned from the following minute of the date of May 29, 1740: "The Commission of Synod did meet last year according to appointment, in order to conclude upon a method for prosecuting the overture respecting the erecting a seminary of learning. The minutes of that proceeding were read, and although herein it is found·that they concluded upon calling the whole Synod together as necessary in that affair, yet the war breaking out between England and Spain, the calling of the Synod was omitted, and the whole affair was laid aside for that time." The war here spoken of would have rendered a voyage to England far more hazardous to those selected to go abroad, or, as the phrase then was, to go home, in ·order to solicit funds for their projected school; and the difficulty of obtaining the requisite aid would have been greatly increased. The entire scheme was not again resumed.

Next year the contentions in the Synod began to come to a head. The meeting was small. No one from the Presbytery of New York was present. The members of the Old Side party were in a majority; and they availed themselves of the opportunity to protest against the members of the New Brunswick Presbytery being permitted " to sit and vote as members of the Synod." The reasons for this remarkable protest can be seen in full on pages 155–158 of the printed minutes. It is sufficient for our purpose to know that the protest led at once to the separation of the New Brunswick Presbytery from the Synod. Sincere and earnest efforts to effect a reconciliation were made the following year by the Presbytery of New York, and were continued until May, 1745, but all to no purpose.

Failing to bring the two parties to such an understanding as would enable them to come to an amicable adjustment, the Presbytery of New York deemed it their duty to withdraw, and to take measures for the formation of another and separate Synod. Both these they did; not because they approved the conduct of their New Brunswick brethren in the matters alleged against them, but solely on the ground that these brethren had been irregularly cut off from the Synod, and denied their rights as members of that body. They believed them to be sincere and faithful servants of Christ, and men owned and blessed of

God in their labors; yet they were not blind to their defects. And before they united with them in a new Synod, all concerned entered into an engagement to abstain from denunciations of their brethren from whom they differed in opinion, from all divisive courses, and to retire peaceably from the new Synod if they could not conscientiously submit to its decisions and orders; terms which would have readily secured their speedy restoration to the old Synod, had they been of a mind to offer or to accept them.

This state of things prevented all further *united* action to secure the erection of a college or seminary of learning. Three of the Presbyteries in connection with the Synod of Philadelphia made provision for establishing a school or academy as early as November, 1743, which in May, 1744, was taken under the care of the Synod. The plan of the school was a very liberal one. It had a succession of able teachers,* and it rendered good service to the cause of religion and learning. But in the unsettled state of affairs then existing, the Presbytery of New York, consisting almost wholly of ministers and churches in East Jersey, although still in connection with the Synod of Philadelphia, could take no part in fostering this institution. It was yet uncertain whether the Presbytery itself could continue its relations to the Synod; and until this matter was de-

---

* The first teacher of this school was the Rev. Francis Allison, pastor of the Presbyterian church in New London, Pennsylvania. He continued to have charge of the school until his removal from New London to Philadelphia, in 1752, at which time he became the principal of a grammar-school in that city. This Philadelphia school was, in 1755, erected into a college, of which Mr. Allison was made viceprovost. The erection of this college and Mr. Allison's connection with it seemed to do away the necessity of a school, of the rank of a college, under the supervision of the Synod; and the Synod's school continued to be only a preparatory school of a high order. As principal of the Synod's school, Mr. Allison was succeeded by his assistant-teacher, the Rev. Alexander McDowell. In 1754 the Rev. Matthew Wilson was appointed teacher of languages, and Mr. McDowell continued to give instruction in logic, mathematics, and in natural and moral philosophy. This school was finally removed to Newark, Delaware, and received a charter from the Proprietaries, under the name of the Newark Academy.

In 1756, Mr. Allison received from Nassau Hall the degree of Master of Arts, and from the University of Glasgow the degree of Doctor in Divinity, and he is said to have been the first Presbyterian minister in this country upon whom this degree was ever conferred.

termined, it was inexpedient to give their countenance and aid
to the Synod's school, or to undertake to erect one to be under
their own control, either virtually or directly. It is therefore
almost certain that nothing was done by the Presbytery of New
York, or by any of the leading members of that body, towards
the erection of a college or seminary of learning, until 1745,
when the Presbytery separated itself from the Synod, and
thereby consummated the first great schism in the Presbyterian
Church. It is not improbable, however, that, before this took
place, Mr. Dickinson, in order to meet present emergencies,
established a private school at Elizabethtown, according to a
commonly received tradition to this effect. It is known that
he instructed certain candidates for the ministry in their theological studies. About this time, also, Mr. Burr had a classical
school at Newark.

After the schism, Messrs. Dickinson, Pierson, Pemberton,
Burr, and others of the Presbytery of New York, unable to
unite with the Synod of Philadelphia in sustaining their school,
not satisfied with the limited course of instruction given at the
Neshaminy school, and having become more or less alienated
from the colleges of New England, turned their thoughts to
the erecting of a college, in which ample provision should be
made for the intellectual and religious culture of youth desirous to obtain a liberal education, and more especially for
the thorough training of such as were candidates for the holy
ministry. That they might the more effectually accomplish
their purpose, they sought to obtain a charter for the erection
of a college in New Jersey. In this undertaking they had no
assistance from either Synod; and most probably at that time
they neither sought nor desired it. The Synod of Philadelphia
were interested in the success of their own school; the Presbytery of New Brunswick in that of the Neshaminy school.
The venerable founder of this school, the Rev. Wm. Tennent,
Sr., was still living when measures were taken to obtain the desired charter. His sons and his pupils were the leading men
in the Presbyteries of New Brunswick and New Castle. His
eldest son, the Rev. Gilbert Tennent, in his famous Nottingham
sermon, had openly expressed his preference for *private* schools

or seminaries, under the care of skilful and experienced Christians (see Dr. Hodge's " History of the Presbyterian Church,"
vol. ii. page 154), "as the most likely method to stock the
Church with a faithful ministry." The Rev. Samuel Blair, one
of the most distinguished scholars and ablest men trained at
the Log College, had established at his residence in Fagg's
Manor, Pennsylvania, and within the limits of the New Castle
Presbytery, a classical and theological school, at which President Davies and other prominent ministers* of the gospel were
prepared for their work. Had there been no rupture of the old
Synod, there is every probability that there would have been
a hearty co-operation on the part of the Presbytery of New
York with the Synod of Philadelphia in the establishment and
endowment of a synodical school. And after the schism, had
the Log College ceased to exist before the formation of the
Synod of New York, it is morally certain that the Synod, as
soon as it was organized, would have promptly given their
countenance to the plan of erecting a college, to be under the
supervision and control of ministers and laymen whose church
relations were with their own body. This is almost evident
from the fact that, two years after, upon an application for another charter with greater privileges, the former friends of the
Neshaminy school became the earnest and devoted friends of
the College of New Jersey. But at the juncture just mentioned it so happened, in the good providence of God, that the
work of initiating the measures for the erection of a college
and for obtaining a charter devolved almost exclusively upon
the leading ministers and laymen of the Presbytery of New
York, most of whom resided in East Jersey, and were men of
high standing in the community and held in great respect for
their wisdom, learning, and piety. In the whole Synod there
were no men so likely to find favor in the sight of the Governor and of his Council, and to obtain from them a compliance
with their petition.

Lewis Morris was Governor of New Jersey during the whole
of the excitement that led to the rupture of the Presbyterian
Church, and he was Governor when the first application was

---

* Dr. John Rodgers, Dr. Robert Smith.

made for a college charter. His son Robert Hunter Morris was the Chief Justice of the Province during the whole of his administration, and for many years after. Both of them must have been more or less familiar with the divisions or parties in the Presbyterian Church; and, although having no particular regard for any one of these parties, it is more than probable that they had a special dislike to the one most nearly allied in views, feelings, and style of preaching to Whitefield and his admirers. This was the party of the Tennents, Blairs, Rowland, Finley, and others of kindred spirit, who were members of the Synod, but not of the Presbytery, of New York.

In 1741 an attempt was made to indict and convict the Rev. John Rowland for horse-stealing, he having been mistaken for a remarkable adventurer of the name of Bell. Robert Hunter Morris presided at the trial, and it is reported that with great severity he charged the grand jury to find a bill against Mr. Rowland. After two refusals and as many reproofs, they complied with the instructions given to them, and found the required bill. Whereupon Mr. Rowland was regularly tried; but he was also acquitted.

The witnesses for the defence were the Rev. William Tennent, Jr., and Messrs. Joshua Anderson and Benjamin Stevens. By the testimony of one or more of these witnesses the fact was fully established that Mr. Rowland was in another Province, and not in New Jersey, on the very day on which the theft was committed. At the same term of the court, for an incorrect statement made by Anderson in reference to another party while giving his testimony in this case, he was, by order of the court, indicted for perjury. It is most probable that the mistake made by him was due to failure of memory, the matter having reference to the time and place when and where he saw this other party.

At a subsequent term of the court, Messrs. Tennent and Stevens were also charged with perjury; and bills were found against them. Mr. Tennent was tried and acquitted. Mr. Stevens was not tried. It is probable that a *nolle prosequi* was entered by the Attorney-General, in view of the evidence adduced in Mr. Tennent's case.

Neither Mr. Rowland nor Mr. Tennent owed anything to the favor or the indulgence of the court, which would have had them both convicted if it had been possible. They were both associated in the public mind with the most active and earnest of the revival preachers; and this whole class of ministers were objects of dislike to such men as Chief-Justice Morris and his father, Governor Morris.

In an application at this time for a college charter, it would have been very indiscreet for any of this class of persons to unite in the petition, even had they been warmly in favor of the project. Their taking part in the matter would have surely resulted in a denial of the request. But, for the reasons which have been given above, they were not disposed at this time to take any part in promoting this enterprise, and the leading men in the Presbytery of New York were left by their brethren in the other Presbyteries to pursue their plan without aid or interference.

The petition for a college charter was refused by Governor Morris, but on what grounds is not certainly known. It may have been that he doubted his authority to grant such a charter as was asked of him, or, having no doubt as to his power, he may have deemed it altogether inexpedient to clothe a body of Dissenters, as he regarded the petitioners, with the power and privileges sought to be attained by a charter for a college to be under the exclusive control of Presbyterian ministers and laymen, however discreet and liberal-minded the petitioners themselves might be. Governor Morris was Chief Justice of New York when a charter was refused once and again, by the Council of that Province, to the First Presbyterian Church in the city of New York, on the ground that there was no precedent for granting corporate privileges to a body of Dissenters. The sole object of the church in seeking to obtain a charter was to secure their property more firmly, which was then held in trust by certain individual members of the congregation.

At the time of their second application, Governor Burnet was Governor of New York as well as of New Jersey, and the Presbyterians in New York City had hope, from the well-known liberal views of his father, Bishop Burnet, and from his

own professions of liberality, that he would have given them
his countenance and aid; but he did not. Upon a second refusal, both the petitioners and the Council requested that the
petition might be sent to the Lords of Trade and Plantations,
in London, for their decision. But the Governor did not send
it until the 16th of May, 1724, nearly four years after he was
requested to do so. Richard West, Attorney-General for Ireland and Solicitor-General to the Board of Trade, and a brother-
in-law of Governor Burnet, to whom the petition was referred,
gave it as his opinion that in the general and abstract view of
the thing there was nothing in the request unreasonable or improper. Yet no charter was obtained until after the American
Revolution, when one was granted by the State of New York.
Perhaps one reason why the Board of Trade did not instruct
Governor Burnet and his Council to give the charter in question was, that Mr. West died in December of that year,—1724,
—and the matter was lost sight of. Whether Governor Morris,
who must have been familiar with the proceedings in this case,
was influenced by this refusal of the New York Council to in-
corporate a body of Dissenters cannot now be known; but that
he refused to grant a charter for a college in New Jersey appears from a statement in the supplement to the " Weekly
Mercury and New York Gazette" of Monday, the 28th of July,
1755. That such an application was made and refused is confirmed by the fact that there was no denial as to this point in the
reply to the supplement, which reply was evidently written by one
familiar with the history of the efforts made to obtain a charter,
and most probably by a Trustee of the College. Had Governor
Morris lived, or had he been succeeded by one of like spirit, no
charter given in the name of the King could have been obtained
by the petitioners from the Governor and Council of New Jersey. And from the time that the eastern and western divisions
of New Jersey were united, in 1702, under the exclusive jurisdiction of the Crown, until the death of Governor Morris, in
1746, there was probably no period when a royal charter could
have been obtained for the erection of a school or college by
a body of Presbyterian ministers and laymen, or by any class
of religionists, whether Churchmen or Dissenters. We might

possibly except from this period the years from 1736 to 1738, when John Anderson and John Hamilton were acting Governors, at the end of which time Lewis Morris received his commission as Governor.

From the accession of Cornbury, in 1702, to that of Morris, in 1738, the Province of New Jersey may to some extent be viewed as an appendage of New York, the Governor of New York being also Governor of New Jersey. The Governors during this period were Lord Cornbury, Lord Lovelace, Robert Hunter, Wm. Burnet, John Montgomerie, and Wm. Cosby. Upon the death of Lord Lovelace, Richard Ingoldsby, the Lieutenant-Governor, had charge of the government for nearly a year. Upon his removal, Wm. Pinhorne, as senior Councillor, for a very short time was at the head of affairs in New Jersey. Upon Governor Hunter's return to England, Lewis Morris, as President of the Council, acted as Governor, and a second time, upon the death of Governor Montgomerie. John Anderson, President of the Council, acted as Governor for a few weeks, upon the death of Governor Cosby; and John Hamilton, upon the death of Anderson. The jurisdiction of the acting Governors here named was limited to New Jersey.

In virtue of the concessions of Carteret and Berkeley, the first Lords Proprietors of New Jersey, to the settlers of this Province, there seem to have been a greater freedom in matters of religion and learning in New Jersey than in New York, and less frequent attempts on the part of the Governors to enforce the instructions given them by the Home Government. These instructions required the Governors of the several Provinces "to give all countenance and encouragements to the exercise of the ecclesiastical jurisdiction of the Bishop of London, as far as conveniently might be done in their respective Provinces;" and particularly directed that "no schoolmaster be hereafter permitted to come from this kingdom, and to keep school within this our said Province, without the license of the Bishop of London; and that no other person now here, or who shall come from other parts, shall be admitted to keep school without your license first obtained." "There is reason," says Wm. Smith, the historian of New York, "to think that this instruction has

been continued from the [English] Revolution to the present
time to the Governors of the Provinces."

Bent upon exercising all the power given to him, and ever
ready to go beyond the spirit of his instructions, Cornbury, in
administering the affairs of New York, " insisted that neither
ministers nor the schoolmasters of the Dutch," the most numerous persons in the Province, " had a right to preach or instruct
within his gubernatorial rule" (see Wm. Smith's " History of
New York," page 172), and this, notwithstanding by the terms
of surrender the Dutch were not to be molested or interfered
with in matters of religion,—the eighth article of the terms
being in these words : " The Dutch shall enjoy their liberty of
conscience in Divine worship and Dutch discipline." (See
Samuel Smith's " History of New Jersey," page 44.)

An avowed friend and supporter of the Church of England,
he was an enemy to all classes of ministers who faithfully and
boldly preached the truth, and who refused to submit to his
arbitrary orders. Attached to the Church, not because it was
the Church of God, but because it was the Church of England
established by law, he imprisoned a truly excellent and devoted
missionary of that Church, the Rev. Thorowgood Moore, for
denouncing certain well-known and indecorous practices of his
Excellency the Governor, and for refusing to administer the
communion to Lieutenant-Governor Ingoldsby on account of
his debauchery and profaneness. These two worthies, the Governor and the Lieutenant-Governor, " par nobile fratrum," had
him arrested in New Jersey and brought to Amboy; and there,
contrary to law, he was forced by their order into a barge,
taken to New York, and committed to the custody of a guard
at the fort. After a confinement of three weeks, he escaped, and,
in company with the Rev. John Brooks, another minister of
the Church of England, a man of kindred spirit, and who had
reason to apprehend like treatment (see S. Smith's " History
of New Jersey," page 333), he went to Marblehead, Massachusetts, where they took passage for England, intending to make
known to the authorities there the situation of affairs here.
Unhappily, the vessel was lost at sea, and all on board perished.
The Rev. Mr. Talbot, a well-known minister of the English

Church, said of these good men, that they were "the most pious and industrious missionaries the Honorable Society ever sent over." (See Hatfield's "History of Elizabethtown.")

Another instance of Lord Cornbury's tyranny is seen in his treatment of the Rev. Francis Makemie and the Rev. John Hampton, two Presbyterian ministers, who, on their way to Boston from their homes on the Eastern Shores of Maryland and Virginia, stopped in New York, and there preached without his Lordship's license, one in a private house in the city, and the other on Long Island. He caused them to be arrested and brought before him, and ordered them to be confined. Mr. Makemie was indicted and tried; and when acquitted by the jury, he was required by the court to pay the costs of trial. In a letter dated October 14, 1706, to the Board of Trade, his Lordship gives his account of the matter, and confirms what is here said of his treatment of these men : he excuses his treatment of them on the ground that they were strolling preachers, and disposed to bid defiance to the government. Mr. Makemie was a native of Ireland, and the first Presbyterian minister ever settled in America as a pastor.

In the very first year that Cornbury entered upon the administration of affairs in New York, he and certain of his officials were guilty of great oppression and gross cruelty, in seizing and imprisoning Samuel Bownas, a preacher of the Society of Friends, for preaching at a private house in Hempstead, Long Island, and speaking in disparaging terms of the Church of England, in relation to the sacrament of baptism. He was confined in a room which two years before had been protested against as an unlawful prison. His friends were denied admittance; and, that he might be chargeable to no man, he learned to make shoes, and earned his food. The grand jury refusing to find a bill against him, he was released, having been in prison nearly a whole year. This act of seizing and imprisoning Bownas is said to have been done by Cornbury at the instigation of two men who had been Quakers, but who had renounced their faith and had turned Churchmen. One of these was the Rev. George Keith, who was a zealous advocate of the Church of England, and a bitter opponent of all non-conformists.

These are a few of the things which made Cornbury so odious to the people in both Provinces, and which contributed to his downfall. His successors in office were men of higher and nobler aims; and yet some of these found it expedient not to bring upon themselves the hostility of the more earnest partisans of the Church of England.

Lord Lovelace, the immediate successor of Cornbury, was greatly respected for his upright administration of affairs, which, however, in consequence of his decease, was of short duration. Had he, or any of his successors, ventured to grant an act of incorporation to the members of any dissenting body, it might and probably would have been a ground of complaint against them, that they had disregarded their instructions. As it was, Governor Hunter, one of the most liberal-minded and popular of these Governors, was complained of for his lack of zeal in behalf of the Church. Against this charge he found it necessary to defend himself; and his friend Lewis Morris, then Chief Justice of New York, united with him in defending his official conduct. To show that he was not unmindful of his duty, Governor Hunter furnished to the Government officials in England evidence of his zeal in behalf of the Church in both the Provinces of which he was Governor; and in the following terms he made a solemn protestation of his devotion "to the true interests of our Holy Mother, in whose communion, ever since I was capable of sober thoughts, I have lived, and, by the blessing of God, I am resolved to die." (See Whitehead's "Contributions," etc., page 153.) At the same time the Governor did not hesitate to speak his mind very freely in regard to some of his clerical opponents. Under the date of October 10, 1711, writing to the Board of Trade, he says, "It is reported that the Bishop of London has appointed Rev. Mr. Vesey as his commissary for New York. Governor Hunter hopes that Mr. Talbot will be appointed his Lordship's commissary for New Jersey, and Mr. Phillips for Pennsylvania: *though I know no good they have ever done, I know no great harm they can do at present.*" (See Whitehead's "Contributions.")

Governor Burnet, the immediate successor of Governor Hunter, interpreted his instructions as giving him authority to

judge of the qualifications of ministers, even of those licensed
by the Bishop of London, and complaint was made against him
for his conduct in this matter, as appears from a letter addressed
to him by his brother-in-law, Richard West, Solicitor-General
of the Board of Trade, who, in writing to the Governor in
regard to the complaint of the Bishop of London, that clergymen licensed by him were subjected by the Governor to a
second examination, says, " Your method is to present him a
text, and give him. a Bible, then lock him up in a room by
himself, and then in case he does not produce, in a given time,
a satisfactory sermon, you refuse to license him. The consequence is that the man must starve. I have seen many complaints against Governors, and no one was surprised. You are
surely the first who ever brought himself into difficulties by
an inordinate care of souls." (See Whitehead's " Contributions.")

It can hardly be supposed that a Governor who was so
watchful of the spiritual instruction given to the members of
his quasi established Church would be anxious to aid in building up churches of other denominations, either by granting
them corporate privileges, or by giving them charters for the
erection of schools and colleges. Aware, no doubt, of the
difficulties of his predecessor arising from his liberal treatment
of non-conformists in the matter of civil appointments, he was
not disposed to bring upon himself the like charge of being
neglectful of his duty to the Church, or of being too indulgent
to Dissenters. And this will account for his conduct in the
matter of a charter for the First Presbyterian Church of New
York, of which mention has been made above.

Of the views and feelings of Governors Montgomerie and
Cosby in regard to the granting of charters upon the petition
of Dissenters, nothing particular is known; and there is no
reason to believe, from anything that is recorded of their respective administrations, that in the matter named they would
have pursued a different course from that marked out by their
predecessors in office.

On the 20th of April, 1730, while Mr. Montgomerie was
Governor of New York and New Jersey, there was passed at
St. James an Order of Council, approving the instructions sent

to all the Governors in America (except of the Leeward Islands, New England, North and South Carolina), directing them to "support the Bishop of London and his commissaries in the exercise of such ecclesiastical jurisdiction as is granted to them." And this included the licensing of schoolmasters as well as of preachers.

During the administration of Governor Cosby occurred the famous trial of John Peter Zenger, printer of the " New York Journal," for a libel against the English Government and the Governor of New York. The trial involved the question whether or no there was freedom for the press in the Province of New York. There was intense feeling on the subject; and for denying the competency of the court to take cognizance of the case, Messrs. Alexander and William Smith, the two most eminent lawyers of New York, who had offered to defend Zenger, were excluded from further practice in the Supreme Court, and their names were stricken from the roll of attorneys; nor were they restored until after the death of Cosby, in 1736. Andrew Hamilton,* a famous lawyer from Philadelphia, and rendered still more famous by his efforts and success in this trial, engaged in the defence, and obtained a verdict for his client, by which it was established that the jury are to decide not only that a paper alleged to be seditious was published by the party accused, but also whether it is of a libellous or seditious character. It is mentioned as a remark of the late Gouverneur Morris, that "the trial of Zenger, in 1735, was the germ of American freedom."† Governor Cosby was evidently no friend to freedom of speech and of the press, and most probably no patron of learning.

Richard Ingoldsby, the Lieutenant-Governor under Cornbury, and who, before the arrival of Lord Lovelace, administered the affairs of the Province, was a man of like views and spirit with Cornbury. Lewis Morris, in virtue of his office as President of its Council, was twice *acting* Governor of New Jersey, —first from the summer of 1719 to the summer of 1720, and

---

* A different person and of a different family from Governor Andrew Hamilton.
† The Forum of Philadelphia, by David Paul Brown.

again from July 1, 1731, upon the death of Governor Montgomerie, to the arrival of Governor Cosby, in 1732. Governor
Cosby dying upon the 10th of March, 1736, John Anderson,
President of the Council for New Jersey, administered the government of this Province until his own death, which occurred
between two and three weeks after he became the acting Governor. He was admitted to the Council by Governor Hunter,
who, in his report of the matter to the Board of Trade, apolo-
gized for displacing an unworthy Churchman and substituting
in his room a worthy Dissenter. He was "a gentleman of the
strictest honor and integrity, justly valued and lamented by all
his acquaintance." He was a brother of the Rev. James Anderson, pastor of the First Presbyterian Church in the city of New
York. He was succeeded by John Hamilton, the next senior
Councillor, who discharged the duties of the Governor until
the accession of Lewis Morris as Governor, in 1738. As early
as 1699, Morris was made President of the Council by Governor Andrew Hamilton; and, with a few short intermissions,
he was a member of the Council until he was appointed Governor. He was active and influential in bringing about the
surrender of the Proprietary Governments in East and West
Jersey, and for this service he was named at that time by the
Lords of Trade for the post of Governor; but Viscount Cornbury, son of the second Earl of Clarendon, and a cousin of
Queen Anne, received the commission. Morris was twice suspended from the Council by Cornbury, on account of his strenuous opposition to his Lordship's administration. But in whatever else they disagreed, they were both professedly earnest
supporters of the Church of England. It is related of Morris
that he made the suggestion "that the Venerable Society for
Propagating the Gospel in Foreign Parts should see to it that
only Churchmen should be sent as Governors of the Colonies;
and that no person should be competent to receive a considerable benefice in England who had not performed three years
of missionary service in America." (See Webster's " History,"
page 81.) His zeal for Episcopacy must, however, have greatly
abated before his death, for in his last Will and Testament, a
remarkable document, these words occur: "I forbid . . . any

man to be paid for preaching a funeral sermon over me. Those who survive me will commend or blame my conduct in life as they think fit, and I am not for paying any man for doing either; but if any man, whether Churchman or Dissenter, in or not in priest's orders, is inclined to say anything on that occasion, he may, if my executors see fit to admit him to do it."

In view of these passages, it can occasion no surprise that he refused to give a charter to an institution to be erected and controlled by a body of Presbyterians, with a special reference to the training of young men for the holy ministry.

But whatever were his errors or feelings, it is due to him to say, that in the course of his long public career of more than fifty years, and embracing within its limits the entire period from the formation of the first Presbytery to the schism of 1745, he rendered several very important services to New Jersey, and indirectly to the interests of religion, learning, and civil liberty. He probably did more than any other one man towards effecting the overthrow of the Proprietary Government in the eastern and western divisions of the Province, and the consequent union of these two divisions under the sole jurisdiction of the Crown. He was also instrumental in securing for New Jersey a Governor separate from the Governor of New York. The first of these measures contributed greatly to the prosperity of the whole Province; and without it the College of New Jersey, in all probability, would never have been established upon its present basis. There might have been an East Jersey College, but not a College of New Jersey. And had the Colonial governments of New York and New Jersey continued under one head, there is reason to believe, as has already been said, that no corporate privileges would have been granted to any body of Dissenters, as all persons who were not of the Church of England were then wont to be called. And in this matter the friends of that Church were in all probability no more unreasonable than the Dissenters themselves would have been, had their respective conditions been reversed. It was reserved for those not connected with established churches to be liberal-minded, and regardful of the rights of others.

In a matter of controversy between the Presbyterians and

Episcopalians of Jamaica, brought before him when he was Chief Justice of New York, he did not permit his preference for the Church of England to influence his decisions, but acted the part of an independent and upright judge.

Another thing for which Governor Morris is to be greatly commended was his earnest opposition to the tyrannical measures of Governor Cornbury;—also for his persistent and successful efforts to have his Lordship removed from an office for which he was utterly unfit.

Governor Morris died in May, 1746, and upon his death the government again devolved upon John Hamilton, Esq., President of the Council. He was the son of Andrew Hamilton, Governor of East and of West Jersey, under the Proprietors, from 1692 to 1702, and for some years also Deputy-Governor of Pennsylvania. Andrew Hamilton was a native of Scotland, and removed with his family to this country in 1686. Both father and son were intelligent and liberal-minded men, and popular Governors. The first and for many years the only laws for the establishing and supporting of public schools in East Jersey were passed while Andrew Hamilton was Governor of the Province. For some years before the surrender of the government he was Postmaster-General for the Provinces of New Jersey and Pennsylvania. (See "East Jersey under the Proprietary Governments," page 229.)

When, in 1746, John Hamilton assumed a second time the administration of affairs, as President of the Council and Commander-in-Chief, the petitioners for a college charter renewed their request, and prepared the form of a charter which they desired to have granted to them. It was granted, and thus the way was prepared for laying the foundations of the College of New Jersey.

It is worthy of notice that this is the first college charter ever granted in this country by a Governor, or acting Governor, with simply the consent of his Council. That of Harvard was granted by the General Court of Massachusetts Bay, with the consent of the Governor; that of Yale, by the General Assembly of Connecticut; that of William and Mary, by their Majesties of those names.

The first Legislative Assembly ever convened in America was that of Virginia, in 1619, and the first attempt to establish a college in this country was made by this Assembly. And although nothing resulted from their action, for the erection and support of a college, it is nevertheless highly creditable to their discernment and good sense, that the members of this body should have directed their attention to a matter of this kind at the very beginning of their legislative career, and almost at the very foundation of their colony.

Mr. Hamilton was the first Governor who ventured to act in a matter of this kind without previously obtaining either the consent of the Provincial Legislature or the special permission of his Majesty's Home Government. Governor Belcher followed the example set him by Mr. Hamilton, and at a later period Governor Franklin did the same, in granting to sundry ministers and laymen of the Dutch Reformed Church a charter for Queen's College, now Rutgers. Governor Bernard, the successor of Governor Belcher, and afterwards Governor of Massachusetts, claimed the right, as the representative of the King, to grant charters for schools and colleges without any action on the part of the Assembly or of the General Court; and a charter for the erection of a college, or collegiate school, in Hampshire County, Massachusetts, was actually prepared and signed by him: but in consequence of an earnest remonstrance from the Overseers of Harvard the Governor did not issue the charter. His right to grant such a charter was questioned by the Overseers, although in their representations to the Governor they did not press this point. Some few at least were of the opinion, and in private gave utterance to it, that, in the charter given to the Province itself, the King had relinquished his own right to interfere in such matters. (See President Quincy's "History of Harvard," vol. ii. pp. 477–479.)

In 1754, Lieutenant-Governor De Lancey, then administering the government of New York, with the consent of the Council, gave to King's College a charter, which was afterwards confirmed by a vote of the Assembly of that Province. This approval by the Assembly was probably obtained by the Trustees of the College in consequence of the objections made to its establishment under a charter given by the acting Governor, in the name of the King, and in order to remove all doubts as to the validity of the charter to which these objections may have given rise.

The Proprietaries of Pennsylvania and Delaware claimed and exercised the right to grant charters for academies and colleges.

The prerogative of the King in this matter was sedulously maintained; and it was never in any case *openly* called into question: but there was no little diversity of opinion as to the respective rights of Governors and of Assemblies in reference to the granting of charters.

Joseph Dudley, who was Governor of Massachusetts from 1703 to 1715, has been highly commended, and very justly, for his boldness in consenting to a resolution to revive the charter given to Harvard in 1650 by the General Court of that Province, and "thus establishing a charter without, and contrary to, the will of the British sovereign," and that after the consent of the Crown had been withheld from several successive charters granted by the provincial authorities between the years 1692 and 1701. The resolution referred to was passed by the Council and by the House of Representatives in December, 1707, and it is believed that it was suggested as well as officially approved by him. (See President Quincy's "History," pages 159-161.)

John Hamilton, the acting Governor of New Jersey in 1746, should be held in no less honor, at least by the College of New Jersey, for his wise and liberal treatment of the founders of this College, in granting to them a charter with ample privileges, and that too in the absence of all precedent in matters of this kind, and with the full knowledge of the fact that his predecessor in office had refused to give them such a charter. His liberality is the more conspicuous from the fact that the petitioners for the charter were Presbyterians, and that he himself was a Churchman.

Just at this time there were in the condition of the civil affairs of the Province several things very favorable to the success of those who were anxious to obtain a charter for their projected institution:

1. The acting Governor was a man of enlightened views, and

friendly to the interests of religion and learning; a member of the Episcopal Church, but not unmindful of the rights of those who were members of other Christian churches.

2. Several members of the Council were Presbyterians: for instance, John Reading, the next senior Councillor to President Hamilton, and his immediate successor as President of the Council; James Hude, a native of Scotland, and the son of a Presbyterian elder who emigrated to this country to escape persecution in his own; and Thomas Leonard, of Princeton. Andrew Johnston, another member of the Council, was an Episcopalian, a gentleman of liberal views, and cordially in favor of the proposed scheme for the erecting of a college. His father, Dr. Johnston, was bail for the Rev. Francis Makemie when he was arrested, imprisoned, and prosecuted by order of Lord Cornbury. Dr. Johnston was a native of Scotland, and came to America in 1685. His son Andrew was born in 1694. These four gentlemen, Messrs. Reading, Hude, Leonard, and Johnston, were all named as Trustees of the College in the second charter given, in 1748, by Governor Belcher. James Alexander, Esq., a native of Scotland, and an eminent lawyer in New York, was also a member of the Council, and, from a liberal gift made by him to the College a few years after, there is good reason to believe that he too was favorable to the wishes of the petitioners.

3. In East Jersey, where most of the petitioners for a college charter resided, the people were divided into two parties, which were known as the Scotch and the English. This distinction had existed for a long time. In a letter of the date of June 16, 1703, addressed to the Lords of Trade by Colonel Quarry, who held at one time the position of a member of Council in five different Provinces, and who was Judge of the Admiralty Court in New York and also in Pennsylvania, the writer says, "The contest in West Jersey was always between the Quakers and those who were not Quakers; in East Jersey between the Scotch and the English,—the Scotch for many years had the advantage of having a Scotch Governor, Colonel [Andrew] Hamilton." The Presbyterian churches in this country all adopted the Doctrine and the Discipline of the Church of Scot-

land; and the Presbyterian Church in New York City was known as the Scotch Church. This in a measure may account for the interest taken in the plan for a Presbyterian college, both by President Hamilton and Mr. Johnston. They doubtless thought that in this land the adherents of the Church of Scotland were entitled to equal favors and privileges with the adherents of the Church of England. And in the case of President Hamilton, the fact that the partisans of the English faction had for a time deprived his father of his office as Governor, on the ground that he was a Scotchman and not an Englishman, and the refusal to grant the Scotch Church in New York their petition for a charter, no doubt rendered him all the more disposed to grant to Presbyterians those privileges for which they could rightfully ask, and which he could lawfully bestow.*

4. The relations between Governor Morris, who had refused to give the sought-for college charter, and President Hamilton, who did give it, were not of the most pleasant kind. Upon his return from England, and before he received his commission as Governor, Morris demanded of Hamilton that he should surrender to him the seals of the Province, which Hamilton refused to do, on the ground that Morris had forfeited his right to administer the government by his absence from the country; and in this Hamilton was sustained by the Home Government. A year or two after, when Morris received his Majesty's commission, he declared it to be his purpose to regard all previous difficulties as bygones; and yet he claimed from Hamilton all the moneys which Hamilton had received for discharging the duties of Governor, on the ground that he, and not Hamilton, was the legal President of the Council during that time. Moreover, although Mr. Hamilton was the second Judge of the Supreme Court of the Province, Governor Morris made his

---

* Another instance of this national feeling is to be seen in the conduct of Lieutenant-Governor Gooch, of Virginia. Sundry gentlemen were brought before him, in 1742, for attending unauthorized religious meetings. As soon as he learned that they held to the doctrinal views and the system of church order set forth in the Westminster Confession of Faith, he said that these gentlemen " were Presbyterians according to the Kirk of Scotland, and could not be molested."

son, Robert Hunter Morris, Chief Justice, who, as compared with Mr. Hamilton, was a mere youth; and the letter of Governor Morris to the Board of Trade, which informed the Board that he had made his own son Chief Justice, also made mention of Mr. Hamilton's resignation as Judge.

In an attack made in 1755 upon the petitioners for the College charter, which passed the seal of the Province in 1746 attested by President Hamilton, it is asserted that he was incompetent, from age and infirmity, to discharge properly the duties of Governor, and that the petitioners availed themselves of his infirm health to obtain from him a charter, which, had he been in the full possession of his faculties, he would never have granted. The paper containing this assault affords evidence that the information of the writer was probably derived, either directly or indirectly, from Chief-Justice R. H. Morris. That this gentleman was no friend to the College appears from an expression in a letter of Governor Belcher's, of the date of January 8, 1749–50, to Mr. Walley, of London, in which the Governor, alluding to the Chief Justice, speaks of "the malevolence of a young gentleman, lately gone from New Jersey, towards the Province and the College."

The statement made by the writer of the paper to which reference is here made is as follows (taken from the supplement to the "New York Mercury" of July 28, 1755, No. 155):

"I have been curious enough to inquire what methods were taken to obtain this charter, and, by the best information I can get, was told that it was done in a public manner, by petition, and passed the seal in same legal manner that other grants of the King do. The reasons of my being so particular in my inquiries of this kind were, that I would endeavor to compare the legality of one grant with the legality of another of the same nature. What I mean is, the grant of the charter of the College of New Jersey. There the Presbyterians, Independents, and the New Lights, for I speak of them as one body, and they are all of a kidney, I am told made their application to the late Governor Morris for a charter. He told them that he could not grant such a charter. He soon after dying, the Government devolved upon the Honorable John Hamilton, Esq., whose age and infirmity had rendered him unequal to the task. This they thought the proper time to get what they wanted; accordingly they applied again, and a draft of the charter was laid before Mr. Hamilton in Council; and the petitioners were ordered to lay a draft of it before the Chief Justice of the Province for his opinion, whether it was legal to grant it or not; but they, well convinced of the illegality of it before the

Chief Justice had time to give his opinion, prepared an engrossed draft on parchment, and got the Governor (by the help of some about him), whom they had properly prepared on the occasion, to pass the charter, at a time when he was unable to read, and scarcely able to sign his name.

" Now, as I am no lawyer, I would beg leave to ask, whether an instance can be found in the law books that a petition to his Majesty for any grant or charter, and that petition referred to the Attorney- or Solicitor-General, or to the Judges, for their opinion, whether he ought to grant the prayer or petition, any grant or charter was ever granted by the King before such opinion was given. I have been informed that some of those gentlemen (whose cunning and deceit equal the society founded by Loyola), because the Judge did not give his opinion, that the charter laid before them was legal, for that reason when he afterward went to England, they represented him there as an Atheist,—a man of no religion; for the great misfortune of most of these people is, that a man has no religion, in their opinion, if he be not possessed of as much cant, hypocrisy, and enthusiasm as themselves. Yet this College has a Presbyterian or Independent President [Mr. Burr], and is a most excellent institution, under the sole inspection and direction of the ' Watch-Tower'; and because that of New York [King's College, now Columbia] is not under their sole direction, it is a most scandalous, pitiful, paltry institution."

The " Watch-Tower" is the title of a series of papers published in the " New York Gazette" in 1754 and 1755. The entire series was edited, and many, if not the greater part, of the articles were written, by Wm. Livingston, Esq., an eminent lawyer of New York, and subsequently Governor of New Jersey, being the first Governor after the Declaration of Independence. The preface to No. XL. of the " Watch-Tower" is avowedly written by the editor; but the paper itself professes to be a letter from a gentleman in the country to his friend in the city, and it contains a reply to some of the statements in the supplement cited above : it is as follows :

" Sir,—The reflections that have been frequently cast on the College of New Jersey by the enemies of the ' Watch-Tower' are so perfectly groundless, and appear so evidently the effects of envy and impotent malice, that I have ever thought them unworthy of the least notice, and I should with the same neglect have treated the spiteful performance which appeared in the Supplement of the ' Mercury,' number 155, had you not judged a few remarks on some points of it necessary for the satisfaction of the Public.

" The present Constitution of the College has no dependence upon the Charter obtained from Governor Hamilton, nor indeed any relation to it, as that by which it is now established is in sundry respects different; the majority of the Trustees being also different persons.

" That Governor Morris [Robert Hunter Morris, who at this time was Deputy-Governor of Pennsylvania as well as Chief Justice of New Jersey] was misrepresented at Home [in England], is to me entirely new, and has not, I am persuaded, the least foundation in Truth. The Trustees of the College of New Jersey are disposed to treat that Gentleman with all suitable respect, and none have the least inclination to enter into a Dispute with him. *But if he requests it*, a particular account of the manner in which the first charter was obtained shall be published, together with a full and candid Disquisition of any Accusation he may be pleased to bring. Till this happens, no notice shall be taken of any ill-natured Reflections made by a Person totally ignorant of his subject, and who will not, I am confident, receive any thanks from the Governor for introducing his name into a controversy with which he had no connexion. The story, as represented from hearsay, as the author himself confesses, is grossly and notoriously false, and that almost in every circumstance, as can be made to appear by sufficient evidence.

" Whether the Charter obtained from Governor Hamilton in his declining state was a valid one, I am not able to determine. The contrary, however, has always appeared to me most probable, and that it was therefore wisely resigned ; though, indeed, the Episcopal Church in Newark is established by a charter obtained of the same gentleman and in the same circumstances, the validity of which I have not heard called in question.

" It is well known that the College at present is established by a Charter, with its usual formalities, from Governor Belcher, with the full consent of his Council, on the petition of several public-spirited gentlemen, who have with great pains and Industry laid a Foundation for a liberal education of Youth in a Province where it was evidently wanted, and in which no undertaking of like nature had ever been attempted.

" And though it must be confessed that the majority of the Trustees thereby incorporated were professed Presbyterians, yet it is worth remarking that his Excellency at the same time generously offered to grant a charter, with equal Privileges, to any Gentlemen of the Episcopal Persuasion who should be willing to embark in the like noble design.

" The present Charter exhibits a most Catholic Plan, and contains no exclusive clauses to deprive persons of any Christian denomination (except Papists) either from its Government or any of its Privileges."   Signed T. T.

If the remark in the last sentence be understood as implying that Papists were excluded from any of the privileges of the College, it will make a wrong impression. No such words, "except Papists," occur in the charter. It is expressly set forth, as one reason for granting the charter, "that the said petitioners have expressed their earnest desire that those of *every religious denomination* may have equal liberty and advantages of education, *any different sentiments in religion notwithstanding*." It is true that the Trustees—*none others*—were required to take certain oaths for the security of his Majesty's person and government, and respecting the succession of the Crown, which " Popish recusants" could not or would not take,

and on that account could not be Trustees of the College.   Upon
the establishment of American Independence these oaths were
no longer required.

There is one matter in this letter in defence of the College
to which exception will be taken when the two charters shall
come more distinctly under consideration; but on the whole
we regard it as a dispassionate and satisfactory reply to the
charges made against the petitioners for the first charter, and
as exposing the ignorance as well as the malevolence of their
assailant.   The object of the writer of this vindication was
rather to defend the College as it was at the time he wrote,
viz., in 1755, than to defend the charter given by President
Hamilton or the conduct of those concerned in soliciting it.
He does indeed say *that the account given of the whole matter*
" *is grossly and notoriously false, and that almost in every circum-*
stance, as can be made to appear by sufficient evidence."

He might have added that it was obviously contradictory
and absurd.   The writer of the supplement admits that the
charter was obtained "in a public manner, by petition, and
passed *the seal* in the same legal manner that other grants of
the King do," and, further, "that a draft of the charter was laid
before Mr. Hamilton *in Council.*"   Had age and infirmity rendered the other members of the Council, as well as the President, unequal to the task devolved upon them ?   Without the
consent of the Council, Mr. Hamilton could not have given the
petitioners a charter, if he had been disposed to do so.   It is
clearly implied, in the charges under consideration, that almost
immediately after the death of Governor Morris the petitioners
applied to Governor Hamilton, *in Council.*   Governor Morris
died on the 21st of May, 1746; the charter was given five
months after, viz., on the 22d of October of the same year.
Surely there was no hot haste in this thing, especially as the
labor of maturing the plan had all been done by the parties
seeking the charter.   It is hardly to be supposed that a Chief
Justice of the acknowledged ability of Chief-Justice R. H.
Morris would require several months to determine whether the
granting of the charter would be illegal, when, according to
the writer of the supplement, the petitioners themselves " were

well convinced of its illegality." With his well-known hostility
to the granting of a charter, if such an inquiry was ever made
of him, it cannot be uncharitable to suppose that he wilfully
deferred making his response as to the legality of the proposed
grant until President Hamilton and the Council, as well as the
petitioners, were annoyed by the delay and determined to wait
no longer. And it is by no means improbable that the writer
of No. XL. of the "Watch-Tower" had allusion to something
of this kind when he made the remark, " But if he [Chief-Justice
R. H. Morris] requests it, a particular account of the manner in
which the first charter was obtained shall be published, together
with a full and candid Disquisition of any Accusation *he* may
be pleased to bring." In these words there is an evident intimation that in the conduct of the Chief Justice relative to the
charter there were things that would not redound to his credit.

While making the intimation just mentioned, the writer of
No. XL. of the "Watch-Tower" says nothing respecting the
statement made by the writer of the supplement, that the petitioners "were ordered to lay a copy of the charter before the
Chief Justice for his opinion, whether it was legal to grant it or
not." Although, possibly for some unexplained reason, this may
have been so, yet it is far more probable that the Chief Justice,
being a member of the Council, requested that all action in regard to the charter might be deferred until he could carefully
examine its provisions and satisfy himself as to the propriety of
his giving his consent, as a member of the Council, to the prayer
of the petitioners. Beyond all question, the usual course in
regard to all important grants was to refer them to the Attorney-
General of the Province for his opinion as to the legality of the
grants therein contained. The Attorney-General at this time
was J. Warrell, Esq., the same gentleman who, upon the granting of the charter of 1748 by Governor Belcher, signed the following declaration at the close of the charter: [L. S.] " I have
perused and considered the written charter, and find nothing
contained therein inconsistent with his Majesty's interest or the
honor of the Crown."

On the charter given in July, 1718, to the Episcopal Church
in Perth Amboy, by Governor Hunter, there is a like declara-

tion, signed by Thomas Gordon, the Attorney-General at that time. But whatever may be the precise facts in the case of the first charter of the College, whether it was referred to the Chief Justice or the Attorney-General, one thing is certain, that the petitioners for a college were under no obligation to the Chief Justice for any favor extended to them by him.

Although President Hamilton was in feeble health during the time he administered the government,—from May 21, 1746, to June 17, 1747, when he died,—he appears to have attended personally to the duties of his office until the latter part of December; and the first official information we have that his health prevented his corresponding with the Home Government is contained in a letter written at his request by Messrs. James Alexander and R. Hunter Morris to the Board of Trade. The date of this letter is the 24th of December, 1746, two months after the College charter had passed the seal of the Province.

The two gentlemen here named were members of the Council. In any record of what Mr. Hamilton did at this time there is no evidence of an infirm state of mind. His consenting to grant the petition for a college charter is in full accord with what would have been expected of him in his best days.

The above sketch shows what was the condition of civil affairs in the Province of New Jersey, and also the state of the Presbyterian Church in the country at large, so far as they had any bearing, either directly or indirectly, upon the erection of the College of New Jersey. It also shows who were the parties engaged in accomplishing this important work, and that the College owes its origin to the need felt by them of more ample provision than any at that time within convenient reach, for the thorough training of candidates for the holy ministry, in both their preparatory and professional studies. But in the erection of this College its founders did not limit their views simply to the educating of candidates for the ministry. It was also their aim to make full provision for the instruction of all classes of youth who might desire to obtain a liberal education and be disposed to avail themselves of the advantages furnished by such a seminary of learning.

With the modes of conveyance then in use, Harvard and Yale, the only Colleges in New England, were too remote for the convenience of youth residing in the middle Provinces. The stand taken by the authorities of these Colleges in opposition to the extravagances which in not a few instances attended the great religious awakening of that period, and seemingly to the awakening itself, alienated from them more or less some of the best and most moderate men in the Presbyterian Church. Suspicions, not fully warranted by the facts of the case, were beginning to find vent that they were tinctured with Arminianism, and were tending to even greater departures from the thorough Calvinism of their founders and early friends.*

It has been said that the College owes its origin to the expulsion of David Brainerd, the celebrated missionary, from Yale College, and to the refusal of the President† and Trustees to admit him to the first degree in the Arts at the same time with the members of his class. The following extract is taken from Dr. D. D. Field's "Genealogy of the Brainerd Family," page 265:

"It is clear enough that the Rev. Jonathan Edwards was not satisfied with the refusal of a degree to David Brainerd by the Faculty and Trustees of Yale College, after all his readiness to confess his faults, and to confess them openly and fully. Others in New England sympathized with him, and others at a distance. Among the former were the Rev. Moses Dickinson, pastor of the church in Norwalk, Connecticut; among the latter, the Rev. Jonathan Dickinson, pastor of the church in Elizabethtown, New Jersey, and the Rev. Aaron Burr, pastor of the church in Newark, who pleaded for Brainerd before the authorities of Yale College in behalf of the Society for the Propagation of Christian Knowledge in Foreign Parts, which had appointed him their missionary.

"And now I will state a fact that may not be known to very many that will read

---

* See Governor Belcher's letter of the 31st of May, 1748, to the Rev. Jonathan Edwards, and also President Quincy's "History of Harvard University," vol. ii. pp. 52 and 67.

† It is to be regretted that a man of the eminent ability and piety of President Clap should not have discriminated more nicely between what was genuine and what was false in the great religious awakening of his day, and that he should have treated with marked severity any of his pupils whose strong religious feelings may have betrayed them into the use of unguarded language or into a disregard of college rules. For his inflexible adherence to what he deemed to be his duty, in those times of high excitement in matters of religion, he is to be held in honor and esteem. There is abundant evidence that he was sound in doctrine, and a faithful servant of Christ.

this book. I once heard the Hon. John Dickinson, Chief Judge of the Middlesex County Court, Connecticut, and son of the Rev. Mr. Dickinson, of Norwalk, say that the establishment of Princeton College was owing to the sympathy felt for David Brainerd, because the authorities of Yale College would not give him his degree, and that the plan of the College was drawn in his father's house.

"Perhaps I have not given every word as he uttered the declaration. But . . . I am certain that I have declared the precise fact that Judge Dickinson uttered. There is evidence that the Rev. Aaron Burr said, after the rise of Princeton College, that it would never have come into existence had it not been for the expulsion of David Brainerd from Yale College. It is a significant fact, that three of the men most conspicuous in their sympathy and efforts for Brainerd were the first three Presidents of that College,—Jonathan Dickinson, Aaron Burr, and Jonathan Edwards."

The evidence here referred to respecting Mr. Burr's declaration, is probably that given in Dr. A. Alexander's work, entitled "The Log College," page 127, in these words: "Some years ago the writer heard the relict of the late Dr. Scott, of New Brunswick, say, that when she was a little girl, she heard the Rev. Mr. Burr declare in her father's house in Newark, if it had not been for the treatment received by Mr. Brainerd at Yale, New Jersey College would never have been erected."

Mrs. Scott was a Miss Crane, daughter of Mr. Elihu Crane, of Newark, and a step-daughter of President Dickinson.

These statements were given from memory long after they were uttered; and if they be in every particular strictly accurate, it does not follow that the College of New Jersey owes its existence to the treatment which Brainerd received from the authorities of Yale College. The originators of the plan for the erection of a college in New Jersey may have needed the stimulus, which that occurrence gave them, to mature, without further delay, their plan for a seminary of learning, which for several years they had deemed necessary to the proper training of candidates for the ministry in their branch of the Church, and for the liberal education of youths designed for other employments; and it may have been that without this additional incitement their plan for such an institution would not have been perfected at that time, nor the requisite steps taken to secure a charter, which in those days was deemed essential to the establishment of a college, or at least to the conferring of literary degrees.

It has also been said that the Log College was the germ of the College of New Jersey, and Whitefield somewhere speaks of the Neshaminy school as having grown into a large college, now erecting in the Jerseys.* But we cannot see the matter in this light. For, as shown in the preceding narrative, the friends and patrons of the Neshaminy school stood aloof when the College of New Jersey was first established. With no more propriety, therefore, can we look to the Log College to discover the origin of the College of New Jersey than we can to the head-waters of the Neshaminy to ascertain the fountain-head of the Delaware, of which river the Neshaminy is but a branch and a tributary.

After the College was in operation, and when it was proposed to enlarge the institution, and to obtain a new charter, the friends of the Log College came into the measure, and became earnest and most efficient friends of the enterprise, and contributed very largely to its success.

In New England the College of New Jersey had many well-wishers, and prominent among these Jonathan Edwards and Moses Dickinson. There is also reason to believe that some of the more extravagant among the Revivalists in New England, after they had seen and renounced their errors, took an interest in the institution designed to promote fervent piety and sound learning, and to be the advocate of such genuine works of grace as were often witnessed in the revivals of those times. In this class may be placed James Davenport and Timothy Allen, men of talent, learning, and piety, yet for a time erratic and even fanatical, but afterwards sober-minded and desirous to repair the evils of their wild and unwarrantable courses. With the aid of some friends, they erected, in New London, Connecticut, an institution called by them "The Shepherd's Tent," *to educate men of the right stamp for the ministry.* They were led to do this in consequence of the opposition of Harvard and Yale to their teaching and measures, and also on account of the severe treatment which Mr. Davenport received at the hands of both the civil and Church authorities of Connecticut. By prohibiting

---

* Dr. Stearns's History of the First Church of Newark.

the establishment of seminaries by private persons, the Legislature of Connecticut compelled the friends of this school to
remove it to Rhode Island, where it lingered for a time, and
was given up.

Mention is made of the "Shepherd's Tent" by the Synod of
Philadelphia in their letter of the 30th of May, 1746, to President Clap, of Yale College,* and, from the manner in which it
is spoken of, it is evident that the Synod had about the same
opinion of it which they had entertained of Mr. Tennent's
school. They assure the President that they will be shy of the
proposals of the New York Synod for a friendly correspondence "till they show us in what way they intend to have their
youth educated for the ministry, and be as ready to discourage
all such methods of bringing all good learning into contempt,
as the 'Shepherd's Tent.'" The Synod of Philadelphia knew
full well that Mr. Dickinson and his friends of the New York
Presbytery were as earnestly in favor of a thorough education
of candidates for the ministry as they themselves were; but the
Synod also knew that the majority of the Synod of New York
were not so; and they were apprehensive that if the Synod of
New York took order in regard to the erection of a school or
college, it would be of the character and standing of the Log
College, or of the Shepherd's Tent. The language of the
Synod of Philadelphia makes it evident that the Synod was not
aware that even before this time the leading members of the
Presbytery of New York had sought to obtain a charter for a
college.

Between the supporters of the Shepherd's Tent and the petitioners for authority to erect a college in New Jersey there
was not at that time a full accord in doctrine, and there was
but little, if any, sympathy. The principal of the Tent and
several other ministers of like mind united in controverting the
views of President Dickinson, as set forth in his dialogue "On
the Display of Divine Grace," and in condemning him, for teaching what they then regarded as an inexcusable error, viz., that
the proof of our justification is to be found in the evidence of

---

* See the printed minutes of the Synod.

our sanctification. (See Webster's "Church History," page 584.) But, as intimated above, Messrs. Allen and Davenport changed their views and openly renounced their errors in doctrine and in practice, and subsequently connected themselves with the Presbyterian Church. For some years they resided in New Jersey, and labored here in the ministry, and were members of the Presbytery of New Brunswick.*   The Rev. Timothy Symes, one of the ministers who had united with Allen in condemning the work of President Dickinson, settled in East Jersey in 1746, and became a member of the Presbytery of New York. As they had become Presbyterians, and had settled within the bounds of a Synod the members of which were *now* all earnestly united in favor of the then only Presbyterian college in the land, they too could not fail to give it their best wishes.

The union of the Synods of New York and of Philadelphia, in 1757, served to promote a friendly feeling towards the College on the part of sundry ministers of the Philadelphia Synod; and in the autumn of 1766 a proposition from a number of gentlemen in Philadelphia and Lewistown, Pennsylvania, was made to the Trustees, that the Faculty of the College should be further enlarged by the appointment of several professors, to be chosen without respect to former divisions or parties in the Church, with the promise of pecuniary aïd in case their proposal should be accepted.

It was found that this arrangement could not be carried into effect. Still, a friendly feeling was promoted.

Thus from the different sources here enumerated, and from others less prominent, including several academies, there were raised up friends for the new College, who all contributed more or less to its prosperity. But for its first establishment, as will be more fully shown, the College was indebted, under God, to Jonathan Dickinson, John Pierson, Ebenezer Pemberton, Aaron Burr, and their immediate friends and helpers. They engaged with earnestness in this undertaking, because they knew and felt the need of just such an institution to train for the Church

---

* See article *Davenport*, in Sprague's Annals of the American Pulpit, vol. iii. page 90.

a pious and learned ministry, and for the other learned professions a body of intelligent and godly men.

May the time be far distant, or, rather, may it never arrive, when this College shall be an "institution devoted exclusively [or even mainly] to the advancement of science or general literature"! On the contrary, may it ever be regarded as an institution consecrated to the service of God for the defence of revealed truth and for the promotion of fervent piety and sound learning!

CHAPTER II.

In tracing the origin of the College, its design was almost necessarily brought into view; but not so fully as the importance of that design demands.

The chief aim of the founders and early friends of the College was to furnish the Church, and more especially their own branch of it, with a pious and learned ministry. But this was not their only aim. It was a part of their plan to provide liberally for the proper intellectual and religious culture of all classes of youths who might be disposed to avail themselves of the facilities afforded by this institution for such culture.

The Trustees under the second charter were in full accord with those under the first, and all had one object in view. Mr. Burr, the first President under the *second* charter, was Mr. Dickinson's successor under the *first* charter; and it is highly probable that all the surviving Trustees of the first charter were Trustees under the charter given by Governor Belcher two years after. The correspondence of the Governor furnishes complete evidence that he and the early friends of the College were all of one mind as to the objects to be attained through the instrumentality of the College, which was already in operation when he entered upon the administration of public affairs in New Jersey. In offering to give the College "a new and better charter," it was *not* his aim *to change the character* of the College, but only to enable it the more readily and effectually to accomplish the design of its founders.

The view here given of this design is fully established by the following extracts from the minutes of the Trustees, and from the minutes of the Synod of New York. At a meeting of the Board, held October 13, 1748, after accepting the charter offered them by Governor Belcher, the Trustees voted to present an address to the Governor, and to "thank his Excellency for the grant of the charter."   The further record of this matter is as follows :

"An address being drawn up by the Rev. Mr. Burr, was read and approved.

"Ordered, That the Rev. Mr. Cowell wait upon his Excellency and present the address to him.

"Ordered, That a copy of the address be taken by the Clerk and inserted in the minutes.

"To His Excellency

"JONATHAN BELCHER, ESQ.,

"Captain-General and Governor-in-Chief of the Province of New Jersey and territories thereon depending in America, and Vice-Admiral of the same:

"The Humble Address of the Trustees of the College of New Jersey.

"May it please your Excellency,—

"We have adored the wise and gracious Providence which has placed your Excellency in the chief seat of government in this Province, and have taken our parts with multitudes in congratulating New Jersey upon that occasion.

"Your long known and well approved friendship to religion and learning left us no room to doubt your doing all that lay in your power to promote so valuable a cause in these parts, and upon this head our most raised expectations have been abundantly answered.   We do, therefore, cheerfully embrace this opportunity of paying our most grateful and sincere acknowledgments to your Excellency for granting so ample and well-contrived a charter for erecting a seminary of learning in this Province, which has been so much wanted and so long desired.

"And as it has pleased your Excellency to intrust us with so important a charge, it shall be our study and care to approve ourselves worthy of the great confidence you have placed in us, by doing our utmost to promote so noble a design.

"And since we have your Excellency to direct and assist us in this important and difficult undertaking, we shall engage in it with the more freedom and cheerfulness; not doubting but by the smiles of Heaven, under your protection, *it may prove a flourishing seminary of piety and good literature;* and continue not only a perpetual monument of honor to your name, above the victories and triumphs of renowned conquerors, but a lasting foundation for the future prosperity of Church and State.

"That your Excellency may long live,—a blessing to this Province, an ornament and support to our infant college,—that you may see your generous designs for the public good take their desired effect, and at last receive a crown of glory that fadeth not away, is and shall be our constant prayer.

"By order of the Trustees.

"THOMAS ARTHUR, *Cl. Cor.*

"NEW BRUNSWICK, October 13, 1748."

To which his Excellency was pleased to return the following answer:

" Gentlemen:

" I have this day received by one of your members, the Rev. Mr. Cowell, your kind and handsome address; for which I heartily return you my thanks; and shall esteem my being placed at the head of this government a still greater favor from God and the King, if it may at any time fall in my power, as it is my inclination, *to promote the kingdom of the great Redeemer, by taking the College of New Jersey under my countenance and protection, as a seminary of true religion and good literature.*

" J. Belcher."

In an address to the Governor by the Trustees, the date being September 24, 1755, mention is made of his ardor for *the promotion of true piety and sound learning* among the inhabitants of New Jersey, and of the indebtedness of the College to him, under God, for its then flourishing state.   In his reply he says:

" It seemed to me that *a seminary of religion and learning* should be promoted in this Province, for the better enlightening the minds and polishing the manners of this and the neighboring colonies. . . . This important affair I have been, during my administration, honestly and heartily prosecuting in all such laudable ways and measures as I have judged most likely to effect what we all aim at, which I hope and believe is the advancing the kingdom and interest of the blessed Jesus and the general good of mankind."

These extracts furnish abundant evidence that *the promotion of true religion and of sound learning was the aim of all concerned in laying the foundations of the College of New Jersey.*

Although the Synod of New York, as a body, took no part in the first efforts to establish the College of New Jersey, but left this important measure to the fostering care of sundry leading ministers and laymen connected with the Presbytery of New York, yet when the new charter was given to the College by Governor Belcher, the entire Synod became interested in promoting the design of the College.   And when, in 1753, the Trustees of the College had obtained the consent of the Rev. Gilbert Tennent and of the Rev. Samuel Davies to visit Great Britain and Ireland, to solicit funds for the erection of suitable buildings, the Synod, upon the petition of the Trustees, appointed these distinguished gentlemen to this work, gave them letters of commendation, and sent with them an earnest appeal to the General Assembly of the Church of Scotland for aid in behalf of the College.   After reciting their utter inability to meet the demand for ministers, to supply the Presbyterian

churches in connection with the Synod, in the Provinces of
New York, New Jersey, Pennsylvania, Maryland, Virginia, and
Carolina, the Synod say:

"Now, it is from the College of New Jersey *only* that we can expect a remedy
for these inconveniences; it is to *that* [college] your petitioners look for the increase of their numbers; it is on *that* the Presbyterian churches through the six
colonies above mentioned principally depend for a supply of accomplished ministers; from *that* has been obtained considerable relief already, notwithstanding the
many disadvantages that unavoidably attend it in its present infant state; and
from that may be expected a sufficient supply, when brought to maturity.

"Your petititioners, therefore, earnestly pray that this very reverend Assembly
would afford the said College all the countenance and assistance in their power.
The young daughter of the Church of Scotland, helpless and exposed in foreign
lands, cries to her tender and powerful mother for relief. The cries of ministers
oppressed with labors, and of congregations famishing for want of the sincere
milk of the word, implore assistance. And were the poor Indian savages sensible
of their own case they would join in the cry, and beg for more missionaries to be
sent to propagate the religion of Jesus among them."

In the conclusion of their address they add:

"Now, as the College of New Jersey appears to be the most promising expedient
to redress these grievances, and to promote religion and learning in these Provinces,
your petitioners most heartily concur with the Trustees, and humbly pray that an act
may be passed by this venerable and honorable Assembly for a national collection
in behalf of said College." (See printed minutes, pp. 255 and 256, of the Synod
of New York.)

Funds more than sufficient to defray the expense of erecting
Nassau Hall was the result of this action of the Synod. The
above extracts from the address of the Synod to the General
Assembly of the Church of Scotland show clearly why the
members of the Synod labored so assiduously to establish
and to sustain with vigor the College of New Jersey. They
regarded it as the most effectual means of supplying their
churches with an able ministry.

The authorities above cited* are amply sufficient to establish
the positions assumed above as to the views and aims of those
who founded and built up this institution. Prompted by a
strong desire to further the interests of religion, and more
especially to furnish their own branch of the Church with an
able and learned ministry, they sought to lay the foundation of

* See also the Rev. David Cowell's letter, urging Mr. Davies to accept the presidency of the College, in Dr. Hall's "History," page 132, or Webster's, page 444.

an institution of learning which should be commensurate with the wants of the whole community, and so to conduct its affairs as to promote, at one and the same time, the welfare of the Church and of the State.

Having obtained a charter, to use their own expression, " so ample and well contrived," the Trustees were not only content, but perfectly satisfied with its provisions. It gave them all they wanted. They were left untrammelled by the State, and yet were under its protection. They enjoyed the confidence of the Church, and yet were perfectly free to adopt such measures as they deemed best adapted to the success of the institution, and through it to advance the civil and religious interests of the country; and, being wise, active, and pious men, their labors were not in vain.

The view here presented accords fully with that given by President Green in his "Historical Sketch of the Origin and Design of the College," as the following extract from that work will fully show:

" It is apparent not only from the motives which so powerfully influenced those who first projected the College, and who labored so long and earnestly to establish it, but from the express and repeated declarations of Governor Belcher, in his replies to the addresses to the original Trustees (those named in the second charter), that this institution was intended, by all the parties concerned in founding it, to be one in which *religion* and *learning* should be *unitedly cultivated* in all time to come. This ought never to be forgotten. There is scarcely anything more unrighteous in itself, or more injurious to society, than disregarding and perverting the design of the founders of charitable, religious, or literary institutions. It is doing base injustice to the dead, and at the same time a powerful and often an effectual discouragement to those among the living, who might, otherwise, make exertions and bestow their property to found and endow establishments of the greatest public utility. It is hoped that the guardians of Nassau Hall will forever keep in mind that the design of its foundation would be perverted if religion should ever be cultivated in it to the neglect of science, or science to the neglect of religion; if, on the one hand, it should be converted into a religious house like a Monastery, or a Theological Seminary, in which religious instruction should claim, almost exclusively, the attention of every pupil; or if, on the other hand, it should become an establishment in which science should be taught, how perfectly soever, without connecting with it, and constantly endeavoring to inculcate, the principles and practice of genuine piety. Whatever other institutions may exist or arise in our country, in which religion and science may be separated from each other by their instructors or governors, this institution, *without a gross perversion of its original design*, can never be one."

It is worthy of note that Governor Belcher and the Trustees, in speaking of the College as an institution designed for the promotion of religion and learning, always mention religion first ; and it is evident from what they said and did with respect to the College, that the religious culture of the pupils was the thing uppermost in their minds, and that to which they attached the most importance.   Between true religion and sound learning there cannot be any real or substantial disagreement; nor will the volume of Nature when thoroughly unfolded be found to contradict the volume of Inspiration properly interpreted. Science, falsely so called, may call into question the teachings of revealed truth, but such a thing as this can never be allowed in this institution, unless its guardians lose sight of its original design and prove recreant to the trust confided to them.   Yea, more, if due regard be had to this sacred trust, the promotion of true religion will ever be regarded by the authorities of the College as having the first claim upon their attention, in all their plans for the extension and the improvement of the course of instruction given in the College.   It must ever be the solemn duty of the Trustees to see to it, in the selection of persons to fill the vacancies in their own Board, that none be chosen in regard to whom any doubt can be entertained as to their approval of the original design of the College, or in regard to their earnest desire to secure the very purposes for which the College was erected.   In the good providence of God, the College has an ample charter, that is equal to all its legitimate aims; and we trust that it will undergo no radical changes, in deference to the varying opinions of the day and to a public clamor for experiment and innovations.   If the College were a State institution, founded, supported, and governed by State authorities, it might with some show of reason be expected to conform its teachings, discipline, and mode of selecting its guardians and instructors to the wishes and whims of those who, from time to time, may represent the opinions of the community at large : but this is not the case with the College of New Jersey.   It was founded, *not* by the State, although with the sanction and under the protection of the civil power, to accomplish certain definite purposes, and in a certain definite way. Nor was it founded directly by the Church, although one branch of the Church extended to it a fostering care, and prominent members of that Church were the first to devise the plan of it and to lay its foundations. The founders of the College were both members of the Commonwealth and members of the Church, and they were in every respect suitable men to be intrusted with the important enterprise of erecting and controlling an institution for the education of youth, in whose education both the State and the Church were deeply interested. In both charters it was stipulated that none should be excluded from the privileges of the College on account of any different religious sentiments, as was the case in the English Universities, but, on the contrary, that all should enjoy equal liberties and privileges; yet the very terms of the stipulation show that the College was expected to have a religious faith, although none were to be required to adopt the religious views embraced by the College authorities as a condition of enjoying the privileges afforded to its members.

The petitioners for the College charter were known to be Presbyterians, and it was also known that the governing motive with them in seeking a charter was to provide for the youth of their own Church, and more especially for their candidates for the ministry, a thorough training in all the various branches of a liberal education, including, as a matter of the highest interest, full instruction in the doctrines of the Christian faith, according to their understanding of them.

Either the superior judgment of those concerned in the foundation of our College, and their great liberality of sentiment, or else the circumstances of their position, perhaps all combined, led them to adopt the very best plan possible for the right founding and the right ordering of such an institution. They made it neither a State College nor a Church College, but committed it to the oversight and care of a select number of the very best men interested in this enterprise, and who had the confidence and respect of the whole community, being leading men both in the Church and in the State.

It has been sometimes a matter of remark and even censure that the Legislature of New Jersey never contributed any funds for sustaining its oldest college, which has been a source of many benefits to the State, and the occasion of large sums of money being expended here.   But in this matter we incline to the opinion that the Legislature has acted wisely for the State and happily for the College.   Had the College been liberally endowed by the State, this might have given the Legislature a pretext, if nothing more, for interfering with the government and course of instruction; which we are happy to say it has never attempted to do.   In the charter of the College the Legislature has never made a change, except at the request of the Trustees; and never refused to make one desired by the Board.   And, further, the Legislature has at different times enacted special laws for the protection of the students from extortion and for the guarding of their health and morals.

Had the College been a State institution, under the control of a Board of Trustees chosen from time to time by the State authorities, and with a course of instruction and a system of government presented by the Legislature, the State would doubtless have regarded it as a duty to do all in its power to sustain the College, and to provide the requisite means for an ample and most liberal course of instruction.   But in this case probably the course of religious instruction, the most important given in any school or college, must have been circumscribed and of a comparatively limited extent, if not wholly excluded: lest the rights of conscience should be invaded.

The only effectual course to guard against such a result is to have this matter of a higher education in the hands of a select number of prominent citizens, bearing the twofold relation of citizens and of church-members, with power to perpetuate themselves, by filling at their own discretion all vacancies in their own body, and let all who are disposed and are able to establish such institutions be encouraged to do so, by granting them corporate privileges without regard to the particular religious denomination with which they are associated.   In this way full provision may be made in the academic curriculum for all the religious instruction which the interests of either the State or the Church call for.   Each pupil, or his parent for him, can select the college he prefers, in view of all the advantages proffered, and neither pupil nor parent can properly complain that the student is required to give attention to the whole of the prescribed course, including the religious as well as the literary and scientific parts of that course.

On this plan, too, each religious denomination will have a guarantee that the children of their own Church will have a sound religious training according to their views of truth. For such colleges must to a great extent depend for their patronage and support upon that religious denomination with which the trustees and teachers are connected; and thus indirectly the Church, or the particular branch of it under whose auspices a college has been established, will have a voice in its management, and that too without being subjected to any of those inconveniences and troubles to which a more direct control might readily and naturally give rise, introducing jealousies and collisions into the ecclesiastical bodies themselves. Happily for the College of New Jersey, it is not and never has been a State or a Church college; yet through the whole period of its existence it has merited and received the countenance and favor of that branch of the Church most interested in its establishment, and also the confidence and protection of the State authorities which gave and confirmed its charter. Yea, more, such from the beginning has been its catholic spirit, that not a few of its warmest friends have been found in other denominations than the Presbyterian; and it has had the honor to educate for other branches of the Church some of their brightest intellects, who have not failed to acknowledge their indebtedness to their Alma Mater.

While, therefore, the friends of this College are not called upon to speak disparagingly of colleges directly under either State or Church control, they may be thankful that the College of their affections was intrusted to the exclusive care of a few wise and select men, who, in the fear of God, laid deep its foundations, and upon them erected an institution for the advancement of piety and learning, and had a special reference to the supplying of their own branch of the Church of Christ with a godly and well-trained ministry.

CHAPTER III.

THE first charter of the College passed the great seal of the Province on the 22d of October, 1746, and it was attested by John Hamilton, Esq., President of his Majesty's Council, and Commander-in-Chief of the Province of New Jersey, as appears from a memorandum made in Book C of Commissions and Charters, etc., page 137, in the office of the Secretary of State for New Jersey.

The charter itself is not given in these records. By the parties to whom it was granted it is spoken of as ".a charter with full and ample privileges," and one by which "equal liberties and privileges are secured to every denomination of Christians, any different religious sentiments notwithstanding."

In an advertisement in the "New York Gazette and Weekly Post Boy" of February 2, 1746–47, it is mentioned that this charter was granted to Jonathan Dickinson, John Pierson, Ebenezer Pemberton, Aaron Burr, ministers of the gospel, and some other gentlemen, as Trustees of said College.

According to a memorandum made by Mr. Nathaniel Fitz Randolph, of Princeton, the gentleman who gave to the College the land upon which Nassau Hall is erected, the whole number of Trustees under the first charter was *twelve*.

This comprises all that is now positively known respecting this charter, of which neither the original nor any copy is to be found.

In his biographical sketches of Presbyterian ministers in this country, the late Rev. Richard Webster mentions that the Rev. Thomas Arthur was one of the original Trustees of the College. This is by no means improbable; but on what authority, or with what understanding of its import, this statement is made,

70

is not known. Mr. Arthur was the pastor of the Presbyterian church in New Brunswick, and a member not of the Presbytery of New Brunswick, but of the Presbytery of New York, of which body Messrs. Dickinson, Pierson, Pemberton, and Burr were all members. Mr. Arthur is named in the second charter as one of the Trustees under that grant.

The second charter was given two years after the first, by Jonathan Belcher, Esq., his Majesty's Governor of New Jersey, and it passed the great seal of the Province on the 14th of September, 1748. Under this second charter the number of clerical and lay Trustees, exclusive of the President of the College, was equal. It is, therefore, most probable that one-half of the Trustees under the first charter were laymen. And as all the ministers who are known to have been Trustees under the first charter, and alive at the date of the second charter, are named as Trustees in this second instrument, so it is probable that most, if not all, of the lay members of the Board under the *first* charter, who were living at the date of the second, continued to be Trustees under the second.

The ministers of the gospel known to have been Trustees under the first charter all resided either in East Jersey or in New York City; and this renders it highly probable that the lay Trustees associated with them were also residents in the same districts.

Of the *lay Trustees* named in the second charter, William Smith and P. V. B. Livingston were members of the First Presbyterian Church in the city of New York, of which church the Rev. Ebenezer Pemberton was the pastor; and *it is certain* that Mr. Pemberton was a Trustee under both charters. Wm. Peartree Smith, who was a Trustee from 1748 to 1793, forty-five years, also resided in the city of New York, at the respective dates of the first and of the second charter. Subsequently he was a prominent citizen of Elizabethtown, New Jersey, and a Trustee of the Presbyterian church there. James Hude, a member of his Majesty's Council for New Jersey, was connected with the Presbyterian church in New Brunswick, under the pastoral care of the Rev. Thomas Arthur. Andrew Johnston, who was not only a Trustee, but also the first person chosen Treasurer of the

College under the second charter, was a member of his Majesty's Council for New Jersey, and a resident of Perth Amboy, the residence of President Hamilton, and the seat of government for East Jersey. Messrs. Hude and Johnston were members of the Council when President Hamilton, with the consent of the Council, granted the first charter. The five civilians here named as included among the Trustees under the second charter were all gentlemen of high standing, and for the reasons suggested above we deem it morally certain that some if not all of them were Trustees of the College under the *first* charter as well as under the *second;* and that Samuel Smith, the earliest historian of New Jersey, was substantially correct in saying that "the College was first founded by a charter from President Hamilton, and enlarged by Governor Belcher." (See Smith's "History of New Jersey," page 490.) Mr. Smith was a personal friend of Governor Belcher, and for some years a townsman.

It is true, indeed, that in the second charter there is no reference made to the one previously granted by President Hamilton of his Majesty's Council; and there appears to have been a disposition upon the part of some of the friends of the College to lose sight of the first charter, and to regard the College under the second charter as a new and distinct institution. Thus, in an account of the College prepared by Mr. Samuel Blair, then a Tutor in the College, under the direction of President Finley, . and published in 1766, we meet with the following statement upon page 7 :

"Yet even in this dark period there were not wanting several gentlemen, both of the civil and of the sacred character, who, forming a just estimate of the importance of learning, exerted their utmost efforts to plant and cherish it in the Province of New Jersey. After some disappointments and fruitless attempts, application was at length made to his Excellency Jonathan Belcher, Esq., at that time Governor of the Province; and in the year 1748 he was pleased, with the approbation of his Majesty's Council, to grant a charter incorporating sundry gentlemen of the clergy and laity, to the number of twenty-three, as Trustees, investing them with such powers as were requisite to carry the design into execution, and constituting his Majesty's Governor, for the time being, *ex officio* their President."

The writer of No. XL. of the "Watch-Tower" uses the following language (see pages 50 and 51, *ante*):

"The present constitution of New Jersey College has no dependence upon the charter obtained from Governor Hamilton, *nor indeed any relation to it;* as that by which it is now established is in sundry respects different, the majority of the Trustees being also different persons. Whether the charter obtained from Governor Hamilton in his declining state was a valid one I am not able to determine. The contrary, however, has always appeared to me most probable, and that it was therefore wisely resigned; though, indeed, the Episcopal church in Newark is established by a charter obtained of the same gentleman and in the same circumstances, the validity of which I have not heard called in question."

The writers of the "Watch-Tower" were opposed to the founding of a college in New York by charter from a Governor, and insisted it should be by an act of the Assembly, of course with the concurrence of the Governor and Council; and they were therefore, in all probability, the more predisposed to question the validity of a charter granted not even by the regularly commissioned Governor, but by one for the time being administering the government; and they were not unwilling to throw doubt upon the right of Lieutenant-Governor De Lancey, then at the head of affairs in New York, to grant a charter for a college to be established in that Province, by giving utterance to any doubt they may have had respecting the validity of the charter granted by the acting Governor of New Jersey.

As to the fact that a majority of the Trustees under the second charter were different persons from those under the first, it has nothing to do in deciding the matter in question, viz., whether the College under the second charter was the same with that under the first charter. Under the first the number of Trustees was *twelve*, and under the second *twenty-three*. Of the former, one at least had died; and this itself would make the *new* Trustees a majority of the whole number under the *second* charter.

It is true that the first charter ceased to be of any force upon the acceptance of the second; and inasmuch as the first was never recorded, and as all persons who could claim any rights or privileges under it had transferred their interests to a new corporation, no formal surrender of it was tendered to the granting power; nor was any such surrender required. This view of the matter accords with what, in a letter of the date of July 4, 1748, Governor Belcher said to the Rev. Gilbert Tennent, and probably in reply to an inquiry made by Mr. Tennent, viz., "as the old charter was not recorded, upon the appearance of the present one the old one would become a nonentity." By "the present one" is meant the charter prepared by himself, or under his instructions, which at the date of his letter was probably ready for revision by the Council.

In a letter dated July 28, 1748, and addressed to the Rev. Mr. Pemberton, Governor Belcher says :

> "The charter has passed the seal, and is ready in all respects, and I think it is best that you and Mr. Burr come hither [to Burlington] as soon as you can, to receive it from me, and that I may talk with you about the College."

And on the 30th of the same month he writes to Mr. Tennent :

> "I have wrote to Mr. Pemberton, desiring he and Mr. Burr would be here as soon as they could, and when they come they should give you notice to come hither also, when I should deliver the charter to you gentlemen on behalf of the Trustees."

In these extracts, written in July, 1748, it is distinctly said that "the *new* charter *has passed* the seal, and is ready in all respects;" and yet it appears from the charter now in the possession of the Trustees, that it was attested by the Governor and passed the seal of the Province on the 14th day of September, 1748. The only solution of the discrepancy here mentioned is this, viz., that Messrs. Pemberton, Burr, and Tennent were not altogether satisfied with some clauses of the charter as at first prepared by the direction of Governor Belcher, and that at their request the charter was altered, and passed the seal a second time on the 14th of September, 1748, the day after its final approval by the Council of the Province.

It was doubtless from viewing the first charter as a nullity upon their acceptance of the *second*, and from their regarding a charter as essential to the very being of a college, that the Trustees, in one of their written addresses to Governor Belcher, viz., in that of November 24, 1755, speak of him as "the *founder*, patron, and benefactor of the College."

As to the validity of the charter given by President Hamilton, there is no more room for doubt than there is with respect to the validity of the one granted by Governor Belcher. From the instructions given to Lord Cornbury, Governor of the Province from 1702 to 1708 (see Smith's "History of New Jersey," pages 258 and 259), it is evident that, upon the death or absence of the Governor and the Lieutenant-Governor, the senior Councillor became the acting Governor, and was in express terms authorized *to exercise all the powers* of the Governor:

. . . "It is our will and pleasure, therefore, that if, upon your death or absence, there be no Lieutenant-Governor or Commander-in-Chief, the eldest Councillor, whose name is first placed in our instructions to you, and who shall be, at the time of your death or absence, *residing* in our said Province of New Jersey, *shall take upon him the administration of the government, and execute our said commission and instructions, with the several powers and authorities therein contained, in the same manner, and to all intents and purposes, as either our Governor or Commander-in-Chief should or ought to do,* in case of your absence, or until your return, or in all cases until our further pleasure be known."

August 23, 1743, the Secretary of the Board of Trade wrote to John Hamilton, Esq., in reply to his letter of June 9, that the Board looked upon him to be the legal President and Commander-in-Chief of New Jersey from the 28th of March, 1736, till Mr. Morris took possession of the government. Upon the death of Governor Morris, 1746, Mr. Hamilton, being the senior Councillor, again took upon himself the administration of the affairs of the Province as President of the Council and Commander-in-Chief; and as such he granted, in the name of the King, with the consent of the Council, the first charter of the College.

It is a far more serious question whether a charter given by a Governor was a valid one before it received the sanction of his Majesty by the advice of his Council. The one hundredth article of the instructions given to Lord Cornbury is in these words:

"And if anything shall happen that shall be of advantage and security to our said Province, which is not herein or by our commission to you provided for, we do hereby allow you, with the advice and consent of our Council of our said Province, *to take order for the present therein, giving to us,* by one of our principal Secretaries of State, and to our Commissioners for Trade and Plantations, *speedy notice thereof, that so you may receive our ratification, if we shall approve the same.*"

Lord Cornbury was the first Governor of New Jersey appointed by the royal authority upon the surrender of the government by the Proprietors of East and West Jersey; and this no doubt accounts for the fulness and particularity of the instructions given to him, as they would serve for the guidance of his successors in office.

There does not appear to have been any subsequent augmentation of the powers intrusted to the Governor, but, on the contrary, further restrictions were imposed.

The granting of charters was regarded by the Crown and its advisers as a special prerogative of the Crown. The Provincial Governors, as representatives of the regal authority, considered themselves authorized to give their consent to legislative acts granting charters for various purposes; and among them were charters to erect institutions for the advancement of knowledge and for its increase among the people. But these charters were liable to be revoked by the royal authority; and in one instance, at least, the royal assent was refused to a charter to Harvard College, viz., to the one granted in 1692 by the General Court of Massachusetts, although it had the sanction of his Majesty's Governor for that Province; and in other instances the Governor refused his consent to the action of the General Court in reference to that institution.

The charters granted by President Hamilton and Governor Belcher—the first charters ever granted by a Governor with merely the consent of his Council—were neither ratified nor revoked by the supreme authority. Although they both passed the seal of the Province, *the first* was *never* recorded, and the one given by Governor Belcher on the 14th of September, 1748, was not recorded until the 4th of October, 1750, more than two years after it had passed the seal; and then it was placed on record by an order of the Trustees, given on the 26th of September immediately preceding. The order was in these words:

"Ordered, That the Clerk take care to have the charter recorded in the Secretary's Office at Amboy and at Burlington, *with all possible speed;* and be allowed to pay the charges out of the Lottery money in the hands of Mr. Hude."

There is scarcely room for doubt that the Trustees were prompted to this measure by the sudden and severe illness of

Governor Belcher at this time, and from an apprehension that
if the charter were not placed on the records of the Province
it might, in case of the Governor's decease, be altered or even
altogether revoked by his successor in office. Of the alarming
illness of the Governor there is abundant evidence. Cadwal-
lader Colden, in a letter of the date of October 6, 1750, to R.
H. Morris, then in London, says, "Governor Belcher has been
seized with palsy while attending Commencement at Newark."
Governor Belcher himself, writing to his son in Ireland, July 3,
1752, says that his paralytic affection had so increased that for
eighteen months he had not been able to hold a pen. His subsequent correspondence shows that he never entirely recovered
from the effects of this shock.

It has been conjectured that the reason why the charter
given by Governor Belcher was not sooner delivered to the
Trustees was owing to the necessity he was under of submitting
it to the inspection of the Home Government and of obtaining
the King's permission before issuing the instrument. (See Dr.
Green's "Notes.") But the correspondence of the Governor
with Messrs. Pemberton, Burr, Tennent, and Edwards, respecting
the charter, shows conclusively that the charter was *not* sent
to England *before* its delivery to the Trustees. Extracts from
this correspondence, establishing this fact, will hereinafter be
given.

That a copy of it was *not* sent to the authorities in London,
after it had passed the seal and had been delivered to the
Trustees, is morally certain from the delay in recording the
instrument and from the circumstance that the recording of it
took place by order of the Trustees themselves, and not in
virtue of any statute requiring it to be done; and it is beyond
dispute that, although given in the name of George the Second,
the charter never received his Majesty's ratification. This is
evident from the "Diary" of the Rev. Samuel Davies, who, in
company with the Rev. Gilbert Tennent, visited England and
Scotland in the years 1753 and 1754 to solicit funds to aid
the Trustees in their efforts to erect suitable buildings for the
recently-established college. Under the head of February 6,
1754, Mr. Davies thus writes:

" Went to Mr. Stennet's, who went with us to introduce us to the Duke of Argyle to deliver Governor Belcher's letter. We found eight or ten Gentlemen and Noblemen waiting in his Grace's Levee. His Grace took us into his Library, a spacious, elegant room. . . . His Grace told us, after reading the letter, that as the College related to the Plantations, we ought first to apply to the Lords of Trade and Plantations, and, if they approved of it, he would willingly countenance it, both here and in Scotland. He advised us to apply to Lord Halifax or Lord Duplin, and Mr. Stennet went to the latter, . . . and showed our Instructions from the Trustees, and the petition we had drawn up. Mr. Stennet told him he applied to him *in confidence,* and his Lordship assured him he would do nothing to injure us. He thereupon told him that we had our Charter only from a Governor, and asked him whether he thought *it would be deemed valid in Court.* His Lordship replied that *he doubted it,* but he would soon satisfy himself by enquiring into the extent of the Governor's commission ; and in case it appeared valid, he would advise us to lay the matter before the Archbishop of Canterbury, and that he himself would go with Mr. Stennet to Mr. Pelham [the Prime Minister] in our Favor, and introduce the matter in Court. For my part, I am afraid of all applications to that Quarter, *lest we lose our Charter and stir up opposition ;* and it is against my mind that the matter has been carried so far. Dined at Mr. Stennet's, who gave us five guineas for the College. *Went home anxious as to the Fate of our Application to the Lords of Trade and to the Court.*"

Monday, February the 11th, there is the following entry:

" Visited Mr. Mill, and delivered Mr. Donald's letter. He and his partner, Mr. Oswald, advised us to apply to the Lords of Trade to encourage our Embassy. But I am afraid of the consequence. Went to Mr. Denham, a Presbyterian minister, and had a long and difficult dispute with him about the importance and necessity of our College, the validity of our Charter, *without the Royal approbation, etc.,* which he managed with great dexterity. It was my happiness to have my thoughts ready, and I made such a defence as silenced him. His name is of great importance, and I was solicitous to obtain it to our Petition, had lost all hope of it, when, to my agreeable surprise, he subscribed."

Under the head of Thursday, the 14th of February, Mr. Davies says:

" Waited on Mr. Stennet to hear Lord Duplin's opinion of the validity of our Charter, but he was indisposed and had not waited on his Lordship."

On Wednesday, the 6th of March, Mr. Pelham, the Prime Minister, died, and his death diverted the attention of Lord Duplin from any further inquiry with respect to the extent of Governor Belcher's powers, and as to the validity of the charter, —matters of more immediate importance at home demanding all his time. At any rate, no further mention of the charter is made in Mr. Davies's " Diary," nor any allusion to it.

In reference to Mr. Pelham's death and its results, mentioned on page 176 of his "Diary," Mr. Davies observes:

"This day died the Honorable Henry Pelham, Esq., Prime Minister, which has struck the town [London] with consternation. He has left a general good character behind him; and the Court is puzzled whom to choose in his place."

Again, under the date of Tuesday, the 19th of March, Mr. Davies writes:

"The Court is all in confusion about choosing one to fill up Mr. Pelham's place, and the King is much perplexed. He says he hoped to spend his old age in Peace, but all his Peace is buried in Mr. Pelham's grave." ("Diary," vol. i. pages 188–89.)

Elections were held soon after in the city of London, and, the state of things there not being favorable to the prosecution of their agency, Messrs. Tennent and Davies left London for Edinburgh; and, although they returned to London before sailing for America, nothing more appears to have been said or done in reference to the charter.

Whether the approval of the King was requisite to give validity to the charter is now, happily, a matter of no moment to the College. Its validity was never called in question by any court in Great Britain or in the Province, and by an act passed the 13th of March, 1780, the Legislature of the State recognized and confirmed its grants.

It is, however, a matter of interest to many friends of the College whether under the second charter it was a new institution, and entirely distinct from the College under the *first* charter, or whether it was the same College under both charters. The facts recited above *tend* to show, if they do nothing more, that the College of New Jersey under the first charter and the College of New Jersey under the second charter were one and the same institution. Its powers and privileges may have been, and doubtless were, somewhat enlarged, and the number of Trustees nearly doubled; but the Trustees and students of the one became Trustees and students of the other; and the Rev. Mr. Burr, who, upon the death of Mr. Dickinson, had the oversight and instruction of the students and the general interests of the College intrusted to him, was unanimously chosen President by the Trustees of the second charter. Before the second charter was prepared, it must have been fully understood that he was to be the President under the second charter, as appears from these two facts: 1st, that the whole number of Trustees, exclusive of the Governor of the Province and the President of the College, was limited to *twenty-one;* and, 2d, that in the charter itself twenty-two names are inserted, and one of them is that of Aaron Burr, who, upon being chosen President, became *ex officio* a Trustee, and this reduced the number to the limit prescribed in the charter itself.

If the view here presented be the correct one, President Dickinson is justly regarded as the first President of the College of New Jersey; and he has a right to the place so long conceded to him in the triennial catalogue of the College as its first President; and *to him and his associates should also be conceded the honor of being the founders of the College.*

The advertisement taken from the "New York Gazette" of February 2, 1746–47, and inserted at the beginning of this chapter, is of itself sufficient to show that the first charter of the College was obtained, not by the *Synod* of New York, but by the most prominent members of the *Presbytery* of New York. Had it been obtained through any action of the Synod, or by any concert among the leading members of that body, there can be no doubt that Gilbert Tennent and Samuel Blair would have been mentioned with Messrs. Dickinson, Pierson, Pemberton, and Burr as those to whom the charter had been granted. They were both far too prominent in the Church not to have been named in such an announcement to the public, had they been Trustees under the first charter, and men of too much influence not to have had their names inserted in the charter, had they consented to take any part in the effort to obtain it. Beyond all question, Mr. Tennent was the most influential member in the Presbytery of New Brunswick, and Mr. Blair the leading man in the Presbytery of New Castle; and had the first efforts to establish the College, and to procure for it a charter, originated with the Synod, the whole matter would not have been given up to the ministers and laymen connected with the Presbytery of New York. The Presbytery of New

Brunswick embraced a larger number of ministers and churches than did the Presbytery of New York, and included several in Pennsylvania, as well as a majority of those in New Jersey.

In the attempt to enlarge the sphere of the College and to increase the number of its friends, the first effort was naturally made to secure the countenance and support of the friends of the Neshaminy school, and to bring into the Board of Trustees Messrs. Gilbert and William Tennent, and some of their particular friends, which was done; and also, as far as practicable, to gain for the College the good will of other gentlemen of position and influence, both in West Jersey and in Pennsylvania. Hence we find in the *second* charter the names of Chief-Justice Kinsey and Judge Edward Shippen, of Philadelphia, and of the Rev. Mr. Cowell, of Trenton, then a member of the Presbytery of Philadelphia, and of the Rev. Samuel Blair, of Fagg's Manor, Pennsylvania.

In the list of ministers whom it was proposed to make Trustees, under the *second* charter, Mr. Blair's name was not included at the first; possibly from a doubt of his willingness to be a Trustee in an institution which might interfere with the one established by himself, or might require him, in case of its success, to change the character of his own school. But whatever may have been the reason, the fact was as here stated; and this is evident from Governor Belcher's letter of the 6th of April, 1748, to the Rev. Mr. Pemberton, in which he says, " I am well pleased to add the name of the Rev. Samuel Blair to the Trustees, for you must remember that we cannot have too many friends in our present infant state."

The circumstance just mentioned, independently of the evidence given heretofore, would of itself make it morally certain that Mr. Blair was not a Trustee under the first charter.

The ground taken above as to *the oneness of the College under both charters is abundantly strengthened by the following extracts* from Governor Belcher's letters. The dates, and the names of the persons to whom the letters are addressed, precede the extracts. Governor Belcher arrived in this country from England August 8, 1747.

October 8, 1747, to President Dickinson:

"I duly received your favor of the 10th ult., enclosing a catalogue, but for some reason I shall not send it forward till I see you, which I hope may be next month, when the Assembly sits here,—the 17th,—and I shall be glad Mr. Pemberton could so order as to come with you, and that you may be prepared to lay something before the Assembly for the service of the *embryo College*, as a Lottery, or anything else."

Mr. Dickinson died on the 7th of October, 1747, the day before this letter was written.

October 8, 1747, to Rev. Mr. Pemberton, of New York:

"Mr. Dickinson has sent me a catalogue, which I have not thought proper to send forward till I shall talk with him and you, and which I hope may be next month, when the Assembly of the Province meets here (17th), and I would have you come prepared to lay something before the Assembly for the service of *our infant College*. I say *our*, because I have determined to *adopt it* for a child, and to do everything in my power to promote and establish so noble an undertaking."

October 8, 1747, to Mr. Smith, New York. After acknowledging the receipt of several other things sent to him by Mr. Smith, the Governor adds:

"I have *also* the Lottery *scheme*, which may be of service in the affair of *our infant College*. What went into the newspapers was carefully done."

These are extracts from three letters written on the same day, but cited in the reverse order from that in which they were written,—one to the President of the College, one to the Rev. Mr. Pemberton, who beyond all doubt was a Trustee under both charters, and the third evidently addressed to one deeply interested in the prosperity *of the then existing College.* The Mr. Smith to whom one of these letters is addressed was probably Mr. Wm. Peartree Smith, of whom Governor Belcher, in a letter to the Rev. Mr. Sergeant, of the date of February 23, 1748, makes mention as being his correspondent in the city of New York. Mr. Smith was one of the Trustees named in the second charter, and most probably he was also a Trustee under the first. In addition to the other reasons for this opinion assigned above, there is a confirmation of it in the form of expression used in his letter to this gentleman, "*our infant College,*" compared with the same expression in the Governor's letter to Mr. Pemberton of the same date, in which he explains his meaning in his use of this phrase, "our infant College:" "I say *our*, for I have determined to adopt it for a daughter." This was a very proper expression in writing to a Trustee of a college recently organized, but not an appropriate one had he been writing to a person who had no particular connection with the College. Mr. Pemberton, we know, was a Trustee at this time, and we infer it to be highly probable that Mr. Smith was also. Mr. Dickinson is urged by the Governor to come prepared to present a petition to the Assembly for a lottery, or for something else, for the service of the College. In his letter to Mr. Smith, the Governor speaks of having also the Lottery *scheme*, which may be of service in the affairs of *our* infant College,—that is, in case the Assembly will authorize the Trustees to raise funds for the College by means of a lottery.

October 2, 1747, to his friend Mr. Walley:

> "There has been a striving at what place the College should be built, but I have persuaded those concerned to fix it at Princeton, and I think as near the centre as any, and a fine situation. I believe *they must have a new and better charter,* which I shall give them."

This letter was written a few days before the death of President Dickinson, and it determines another point of interest,—viz., that the question of another charter was agitated *before* the death of President Dickinson.

November, 1747, to Mr. Pemberton:

> "I shall be glad to see you here *for the sake of the College.* . . . The death of that eminent servant of God, the learned and pious Dickinson, is a considerable Rebuke of Providence, and is to remind us that we have such precious treasure in earthen vessels, and that our eyes and hearts must be lifted to the great head of the Church, who holds the stars in his right hand. Then let us not despond or murmur."

December 15, 1747, to Mr. Allen, of Boston:

> "The death of the late excellent, now ascended, Dickinson, is indeed a considerable loss to *my adopted daughter;* but God lives, and is always better than we deserve, and with whom we must wrestle for his mercy and blessing to fall upon *our Infant College,* so shall it rise into youth, and in God's best time become an Alma Mater for this and the neighboring colonies."

January 25, 1747–48, to Mr. Pemberton:

> "As to a *new* charter, if you and the rest of the gentlemen will digest that matter, and with enlargement, in the best manner you can, and let me have a Rough of it, to see if it can be made better, you will be sure of all my Protection."

This last extract shows that at the date of this letter nothing had been done towards the preparing of a *new* charter.

March 21, 1747–48, to Mr. Burr, the successor of President Dickinson:

"You cannot be more thoughtful or solicitous for *the growth and prosperity* of my adopted daughter, and our future Alma Mater, than I am. In order to the perfecting of the charter, you know it will be necessary for me to go to Philadelphia, and which I intend soon. *You say Commencement is designed the third Wednesday of May next; so I will try to get the charter to you before that time.* I much approve a wise frugality at the solemnity you mention, more especially in our Infant Days, for I think the too common Extravagances and Debauchery at such times be no honor to what may laudably pride itself in being called a Seminary of Religion and Learning. So soon as the charter shall be completed, a meeting of the Trustees will be very proper and necessary."

The above extract shows that the Governor had no expectation that the charter would be ready much before the third Wednesday of May. It was not, however, prepared and issued until the 14*th of September*, and the Commencement was postponed from time to time until the 9th of November, at the request of Governor Belcher.

May 31, 1748, to the Rev. Jonathan Edwards:

"As to our Embryo College, it is a noble design, and if God pleases may prove an extensive blessing. *I have adopted it for a daughter*, which I hope in time may become an Alma Mater to this and the neighboring Provinces. . . . I am getting the best advice and assistance I can in a draft of a charter which I intend to give our Infant College; and I thank you for all the kind hints you have given for the service of this excellent undertaking," etc.

This is conclusive as to the fact that the charter was not matured at the date of this letter, May 31.

June 18, 1748, to the Rev. Gilbert Tennent. In this letter the Governor alludes to the first charter, viz., the one given by President Hamilton, in these words:

"Perhaps it may be more satisfactory to a majority of the intended Trustees *to proceed on the old Patent*, in which I am quite easy." And he adds, "If I have any further to do in the matter, I shall immediately send it [the charter] to Mr. Gillnawary of your city [Philadelphia] to be engrossed, who I think did the last."

This extract shows that the charter had not been engrossed as late as the 18th of June.

Extracts from other letters, showing the same facts, might be given; but the above will probably be regarded as more than sufficient to establish these two points: 1, that the charter given by Governor Belcher could not have been sent to England for the King's approbation before its delivery to the Trustees; and, 2, that it was given, not for a *new* college, but for the College of New Jersey, already established and in operation, under a charter granted, in the name of the King, by President Hamilton, of his Majesty's Council for New Jersey. It is not for a new institution, but for a new charter, that we are indebted to Governor Belcher. An infant is not a nonentity, nor a something that is to be, but a reality, a thing in actual existence. So in this case, the infant College of New Jersey, the adopted daughter of the Governor, was in being and engaged in its appropriate work *before* Governor Belcher gave it " a new and better charter," and even *before* his arrival in the Province. The charter of 1748 doubtless gave increased vigor to the institution, and added largely to the number of its friends. Under this new charter the College became, what its name indicates it aspired to be, " The College of New Jersey," and not simply of East Jersey, sending abroad throughout the land a wholesome influence for the promotion of genuine piety and sound learning. Under this charter additions were made to the number of the Trustees, by introducing into the Board several distinguished ministers and laymen in Pennsylvania and New Jersey,—and among these the most prominent members of the Presbyteries of New Brunswick and of New Castle,— and thus securing to the College the friendship and patronage of the entire Synod of New York.

It has been conjectured that the reason why the first charter was never recorded was this, that its grants were of so limited a character that the founders of the College were much dissatisfied with it, and, knowing that Governor Belcher was to be the Governor of the Province, they hoped that he would give them one with ampler powers and privileges. Dr. Green, in his Sketch of the Origin and Design of the College, takes this view of the matter; and most others, if not all, who have had occasion to advert to it have done the same. Had they ever met with the advertisement respecting the College inserted in the "New York Gazette" of February 2, 1746–7, they would have seen that the conjecture was not well founded as to any dissatisfaction with the charter granted by President Hamilton. Had there been any such dissatisfaction, the Trustees in their notice to the public could *not* have used the language they did: "Whereas *a charter with full and ample Privileges* has been granted by his Majesty, under the seal of the Province of New Jersey, bearing date the 22d of October, 1746, for erecting a college within said Province, . . . by which charter equal Liberties and Privileges are secured to every denomination of Christians, different religious sentiments notwithstanding," etc. There is some evidence that the charter was drawn by the petitioners, and that they obtained all they asked for. (See chap. i., "On the Origin of the College," page 44.) However this may be, the acknowledgment by the Trustees, that they had received a charter of the description just mentioned, takes away entirely the foundation of the above conjecture as to the reason why the first charter was not recorded.

Was the *second* charter left unrecorded for two years or more because of any dissatisfaction with it?

The first charter may not have been in all respects as liberal as the second; but in what the second differed from the first, excepting with respect to the larger number of Trustees, and in making the Governor of the Province for the time being President of the Board, can now be only a matter of conjecture. Possibly the first charter was more restrictive as to the power of conferring degrees, and as to the amount of productive property which the Trustees were permitted to hold. In its liberal provision for the admission of all classes of Christians to the privileges of the College, the first was on the same footing with the second; and, *in fact, the language of the second as to this matter is evidently taken from the first.* The reference in the second charter to the concessions of Carteret, seemingly for the purpose of assigning a good and sufficient reason why all should be admitted to the privileges of the College, in accordance with the prayer of the petitioners, was also probably intended to meet, by indirection, the objection to granting corporate powers to a body of Dissenters; the right to do which had been called in question upon an application for a church charter for the First Presbyterian Church in the city of New York. The connection in which these things occur in the second charter renders it highly probable that the provision for admitting all classes of Christians, and the reference to the concessions of Carteret, were both borrowed from the *first* charter.

William Smith, the most distinguished lawyer of his day in New York, was a prominent member of the Presbyterian Church in that city. For reasons given near the beginning of this chapter, it is more than probable that he was a Trustee of the College under both charters; and it is by no means improbable that he prepared the first charter, and also "the rough" of the second, which Governor Belcher desired Mr. Pemberton to send him for his inspection. There was no person among Mr. Pemberton's friends better, if so well, qualified to do this work, and no one upon whom Mr. Pemberton would be so likely to call for just such a service. For many years, and to the end of his life, Mr. Smith was an earnest friend of the College, and one of the most honored and influential members of the Board.

Governor Belcher was disposed to possess himself of the views and wishes of those interested in the College, but at the same time he purposed to mould the charter to suit his own views; and therefore, while he sought, and in some cases accepted, advice, he desired not to have a charter fully prepared for his approval and signature, but only the "rough" of one, which he might examine and see if it could be made better. He was to give "a new and better charter," and he must decide for himself what that new and better charter must be; and to this end he had it prepared under his own direction, as is fully evident from his letters to Messrs. Pemberton and others. He introduced in the second charter the clause making the Governor of the Province *ex officio* President of the Board of Trustees, in opposition to the wishes of some of the friends of the College and the earnest remonstrance of the Rev. Gilbert Tennent. But the Governor was inflexible as to this point, and said he could not give a charter without such a provision. It is not to be supposed that Mr. Tennent, or any other friend of the College, had any objection to making Governor Belcher President of the Board: the objection was to establishing it as a fixed rule that the Governor for the time being should be President of the Board. The opposition to this measure doubtless arose from an apprehension that it would sometimes happen that the Governor would not be in sympathy with the Trustees, and that he might embarrass their deliberations, even if he should not directly oppose their measures. But the experience of more than a hundred years has shown that there was no sufficient cause for any such apprehension, and that the measure has worked to the advantage of the College, and not to its injury. It is but right that the State to which the College is indebted for its corporate privileges, and which has a deep interest in the proper training of her youth, should be represented at the Board and have a voice in directing the affairs of the institution; and the Chief Magistrate of the State seems to be the proper person to represent her in her highest seats of learning, and to see that the interests of the State are properly cared for and the directions of the charter properly observed. From a remark made by Governor Belcher in his letter of April 2, 1748, to Mr. Pemberton, it is not improbable that the Governor would have been disposed to make several members of Council *ex officio* members of the Board of Trustees, as well as the Governor of the Province, for in this letter he says:

"As to the matter of the President of the Trustees, I think Mr. Burr was convinced with what I said, that it would be best to be always the King's Governor for the time being, which may be of service on many accounts. He is to be confined to a single vote, nor is he to call, or adjourn, a meeting but in conformity to the constitution. It is now thirty years since my first being one of the Trustees of Harvard College, by virtue of my being one of his Majesty's Council for the Massachusetts Bay. I could never observe any Inconvenience in that part of the Charter. However, I will consider and talk further with some of the Trustees on this article."

The first four persons named as Trustees of the College in the charter given by Governor Belcher were members of his Majesty's Council for New Jersey, but they were not Trustees *ex officio*, but by special designation. There was probably an earnest desire on the part of the friends of the College to have these gentlemen for Trustees, but they never would have assented to have their successors in his Majesty's Council to be *ex officio* their successors in the Board of Trustees.   The College was a Presbyterian College, established by Presbyterians, supported by Presbyterians, and controlled by Presbyterians, and they never would have consented to run the risk that might arise, either to the religious or Presbyterian character of their institution, from having so large a number of the Board chosen, not by the other Trustees, but by the civil power.   Knowing the feeling on this subject on the part of the friends of the College, Governor Belcher, even if willing to make sundry members of the Council *ex officio* members of the Board, was content with carrying out his plan of making the Governor for the time being President of the Board.   In doing this he did the College good service.   Had he gone further in this direction, he would have turned away from the College some of those who proved to be among its most efficient friends and advocates.

The following extract is from a letter of Rev. Jonathan Edwards to Rev. Dr. John Erskine, of Scotland, of the date of May 20, 1749, and written from Northampton :

"I have heard nothing new that is very remarkable concerning the College in New Jersey. It is in its infancy; there has been considerable difficulty about settling their charter. Governor Belcher, who gave the charter, is willing to encourage and promote the College to his utmost, but differs in his opinion concerning the Constitution which will tend most to its prosperity from some of the principal ministers that have been concerned in founding the Society. He insists upon it that the Governor for the time being and four of his Majesty's Council for the Province should always be of the Corporation of Trustees, and that the Governor should always be the President of the Corporation. The ministers are all very willing that the present Governor, who is a religious man, should be in this standing; but their difficulty is with respect to the future Governors, who they suppose are as likely to be men of no religion and Deists as otherwise. However, so the matter is settled, to the great uneasiness of Mr. Gilbert Tennent, who, it is feared, will have no further concern with the College on this account. Mr. Burr, the President of the College, is a man of religion and singular learning, and I hope the College will flourish under his care."

The following is a list of the gentlemen named in the charter given by President Hamilton in 1746, as far as positive evidence exists on this head, viz., Jonathan Dickinson, John Pierson, Ebenezer Pemberton, and Aaron Burr.

The following is a list of the Trustees named in the charter given by Governor Belcher in 1748, viz., John Reading, James Hude, Andrew Johnston, Thomas Leonard, John Kinsey, Edward Shippen, William Smith, Peter Van Brugh Livingston, William Peartree Smith, Samuel Hazard, John Pierson, Ebenezer Pemberton, Joseph Lamb, Gilbert Tennent, William Tennent, Richard Treat, Samuel Blair, David Cowell, Aaron Burr, Timothy Johnes, Thomas Arthur, and Jacob Green.

As already shown, it is *very probable* that at least nine of the gentlemen here named were Trustees under the first charter.

CHARTER OF THE COLLEGE OF NEW JERSEY.

GEORGE THE SECOND, by the grace of God, of Great Britain, France, and Ireland, king, defender of the faith, &c., to all to whom these presents shall come, greeting—

Preamble.   WHEREAS sundry of our loving subjects, well-disposed and public-spirited persons, have lately, by their humble petition, presented to our trusty and well-beloved Jonathan Belcher, Esquire, governor and commander in chief of our province of New Jersey in America, represented the great necessity of coming into some method for encouraging and promoting a learned education of our youth in New Jersey, and have expressed their earnest desire that a college may be erected in our said province of New Jersey in America, for the benefit of the inhabitants of the said province and others, wherein youth may be instructed in the learned languages, and in the liberal arts and sciences. AND WHEREAS by the fundamental concessions made at the first settlement of New Jersey by the Lord Berkley and Sir George Carteret, then proprietors thereof, and granted under their hands and the seal of the said province, bearing date the tenth day of February, in the year of our Lord one thousand six hundred and sixty-four, it was, among other things, conceded and agreed, that no freeman within the said province of New Jersey should at any time be molested, punished, disquieted or called in question, for any difference in opinion or practice in matters of religious concernment, who do not actually disturb the civil peace of the said province; but that all and every such person or persons might, from time to time, and at all times thereafter, freely and fully have and enjoy his and their judgments and consciences, in matters of religion, throughout the said province, they behaving themselves peaceably and quietly and not using this liberty to licentiousness, nor to the civil injury or outward disturbance of others, as by the said concessions on record in the secretary's office of New Jersey, at Perth Amboy, in lib. 3, folio 66, &c., may appear. WHEREFORE and for that the said petitioners have also expressed their earnest desire that those of every religious denomination may have free and equal liberty and advantages of education in the said college, any different sentiments in religion notwithstanding. WE being willing to grant the reasonable requests and prayers of all our loving subjects, and to promote a liberal and learned education among them—

KNOW YE THEREFORE, that we, considering the premises, and being willing for the future that the best means of education be established in our said province of New Jersey, for the benefit and advantage of the inhabitants of our said province and others, do, of our special grace, certain knowledge and mere motion, by these presents, will, ordain, grant and constitute, that there be a college erected in our said prov- *College founded.* ince of New Jersey, for the education of youth in the learned lan- guages and in the liberal arts and sciences;* and that the trustees of *Trustees a corporation.* the said college and their successors for ever, may and shall be one body corporate and politic, in deed, action and name, and shall be called, and named and distinguished, by the name of THE TRUSTEES *Corporate* OF THE COLLEGE OF NEW JERSEY—and further, we have willed, *name.* given, granted, constituted and appointed, and by this our present charter, of our special grace, certain knowledge, and mere motion, we do, for us, our heirs and successors, will, give, grant, constitute, and ordain, that there shall, in the said college from henceforth for ever, be *Charter per-* a body politic, consisting of trustees of the said College of New Jersey. *petual.* And for the more full and perfect erection of the said corporation and body politic, consisting of trustees of the College of New Jersey, we, of our special grace, certain knowledge and mere motion, do, by these presents, for us, our heirs and successors, create, make, ordain, consti- tute, nominate and appoint, the governor and commander in chief of our said province of New Jersey, for the time being, and also our trusty and well-beloved John Reading, James Hude, Andrew Johnston, *Names of* Thomas Leonard, John Kinsey, Edward Shippen and William Smith, *corporators.* Esquires, Peter Van-Brugh Livingston, William Peartree Smith and Samuel Hazard, gentlemen, John Pierson, Ebenezer Pemberton, Joseph Lamb, Gilbert Tennent, William Tennent, Richard Treat, Samuel Blair, David Cowell, Aaron Burr, Timothy Johnes, Thomas Arthur and Jacob Green, ministers of the gospel, to be trustees of the said College of New Jersey.

That the said trustees do, at their first meeting, after the receipt of *Oaths to be* these presents, and before they proceed to any business, take the oath *taken by* appointed to be taken by an act, passed in the first year of the reign *trustees.* of the late king George the First, entitled, "An act for the further security of his Majesty's person and government, and the succession of the crown in the heirs of the late princess Sophia, being protest- ants, and for extinguishing the hopes of the pretended prince of Wales and his open and secret abettors;" as also that they make and subscribe the declarations mentioned in an act of parliament, made

---

* Extended by the Act of March 11, 1864.

in the twenty-fifth year of the reign of king Charles the Second, entitled "An act for preventing dangers which may happen from popish recusants;" and likewise take an oath for faithfully executing **By whom** the office or trust reposed in them, the said oaths to be administered **oaths to be** to them by three of his Majesty's justices of the peace, *quorum unus;* **adminis-** **tered.** and when any new member or officer of this corporation is chosen, they are to take and subscribe the aforementioned oaths and declarations before their admission into their trusts or offices, the same to be administered to them in the presence of the trustees, by such person as they shall appoint for that service.*

Notice of That no meeting of the trustees shall be valid or legal for doing any **meeting of** business whatsoever, unless the clerk has duly and legally notified each **trustees.** and every member of the corporation of such meeting; and that before the entering on any business, the clerk shall certify such notification under his hand, to the board of trustees.

To fill va- That the said trustees have full power and authority or any †*thirteen* **cancies.** or greater number of them, to elect, nominate and appoint, and associate unto them, any number of persons as trustees upon any vacancy, **Number of** so that the whole number of trustees exceed not ‡*twenty-three*, whereof **trustees.** the president of said college for the time being, to be chosen as hereafter mentioned, to be one, and twelve of the said trustees to be always **Residence.** such persons as are inhabitants of our said province of New Jersey. And we do further, of our special grace, certain knowledge, and mere motion, for us, our heirs and successors, will, give, grant and appoint, that **Perpetual** the said trustees and their successors shall, for ever hereafter, be in **succession.** deed, fact and name, a body corporate and politic; and that they, the said body corporate and politic, shall be known and distinguished in all deeds, grants, bargains, sales, writings, evidences, muniments or otherwise howsoever, and in all courts for ever herereafter, plead and be impleaded, by the name of THE TRUSTEES OF THE COLLEGE OF NEW JERSEY.

Property. And that they the said corporation, by the name aforesaid, shall be able and in law capable, for the use of the said college, to have, get, acquire, purchase, receive and possess lands, tenements, hereditaments, jurisdictions and franchises, for themselves and their successors, in fee simple or otherwise howsoever; and to purchase, receive or build, any house or houses, or any other buildings, as they shall think needful or convenient for the use of the said College of New Jersey, and in such place or places in New Jersey, as they the said trustees shall agree upon, and also to receive and dispose of any goods, chattels, and

---

* The entire clause relative to oaths repealed and supplied by Act of March 13, 1780.

† Altered to *nine*, provided that the Governor of the State, or the President of the College, or the senior Trustee, be one of the nine; by the Act of November 2, 1781, p. 18.

‡ Altered to *twenty-seven* by the Act of April 6, 1868.

other things of what nature soever, for the use aforesaid: and also to have, accept and receive any rents, profits, annuities, gifts, legacies, donations and bequests of any kind whatsoever, for the use aforesaid, so, nevertheless, that the yearly clear value of the premises do not exceed the sum of * *two thousand pounds sterling:* And therewith or otherwise to support and pay, as the said trustees and their successors, or the major part of such of them as (according to the provision herein afterwards) are regularly convened for that purpose, shall agree and see cause, the president, tutors and other officers or ministers of the said college, their respective annual salaries or allowances, and all such other necessary and contingent charges as from time to time shall arise and accrue, relating to the said college; and also to grant, bargain, sell, let, set or assign, lands, tenements or hereditaments, goods or chattels, contract or do all other things whatsoever, by the name aforesaid, and for the use aforesaid, in as full and ample manner, to all intent and purposes, as any natural person or other body politic or corporate is able to do, by the laws of our realm of Great Britain, or of our said province of New Jersey. *[margin: Limitation of value of estate. Salaries. Contracts.]*

And of our further grace, certain knowledge and mere motion, to the intent that our said corporation and body politic may answer the end of their erection and constitution, and may have perpetual succession and continue for ever, WE do for us, our heirs and successors, hereby will, give and grant, unto the said trustees of the College of New Jersey, and to their successors for ever, that when any *thirteen* of the said trustees or of their successors are convened and met together as aforesaid, for the service of the said college, the governor and commander in chief of our said province of New Jersey, and in his absence, the president of the said college, and in the absence of the said governor and president, the eldest trustee present at such meeting, from time to time, shall be president of the said trustees in all their meetings: and at any time or times such *thirteen* trustees convened and met as aforesaid, shall be capable to act as fully and amply, to all intents and purposes, as if all the trustees of the said college were personally present; provided always, that a majority of the said *thirteen* trustees be of the said province of New Jersey, except after regular notice they fail of coming, in which case those that are present are hereby empowered to act, the different place of their abode notwithstanding; and all affairs, and actions whatsoever, under the care of the said trustees, shall be determined by the majority or greater number of those *thirteen*, so convened and met together, the president whereof shall have no more than a single vote. *[margin: Who to preside. Quorum. Majority of quorum to decide.]*

And we do for us, our heirs and successors, hereby will, give and grant, full power and authority, to any six or more of the said trustees, to call meetings of the said trustees, from time to time, and to order *[margin: Meetings, how called.]*

---

* Altered to *one hundred thousand dollars,* by the Act of March 11, 1864.

notice to the said trustees of the times and places of meeting for the service aforesaid.

Election of President. And also we do hereby for us, our heirs and successors, will, give and grant, to the said trustees of the College of New Jersey, and to their successors for ever, that the said trustees do elect, nominate and appoint such a qualified person as they, or the major part of any *thirteen* of them convened for that purpose as above directed, shall think fit, to be the president of the said college, and to have the immediate care of the education and government of such students as shall be sent to, and admitted into the said college for instruction and education; and also

Tutors and Professors. that the said trustees do elect, nominate and appoint so many tutors and professors, to assist the president of the said college, in the education and government of the students belonging to it, as they, the said trustees, or their successors, or the major part of any *thirteen* of them, which shall convene for that purpose as above directed, shall, from time to time, and at any time hereafter, think needful and serviceable to the interests of the said college; and also, that the said trustees and their successors, or the major part of any *thirteen* of them, which shall con-

Power of removal. vene for that purpose, as above directed, shall at any time displace and discharge from the service of the said college such president, tutors and professors, and to elect others in their room and stead; and also, that

Other officers. the said trustees or their successors, or the major part of any *thirteen* of them, which shall convene for that pupose, as above directed, do from time to time, as occasion shall require, elect, constitute and appoint a treasurer, a clerk, an usher, and a steward, for the said college, and appoint to them, and each of them, their respective business and trusts, and displace and discharge from the service of the said college such treasurer, clerk, usher or steward, and to elect others in their

Powers of officers. room and stead; which president, tutors, professors, treasurer, clerk, usher and steward, so elected and appointed, we do for us, our heirs and successors, by these presents, constitute and establish in their several offices, and do give them, and every of them, full power and authority to exercise the same in the said College of New Jersey, according to the direction, and during the pleasure of the said trustees, as fully and freely as any other, the like officers in our universities or any of our colleges, in our realm of Great Britain, lawfully may and ought to do.

Election of trustees. And also that the said trustees, and their successors, or the major part of any *thirteen* of them, which shall convene for that purpose as above directed, as often as one or more of the said trustees shall happen to die, or by removal or otherwise shall become unfit or incapable, according to their judgment, to serve the interest of the said college, do, as soon as conveniently may be, after the death, removal or such unfitness or incapacity of such trustee or trustees to serve the interest of the said college, elect and appoint such other trustee or trustees as shall supply the place of him or them so dying, or otherwise becoming unfit or incapable to serve the interest of the said college; and every trustee so elected and appointed shall, by virtue of these presents, and of such election, and appointment, be vested with all the power and privileges which any of the other trustees of the said college are hereby invested with.

And we do further, of our special grace, certain knowledge and mere motion, will, give and grant, and by these presents do, for us, our heirs and successors, will, give and grant, unto the said trustees of the College of New Jersey, that they and their successors, or the major part of any *thirteen* of them, which shall convene for that purpose as above directed, may make, and they are hereby fully empowered from time to time, freely and lawfully to make and establish such ordinances, orders and laws, as may tend to the good and wholesome government of the said college, and all the students and the several officers and ministers thereof, and to the public benefit of the same, not repugnant to the laws and statutes of our realm of Great Britain, or of this our province of New Jersey, and not excluding any person of any religious denomination whatsoever from free and equal liberty and advantage of education, or from any of the liberties, privileges, or immunities of the said college, on account of his or their being of a religious profession different from the said trustees of the said college; and such ordinances, orders and laws, which shall be so as aforesaid made, we do, by these presents, for us, our heirs and successors, ratify, allow of and confirm, as good and effectual, to oblige and bind all the said students and the several officers and ministers of the said college; and we do hereby authorize and empower the said trustees of the college, and the president, tutors and professors by them elected and appointed, to put such ordinances and laws in execution, to all proper intents and purposes. *[margin: Laws for the government of the college.]*

And we do further, of our especial grace, certain knowledge and mere motion, will, give and grant, unto the said trustees of the College of New Jersey, that, for the encouragement of learning and animating the students of the said college to diligence, industry, and a laudable progress in literature, that they and their successors, or the major part of any *thirteen* of them, convened for that purpose as above directed, do, by the president of the said college for the time being, or by any other deputed by them, give and grant any such degree and degrees to any of the students of the said college, or to any others by them thought worthy thereof, as are usually granted in either of our universities or any other college in our realm of Great Britain;* and that they do sign and seal diplomas or certificates of such graduations, to be kept by the graduates as perpetual memorials or testimonials thereof. *[margin: Degrees.]* *[margin: Diplomas.]*

And further, of our especial grace, certain knowledge and mere motion, we do, by these presents, for us, our heirs and successors, give and grant unto the said trustees of the College of New Jersey and to their *[margin: Seal.]*

---

* Extended by the Act of March 29, 1866.

successors, that they and their successors shall have a common seal, under which they may pass all diplomas, certificates of degrees, and all other the affairs and business of and concerning the said corporation, or of and concerning the said College of New Jersey, which shall be engraven in such form and with such inscription as shall be devised by the said trustees of the said college, or the major part of any *thirteen* of them, convened for the service of the said college as above directed.

Inferior offi-
cers.

And we do further, for us, our heirs and successors, give and grant unto the said trustees of the College of New Jersey and their successors, or the major part of any *thirteen* of them, convened for the service of the college as above directed, full power and authority from time to time, to nominate and appoint all other inferior officers and ministers, which they shall think to be convenient and necessary for the use of the college, not herein particularly named or mentioned, and which are accustomary in our universities, or in any of our colleges in our realm of Great Britain, which officers or ministers we do hereby empower to execute their offices or trusts as fully and freely as any other the like officers or ministers, in and of our universities or any other college in our realm of Great Britain, lawfully may or ought to do.

And lastly, our express will and pleasure is, and we do by these presents for us, our heirs and successors, give and grant unto the said trustees of the College of New Jersey and to their successors for ever, that these our letters patent, or the enrolment thereof, shall be good and effectual in the law, to all intents and purposes, against us, our heirs and successors, without any other license, grant or confirmation from us, our heirs and successors, hereafter by the said trustees to be had or obtained; notwithstanding the not reciting or misrecital, or not naming or misnaming of the aforesaid offices, franchises, privileges, immunities, or other the premises, or any of them: and notwithstanding a writ of *ad quod damnum* hath not issued forth to inquire of the premises or any of them, before the ensealing hereof; any statute, act, ordinance or provision, or any other matter or thing to the contrary notwithstanding; to have, hold and enjoy, all and singular the privileges, advantages, liberties, immunities and all other the premises herein and hereby granted and given, or which are meant, mentioned, or intended to be herein and hereby given and granted, unto them the said trustees of the said College of New Jersey, and to their successors for ever.

IN TESTIMONY whereof we have caused these our letters to be made patent, and the great seal of our said province of New Jersey to be hereunto affixed. WITNESS our trusty and well-beloved *Jonathan Belcher*, Esquire, governor and commander in chief of our said province of New Jersey, this fourteenth day of September, in the twenty-second year of our reign, and in the year of our Lord, one thousand seven hundred and forty-eight.

I have perused and considered the written charter of incorporation, and find nothing contained therein inconsistent with his Majesty's interest or the honor of the Crown.

J. WARRELL, *Att. Gen'l.*

September the 13th, 1748.—This charter, having been read in Council, was consented to and approved of.

CHA. READ, *Cl. Con.*

Let the Great Seal of the Province of New Jersey be affixed to this charter.

J. BELCHER.

To the Secretary of the Province of New Jersey.

CHAPTER IV.

THE Governor was *not*, properly speaking, *the founder* of the College, in the sense of being its originator, for the College was in existence, and in active operation, before his arrival. He was not, therefore, to use a phrase of Lord Coke's, its " *Fundator Incipiens*," although, in view of what he did towards the building up of the institution, he may be regarded as its " *Fundator Perficiens;*" and in this latter sense only can the statement in one of the addresses of the Trustees to the Governor be justified, when they assign as a reason why the first College edifice should be called "Belcher Hall," that "the College of New Jersey views you in the light of its *founder*, patron, and benefactor." That this view of Governor Belcher's relations to the College is a perfectly accurate one is evident from the extracts given in this work from his letters to various correspondents, and from his replies to the addresses presented to him by the Trustees of the College. The extracts here referred to are those given in the narrative of the two charters of 1746 and of 1748, in the chapter on the Design of the College, and in the History of President Burr's Administration.

Governor Belcher was the son of the Hon. Andrew Belcher, of Cambridge, one of his Majesty's Council for Massachusetts Bay, and he was born on the 8th of January, 1682. He was graduated at Harvard in 1699; and soon after he went to Europe, where he resided six years. During this period he formed an acquaintance with the Princess Sophia Dorothea, of Hanover, and with her son, George Augustus, which opened the way for his future advancement, upon the accession of this prince, in 1727, to the throne of England, as George the Second.

98

On his return he married and settled in Boston, where he became a merchant of great reputation and considerable wealth. His wife was a daughter of Lieutenant-Governor Partridge, of New Hampshire. She died on the 1st of October, 1736. He was appointed a member of the Provincial Council, and in 1729 he was sent to England as agent of the Province; and on the 29th of November of the same year he was made Governor of Massachusetts and of New Hampshire, which office he held for twelve years. Upon becoming Governor he relinquished his mercantile pursuits and devoted himself to his official duties. His home was distinguished for its elegant hospitality, and he is said to have impaired his private fortune in upholding the dignity of his office, of which, both in Massachusetts and in New Jersey, he had a very high estimate.

We learn from President Quincy's "History of Cambridge University" that Governor Belcher, as Governor Burnet had done before him, made a formal and public visit to Harvard. Of this visit the President gives the following account:

> "The visit of Governor Belcher to the College appears, according to the records, to have been attended with like ceremonies. He was, on the 9th of September, 1730, accompanied to Cambridge by a 'military troop, then waited on by two companies of foot.' When he arrived at the College, after having been for a while in Mr. Flynt's chamber, the bell tolled, and the scholars assembled in the Hall, into which the Governor and Corporation having entered, Mr. Hobby made a Latin oration, and his Excellency made a very handsome answer in Latin. This done, and his Excellency the Governor, his Majesty's Council, the Tutors, Professors, and sundry gentlemen, who came on the occasion, dined together in the library, with the Corporation.
>
> "These forms and ceremonies, of the last and preceding age," adds President Quincy, "are interesting as characteristic of the customs and manners of Massachusetts under the Colonial and Provincial Governments."

The "History of the College of New Jersey" furnishes examples of somewhat similar ceremonies, on occasions of the first visits made to the College by the Colonial Governors.

On the death of President Wadsworth, of Harvard, which occurred on the 16th of March, 1737, the other members of the Corporation were equally divided in opinion as to the proper person to be chosen his successor, one half being in favor of electing the Rev. Mr. Holyoke, a minister of Marblehead, and the other half being for the Rev. Joshua Gee, whom President Quincy describes as a man of considerable genius, not deficient in learning, holding all the peculiar doctrines of Calvin with a bigoted pertinacity, and naturally of a fiery zeal, which, if it had not been quenched by constitutional indolence, would probably have rendered him a firebrand among the churches. Perhaps this description of a rigid Calvinistic divine, by one of such liberal views in matters of religion as President Quincy, should be taken *cum grano salis*. Still, it may be sufficiently near the mark to account for Governor Belcher's influence being finally cast in favor of Mr. Holyoke, of whose thorough Calvinism some of the stricter sort stood in doubt, without ascribing the Governor's course "to *the tact of a politician*, who saw clearly that the times of denunciation and exclusion were fast passing away," and who was satisfied, or *willing to appear to be convinced*, upon the sole authority of Barnard" (also a minister of Marblehead, and an intimate friend of Holyoke), "although the terms in which he vouched for the Calvinism of Holyoke placed his catholicism and liberality in high relief, and conveyed a severe sarcasm on those who were counteracting his election by scattering doubts concerning the soundness of his principles." Upon hearing Mr. Barnard's account of the character and religious views of Mr. Holyoke, Governor Belcher said, "Then I believe he must be the man." "And accordingly," adds President Quincy, "he was the man, and was elected in both Boards* unanimously." This statement shows at once the sound judgment of his Excellency, his freedom from undue bias, and his great influence, at that time, in shaping the measures of the authorities of Harvard.

Governor Belcher presided at the inauguration of President Holyoke, and also on this occasion made a speech in Latin, in the course of which he delivered to the President the charter, key, etc. The President replied in Latin. Governor Belcher's

---

* The Boards referred to above were the *Corporation*, consisting of the President and six Fellows, whose privilege it was to nominate the officers of the College, and the *Board of Overseers*, consisting of the Governor, Deputy-Governor, members of the Council, and others, who had the power to confirm or to reject.

course with respect to the University was such as naturally tended to gratify the friends of the institution generally; and had he been equally fortunate in pleasing the supporters and opponents of his administration, he might possibly have held the government during life. But his insisting, as his predecessors had done, that a sufficient and fixed salary for the support of the Governor should be voted by the General Court, and his opposition to a measure known as "the land bank company," helped to undermine his influence and to prepare the way for his removal. As the representative of the King, he was *not* indisposed to exercise all the authority given him in his commission; and in deciding upon the course he ought to pursue in reference to measures bearing upon the honor of the Crown, the welfare of the Province, or the interests of religion and learning, he was not distrustful of his own judgment, although as to particular points he deemed it prudent to avail himself of the opinions of others whose position, ability, and good sense commanded his respect and confidence; and sometimes, though not always, he yielded his own judgment to theirs. In religion he was a decided Calvinist; also an ardent friend to revivals, and a favorite of those engaged in promoting them. That eminent evangelist, the Rev. George Whitefield, was most kindly received by him, both in Massachusetts and in New Jersey.

His freedom in the utterance of his opinions was very marked, and not always the most discreet; and this is said to have been one and a principal cause of the hostility against him on the part of those who succeeded in their efforts to have him removed from his office as Governor of Massachusetts and New Hampshire.

That he had been misrepresented by his political enemies, he gave to King's Council, at the English Court, such clear evidence that he was promised the first vacancy in the gubernatorial chairs of the American Provinces; and happily for the interests of the country, and more especially for the interests of sound learning and fervent piety, this first vacancy occurred in the Province of New Jersey, in which, at this very time, efforts were making to establish the institution ever since known as " The College of New Jersey," although it is not unfrequently

spoken of under the names of " Princeton College" and " Nassau
Hall."

Upon being superseded by Governor Shirley, in 1741, Governor Belcher went to England, and did not return to America
until the summer of 1747, when he came back with the commission of Captain-General and Governor of the Province of New
Jersey, etc.   The date of his commission was that of July 18,
1746, and it was approved in Council August 22 of that same
year ; but such appear to have been the straitened circumstances of the Governor at this time, that he was unable for
many months to pay the requisite fees ; and for the funds with
which they were paid he was indebted to the liberality of sundry
persons, members of the Society of Friends, in England.

Sailing from England in the Scarborough, an English vessel
of war, he arrived here on the 8th of August, 1747, after a
tedious passage of nearly ten weeks; and, as mentioned by him
in a letter of the 16th of September, to a friend in London
(Rev. Mr. Bradbury), he was received by the people with all
possible appearance of respect and satisfaction.   In this letter
he also speaks of putting forward the building of a college,
and in a letter to the Committee of the West Jersey Society of
London he says:

> " The people of New Jersey are in a poor situation for educating their children,
> and the project for a college had been started before my arrival, and where it
> should be placed was a matter of dispute between the gentlemen of East and West
> Jersey, but I have got them to agree upon Princeton."

And in a letter of October 2, of the same year, he says, to
another friend (Mr. Walley):

> " Princeton is fixed upon for the site of the College, and such a nursery for
> religion and learning is much wanted."

We are not to infer from these statements that there was any
formal vote or agreement among the friends of the College that
it should be permanently established at Princeton, but that those
of them with whom the Governor conversed had intimated to
him a willingness to accede to his suggestion, "if," to use an
expression common in ecclesiastical parlance, "the way should
be clear."

For ten years Governor Belcher administered, with great ability and much to the satisfaction of the people generally, the government of this Province. The disturbances existing before his coming were quelled by his mild and conciliatory course, and he had the esteem and encouragement of the friends of evangelical piety and sound learning in his efforts to place upon a firm foundation the College which, to use his own expression, " he had adopted as a daughter."

Governor Belcher was the first to follow the notable example set by acting Governor John Hamilton, in granting a charter, with the consent of Council, without any reference to the Assembly, and without waiting for any special instructions from the English Court. (See chapter i., page 45.) In this respect, Hamilton first, and Belcher next, in boldness and consummate judgment, went beyond the much-lauded measure of Governor Dudley, of Massachusetts, in prompting and approving the declaration by the General Court of that Province in 1707, that the act of 1650, respecting Harvard College, having never been repealed, was to be deemed the law governing that institution, and thus secured its perpetuity and its freedom from further interference by the Crown, which had annulled its charters, granted subsequently to that act. The example of President Hamilton was followed not only by Governor Belcher, but by other of the Provincial Governors, as in the cases of King's College, New York City; Dartmouth College, New Hampshire; Queen's College, New Jersey; which were all, in a measure at least, indebted for their existence to these precedents of 1746 and of 1748.

Of the Rev. Jonathan Dickinson, and of the Rev. Aaron Burr, Trustees of the College under the first charter, memoirs will be given in connection with the narratives of their administrations as Presidents of the College.

The Rev. John Pierson, a Trustee under both charters, was pastor of the Presbyterian church in Woodbridge, Middlesex County, New Jersey. He was a graduate of Yale in 1711, and was a son of the Rev. Abraham Pierson, the first rector or President of that College; and he was the maternal grandfather of the Rev. Dr. Ashbel Green, the eighth President of the College of New Jersey. Mr. Pierson was the Moderator of the Synod of New Jersey in 1749.

The Rev. John Pemberton, D.D., also known to be a Trustee under both charters, was graduated at Harvard College in 1721. His father, of the same name, was at this time minister of the South Church, Boston. Dr. Pemberton, the Trustee, was pastor of the Presbyterian church in the city of New York from 1727 until 1753 or 1754, when he removed to Boston and took charge of a church in that city. In 1746 he was the Moderator of the Synod of New York. He died on the 9th of September, 1777, at the age of seventy-two years. It was only during his residence in New York that he held the position of Trustee.

The Hon. John Reading, the first person named as a Trustee in Governor Belcher's charter, was a resident of Hunterdon County, and the *senior* member of the Governor's Council at the time this charter was given; and upon the death of Governor Belcher he became the acting Governor of the Province, as he had been for nearly a year before Governor Belcher's arrival.

Hon. James Hude, a native of Scotland, emigrated to this country while yet a young man, and made New Brunswick the place of his residence. He took an active part in the erection of the First Presbyterian Church in that city, of which church he was an elder during the pastorate of the Rev. Mr. Arthur. Mr. Hude was for some time Mayor of New Brunswick, and at the time of his appointment as Trustee of the College he was a member of Governor Belcher's Council.

Hon. Andrew Johnston was a resident of Perth Amboy, an attendant at the Episcopal church of that city, a member of Governor Belcher's Council, Treasurer of East Jersey, and was the first person chosen Treasurer of the College.

Both Mr. Hude and Mr. Johnston were members of the Provincial Council when the Honorable John Hamilton, President of the Council, gave the first charter, and it is quite probable that they were Trustees of the College under that charter also. (See page 47.)

Hon. Thomas Leonard was a member of Governor Belcher's

Council, a resident of Princeton, and a gentleman of wealth and influence. He laid the corner-stone of " Nassau Hall."

The Leonards of New Jersey were of English origin, and they were descended from a family of that name settled at Raynham, Massachusetts, in 1652. At this place they introduced the first forge set up in America, and in 1797 it was in the possession of this family of the sixth generation. The Leonards were remarkable for their longevity, promotion to public office, a hereditary attachment to the manufacture " of iron, and kindness to the Indians." " Of the great ages attained by this family, it is stated that in 1793 it was known that one had died aged *one hundred,* two over *ninety,* seventeen over *eighty,* fifty-three over *seventy-three.* Thirteen had been graduated at Cambridge." *

King Philip's hunting-house stood a mile and a quarter from the forge, and Philip and the Leonards lived on such friendly terms that as soon as the war of 1675 broke out, which ended in the death of the King and in the ruin of his tribe, "he issued strict orders to all his Indians never to hurt the Leonards." * As early as 1721, Mr. Leonard was a member of the Assembly of New Jersey, from Somerset County; and he died in 1760.

The Hon. John Kinsey, the next in the list of Trustees, was, at the date of the charter, Chief Justice of Pennsylvania. He was a member of the Society of Friends. In the preparation of this instrument Governor Belcher sought his advice, and he placed it in his hands for revision before submitting it to the Attorney-General of New Jersey for his approval. At the earnest desire of Governor Belcher, Chief-Justice Kinsey continued to serve as a Trustee.

He was a native of England, and upon coming to this country settled first in New Jersey. In 1716 he was a representative to the Provincial Assembly from Middlesex County, and the same year, and for several years in immediate succession, he was chosen Speaker of this body; and again in 1730 and 1733. From New Jersey he removed to Philadelphia, where he was elected a member of the Pennsylvania Assembly, of

* Morse's American Gazetteer.

which he was the Speaker for several sessions. (See Elmer's " Reminiscences.")

David Paul Brown, author of the " Forum and Bar," speaks of Mr. Kinsey as being for some years, with Andrew Hamilton, the only great lawyer in the Province. In the case of the Rev. Wm. Tennent, tried for perjury, Mr. Kinsey was associated with Mr. Wm. Smith, of New York, and with Mr. John Coxe, of New Jersey, as counsel for the defence.

A few years after the establishment of the Court of Chancery in Pennsylvania by Governor Sir W. Keith, he caused Mr. Kinsey's hat to be taken off by an officer of the court, whilst Mr. K. was attending to some business before him as Chancellor. This gave great offence to the Quakers, and, although they were afterwards allowed to wear their hats, the court itself was soon after entirely set aside. (See Field's " Provincial Courts" and Proud's " History of Pennsylvania.")

In 1738, Mr. Kinsey was Attorney-General of Pennsylvania, and in 1743 he was made Chief Justice of that Province : this latter office he retained until his death, which occurred at Burlington, New Jersey, in May, 1750.

In writing to Mr. Richard Partridge, then in London, Governor Belcher, in a letter of the date of April 22, 1748, says of Mr. Kinsey, " He is the next man in honor and power to the Governor of Pennsylvania." And again, in writing to the same gentleman, in November, 1750, he says, " My friend Kinsey is ·dead."

Hon. Edward Shippen was by profession a merchant, but in 1749 he was made a Judge of the Common Pleas, and also of the Orphans' Court and Quarter Sessions, of Philadelphia. He had for his associates on the bench Franklin, Lawrence, and Maddox. (See Brown's " Forum.")

He was evidently a man of note and influence, and took an active part in promoting the interests of the College. Owing to his advanced age, he resigned his place at the Board in 1767.

His son, Edward Shippen, was for some years Chief Justice of the State of Pennsylvania ; and his younger son, Joseph Shippen, a graduate of the College in 1753, was Secretary of the *Province* of Pennsylvania. Judge Shippen was a scholarly man, and occasionally corresponded with his sons in the Latin and French languages.

Hon. Wm. Smith was an eminent lawyer of New York City. He was born in Buckinghamshire, England, in 1696, and emigrated to America in 1715. He was graduated at Yale College in 1719, and was a Tutor in the same from 1722 to 1724. In 1736 he was made Recorder of the city of New York, and subsequently a member of the King's Council, and also a Judge of the Supreme Court of the Province. Of the part he took in the Zenger trial for libel, and of the consequences to himself and to his friend James Alexander, Esq., mention was made in the first chapter of this work; but nothing is there said of the grounds of the exceptions taken by them to the competency of the court to try the case. They were these :

" 1. Because the commission was granted during pleasure, whereas it ought to be granted during good behavior.

" 2. That the commission was granted by a Justice of the Common Pleas, whereas it could only be granted by a Judge of the King's Bench.

" 3. That the form of the commission was not warranted by law.

" 4. It appears that the commission was allowed by William Cosby, Esq., Governor of the Colony, and without the advice or consent of his Majesty's Council of this Colony, without which the Governor could not grant the same.

" When these exceptions were offered to the Court, April 15, 1735, the Chief Justice said to Messrs. Alexander and Smith that they ought well to consider the consequences of what they offered; to which they answered, they had well considered the consequences; and Mr. Smith further said, that he was so well satisfied of the right of the subject to take an exception to the commission of a judge, if he thought such commission illegal, that he durst venture his life upon that point.

" The next day Mr. Smith asked to be heard by the Court on these two points :

" 1. Whether the subject has the right to take such exceptions.

" 2. That the exceptions were legal and valid.

" To which the Chief Justice said, ' That they would neither hear nor allow the exceptions; . . . and that either we must go from the bench or you from the bar.'

" Accordingly, by order of the Court, they were 'excluded from any further practice in this Court.' " (See Brown's " Forum," pp. 287, 288.)

" In 1754, with the aid of Messrs. James Alexander, P. V. B. and W. Livingston, and J. Morin Scott, he raised £600 to buy books to lend to the people, which led to the establishment of the New York Society Library." (Duer's " Life of Lord Stirling.")

The following obituary notice of Mr. Smith appeared in the " New York Gazette," November 22, 1769:

" Last Wednesday morning departed this life, in the seventy-third year of his age, the Honorable Wm. Smith, Esq., one of the Justices of the Supreme Court, and late one of his Majesty's Council for this province. He was born in England, and arrived here in 1715. He practised the law with great reputation, and was esteemed one of the most eminent in his profession. In 1753 he was made one of his Majesty's Council, which office he afterwards resigned, and in the year 1763 he was made one of the Judges of the Supreme Court. He was a gentleman of great erudition, and was the most eloquent speaker in the province. He was of an amiable and exemplary life and conversation, and a zealous and inflexible friend to the cause of religion and liberty."

Peter Van Brugh Livingston, Esq., was an eminent merchant in the city of New York, and a man of great public spirit. He was a son of Philip Livingston, of Livingston Manor, and the eldest brother of Governor Livingston, of New Jersey. He was graduated at Yale in 1731. He married Mary, a daughter of James Alexander, above mentioned. In the latter part of his life he removed to Elizabeth, New Jersey, in the vicinity of which he purchased a farm, that has remained in possession of his family ever since, the present proprietor being John Kean, Esq.

Wm. Peartree Smith was the grandson of Wm. Smith, Governor-General of the island of Jamaica, who was married at Port Royal to Frances Peartree, and who died at New York April 2, 1714, leaving two sons, the younger of whom, William, was the father of William Peartree Smith, who was born in New York in 1723. He was graduated at Yale College in 1742, and studied law, but did not engage in the practice of it, finding sufficient employment in attending to his own estate and in promoting useful objects. Governor Belcher, as early as 1748, speaks of him as his correspondent in New York, and as being "a very worthy and religious young man." The family was one of much taste and refinement. He married Mary Bryant, daughter of Captain Bryant, of Amboy, and left one daughter, the wife of the Hon. Elisha Boudinot, and one son, Wm. Pitt Smith, M.D. Ten other children died in early life. He joined Cummings, Livingston, and Scott in publishing the "Watch-Tower," in the city of New York, in 1755. He was an ardent patriot, and took a great interest in the struggle between the Provinces and the mother-country, and lost much of his property by the depreciation of the currency. " He was," says Dr. Hatfield, "one of the most distinguished civilians of the day." Upon the marriage of his daughter he removed to Elizabethtown, New Jersey, and while living there he was arrested by the British and taken to New York, and, had it not been for the interposition of his numerous friends in that city, would have been sent to the prison-ship. He resigned his place at the Board in 1793, having been for at least forty-five years a trustee of the College. He died in 1801.

Samuel Hazard, Esq., was the second son of Nathaniel Hazard, a merchant of New York. He removed to Philadelphia, and continued to reside there. He had two sons, one of whom, Ebenezer Hazard, a graduate of Nassau Hall, succeeded Mr. Bache as Postmaster-General of the United States.

Mr. Hazard, the Trustee, and Mr. Robert Smith, the Architect, were a committee to select the site for Nassau Hall.

Of the Rev. John Pierson and the Rev. Ebenezer Pemberton, the first two ministers of the gospel named in the second charter, mention was made above as being Trustees under the first charter.

The next in order is the Rev. Joseph Lamb. He was graduated at Yale in 1717, and was ordained by the Presbytery of Long Island, and installed pastor of Mattituck. Being called to Baskingridge, May, 1744, he joined the New Brunswick Presbytery. He was the Moderator of the Synod of New York in 1748, his predecessors in that office being, Jonathan Dickinson, 1745; Ebenezer Pemberton, 1746; Gilbert Tennent, 1747. Mr. Lamb died in July, 1749.

The Rev. Gilbert Tennent and the Rev. William Tennent were born in Ireland, and came to America with their father, the Rev. William Tennent, Senior, September, 1716. Their father accepted a call to Neshaminy in 1726, at which place he established the famous Log College, "at which," says Whitefield, "eight ministers trained by him were sent out before the autumn of 1739. Of these, four were his own sons." As frequent mention will be elsewhere made in this history of these two distinguished and devoted servants of Christ, and our object being mainly to identify, as far as can be done, the first Trustees under each of the two College charters, we shall merely state in this connection that the Rev. Gilbert Tennent, D.D., was first settled as pastor of the Presbyterian church at New Brunswick, in 1726, and removed to Philadelphia in 1744, where he had charge of the Second Presbyterian Church until his death, in January, 1764. He was an eloquent preacher, and an earnest controversialist, both in the pulpit and out of it, making a liberal use of the press in maintaining his own opinions, and in attacking, and not always in the mildest terms, the opinions of those from whom he differed. He was beyond question the leading man among his brethren of the Presbytery of New Brunswick—not to say of the Synod of New York—after the death of Mr. Dickinson.

Of Dr. Gilbert Tennent, and also of his father and three brothers, William, Jr., John, and Charles, interesting memoirs are given in Dr. A. Alexander's " History of the Log College."

The Rev. William Tennent, Jr., was ordained by the Presbytery of Philadelphia in October, 1733, and succeeded his younger brother, John Tennent, as pastor of the Freehold Presbyterian church, now known as the Tennent Church, Monmouth County, New Jersey. On different occasions he was chosen *pro tem.* President of the College. A sketch of his life, recording several extraordinary incidents, was published by Hon. Elias Boudinot, LL.D., in " The Assembly's Missionary Magazine" of 1806.

The accuracy of this sketch with respect to some matters connected with Mr. William Tennent's trial, on the charge of perjury in the case of Mr. Roland, before Chief-Justice Robert Hunter Morris, has been called in question by two such eminent lawyers as Judge R. S. Field and Chancellor H. W. Green, who, in the opinion of the writer, have made good the exceptions taken by them to some of the details. Chancellor Green's paper was published in the " Princeton Review" for 1868, and Judge Field's in the " Proceedings of the New Jersey Historical Society," vol. vi.

The errors in the narrative of the trial can be readily accounted for, if we bear in mind that it was written between sixty and seventy years after the trial took place, and about thirty years after Mr. Tennent's decease; and further, that the incidents mentioned were given upon the authority of persons who had no personal knowledge of any of the facts, and whose belief in the truthfulness of what they had heard respecting the trial rested solely upon mere traditions, in which the facts were so intermingled with wrong deductions from them as to give to the entire narrative an air of fiction. If all the incidents, both those known and those unknown to the author of the narrative, had been given in their proper order, there would have been no difficulty in showing that they were such as might have occurred in the usual course of divine providence, without requiring any supernatural interposition through the medium of dreams. Granting that two of the witnesses had the very dreams they are reported to have had, it is far more likely that *the dreams* were *in consequence* of what they had previously heard respecting the bills of indictment found against Mr. Tennent and Mr. Stevens, than that *their first information* on the subject was derived from the dreams; which, indeed, is not directly affirmed, but is left to be inferred from the manner in which they are introduced into the narrative. The trial took place in June, 1742, ten months after the indictment, and of course there was ample time to summon all the witnesses required in the case.

There is another objection to the narrative, inasmuch as it exalts Mr. Tennent's piety at the expense of his judgment, the right exercise of which would have led him, contrary to what is said in the narrative, to employ every lawful means within his reach to meet the unjust and cruel charge brought against him, and from which he was triumphantly vindicated by the testimony adduced at the trial and by the verdict of the jury.

The Rev. Richard Treat, D.D., was born in Milford, Connecticut, September 25, 1705, and was a descendant or near relative of Governor Robert Treat. He was graduated at Yale in 1725, and was ordained by the Presbytery of Philadelphia, and installed pastor of the church of Abington, December 30, 1731. But upon the division in the Synod of Philadelphia, by which the Presbytery of New Brunswick and their adherents were excluded from the Synod, he joined this Presbytery, of which he was an influential member.   He died November 20, 1778.

Rev. Samuel Blair was born in Ireland, June 14, 1712; he came to this country while yet a lad.   He pursued his studies at the "Log College," and was licensed November, 1733, at Abington, by the Philadelphia Presbytery.   He accepted a call to Middletown and Shrewsbury, New Jersey, and was ordained by the East Jersey Presbytery in 1734.   At the earnest invitation of the people at Fagg's Manor, Pennsylvania, he removed to that place, and was installed pastor of their church in April, 1740.   Here he established a classical and theological school, which under his wise and skilful guidance, and that of his brother, the Rev. John Blair, his successor at Fagg's Manor, rose to be an institution of much note.   He died July 5, 1751. The Rev. Samuel Davies, in writing to the Rev. Dr. Bellamy, says, "The greatest light in these parts is just about to take wing." (See Rev. R. Webster's "History.")

Rev. David Cowell was born in Dorchester, Massachusetts, in 1704, and was graduated at Harvard in 1732.   He was ordained by the Presbytery of Philadelphia, November 3, 1736, and installed pastor of the church at Trenton.   He was an ardent and devoted friend of the College, and had much to do in placing Mr. Davies in the presidency of that institution.   To Mr. D. he wrote, "I am sensible that your leaving Virginia is attended with great difficulties, but I cannot think your affairs are of equal importance with the College."

He died December 1, 1760, and his funeral sermon was preached by President Davies, who said of him, "In the charter of the College of New Jersey he was nominated one of the Trustees, and but few invested with the same trust discharged it with so much zeal, diligence, and alacrity;" adding, "The College of New Jersey has lost a father, and I have lost a friend." (See Rev. Dr. Hall's "History of the First Church, Trenton.")

He was the only member of the Synod of Philadelphia whose name appears in the charter; for, although Drs. Tennent and Treat resided in Pennsylvania, they were members of the Synod of New York.

Rev. Timothy Johnes, D.D., was of Welsh descent, and was born at South Hampton, Long Island, New York, May 24, 1717. He was graduated at Yale in 1737. He was ordained February 9, 1743, and was pastor of the church at Morristown until his death, September, 1794, at the age of seventy-eight years. In 1783 he received from Yale the degree of Doctor in Divinity.

Rev. Thomas Arthur was graduated at Yale in 1743, and was ordained by the Presbytery of New York in 1746, and settled as pastor of the Presbyterian church at New Brunswick, at which place he died, February 2, 1751, aged twenty-seven. "He was a good scholar, a graceful orator, and a finished preacher." ·

Rev. Jacob Green was born at Malden, Massachusetts, January 22, 1723. He was graduated at Harvard in 1744. He came to New Jersey, and was ordained and installed at Hanover in 1746.

On the 22d of November, 1758, he was chosen Vice-President of the College *pro tem.*, and for six months discharged the duties pertaining to the office of President.

He was father of the Rev. Dr. Ashbel Green, the eighth President of the College. He was a member of the Provincial Congress of New Jersey of 1776, and the chairman of the committee that prepared the first Constitution of the State.

In the second charter the names of the lay Trustees appear to be inserted in the order of their rank, if they held office, and of their age or social position, if not in office. Hence the names of the members of the Governor's Council are given first. Then occur the names of Chief-Justice Kinsey and Judge Shippen, of Pennsylvania. The name of William Smith, the distinguished attorney and counsellor of New York, comes next. He was not made a judge till 1763. After him are named Peter V. B. Livingston, William Peartree Smith, and Samuel Hazard, in order of age, most probably.

The names of the clergy are given according to the dates of their respective ordinations.

CHAPTER V.

In the Introduction to this work it has been made to appear that the College owed its origin mainly to the foresight and efforts of the Rev. Messrs. Dickinson, Pierson, Pemberton, Burr, and their coadjutors.

The first named of these eminent and good men was the one selected by his associates to take the oversight of their infant seminary of learning.

In the triennial catalogue of the College, Mr. Dickinson is spoken of as President in 1746; but this is an error, and it arose from confounding the date of the first charter with the time when Mr. Dickinson was chosen President of the College, which most probably took place in April, 1747, and certainly not before February of that year. For on the 2d of February, O. S., corresponding to the 13th of February, N. S., the Trustees announced to the public that a charter for a College had been granted to them, and that the College would be opened some time in May next, at the latest; but in this their first advertisement they make no mention of the choice of a President, nor of the location of the College. In their next public notice, of the date of April 27, 1747, they say that "the Trustees of the College of New Jersey have appointed the Rev. Jonathan Dickinson President of said College, which" (they add) "will be opened in the fourth week of May next, at Elizabethtown. At which Time and Place all Persons suitably qualified may be admitted to an Academic Education."

That the first term of the College began at the time here specified there can be no reasonable doubt; and the evidence adduced shows that the charter under which Mr. Dickinson

114

conducted the instruction and the government of the College was in full force until it was superseded by the one given by Governor Belcher in 1748.*

Within one year from the opening of the College there were several students ready to receive their first degree in the Arts. And this fact renders it morally certain that some of these candidates, if not all, had been in training under the supervision and instruction of President Dickinson. As just mentioned, the first term began in the fourth week of May, 1747. Mr. Dickinson died on the 7th of October of the same year. The third Wednesday of May, 1748, was the day selected for the first Commencement; and had it taken place at that time the first graduates of the College of New Jersey would have been admitted to their Bachelor's degree under the charter given by President Hamilton in 1746. But Governor Belcher, desirous that they should receive this honor from himself and the gentlemen to be associated with him as Trustees under the charter which he was then preparing, requested that the Commencement might be deferred for a fortnight, in order that he might have it in his power to attend the Commencement, and to deliver the new charter to the Trustees on that occasion. The promised charter was not ready at the time the Governor expected, and a further delay occurred in the holding of the first Commencement. And when the charter prepared under the direction of Governor Belcher was ready to be delivered to the Trustees therein named, it did not prove to be in all respects satisfactory to the leading friends of the College. It was therefore altered, and it passed the seal of the Province a second time on the 14th of September, 1748; and this delay in the preparation of the second charter occasioned a still further postponing of the Commencement, which finally took place at Newark on the 9th of November of that year, when the expectant candidates received their deferred honors. From the above statement it is evident that these first graduates are to be regarded as foster-sons of the College under the first charter rather than under the second, and as connected with the ad-

* See extracts from the Governor's letters on pages 82–84.

ministration of President Dickinson as well as with that of President Burr.

Of the course of study or of the number of pupils during Mr. Dickinson's administration, so far as is now known, there is no official record, nor is there any memorandum of these matters by any person conversant with the condition of the College at that time.   With respect to the number of students during the presidency of Mr. Dickinson, different estimates have been made; but, as they can be little else than mere conjectures, they hardly call for particular consideration.

From the well-known ability and learning of the President, and from the character of the prominent gentlemen associated with him, there can be no doubt that they sought to establish a curriculum which would compare well with those of the older colleges; and further, it is certain beyond all question, that in ordering the course of instruction they had a special reference to the training of young men for the gospel ministry.   Not only was this their avowed object and their strongest inducement to engage in this enterprise, but the catalogue of graduates shows that the first class consisted of *six* members, *five* of whom became ministers of the gospel; and that of the *seven* graduates of the following year, *five* entered the ministry. Another of the seven, of whose professional pursuits nothing is known, died about two years after leaving College.

It is said by Dr. Hatfield, in his "History of Elizabeth," that President Dickinson was assisted in the instruction of the students by the Rev. Caleb Smith, a graduate of Yale College, and that this gentleman was the first Tutor of the College of New Jersey.   It is quite probable that it was so; although the evidence is not so complete as we could desire.   From a "Brief Account of Mr. Smith," published in 1765, and within two or three years after his decease, it appears that he was teaching at Elizabeth, and pursuing his theological studies there under the direction of Mr. Dickinson; and that he was licensed to preach the gospel by the Presbytery of New York in April, 1747, which was about the time that Mr. Dickinson was chosen President of the College.   If not formally appointed a Tutor by the Trustees, he may have been, and most probably was, employed by the President under an authority given him by the Trustees to engage for a limited time the services of a competent assistant. From what is known of Mr. Smith's talents and scholarship, he must have been a very suitable person for such a position. There is reason to believe that Mr. Smith continued to reside at Elizabethtown after the decease of Mr. Dickinson, until his ordination and settlement at Newark Mountains, now Orange, in the autumn of 1748. Of the character of this early friend of the College, and of the important services which he rendered to it, we hope to have an opportunity to speak more fully than we can in this connection.

A BRIEF SKETCH OF THE LIFE AND LABORS OF PRESIDENT DICKINSON.*

President Dickinson was born in Hatfield, Massachusetts, on the 22d of April, 1688. His father was Hezekiah Dickinson, and his grandfather was Nathaniel Dickinson, one of the first settlers of Wethersfield, Connecticut. His mother was Abigail, daughter of Samuel, and granddaughter of the Rev. Adam Blackman, or Blakeman, the first minister of Stratford, Connecticut, and a graduate of the University of Oxford.

Mr. Dickinson was graduated at Yale College in 1706, and while there he was a pupil of the Rev. Abraham Pierson, the first Rector or President of that institution, which was founded in 1701 and incorporated in 1702, and to which the College of New Jersey is indebted for the academic training of her first three Presidents,—Dickinson, Burr, and Edwards.

After leaving college, Mr. Dickinson engaged in the study of theology, but under whose guidance we have no tradition. He went to Elizabethtown in 1708, and his preaching was so acceptable to the people of that place that he was invited to become their pastor, and, accepting this invitation, he was ordained on Friday, the 29th of September, 1709. The services on this occasion were performed by the ministers of Fairfield

---

* In preparing this sketch, the writer has freely availed himself of the labors of Drs. Green, Sprague, Stearns, and of the Rev. Richard Webster; but more especially of the admirable sketch of " President Dickinson's Life and Labors," by the Rev. Dr. Edwin F. Hatfield, in his " History of Elizabeth, New Jersey."

County, Connecticut, who the year before had formed a consociation according to the Saybrook Platform, and who on this occasion were assisted by the pastors of some of the churches in New Jersey.

At the time of his ordination and of his engaging in pastoral labors Mr. Dickinson was not twenty-one years of age.

"It was," says Dr. Hatfield, "a weighty charge to be laid on such youthful shoulders. And yet not too weighty, as the sequel proved. Quickly and diligently he applied himself to his work, and his profiting presently appeared to all. It was not long before he took rank among the first of his profession."

Some months before his ordination, and while supplying the pulpit of the church at Elizabethtown, he married Joanna Melyen, daughter of Jacob Melyen, and sister of the Rev. Samuel Melyen. The father was one of the associates in the purchase of the Elizabethtown tract, under Governor Nicolls's grant; the brother was for two or three years pastor of the church of that place prior to Mr. Dickinson's settlement there.*

The church at Elizabethtown was originally Independent, and conducted its affairs after the model of the Congregational churches of New England. At the time Mr. Dickinson became the pastor of this church it had been established about forty years, and for several years after his settlement it continued to be an Independent church. But, influenced more or less by his

---

* The family was from Holland, and Cornelis Melyn, the grandfather of Mrs. Dickinson, was a patroon, or large landed proprietor, having obtained of the Dutch Government a grant of Staten Island, which he afterwards relinquished to the West India Company.

Mr. and Mrs. Dickinson had nine children. Their youngest daughter, Martha, was married to the Rev. Caleb Smith, of Newark Mountains, now Orange, and their eldest to Jonathan Sergeant, the father of the Hon. Jonathan Dickinson Sergeant and the grandfather of the Hon. John Sergeant and of the Hon. Thomas Sergeant, of Philadelphia, and also of Mrs. Sarah Sergeant Miller, wife of the Rev. Dr. Samuel Miller, of Princeton.

Mr. and Mrs. Smith's descendants are numerous, and several of them highly distinguished in their respective callings. Among these are John C. Green, Esq., of New York, who has reared a noble monument to his eminent ancestor, in the erection of Dickinson Hall, at Princeton, the Hon. Henry M. Green, LL.D., late Chancellor of New Jersey, and the Rev. William Henry Green, D.D., LL.D., Professor in the Princeton Theological Seminary, and who in the spring of 1868 was chosen President of the College, but declined the appointment.

views and wishes, the members consented to change their form of government, and placed themselves under the care of the Presbytery of Philadelphia. This change probably occurred in the spring of 1717, as in the autumn of that year Mr. Dickinson's name is given in the list of members present at the meeting of the *Synod* of Philadelphia, which held its first sessions in the *city* of Philadelphia, in September, 1717. Although it appears from certain memoranda kept by the Presbytery that Mr. Dickinson was present and took part in the ordination of the Rev. Robert Orr, on the 20th of October, 1715, yet there is no reason to believe that he was at that time a member of the Presbytery, as his name does not appear in the list of members at that meeting, or at any previous one. He was also present at the ordination of his friend the Rev. John Pierson, at Woodbridge, New Jersey, on the 29th of April, 1717; and, as he was a member of the Synod in the following autumn, he was probably received as a regular member at the meeting held for Mr. Pierson's ordination.

The first Presbytery in this country, viz., that of Philadelphia, was organized in 1705. It increased rapidly, and in 1716 it resolved itself into a Synod, consisting of three Presbyteries, one of them retaining the name of the Presbytery of Philadelphia. Of this body Mr. Dickinson was a member until the formation of the Presbytery of East Jersey, in 1733. This last-named Presbytery comprised most if not all of the ministers in the eastern division of the Province, and to it was united, in 1738, the small Presbytery of Long Island. Upon the union of the two they received the name of the Presbytery of New York; and of this Presbytery Mr. Dickinson was the leading member until his decease, in the autumn of 1747. It was as a member of this Presbytery that Mr. Dickinson took the prominent part mentioned in the Introduction to this work, in favor of establishing a seminary of a high order for the education of candidates for the holy ministry.

Mr. Dickinson was held in great reverence by his brethren in the sacred office. He was twice chosen Moderator of the Synod of Philadelphia,—once in 1721 and again in 1742,—and he was the *first* Moderator of the Synod of New York, organ-

ized in 1745. He was also from year to year a member of
the most important committees of the Synod. From choice a
Presbyterian, he was nevertheless not forgetful of his training
as an Independent, and he was altogether indisposed to countenance the assumption, by Presbytery or Synod, of any doubtful power. Hence, at the meeting of the Synod in 1721, he
drew up a protest against the action of the Synod in adopting
a certain measure which, he apprehended, would prepare the
way for the introduction of rules and regulations touching the
government and discipline of the Church, the enacting of which
by the Synod would, according to his view of the case, transcend
its legitimate powers as a Church court. At the next meeting
of Synod, as Moderator of the previous one, he preached the
opening sermon, and in this discourse he took occasion to
define fully and clearly his own views in regard to the limits
of ecclesiastical authority. This full discussion of the subject
led to the withdrawal of the protest of the year before, and to
the presentation of a paper by Mr. Dickinson and his friends,
in which paper the true limits of Church power were so satis-
factorily exhibited that it commanded the hearty approval of
the entire body, and its unanimous adoption called forth, on
the part of the Synod, to use the words of the minute, "a
thanksgiving prayer and joyful singing of the 133d Psalm."

In the autumn of 1728 an overture was introduced into the
Synod, "having reference to the subscribing of the [West-
minster] Confession of Faith, and proposing that every minister
and candidate should be required to give his hearty consent to
it." Deeming this proposition to be one of grave importance,
the Synod deferred the consideration of it until the following
year. In the mean while the overture was printed, and Mr.
Dickinson published an answer to it, although he was an earnest Calvinist and cordially assented to the system of doctrine
set forth in the Confession and the Catechisms of the Westminster Assembly. When this subject again came before the
Synod, it was referred to a committee, of which Mr. Dickinson
was a member. After an evidently careful survey of the whole
matter, the committee agreed upon a unanimous report, and
presented the overture with such alterations as secured for it

the assent of the entire Synod, with the exception of one member, who declared that he was not prepared to vote. The changes made in the overture are ascribed to the ground taken by Mr. Dickinson, and the paper as adopted by the Synod is known, in the Presbyterian Church, as "*the Adopting Act.*"

The record of this act is accompanied by the following . minute: "The Synod, observing that unanimity, peace, and unity which appeared in all their consultations and determinations relating to the affair of the Confession, did unanimously agree in giving thanks to God in solemn prayer and praises."

It was Mr. Dickinson's constant aim to promote harmony among his brethren, and to engage them in earnest endeavors for the advancement of sincere and fervent piety and of sound learning. He was a man of great practical wisdom, and of untiring industry. These qualities, together with his learning and piety, gave him a commanding influence in the Church and in the community at large, and enabled him to accomplish the great and good work which in the providence of God he was called to do.

He was an earnest advocate of missionary labor among the Indians, and with his younger yet intimate friends, Messrs. Pemberton and Burr, he made a successful appeal to the Honorable Society for Promoting Christian Knowledge * in behalf of the Indians on Long Island, in New Jersey, and in Pennsylvania. The three who united in this appeal, and who were afterwards united in other important labors, were appointed correspondents of the Society, and they were authorized to employ missionaries to instruct the Indians, in whose welfare they had taken so deep an interest. The first missionary employed by them was the Rev. Azariah Horton ; the second, the Rev. David Brainerd, whose name is so dear to all friends of Christian missions. From the time that Mr. Brainerd came to New Jersey he was ever a welcome guest at the house of Mr. Dickinson ; and their intimate friendship lasted till death.

Mr. Dickinson was also an earnest advocate and defender of *revivals;* that is to say, of those remarkable religious excite-

* Formed at Edinburgh in 1709.

ments which from time to time have been witnessed in the
churches of Christ, when the truth of God accompanied with
unusual power from on high has aroused the attention of the
hearers to the most serious and devout contemplation of their
spiritual condition, and has led them, sometimes in large numbers, to seek a vital union with Christ, if unconverted, or clearer
evidence of such union, if they are already one with Him,
through sanctification by the Holy Spirit and a belief of the
truth.

It can therefore occasion no surprise to learn that Mr. Dickinson was earnestly desirous that his own Church should share
in that wondrous outpouring of the Spirit which occurred in so
many of the churches in this country at the time of "the Great
Awakening," as the event here alluded to is commonly designated by the Revivalists and their friends of that day. His
prayers and his faithful labors were graciously and abundantly
rewarded. Writing to Mr. Foxcroft, of Boston, September 4,
1740, he says, "I have had more young people address me for
direction in their spiritual concerns in this three months than
in thirty years before." (See Dr. Hatfield's "History.") By
invitation of Mr. Dickinson, Mr. Whitefield preached on two
different occasions at Elizabethtown.

Although warmly in favor of revivals, Mr. Dickinson was not
indifferent to the abuses and errors sometimes connected with
them ; and to guard his own people and others against these
errors, he prepared and published a discourse from the words,
"The Spirit itself beareth witness with our spirit, that we are
the children of God." A second edition was published in 1743.
It was entitled "The Witness of the Spirit. A Sermon preached
at Newark, May 7, 1740." It gave *offence* to some of the
friends of revivals ; and even by the Tennents it was regarded
as being of a hurtful tendency to the interests of religion.
(See Webster's "History," pages 148 and 152.) Yet in the
estimation of the most sober-minded advocates of revivals,
the views entertained by Mr. Dickinson are in entire accord
with the teachings of the gospel.

As a preacher, and as a theological writer, Mr. Dickinson
attained to great distinction. He was esteemed one of the best

preachers in the Presbyterian Church, and the ablest defender of its doctrine and order. Several of his works were republished in Great Britain, and were much commended.

The following is a list of his published works:

1. In 1722. The sermon already spoken of as preached before the Synod of Philadelphia on " Ecclesiastical Jurisdiction."

2. In 1724. " A Defence of Presbyterian Ordination," published at Boston, being a *reply* to a pamphlet entitled " A Modest Proof of the Order and Government settled by Christ and his Apostles in the Church." This was followed by another from Mr. Dickinson's pen, both of which were afterwards revised, enlarged, and published by the author.

3. In 1729. " An Answer to the Rev. John Thomson's Overture urging the Synod to adopt by a Public Agreement the Standards of the Church of Scotland."— R. Webster.

4. In 1732. A work entitled " The Reasonableness of Christianity, in Four Sermons. Wherein the Being and Attributes of God, the Apostasy of Man, and the Credibility of the Christian Religion are demonstrated by Rational Considerations, and the Divine Mission of our Blessed Saviour proved by Scripture Arguments, both from the Old Testament and the New," with a preface by Mr. Foxcroft, of Boston, and published in that city.

Of these discourses the Rev. Dr. Hatfield makes these remarks: " They are admirable discourses, learned, discriminating, and logical; full of pith and power; pointed and impressive. Happy the people favored with the ministry of such a teacher! Happy the children whose early years were blessed with such instruction!"

5. In 1733. " The Scripture Bishop vindicated," published at Boston.—Dr. Hatfield.

6. In 1733. A sermon preached at the funeral of Mrs. Ruth Pierson, the wife of his friend the Rev. John Pierson, of Woodbridge, New Jersey, and daughter of the Rev. Timothy Woodbridge, of Hartford, Connecticut. Printed at New York.—Dr. Green's " Notes."

7. In 1735. " Remarks on a Letter to a Friend in the Country, containing the Substance of a Sermon preached at Philadelphia, in the Congregation of the Rev. Mr. Hemphill." Published September, 1735.

8. In 1736. A sermon preached at Newark, Wednesday, June 2, 1736, and published with the title, " The Vanity of Human Institutions in the Worship of God."

9. In 1737. A defence of this sermon.

10. In February, 1737-38. A second defence of this sermon, entitled " The Reasonableness of Non-conformity to the Church of England in Point of Worship."

11. In 1740. His sermon on the " Witness of the Spirit," of which mention has already been made.

12. In 1741. " The True Scripture Doctrine concerning some Important Points of Christian Faith, particularly Eternal Election, Original Sin, Grace in Conversion, Justification by Faith, and the Saint's Perseverance, represented and applied in Five Discourses." This able work has been several times republished in this country and in Scotland.

13. In 1742. "A Display of God's Special Grace, in a Familiar Dialogue between a Minister and a Gentleman of his Congregation. About the Work of God in the Conviction and Conversion of Sinners, so remarkably of late begun and going on in these American Parts. Wherein the Objections against some Uncommon Appearances among us are distinctly considered, Mistakes rectified, and the Work itself particularly proved to be from the Holy Spirit: with one Addition, in a Second Conference, relating to Sundry Antinomian Principles beginning to obtain in some Places."

It was published first at Boston, and a second time at Philadelphia, in 1743. The first edition was without the author's name, but with an attestation by the Rev. Messrs. Coleman, Sewell, Prince, Webb, Cooper, Foxcroft, and Gee, all ministers of Boston, and most of them men of note.

The second edition appeared having the hearty commendation of the Rev. Messrs. Gilbert and William Tennent, Samuel and John Blair, Treat, and Finley.

Of this work Dr. Green, in his "Notes," observes that "no cotemporaneous publication was probably so much read, or had as much influence."

14. In 1743. "The Nature and Necessity of Regeneration, considered in a Sermon from John iii. 3, preached at Newark, at a Meeting of the Presbytery there. To which are added some Remarks on a Discourse of Dr. Waterland's, entitled and explained according to Scripture Antiquity."

Rev. Dr. Hatfield observes, "Dr. Waterland's book had been imported by the Episcopal ministry, and circulated as an antidote to the revival doctrines of Whitefield and his sympathizers. Dickinson's drew forth, in 1744, from the Rev. John Wetmore, rector of the parish church of Rye, New York, a defence of Waterland's discourse on 'Regeneration.' This was answered promptly by Mr. Dickinson."

In 1745 he published his "Familiar Letters to a Gentleman, upon a Variety of Seasonable and Important Subjects in Religion." A work of great ability, in which the Evidences of Christianity, the Doctrine of God's Sovereign Grace in the Redemption of Men, the Way of Salvation, and the Dangers of Antinomianism are fully set forth. It has been reprinted several times, both at home and abroad. It is from a print in the Glasgow edition of this work that the portrait of President Dickinson in the College collection of portraits, and the portraits of him in several sketches of his life published in this country, were copied.

In this same year he published his work entitled "A Vindication of God's Sovereign Free Grace. In some Remarks upon Mr. J. Beach's Sermon, with some Brief Reflections upon Mr. H. Caner's Sermon, and on a pamphlet entitled 'A Letter from Aristocles to Anthades.'" This letter was from the pen of the Rev. Dr. Samuel Johnson, of Hartford, Connecticut. This work called forth *a reply* by Dr. Johnson, which induced Mr. Dickinson to prepare "A Second Vindication of God's Sovereign Free Grace," which was published after his death by his brother, the Rev. Moses Dickinson.

HIS DEATH.

Mr. Dickinson died of pleurisy, October 7, 1747, in the sixtieth year of his age. In reply to an inquiry made by a friend who visited him when he was on his dying bed, he said, "Many days have passed between God and my soul, in which I have solemnly dedicated myself to Him, and I trust what I have committed unto Him He is able to keep until that day."

The following notice of his death and burial appeared in the "New York Weekly Post Boy" of October 12, 1747 :

"ELIZABETHTOWN, IN NEW JERSEY, October 10.

"On Wednesday morning last, about four o'clock, died here, of a pleuritic illness, that eminently learned and pious minister of the Gospel and President of the College of New Jersey, the Rev. Mr. Jonathan Dickinson, in the sixtieth year of his age, who had been Pastor of the first Presbyterian Church in this Town for nearly forty years, and was the Glory and Joy of it. In him conspicuously appeared those natural and acquired moral and spiritual Endowments which constitute a truly excellent and valuable man, a good Scholar, an eminent Divine, and a serious, devout Christian. He was greatly adorned with the gifts and graces of the Heavenly Master, in the Light whereof he appeared as a star of superior Brightness and Influence in the Orb of the Church, which has sustained a great and unspeakable Loss in his Death. He was of uncommon and of very extensive usefulness. He boldly appeared in the Defence of the great and important Truths of our most holy Religion, and the Gospel Doctrines of the free and sovereign Grace of God. He was a zealous Professor of godly Practice and godly Living, and a bright ornament to his Profession. In Times and cases of Difficulty he was a wise and able Counsellor. By his death our Infant College is deprived of the Benefit and Advantage of his superior Accomplishments, which afforded a favor-able prospect of its future Flourishing and Prosperity under his Inspection. His remains were decently interred here yesterday, when the Rev. Mr. Pierson, of Woodbridge, preached his funeral sermon ; and as he lived desired of all, so never any Person in these Parts died more lamented. Our Fathers, where are they? and the Prophets, do they live forever?" *

Dr. Hatfield remarks that "this notice was probably written by the Rev. Mr. Pemberton, of New York, with whom Mr. Dickinson had been intimately associated for years in the defence of the truth and the promotion of the cause of Christ."

This testimony to the worth of Mr. Dickinson is not exaggerated. He was all that he is here represented to have been. President Edwards, the Rev. Dr. Bellamy, Dr. John Erskine, of Scotland, Governor Belcher, all confirm its truthfulness. Edwards speaks of him as the late learned and very excellent Mr. Jonathan Dickinson. Bellamy calls him the great Mr. Dickinson. Erskine, speaking of Dickinson and Edwards, says, "The

---

* Dr. Stearns's "First Church, Newark," and Dr. Hatfield's "History of Elizabeth."

British Isles have produced no such writers on divinity in the
eighteenth century." Belcher, in his letter of the 13th of November, 1747, to Mr. Pemberton, speaks of him as " that eminent
servant of God, the learned and pious Dickinson."

" It may be doubted," says Dr. Sprague, " whether, with the
single exception of the elder Edwards, Calvinism has ever found
an abler or more efficient champion in this country than Jonathan Dickinson." If the writer may venture to institute a
comparison between those two admirable men : for *profound*
thinking, but *not always correct*, he would assign the palm to
Edwards; but for sound judgment and practical wisdom, to
Dickinson. Both of them were eminently good, and both
eminently great.

From the autobiography of the Reverend Jacob Green, in
early life a pupil of Dr. Dickinson's, and the father of the
Rev. Dr. Ashbel Green, the eighth President of the College, it
appears that both Mr. Dickinson and Mr. Burr differed from
President Edwards in regard to the qualifications requisite for
admission to the sacraments; and that in regard to this important question they held, or inclined to, the views of Mr.
Stoddard, the maternal grandfather of President Edwards.

CHAPTER VI.

UPON the decease of President Dickinson, the Rev. Aaron Burr took charge of the College,* and the students were removed from Elizabethtown to Newark, the place of Mr. Burr's residence. Whether Mr. Burr was *formally* invested with the office of President at this time is uncertain, there being no College records of that date, or other cotemporary authority to determine this question. But *it is certain* that he discharged *the duties* of the President while the College was yet under the *first* charter.

The charter given by Governor Belcher was accepted by the Trustees therein named on the 13th of October, 1748, O. S., and on the 9th of November following, at a meeting of the Trustees at Newark, Mr. Burr was unanimously chosen President of the College as reorganized under the second charter.

In his sketch of the College, Dr. Green observes:

" It will be seen from the following extracts from the minutes of the Trustees that a class was in readiness to receive their Bachelor's degree within one month from the time that Belcher's charter took effect; and that under that charter the degrees were conferred by Mr. Burr on the very day that he was elected President. Everything, therefore, must have been previously prepared and arranged with a view to this event."

If the reverend and learned author of this sketch had had access to Governor Belcher's correspondence with Messrs. Burr, Pemberton, and Gilbert Tennent respecting the second charter, he would have learned from that correspondence that there was a class in readiness to receive their first degree in the

---

* See obituary notice of President Burr, in the "New York Mercury," September 29, 1757, or Dr. Stearns's "History," p. 206.

Arts six months before they did receive it, and he would also have known the reason of the delay in conferring upon them this distinction.*

In the minutes of the Trustees there is no reference or allusion to either of these things; yet they are important from their bearing upon the question, whether the College under the *first* charter and the College under the *second* charter were one and the same institution.

The following is *the entire record* respecting the first Commencement, and the conferring of degrees on that occasion :

"Agreed, that the commencement for graduating the candidates, that had been examined and approved for that purpose, go on to-day.

" It was accordingly opened this forenoon by the president with prayer, and publickly reading of the charter in the meeting house.

"Adjourned till two o'clock in the afternoon.

"In the afternoon the president delivered a handsome and elegant Latin Oration. And after the customary scholastic disputations, the following gentlemen were admitted to the degree of Bachelor of Arts, viz., Enos Ayres, Israel Read, Benjamin Chestnut, Richard Stockton, Hugh Henry, Daniel Thane.

" After which his Excellency the Governor was pleased to accept of a degree of Master of Arts; this was succeeded by a salutatory oration by Mr. Thane, and the whole concluded with prayer by the president."

The above-named gentlemen, the first graduates of the College, were prepared to receive this their first academic honor while the first charter was yet in force. Apart from the evidence on this head furnished by Governor Belcher's letters, referred to above, the fact that they were admitted to their first degree on the very day that Mr. Burr was chosen and inaugurated President of the College under the second charter is sufficient to establish the truth of this statement. It appears, also, that this honor was conferred *after* the candidates had been examined and approved. By whom, and under whose authority, was this examination held? Assuredly not by the authority of the Trustees acting under the *second* charter, or by persons designated by them. For at the meeting on the 13th of October—their only one previous to the election of Mr. Burr and the holding of the first Commencement—no provision whatever was

---

* See extracts from Governor Belcher's letters, in the third chapter of this work.

made for this examination. The candidates must therefore have been examined and approved by the President and others acting under an authority given in the first charter, although they were admitted to their first degree in the Arts by a vote of the Trustees of the second charter, the transition of the College from the control of the one to that of the other being completed on the very day on which the degrees were conferred.

"Its first Commencement," says Mr. Moore, the Librarian of the New York Historical Society, "was celebrated with circumstances of great pomp and ceremony equally novel and interesting. The following report of the proceedings was prepared at the request of the Trustees of the College, by WILLIAM SMITH, at that time a leading lawyer of the New York Bar, and published in the principal New York newspaper."

[*From Parker's Gazette and Post Boy, Nov. 21, 1748.*]

" MR. PARKER:

"*As the Acts of a publick Commencement are little known in these Parts, perhaps the following Relation from an Eye and Ear Witness, may be agreeable to many of your Readers.*

"On Wednesday the ninth Instant, was held at *Newark*, the first commencement of the College of *New-Jersey;* at which was present his Excellency JONATHAN BELCHER, Esq., Governor and Commander in Chief of the said Province, and President of the Trustees, and sixteen Gentlemen, being other Trustees named in the Royal CHARTER: Who after they had all taken and subscribed the Oaths to the Government, and made and signed the Declaration which are appointed by divers Statutes of *Great Britain*, and had taken the particular Oath for the faithful performance of their Trust, all which were required by the said Charter, they proceeded to the Election of a President of the said College; whereupon the Reverend Mr. AARON BURR, was unanimously chosen.

" Which being done, his Excellency was preceded from his Lodgings at the President's House; first by the Candidates walking in Couples uncovered; next followed the Trustees two by two being covered, and last of all his Excellency the Governor, with the President at his Left Hand. At the Door of the Place appointed for the Publick Acts, the procession (amidst a great number of Spectators there gathered) was inverted, the Candidates parting to the Right and Left Hand, and the Trustees in like Manner. His Excellency first entered with the President, the Trustees next following in the Order in which they were ranged in the Charter; and last of all the Candidates. Upon the Bell ceasing, and the Assembly being composed, the President began the Publick Acts by solemn Prayer to God in the *English* Tongue, for a Blessing upon the publick Transactions of the Day; upon his Majesty King GEORGE the Second, and the Royal Family; upon the *British* Nations and Dominions; upon the Governor and Government of *New-Jersey;* upon all Seminaries of true Religion and good Literature; and particularly upon the infant College of *New-Jersey.*

"Which being concluded, the President attended in the Pulpit with the Reverend Mr. *Thomas Arthur*, who had been constituted Clerk of the Corporation, desired in the *English* tongue, the Assembly to stand up and hearken to his Majesty's Royal CHARTER, granted to the Trustees of the College of *New-Jersey*.

"Upon which, the Assembly standing, the Charter was distinctly read by the Reverend Mr. *Arthur*, with the usual Indorsement by his Majesty's Attorney General, and the Certificate signed by the Secretary of the Province, of its having been approved in Council, with his Excellency's *Fiat* for the Province Seal, signed with his Excellency's own Hand.

"After this, the Morning being spent, the President signified to the Assembly, that the succeeding Acts would be deferred till two o'clock in the Afternoon.

"Then the Procession, in Return to the President's House, was made in the Order before observed.

"The like procession being made in the Afternoon as in the Morning, and the Assembly being seated in their places, and composed; the President opened the publick Acts, first by an elegant Oration in the *Latin* Tongue, delivered *memoriter*, modestly declaring his Unworthiness of, and unfitness for so weighty and important a Trust as had been reposed in him; apologizing for the Defects that would unavoidably appear in his part of the present Service; displaying the manifold Advantages of the liberal Arts and Sciences, in exalting and dignifying the humane Nature, enlarging the Soul, improving its Faculties, civilizing Mankind, qualifying them for the important Offices of Life, and rendering them useful Members of Church and State: That to Learning and the Arts, was chiefly owing the vast Pre-eminence of the polished Nations of Europe, to the almost brutish Savages of America; the Sight of which last was the constant Object of Horror and Commiseration. Then the President proceeded to mention the Honours paid by our Ancestors in *Great Britain* to the Liberal Sciences; by erecting and endowing those illustrious Seminaries of Learning which for many Ages had been the Honour and Ornament of those happy Islands, and the source of infinite Advantage to the People there: Observing, that the same noble Spirit had animated their Descendants, the first *English* Planters of *America;* who, as soon as they were formed into a civil State in the very infancy of Time, had wisely laid Religion and Learning at the Foundation of their Commonwealth; and had always regarded them as the firmest pillars of their Church and State—That hence very early arose *Harvard* College, in *New-Cambridge*, and afterwards *Yale* College, in *New-Haven*, which have now flourished with growing Reputation for many Years, and have sent forth many hundreds of learned Men of various Stations and Characters in Life, that in different Periods have proved the Honour and Ornament of their Country, and of which, the one or the other had been the ALMA MATER of most of the *Literati* then present. That Learning, like the Sun in its Western Progress, had now begun to dawn upon the Province of *New-Jersey*, through the happy Influence of its generous Patron their most excellent Governor; who from his own Experience and an early Acquaintance with Academic Studies, well knowing the Importance of a learned Education, and being justly sensible that in nothing he could more subserve to the Honour and Interest of his Majesty's Government, and the real Good and Happiness of his Subjects in *New-Jersey*, than by granting them the best Means to render themselves a *religious, wise* and *knowing* people; Had therefore, upon his happy Accession to his Government, made the Erection of a College in this Province for the Instruction of Youth in the liberal Arts and Sciences, the immediate Object of his Attention and Care : The clearest Demonstration whereof they had by the Grant of his most gracious Majesty's ROYAL CHARTER in the Morning published in that Assembly, which had been conveyed to them through his Excellency's Hands; which appears to have been founded in the noblest Munificence, granting the most ample Privileges consistent with the natural and religious Rights of Mankind, and calculated for the most extensive Good of all his Majesty's Subjects.   That therein we see the Ax laid to the Root of that ANTICHRIS-TIAN BIGOTRY that had in every Age (wherever it had prevailed) been the Parent of Persecution, the Bane of Society, and the Plague of Mankind : That by the Tenour of his Majesty's Charter, it could assume no Place in the College of *New-Jersey ;* but as a *foul Fiend* was banished to its native Region, that *infernal* PIT from whence it sprung.

"These, and many other Particulars having, *more Oratorio,* taken up about three Quarters of an Hour, and the printed *Theses* being dispersed among the Learned in the Assembly, the Candidates, by the Command of the President, entered upon the publick Disputations in *Latin,* in which six Questions in Philosophy and Theology were debated.   One of which was :

"'*An Libertas agendi Secundum Dictamina Conscientiæ, in Rebus merè religiosis, ab ullâ Potestate humana coerceri debeat ?*'

"In *English,* Whether the Liberty of acting according to the Dictates of Conscience, in Matters merely religious, ought to be restrained by any humane Power?

"And it was justly held and concluded, That that Liberty ought not to be restrained.   Then the President addressing himself to the Trustees in *Latin,* asked, Whether it was their Pleasure that these young Men who had performed the publick Exercises in Disputation should be admitted to the Degree of Batchelor of the Arts ?

"Which being granted by his Excellency in the name of all the Trustees present, the President descended from the Pulpit, being seated with his Head covered, received them two by two; and according to the Authority to him committed by the Royal *Charter,* after the Manner of the Academies in *England,* admitted six young Scholars to the Degree of Batchelor of the Arts.

"In the next Place, his Excellency JONATHAN BELCHER, Esq., Governor and Commander in Chief of the Province of *New-Jersey,* having declared his desire to accept from that College the Degree of Master of Arts; the other Trustees in a just Sense of the Honour done the College by his Excellency's Condescension, most heartily having granted his Request, and the President rising uncovered addressed himself to his Excellency; and according to the same Authority committed to him by the Royal CHARTER, after the Manner of the Academies in *England* admitted him to the Degree of Master of Arts.

"Then the President ascended the Pulpit, and commanded the *Orator Salutatorius* to ascend the Rostrum, who being Mr. *Daniel Thane,* just before graduated Batchelor of Arts; he in a modest and decent manner, first apologizing for his Insufficiency, and then having spoken of the Excellency of the liberal Arts and Sciences, and of the Numberless Benefits they yield to Mankind in private and social life; addressed himself in becoming Salutations and Thanks to his Excellency and the Trustees, the President and whole Assembly: All which being performed in good Latin from his Memory in a handsome oratorical Manner in the

Space of about half an Hour. The President concluded in English, with Thanksgiving to Heaven for the Favours received and Prayers to God for a Blessing upon
the Scholars that had received the publick Honours of that Day, and for the Smiles
of Heaven upon the infant College of *New-Jersey*, and dismissed the Assembly.
All which being performed to the great Satisfaction of all present, his Excellency
with the Trustees and Scholars, returned to the House of the President in the Order
observed in the Morning; where, after sundry By-Laws were made, chiefly for
regulating the Studies and Manners of the Students, they agreed upon a Corporation Seal with this Device: In the upper Part of the Circle, a Bible spread open,
with *Latin* Characters inscribed on the Left Side, signifying the *Old Testament*, and
on the right side the *New*, with this Motto over it: Vitæ Lumen Mortuis Reddit;
with a view to that Text, *Who hath abolished Death, and hath brought Life and
Immortality to Light through the Gospel.* Underneath on one Side a Table with
Books standing thereon, to signify the proper Business of the Students; on the
other a *Diploma*, with the College Seal appended over it, being written Meriti
Præmium, to signify that the Degrees to be conferred are only to be to those that
deserve them. On the outside of the Circle, Sigillum Collegii Neo Cæsari-
ensis in America; *the Seal of the College of New-Jersey, in America;* and then
appointed the succeeding Commencement to be at *New-Brunswick* on the last
Wednesday of September next. Thus the first Appearance of a College in *New-
Jersey* having given universal Satisfaction, even the Unlearned being pleased with
the external Solemnity and Decorum which they saw, 'tis hoped that this infant
College will meet with due Encouragement from all publick spirited generous
Minds; and that the Lovers of Mankind will wish its Prosperity, and contribute to
its Support."

In the evening of Commencement-day the Trustees held
another session, and took into consideration several important measures for the welfare of the College, the first of them
having reference to its government, the minute respecting
which is as follows:

"A set of laws were laid before the Trustees for their approbation; and, after a
second and third reading, and some alterations and amendments, they were unanimously received, and ordered to be inserted with the minutes, as the laws of the
College of New Jersey."

It is morally certain that these laws were prepared by President Burr, and that they were the product of his experience
in conducting the government of the College for the twelve
months preceding.

The following were the rules relating to the admission of
students:

"1. None may expect to be admitted into College but such as being examined
by the President and Tutors shall be found able to render Virgil and Tully's Ora-

tions into English; and to turn English into true and grammatical Latin; and to be so well acquainted with the Greek as to render any part of the four Evangelists in that language into Latin or English; and to give the grammatical connexion of the words.

" 2. Every student [that] enters College shall transcribe the Laws, which being signed by the President, shall be testimony of his admission, and shall be kept by him, while he remains a member of the College, as the rule of his Behavior."

So far as a knowledge of Latin and Greek is concerned, it is doubtful whether any advance has been made in the requisites for admission into the Freshman or lowest class since the time that the first of these two rules was adopted. For although a more extensive reading of authors in these languages is now required of candidates, yet the instances are very rare in which they are found able to translate any part of the four Gospels from Greek into Latin, or to turn English into true and grammatical Latin. In those days a knowledge of Latin and Greek was more generally and highly appreciated by educated men than it is now; not that the first classical scholars of those times were superior or even equal to the best in our own times in matters of critical nicety and in a thorough acquaintance with the grammatical structure of these ancient languages. Many a man can speak his own language well and fluently, and with readiness quote from eminent writers passages committed by him to memory, who possesses little or no ability to analyze his own modes of speech, much less the expressions of others, and weigh with exactness the import of the several words and sentences. So classical scholars of the last century, in this country, could quote and speak and write Latin with far greater facility than students of the same relative position at the present day are able to do, but in sound and thorough criticism they have been surpassed by their successors. What is wanting in our schools and colleges is the union of both systems, of which there is little hope, seeing the number and variety of subjects pressing their claims for a place in our curriculums of study.

The next thing, after adopting a college code, was a vote:

" That the annual Commencement for the future be on the last Wednesday of September, and that the next Commencement be held at New Brunswick."

The reason for selecting the last day of September as the

day for the annual Commencement was probably owing to the circumstance that at that time the Commencement at Harvard took place on the second Wednesday in September in each year, and that at Yale on the third Wednesday of the same month.

Notwithstanding Governor Belcher's strong preference for Princeton as the permanent seat of the College, some of the Trustees, perhaps a majority, were in favor of locating the institution at New Brunswick, and by holding the next Commencement there they hoped to interest the people of that place in the College, and to induce them to offer liberal pecuniary aid towards the erection of suitable buildings.

The appointment of a Treasurer next claimed their attention, and the minute respecting it is this:

"Voted, That the Honorable Andrew Johnston, Esq., be desired to accept the office of Treasurer to the corporation."

Mr. Johnston was the Treasurer of East Jersey, and a member of the Council, and in the list of Trustees mentioned in Governor Belcher's charter his name stands third.   He was present at the meeting, on the 13th of October, 1748, when the new charter was accepted, and was qualified by taking the prescribed oaths.   He was not present at this meeting.   It is not said in the minutes of the Board that he accepted the office thus tendered him, but it is probable that he did, as there is no mention made of the appointment of another person to this office until nearly two years after, and then only incidentally, as seen in the following extract from the minutes:

"Mr. Hude was appointed to administer the oaths required by the charter to Messrs. Caleb Smith and Mr. Woodruff, Trustees, Mr. Sergeant, Treasurer, Mr. Sherwood and Mr. Maltby, Tutors."   .

Mr. Sergeant was probably appointed Treasurer at this time, September 26, 1750, as his name does not appear in the minutes before this meeting, and as in a previous minute of this same meeting it is said, "Rev. John Frelinghuysen and Rev. Caleb Smith chosen Trustees in the room of John Kinsey, Esq., deceased, and of the Hon. Andrew Johnston, *resigned.*"   It is not improbable that Mr. Johnston resigned *both* offices at the same time, while it is possible that he may *never* have acted as Treasurer, and that the President of the College may have attended to the fiscal concerns of the institution until the appointment of Mr. Sergeant.

The other items of business at this meeting may be learned from the following extracts from the minutes :

"Voted, That the seal prepared by Mr. P. Smith [one of the Trustees] be accepted as the common seal of this corporation, and that the thanks of the corporation be returned to Mr. Smith for his care in devising the same.

"And that he be desired to get two seals engraven, of the same device, for the use of the corporation, and that the Trustees be answerable for the expense thereof.

"Voted, That all diplomas and certificates of degrees be signed by the President and at least six of the Trustees.

"Voted, That William Smith, Esq., be appointed to draw up an account of the proceedings of the Commencement, and to get it into the ' New York Gazette' as soon as he conveniently can.

"That Messrs. Pierson, Cowell, Johnes, Arthur, be appointed to make application to the General Assembly of this Province, now sitting at Perth Amboy, in order to get their countenance and assistance for the support of the College.

"Voted, That the following gentlemen be desired to take in subscriptions for the College, viz., Messrs. Kinsey, Hazard, at Philadelphia; P. Van Brugh Livingston, P. Smith, New York; Read and Smith, at Burlington; Read and Cowell, at Trenton; John Stevens, Amboy; Samuel Woodruff, Elizabethtown; Thomas Leonard, John Stockton, Esqs., Princeton; James Hude, Esq., and Thomas Arthur, at Brunswick; Henderson and Furman, Freehold; John Pierson, Woodbridge; Major Johnson, at Newark.

"That all the Trustees shall use their utmost endeavors to obtain benefactions to the said College, and that this vote go into the New York and Philadelphia gazettes.

"That this meeting be adjourned to the third Tuesday in May, to be held at Maidenhead [now Lawrenceville]. Mr. Tennent concluded with prayer."

It is evident, from the variety and importance of the matters handled by the Trustees on the day of the first Commencement, that they must have devoted themselves very earnestly to the business before them, viz., the election of a President, his inauguration, the public reading of the charter, attendance on the Commencement exercises, including the President's Latin address, the conferring of degrees, and the adopting of a body of laws, besides the various matters mentioned in the above extract.

The next record in the minutes is in these words :

"TRENTON, May 18, 1749.

" According to adjournment, met at Maidenhead [Lawrenceville] sundry of the Trustees of the College, but were frustrated of a Quorum by the absence of several members. The Trustees, however, thought proper to wait upon his Excellency the Governor, who was come to Trenton on his way to the meeting of the Corporation, where several things were disposed of with respect to the College.

" Upon the recommendation of Mr. President, the Trustees present do approve of Mr. Maltby to be employed as Tutor of the College, and do recommend it to the Trustees at their next meeting to establish him in that capacity. It is farther recommended to the Committee appointed to wait upon the Assembly [of the Province], that they renew their application to them, at their next session, at Perth Amboy, and that they do Expressly request that a Lottery be granted them, for the service of the College."

Public attention had not yet been called to the evils of the lottery system; and, as a lottery scheme furnished great facilities for the raising of funds, the Trustees of the College at that time did not scruple as to the propriety of their taking part in one, provided they could obtain permission so to do.

At the next regular meeting of the Board, held at New Brunswick, September 27, 1749, the committee to ask aid from the General Assembly of the Province was enlarged by the addition of four members, and was instructed to apply for authority to raise by a lottery a sum not exceeding three thousand pounds *proc.*, equal to eight thousand dollars.

The application was made; but the final report to the Board on this subject was, that "the Provincial Assembly absolutely refused to grant the petition for a Lottery," and that the committee, "with the concurrence of the generality of the Trustees, had agreed to erect a Lottery in Philadelphia to raise money for the benefit of the College; and that the said Lottery had been drawn." This report was made at a meeting of the Trustees, held at Newark, September 26, 1750. The thanks of the Board were presented to the gentlemen who took upon themselves the management of the lottery, and provision was made for settling all matters connected with it.*

It was ordered, that all moneys remaining in the hands of the managers after the expiration of six months be paid to the Treasurer. The committee appointed to settle with the managers consisted of the President, the Treasurer, the Clerk of the Board, and Messrs. Woodruff and Neilson. Subsequently,

---

* There does not appear to have been at this time in Pennsylvania any law prohibiting the drawing of lotteries in that Province.

viz., in the year 1753-4 (see "Minutes of the Board," pages 37 and 39), upon a petition from the Trustees, the General Court of the Colony of Connecticut granted them the privilege of drawing a lottery within the limits of that Colony, and in 1761-2 the General Assembly of New Jersey gave them authority to draw one in this Province. What sums of money were received from these lotteries cannot now be ascertained, the books of the Treasurer at those periods not having been preserved. It is most probable that the College received but little, if any, addition to its funds from these sources. The last application to the Legislature of New Jersey for a lottery was made in the winter of 1813-14, soon after Dr. Ashbel Green became President of the College, and it met with the same fate that most of the previous ones had done,—it was refused.

In his notes respecting the College, and in reference, more particularly, to the failure of the first efforts made to obtain aid from the General Assembly of the Province, Dr. Green thus writes:

"Petitions of the most urgent kind were addressed to the legislature of the province of New Jersey in behalf of the College. But even a petition for a lottery was 'absolutely rejected.' Whatever was the influence of Governor Belcher or the popularity of President Burr, their united exertions could never prevail upon the legislature of the province in which the College was founded, whose name it bore, and of which it was the greatest ornament, to show it patronage or favor of any kind. It is as grievous to the writer to record this want of liberality in the legislature of his native State, as it can be to any other inhabitant to read the record. But historical fidelity requires that the fact should not be suppressed. All the State patronage which the College has ever received shall, in its proper place, be faithfully stated. The writer has only to regret that the statement will so easily be made."

As the "Historical Sketch of the Origin of the College of New Jersey," from which the above is copied, does not extend over a period of twenty years, but ends with the administration of President Finley, who died while yet President, in 1766, no allusion or reference is again made to this matter in the notes of President Green, except the mention of the fact that in the year 1761 the General Assembly of New Jersey authorized the drawing of a lottery for the benefit of the College.

To the view here presented of the want of liberality on the part of the Legislature the writer of this history cannot assent; and for these reasons. The College of New Jersey, although bearing the name of the State, was never a State institution. It was not established by the Legislature. In the exercise of its granted and legitimate powers it is not subject to the control of that body, and therefore has no special claims upon its liberality. On the other hand, after the American Revolution, the Legislature confirmed the charter of the College, with only such changes as the altered condition of the civil affairs of the country required, enlarged its powers, and never refused to pass any measure desired by its friends for the protection of its interests.

The good will uniformly exhibited towards the College by the authorities of the State calls for a grateful acknowledgment on the part of the friends of the College, and they may be glad that the applications to the Legislature for pecuniary aid were unsuccessful. Had the aid sought been granted, this might have led to more or less interference by the Legislature in the management of the institution, under the plea of seeing that the funds given by the State were wisely expended, or employed in accordance with the design and the terms of the different grants. From any and all such interference the College, happily, has ever been free.

The matters which more especially demanded and received the attention of the Trustees during the presidency of Mr. Burr were provision for the instruction of the students, the selection of a permanent seat for the College, the erection of suitable buildings, and the raising of the funds required for these purposes.

To provide the necessary instruction, the Board, at a meeting held September 27, 1749, authorized the President, "with the advice of any four of the neighboring Trustees, to employ any such person or persons as they shall think proper to assist him in the government and instruction of the College till their next meeting." Previously to this action, as appears from a minute cited above, sundry Trustees, but not a quorum, met Governor Belcher at Trenton, May 18, 1749, and those present expressed their approval of employing Mr. Maltby as a Tutor, and also recommended "that at their next meeting the Trustees should establish him in that capacity." The form of the minute seems to indicate that he had been assisting President Burr, or at least that he was expected to do so, from that time, which corresponded with the beginning of the second term under the second charter. Whether at their next meeting, of September 27, 1749, the Trustees did establish Mr. Maltby in the office of Tutor, the minutes of that meeting do not indicate. But the minute, already cited, authorizing the President to employ such assistants as he might need, with the consent of any four of the neighboring Trustees, was a virtual confirmation of Mr. Maltby's appointment; and at the next meeting of the Board, at Newark, September 27, 1750, this gentleman took the required oaths of office as a College Tutor, as also did Mr. Samuel Sherwood, who was chosen a Tutor at this time.

It is a matter of some doubt whether for the first six months Mr. Burr had any assistance in the government and the instruction of the College. He may have employed Mr. Maltby on trial before he recommended his appointment by the Trustees; but this is uncertain. For the next eighteen months he was aided by this gentleman, and from the beginning of the third College year until the end of his administration there were, without any intermission, two Tutors associated with him, who with him constituted the College Faculty.

The names of the several Tutors during Mr. Burr's time are John Maltby, Samuel Sherwood, Jonathan Badger, Alexander Gordon, George Duffield, William Thompson, Benjamin Youngs Prime, John Ewing, Isaac Smith, and Jeremiah Halsey. Some of these gentlemen became eminent in their professions, and of them further mention will be made at the end of this memoir of President Burr and his administration.

What was the full course of instruction at this period in the history of the College we have no means of ascertaining definitely, as the Faculty minutes of that time are lost. But from what is known of the opinions prevalent among the early friends of the College, and from the varied attainments of Mr. Burr and of the Tutors associated with him, and also the usual scholastic exercises at the Commencements of those days, we may safely conclude that the College curriculum embraced the study of the Latin and Greek languages, the Elements of Mathematics, Natural Philosophy, Moral Philosophy, Rhetoric and Logic, together with declamations and discussions. The students were also well instructed in the doctrines and precepts of the Christian faith, their religious teacher being the President of the College.

In the school under the care of the Synod of Philadelphia, established three years before the first charter of the College of New Jersey was obtained, the course of instruction included "languages, philosophy, and divinity;" and from a minute of the Synod of Philadelphia, May 23, 1754, it appears that Mr. Alexander McDowell, the Principal of the school at that time, was to continue to give instruction in "logic, mathematics, natural and moral philosophy," etc., and that Mr. James P. Wilson, just appointed to assist him, was "to teach the languages."

It is not to be presumed that in the College of New Jersey, under the government and instruction of President Burr, a graduate of Yale, and one of the first scholars of his day, the prescribed course would fall short of that existing in the school of the Synod of Philadelphia, as it was the aim and desire of the early friends of the College to provide for the young men of the middle Provinces an education equal to that furnished by Harvard and Yale to the youth of New England.

The view here presented of the course of instruction given by President Burr and his assistants is confirmed by sundry occasional remarks of Mr. Joseph Shippen, of ·Philadelphia, a student of the College, in his correspondence with his father, Judge Edward Shippen, and with other friends. It is only very recently (May, 1876) that the writer has had access to this correspondence, and for this privilege he is indebted to the courtesy of the Hon. J. C. G. Kennedy, of Washington City.

In his letters, written in 1750, 1751, 1752, and 1753, Mr. Shippen does not profess to give a particular account of the College curriculum, but, as the occasion calls for it, he mentions the subjects of study pursued by his class, and the works of which he had need, or which would be useful to him, in the prosecution of his studies. For example, he says to his father, in a letter written in French, and dated February 13, 1750, at which time he was a member of the Freshman class, "But I must give you an account of my studies at the present time. At *seven* in the morning we recite to the President lessons in the works of Xenophon, in Greek, and in Watts'

'Ontology.' The rest of the morning, until dinner-time, we study Cicero de Oratore and the Hebrew Grammar, and recite our lessons to Mr. Sherman (the College Tutor). The remaining part of the day we spend in the study of Xenophon and Ontology, to recite the next morning. And besides these things, we dispute once every week after the syllogistic method; and now and then we learn Geography." Two months later, April 19, he requests his father to send him Tully's "Orations," which, he adds, "I shall have occasion to use immediately." In a subsequent letter, of May 12, 1750, he says, "I believe I shall not want any more books till I come to Philadelphia, when I can bring them with me; which will be Gordon's 'Geographical Grammar' and (it may be) Watts' 'Astronomy' and a book or two of Logick. . . . We have to-day a lesson on the Globes."

" As I have but little time but what I must employ in my studies I can't enlarge, otherwise I would give some account of our College, as to the constitution, method, and customs, but must leave that till I see you." In a letter of the 8th of June, he says, "I shall learn Horace in a little while ; . . . but my time is filled up in studying Virgil, Greek Testament, and Rhetoric, so that I have no time hardly to look over any French, or Algebra, or any English book for my improvement. However, I shall accomplish it soon. . . . The President tells our class that we must go into Logick this week, and I shall have occasion for Watts' 'Book of Logick.'"

Such it seems was the course of study pursued by the Freshman class in 1750. As portions of Virgil and the four Gospels were required for admission to this class, it is probable that at or near the end of the year they revised these for another examination upon them, in connection with the regular studies of the year. In the Sophomore year attention was paid to Rhetoric, Ontology, and Mathematics. In his letter of the 21st of December, 1750, at which time he was a member of the Sophomore class, referring to a course of lectures then being delivered in Philadelphia, on several branches of Natural Philosophy, Mr. Shippen remarks, "The Astronomical parts, I perceive, are to be illustrated by a fine Orrery,* which . . . will represent to you the most adequate idea of the system of the world and the various motions of the Heavenly Bodies, which· [it] would give me great pleasure to see, *because these things are a part of my studies every day.*" It is probable that these subjects were attended to in connection with the study of the globes previously mentioned. From the same letter it appears that at this time he was reading the second book of Homer, and would shortly enter upon the study of the third book, and that in the spring he would have need of Martin's "Natural Philosophy," *in two volumes*, of which he seems to have a just appreciation when he says, "that it is by far the best that is extant, and which," he adds, "the President now uses in the instruction of the upper [Senior] class."

On the 29th of May, 1751, President Burr wrote to Mr. James David Dove, of Philadelphia, and made an arrangement with him for the use of *an apparatus* suited to the illustration of a course of twelve lectures on Natural Philosophy, by Mr. Lewis Evans. It does not appear what compensation Mr. Evans was to receive for his lectures, but Mr. Burr engaged to pay to Mr. Dove ten pounds *proclamation* when the lectures are finished. These lectures were the same as those delivered by Mr. Evans in the cities of Philadelphia and New York, and concerning which Mr. Shippen thus speaks in his letter to his father, of the date of September 14,

---

* This was not Rittenhouse's famous orrery.

1751: "Mr. Lewis Evans has already exhibited eight of his lectures, . . . to the general satisfaction of all attending thereon.   And as to his Lecture on Electricity, his great knowledge in it, and his accurateness in performing the experiments, have given us abundant Light into the Nature and properties thereof, of which I was entirely ignorant before.   And as several Phenomena in Nature can be accounted for from the knowledge of this newly-discovered Element (I mean the Electrical Fluid), and are dependent thereon, I have taken this good opportunity, while Mr. Evans is here, and has *a globe* to spare, to procure myself a small Electrical Machine, particularly for my instruction in this useful branch of Philosophy."

From a letter of Governor Belcher to Mr. [Dr.] Franklin, of the date of January 20, 1752, it appears that President Burr had possessed himself of an Electrical Machine, and that he experimented with it upon the Governor himself, for his relief from the paralysis under which he was suffering at the time.   The relief, however, afforded by the use of electricity in the Governor's case was but little, if any.   Dr. Franklin had kindly offered to wait upon the Governor for a like purpose, and sent him one of his machines, the "glass globe" of which unfortunately was broken on its way to the Governor's residence; and this was the occasion of Mr. Burr proffering his services.   As Mr. Burr instructed the students in Natural Philosophy, this doubtless was the chief reason for his purchase of this Electrical Machine.   Dr. Franklin's great discovery of the identity of lightning and ordinary electricity was made in 1752.

In a letter of December 2, 1751, Mr. Shippen says, "Mr. Burr has collected this Fall subscriptions to the value of £200, Penn's currency, for the apparatus, about £100 whereof Col. Alford very generously subscribed, he being one of the greatest friends our College is blessed with."   Further on Mr. Shippen adds, "I am beginning to read Ethics (or Moral Philosophy), and shall have occasion for Grove's 2 vols. on that branch."   Again, in a letter of May 23, 1752, "Since you were here, the President has been instructing two or three of us in the calculation of Eclipses, for which we made use of Whiston & Brent's Astronomical Tables."   And in a letter of the 25th of July, 1752, to his father, Mr. Shippen, "I received your letter of the 23d of May, with Hodgson's 'Theory of Navigation' and Street's 'Tables,' for which I am very thankful, though I am sorry that I cannot now employ my thoughts in studying anything of them, as I am fully engaged in the necessary exercises of the College."   From this remark and the one preceding, it is probable that the calculating of Eclipses and study of Navigation were optional studies, to which the students in general were not required to give attention, but for instruction in which, if desired, they could have all needed help.

In August, 1752, Mr. Shippen, with the consent of his father, and of Mr. Burr, went for a few weeks to New Rochelle, to be with a French family and learn the French language more perfectly.

THE LOCATING OF THE COLLEGE.

The second thing mentioned as an object of special interest at this time was the choice of a permanent seat for the College. At a meeting of the Trustees, at Newark, September 26, 1750, the time of the annual Commencement, it was *voted,*

" That a proposal be made to the Towns of Brunswick and Princetown to try what sum of money they can raise for Building of the College, by the next meeting, that the Trustees may be better able to judge in which of these places to fix the place of the College."

At the next meeting, held at Trenton, May 15, 1751, the Trustees decided,

" That New Brunswick be the place for the building of the College, *provided* the Inhabitants of said Place agree with the Trustees upon the following terms, *viz.* that they secure to the College a Thousand Pounds *proc.* money, ten acres of land contiguous to the College, and two hundred acres of wood-land, the furthest part of it not to be more than three miles from the town."

At this meeting there was an offer made by the inhabitants of Princeton, and it was next ordered,

" That Mr. Sergeant, the Treasurer, and some other person, whom he shall see fit, view the above promised land at Princetown, and also that to be given by the Inhabitants of New Brunswick, and make a report of the same to the Trustees at their meeting in September next."

This meeting was held at Newark, on the 25th of September, at which time the following record was made :

" When the Board of Trustees had laid before them the proposals of the Inhabitants of New Brunswick, relating to the College being fixt there, for want of some particular steps being taken respecting that matter, the Trustees judged that they could not at present come to any conclusion in the affair, and so deferred the further consideration of it to their next meeting."

The Trustees also ordered,

" That Mr. Sergeant, with any person he shall choose, view the land at New Brunswick and at Princetown, and make a report what they shall deem an equivalent at the next meeting."

This is substantially the same order with one given at the previous meeting, but differing in this respect, as they were to give their judgment as to what would be an equivalent for the land promised the College.

The next meeting of the Board was held at Elizabeth, May 14, 1752, but it does not appear from the minutes that any action was had in reference to the erection of a College building. At the meeting held at the time of the next Commencement,

September 27, 1752, the following entry was made in the minutes:

"The Trustees taking into consideration that the people of New Brunswick have not complied with the terms proposed to them for fixing the College in that place, by the time referred to in the offer of this Board, now Voted, That they are free from any obligation to fix the College at New Brunswick, and are at liberty to place it where they please. The Trustees agree that it shall be put to Vote in what place the College shall be fixed, upon such conditions as the Board shall propose.

"Voted, That the College be fixed at Princetown, upon condition that the inhabitants of said Place secure to the Trustees those two hundred acres of wood-land, and that Ten Acres of cleared land which Mr. Sergeant viewed; and also one thousand Pounds proc. money. The one half of which sum to be paid within two months after the foundation of the College is laid, and the other half within six months afterwards; and that the people of said Place comply with the terms of this vote within three months from this time by giving in Bonds for said money, and making a sufficient Title for said land to be received by such persons as the Board shall appoint, or else forfeit all privilege from this Vote; and that the Treasurer be empowered to give them a bond for the fulfilment of this Vote on the part of the Trustees.

"The Trustees appoint Messrs. President Burr, Samuel Woodruff, Jonathan Sergeant, Elihu Spencer, Caleb Smith, to be a committee to transact the above affair with the Inhabitants of Princetown, and that Elizabethtown be the place for accomplishing the same."

At this meeting Governor Belcher earnestly urged the Trustees to go on with the erection of a College building, and of a house for the President and his family. The Governor's speech is given at length in the minutes of the Board.

The next meeting of the Trustees was held at Princeton, on the 24th of January, 1753, when it was voted by the Board,

"That said People (when Mr. Randolph has given a Deed for a certain tract of Land four hundred feet Front and thirty Poles depth, in lines at right angles with the broad street where it is proposed that the College shall be built) have complied with the terms proposed to them for fixing the College at said place."

Mr. Nathaniel Fitz Randolph here referred to did give the required deed, and through his liberality and that of the gentlemen who contributed the thousand pounds *proc.*, and who paid for the rest of the land given to the College, the permanent seat of the College was fixed at Princeton.

Among certain memoranda made by Mr. Randolph is the following:

"January 25, 1753. Gave a deed to the Trustees for (4½) four and one-half acres of Land for the College."

The consideration mentioned in the deed was (£150) one hundred and fifty pounds; but it is added by Mr. Randolph,

" I never did receive one penny for it : it was only to confirm the title."

He also gave twenty pounds in addition to the land and his services in obtaining subscriptions.

From a comparison of dates, it appears that the deed was given the third day after the meeting of the Board in Princeton to conclude their agreement with the inhabitants of that place, viz., on the 25th of January, 1753.

THE ERECTION OF COLLEGE BUILDINGS.

At the meeting in Princeton just mentioned, Thomas Leonard, Esq., Samuel Woodruff, Esq., and the Rev. Messrs. Cowell, William Tennent, Burr, Treat, Brainerd, and Smith, were appointed a committee "to act in behalf of the Trustees in building the College, according to the plan agreed upon by the Board." This committee was also authorized to build a house for the President, and to draw upon the Treasurer of the College for the requisite funds. The plan adopted was, "in general," one drawn by Dr. Shippen and Mr. Robert Smith, of Philadelphia. Mr. Samuel Hazard and Mr. Robert Smith were a committee to select the spot and to mark out the ground. Dr. Shippen and Mr. Hazard were Trustees. Mr. Smith was the Architect for the building.

It was first ordered, " That the College be built of brick, if good brick can be made at Princeton, and sand be got reasonably cheap, and that it be three stories high, and without any cellar." At a subsequent meeting it was " Voted, That the College be built of stone, and the President's house of wood." The outer walls of the College were accordingly built of stone obtained from a quarry near the village, but the President's house was built of brick. (See Minutes of the Board for July 22, 1754, and for September 25 of the same year.)

The land upon which these buildings were erected was

given by N. F. Randolph, from whose memoranda* we gather the following particulars respecting the College building, viz., that the ground for this building was first broken on the 29th of July, 1754, under the direction of Joseph Morrow, and that the first corner-stone was laid at the northwest corner of the cellar, by Thomas Leonard, John Stockton, John Hornor, William Worth (the mason who did the stone and brick work), N. F. Randolph, and many others. From which we may infer that the corner-stone was laid by Mr. Leonard, the Chairman of the Building Committee, in the presence and with the assistance of some of the other persons named. Mr. Randolph adds that in November, 1755, "the roof of said College was raised by Robert Smith, the carpenter who did the wood-work of the College."

This building was originally one hundred and seventy-six feet in length, fifty-four in width at the two ends, with projections in the front and in the rear, the front one extending three or four feet, the one in the rear about twelve feet. The middle of the roof was surmounted by a cupola. There were three stories, with a basement, and, exclusive of the Chapel, there were in all *sixty* rooms, sixteen of them in the basement, or what is now the cellar. From the account of the College prepared by Mr. Samuel Blair, under the direction of President Finley, and published in 1764, it appears that forty-nine of these rooms were assigned to the lodging of students, and that they were deemed sufficient for one hundred and forty-seven, reckoning three to a chamber. The other rooms were used for recitation, library, refectory, dining-room, etc. Since the burning of Nassau Hall, in 1855, none of the sixteen rooms above mentioned have been fitted up for the accommodation of students, as was the case before that time.

At the time of its erection this College building was the largest edifice of its kind in the British Provinces of North

---

* Copies of these memoranda and of other papers of the Randolph family were very kindly furnished the writer by Colonel J. Ross Snowden, of Philadelphia, Miss Frances W. Morford, formerly of Princeton, but now of Lynchburg, Virginia, and Mrs. John S. Hart, all of whom are descendants of the Randolphs of Princeton.

America, and in view of the very important services rendered
to the College by Governor Belcher, the Trustees, in a very
flattering letter addressed to the Governor, requested his permission to call this building "Belcher Hall."

With a rare modesty he declined the honor, and at the same
time expressed an earnest desire that the building should be
called "Nassau Hall," in honor of King William *the third*,
"who was a branch of the illustrious House of Nassau." It
was therefore ordered by a vote of the Trustees, "that the said
edifice be, in all time to come, called and known by the name
of Nassau Hall."

From the name given to this first College edifice the College
itself is extensively known under this appellation.

THE RAISING OF FUNDS.

Of necessity this important matter demanded the attention
of the Trustees from the very beginning of their efforts to erect
a College. But it was altogether beyond their ability to make
provision for the current expenses of the institution, and at the
same time to erect such buildings as were deemed essential to
the complete success of their enterprise. The erection of a
large and commodious College building was regarded by them
as scarcely of less importance than the charter itself. It would
seem from some of Governor Belcher's letters, written soon
after his arrival in the Colony, that he too regarded the erection of a suitable building and the full establishment of the College as almost one and the same thing, or at least he was of
the opinion that without such a building the attempt to establish a College must prove a failure. In a letter to the Rev.
Gilbert Tennent, of the date of July 30, 1748, the Governor
says, . . . "and if, finally, money cannot be raised for *the House*
and to support the necessary officers, the thing must be given
up." In a letter, written as early as September 18, 1747, to a
committee of the West Jersey Society, the Governor says, " I
find the people of this Province are in a poor situation for educating their children. I am therefore for promoting the building of a College for the Instruction of Youth. *This affair was
agitated before my arrival,* and much contested between the

gentlemen of the Eastern and those of the Western Division, where it should be placed, and I have got them to agree to have it built at Princetown, in the Western Division, being (I apprehend) nearest to the centre of the Province." And in a letter to his friend Mr. Walley, of Boston, of the date of October 2, 1747, he writes: "The People . . . in many parts of the Province show a great desire to enjoy the Gospel in Its purity. There has been striving at what place the College should be *built*, and I have persuaded those concerned to fix it at Princetown, and I think it as near the centre of the Province as any, and a fine situation. . . . By the Scarborough I have wrote to several of my rich Friends in England of this noble design, and I doubt not of obtaining some Donations from them, and, God sparing my life, they will find me a faithful friend. These southern Provinces greatly want such a nursery of Religion and Learning."

Neither the Governor nor the Trustees ever lost sight of the importance of erecting a College building, and to the obtaining of the requisite funds for this purpose they gave much thought. Before Governor Belcher entered upon his administration of the Province the Trustees had gotten subscriptions to the amount of eight hundred pounds (see letter of Governor Belcher to Rev. G. Tennent), and before the selection of the permanent seat of the institution they had received some valuable gifts, which, in the low state of the College treasury, were of great service to their undertaking. Still, they found that they needed larger funds than could be had in this country; and they therefore turned their thoughts to the securing of aid from abroad. The Rev. Dr. Pemberton, of New York, was the person first chosen to visit Great Britain; but he having declined, Mr. Burr was requested to take upon himself the burden of soliciting funds in England and Scotland. With no little hesitation Mr. Burr consented to do so, provided his friend the Rev. Caleb Smith, then pastor of the church in Newark Mountains, now Orange, would agree to take the oversight of the College during his absence. Mr. Smith, although disposed to render the College every assistance in his power, shrank from this responsibility, on the ground that he did not think

himself equal to the task. It is no slight evidence of this gentleman's great worth, as well as of his modesty, that the estimate
of his talents and learning by those best acquainted with them
was far higher than his own.

The Trustees next requested Rev. Messrs. Gilbert Tennent
and Samuel Davies to visit Great Britain and to solicit aid in
behalf of the College; and having obtained the consent of these
distinguished ministers, they next applied to the Synod of New
York for their sanction, which was unanimously given by that
body. An address to the General Assembly of the Church of
Scotland was prepared, and, after a revision by a committee,
was unanimously approved by the Synod. Certificates of their
appointment by the Synod were also given to Messrs. Tennent
and Davies, and provision was made for supplying their pulpits
during their absence. The address of the Synod is well worthy
of a place in any and every history of the College, and it may
perhaps be as well inserted in this connection as in any other.

A COPY OF THE ADDRESS TO THE GENERAL ASSEMBLY OF THE CHURCH OF SCOTLAND.

"To the very venerable and the very honourable the moderator and other
members of the General Assembly of the Church of Scotland, to meet at Edinburgh, May, 1754. The petition of the Synod of New York, convened at Philadelphia, October 3, 1753, humbly showeth :—

"That a college has lately been erected in the province of New Jersey, by his
Majesty's royal charter, in which a number of youth have been already educated,
who are now the instruments of service to the church of God; and which would
be far more extensively beneficial were it brought to maturity. That after all the
contributions that have been made to said college, or can be raised in these parts,
the fund is far from being sufficient for the erection of suitable buildings, supporting
the president and tutors, furnishing a library, and defraying other necessary expenses; that the trustees of said college, who are zealous and active to promote it
for the public good, have already sent their petition to this venerable house for some
assistance in carrying on so important a design; and also petitioned the Synod to
appoint two of their members, the Rev. Messrs. Gilbert Tennent and Samuel
Davies, to undertake a voyage to Europe in behalf of said college.

" Your petitioners therefore most heartily concur in said petition of the trustees
to the Reverend Assembly, and appoint the said Messrs. Tennent and Davies to be
their commissioners for that purpose.

" And as your petitioners apprehend the design of said petition to be of the utmost
importance to the interests of learning and religion in this infant country, and are
confident of the zeal of so pious and learned a body as the General Assembly of

the Church of Scotland to promote such a design, they beg leave to lay before this venerable house a general representation of the deplorable circumstances of the churches under their Synodical care, leaving it to the commissioners to descend to particulars.

"In the colonies of New York, New Jersey, Pennsylvania, Maryland, Virginia, and Carolina a great number of congregations have been formed upon the Presbyterian plan, which have put themselves under the Synodical care of your petitioners, who conform to the Constitution of the Church of Scotland, and have adopted her standards of doctrine, worship, and discipline. There are also large settlements lately planted in various parts, particularly in North and South Carolina, where multitudes are extremely desirous of the ministrations of the gospel; but they are not yet formed into congregations, and regularly organized, for want of ministers. These numerous bodies of people, dispersed so widely through so many colonies, have repeatedly made the most importunate applications to your petitioners for ministers to be sent among them; and your petitioners have exerted themselves to the utmost for their relief, both by sending their members and candidates to officiate some time among them and using all practicable measures for the education of pious youth for the ministry.

"But, alas, notwithstanding these painful endeavours, your petitioners have been utterly incapable to make sufficient provision for so many shepherdless flocks; and those that come hundreds of miles crying to them for some to break the bread of life among them, are often obliged to return in tears, with little or no relief, by reason of the scarcity of ministers.

"Though every practicable expedient which the most urgent necessity could suggest has been used to prepare labourers for this extensive and growing harvest, yet the number of ministers in the Synod is far from being equal to that of the congregations under their care. Though sundry of them have taken the pastoral charge of two or three congregations for a time, in order to lessen the number of vacancies; and though sundry youth have lately been licensed, ordained, and settled in congregations that were before destitute, yet there are no less than forty vacant congregations at present under the care of this Synod, besides many more which are incapable at present to support ministers; and the whole colony of North Carolina, where numerous congregations of Presbyterians are forming, and where there is not one Presbyterian minister settled.

"The great number of vacancies in the bounds of this Synod is owing, partly, to new settlements lately made in various parts of this continent, partly to the death of sundry ministers belonging to this Synod, but principally to the small number of youth educated for the ministry, so vastly disproportionate to the numerous vacancies; and unless some effectual means can be taken for the education of proper persons for the sacred character, the churches of Christ in these parts must continue in the most destitute circumstances, wandering shepherdless and forlorn through this wilderness, thousands perishing for lack of knowledge, the children of God hungry and unfed, and the rising age growing up in a state little better than that of heathenism with regard to the public ministrations of the gospel.

"The numerous inconveniences of a private, and the many important advantages of a public education are so evident, that we need not inform this venerable Assembly of them, who cannot but be sensible, from happy experience, of the many extensive benefits of convenient colleges.

" The difficulty (and in some cases the impossibility) of sending youth two, three, four, or five hundred miles or more, to the colleges of New England, is evident at first sight. Now it is from the College of New Jersey only that we can expect a remedy of these inconveniences ; it is to *that* your petitioners look for the increase of their numbers ; it is on *that* the Presbyterian churches through the six colonies above mentioned principally depend for a supply of accomplished ministers ; from *that* has been obtained considerable relief already, notwithstanding the many disadvantages that unavoidably attend it in its present infant state ; and from *that* may be expected a sufficient supply when brought to maturity.

" Your petitioners, therefore, most earnestly pray that this very reverend Assembly would afford the said college all the countenance and assistance in their power. The young daughter of the Church of Scotland, helpless and exposed in this foreign land, cries to her tender and powerful mother for relief. The cries of ministers oppressed with labours, and of congregations famishing for want of the sincere milk of the word, implore assistance. And were the poor Indian savages sensible of their own case they would join in the cry, and beg for more missionaries to be sent to propagate the religion of Jesus among them.

" Now, as the College of New Jersey appears the most promising expedient to redress these grievances, and to promote religion and learning in these provinces, your petitioners most heartily concur with the trustees, and humbly pray that an act may be passed by their venerable and honourable Assembly for a national collection in favour of said college. And your petitioners, as in duty bound, shall ever pray," etc.

A COPY OF THE CERTIFICATE FOR MESSRS. GILBERT TENNENT AND SAMUEL DAVIES.

" The Rev. Messrs. Gilbert Tennent and Samuel Davies, the bearers hereof, undertaking a voyage to Europe by the appointment of the Synod, in concurrence with the trustees of the College of New Jersey, for services of said college ; the Synod do hereby certify, that the above reverend gentlemen are worthy and well-approved members of their body, and do recommend them to the acceptance of the church of God and the work of their mission, wheresoever Divine Providence may call them, imploring the Divine Presence with them and success to their important undertaking.

" Signed by order of the Synod."

The appointment of these two gentlemen, Messrs. Tennent and Davies, was a most happy one for the College. Going with an earnest recommendation from the Synod, and with letters from Governor Belcher, they were cordially received by the Presbyterians of Scotland and Ireland, and the Baptists and Independents of England, and kindly treated by some of the prominent statesmen of that day. Their mission was successful beyond all expectation, and they obtained an amount of funds which enabled the Trustees to proceed without further delay in the erection of their proposed College Hall, and also of a house for the President and family. What was the precise sum collected in Great Britain and Ireland cannot now be stated, as the books of the Treasurer of the College have been lost ; but the minutes of the Board for the 24th of September, 1755, set forth the fact that the funds were amply sufficient to defray the expenses incurred in the erection of the buildings above mentioned ; and that three hundred and fifty pounds sterling, or more, were also obtained from divers friends in Great Britain for the education of pious and indigent youth for the gospel ministry.*

Messrs. Tennent and Davies received in the city of London alone about twelve hundred pounds sterling. On their return from Edinburgh to London, Mr. Tennent went to Ireland, and to some of the towns in the west of England, and obtained on this tour five hundred pounds sterling. And Mr. Davies collected in the several towns visited by him about four hundred pounds. And these sums are exclusive, in a great measure at least, of the collections made in the churches in Scotland and Ireland, by order of the General Assembly of the Church of Scotland, and by the Synod of Ulster.

The youth to be aided from this fund were to be selected by the Synod, and to receive their education at the College of New Jersey. This doubtless may be regarded as the foundation of the charitable funds of the College, which have been of no little service to the institution, as well as to the Presbyterian Church, by assisting in the support of a valuable class of students, whose desire and aim were to become ministers of the gospel. Of the several contributions to this fund mention will be made hereafter.†

For the liberality and kindness of the General Assembly of the Church of Scotland, the Trustees, by a formal vote, expressed their grateful acknowledgments.

In Guild's " History of Brown University" there is a copy of a letter written from London, April 26, 1768, by the Rev.

---

* For a list of the contributors to this particular fund, see printed " Minutes of the Synod of New York," pages 264, 265.

† In Minutes, page 43.

Morgan Edwards to President Manning, in which letter the following passage occurs respecting Messrs. Tennent and Davies, and two other well-known gentlemen, who had visited Great Britain and Ireland to solicit funds in aid of the important and benevolent objects of their several missions:

" You must observe also that in England, as in Ireland, I solicit money towards endowing the College, and therefore take care that you attend to the design of the donors.

" Indeed, you have a list of all the sums I received in Ireland, which list was distributed in the several places where I have been. The design was to let every one of them see that I gave true credit for what I have received. *Had Tenn—nt, D—vis, and Be—ty and Whit—r, done so, they would have prevented suspicions very injurious to themselves, and to those that come after them on the like errand. Mr. Raffey told me that he had been called a rogue for aiding the said persons to raise money in London.*"

Mr. Guild, not content to let the letter speak for itself, must needs add the following note, lest the reader of his book might not otherwise know who were the gentlemen referred to by Mr. Edwards:

"In 1753, by request of the Trustees of the College of New Jersey, the Presbyterian Synod of New York appointed the Rev. Gilbert Tennent, in conjunction with the Rev. (afterwards President) Samuel Davis, to cross the Atlantic and solicit funds for that Institution. The mission was eminently successful; but the only account of it that remains is found in the diary of Mr. Davis. About the same time, or a little later, the Rev. Nathaniel Whitaker, accompanied by Samson Occum, an Indian preacher, solicited funds for Moor's Indian Charity School, afterwards Dartmouth College. Who the other person was to whom Edwards refers we are not informed."

This information it is in the writer's power to supply. He was the Rev. Charles Beatty, a man without reproach and of eminent piety, who was sent by the Synod of New York and Philadelphia to solicit contributions for the establishment of a fund to assist aged and disabled ministers and the families of deceased ministers. All the gentlemen named discharged their respective trusts, in collecting funds and in making report thereof, to the entire satisfaction of those whose agents they were. And although there be not *now* any account of the moneys collected by Messrs. Tennent and Davies but what is given in the diary of Mr. Davies, *yet it would be perfectly absurd to imagine* that they did not give a detailed report of all the moneys received by them for the College; and for the collecting of which the Trustees of the College gave them their thanks, and to each a present of £50, in addition to the expenses of their agency and of supplying the pulpits during their absence. The Treasurer's books and papers of that day have long been lost, but whether during the ravages of the Revolutionary War or by the fire of 1802, which consumed the College edifice, known as Nassau Hall, together with the Library, Philosophical Apparatus, and other valuables, is unknown. The election of Mr. Davies, a few years later, as President of the College, in the absence of all other evidence, would be conclusive as to the fact that his agency had given the Trustees entire satisfaction; and it shows that the currency given to what was doubtless the grossly exaggerated statement of Mr. Raffey, as reported by Mr. Edwards, was a discourteous treatment of gentlemen in every respect his equals, not to say his superiors.

The Rev. Dr. Manning, the first President of Brown University, to whom Mr. Edwards's letter was addressed, was a graduate of the College of New Jersey in 1762. He was an eminently active and useful man, and was held in high repute as a teacher, a minister, and a patriot. In 1786 he represented Rhode Island in the Continental Congress.

THE REMOVAL TO PRINCETON.

The College edifice and the house for the President were both so far completed by the autumn of 1756 that the Trustees, at their meeting in September of that year, the time of the annual Commencement, passed an order for the removal of the students from Newark to Princeton, and it took place accordingly. The words of this order were: " *Voted*, That the President move the College to Princeton this Fall, and that the expense thereof be paid by the Treasurer."

In Dr. Finley's account of the College it is said to have taken place in 1757. Dr. Green suggests that President Finley "probably spoke of what might be called a collegiate year, reckoning from one Commencement to another."

That the removal actually occurred in the autumn of 1756 we have the testimony of Mr. N. F. Randolph, who, in his "Memoranda," says that, "in 1756, Aaron Burr, President, preached the first sermon, and began the first school in Princeton College." And it also appears from a minute in the Records of the Synod of New York for 1757, that a committee of the Synod met at Princeton on the 23d of November, 1756, to examine such students as were candidates to receive assistance from the fund designed for the support of pious youths.

At this time, it is estimated that there were seventy pupils in the College. Everything appeared bright and promising. Governor Belcher and Mr. Burr had seen their fondest hopes in regard to the College realized. Their efforts to obtain funds in Great Britain and Ireland had surpassed their expectations. A college edifice sufficient for the accommodation of more than one hundred students had been erected. A house for the President of the College had also been built. The College was in good repute at home and abroad, with a prospect of increase in the number of the pupils and in the resources of the institution. At the meetings of the Synods of New York and of Philadelphia in May, 1757, effectual measures were taken for the union of these two Synods, thus bringing together into one harmonious body all the Presbyterian ministers and churches in the several Provinces, and giving hope to the friends of the College of increased patronage from a united Church.*

But scarcely were these things realized, or rather looked forward to with confident expectation, when the two principal supports of the College were removed from their earthly labors; and neither of them lived to see a class graduated at Princeton, —Governor Belcher having died on Wednesday, the 31st of August, and President Burr on Saturday, the 24th of September, 1757, four days before the annual Commencement, which took place on Wednesday, the 28th of September.

From the day on which Mr. Burr was inaugurated President of the College, under the second charter, to the Commencement, which occurred on the fourth day after his decease,—that is, from the 9th of November, 1748, to the 28th of September, 1757,—there were admitted to the first degree in the Arts *one hundred and fourteen* young gentlemen who had pursued their studies under his guidance, and of these, *sixty-two* entered the ministry. Thus far, it appears, the College had answered the design of its founders.

The first general revival of religion in the College took place in the last year of President Burr's administration and of his life, the Lord permitting him to see that the blessing of the

---

* The union was consummated in May, 1758.

Almighty had attended his labors for the promotion of piety and learning in happy union.

The names of the several Tutors during Mr. Burr's administration are as follows, viz.:

1. John Maltby, from 1749 to 1752. Mr. Maltby was a graduate of Yale, and was a descendant of the Rev. Abraham Pierson, the first President of that College. For several years he was "the much-loved pastor" of a church in the island of Bermuda. He died in 1771.

2. Samuel Sherwood, from 1750 to 1752.

3. Jonathan Badger, from 1752 to 1755.

4. Alexander Gordon, from 1752 to 1754.

5. George Duffield, from 1754 to 1756.

6. William Thompson, from 1755 to 1756.

7. Benjamin Y. Prime, from 1756 to 1757.

8. John Ewing, from 1756 to 1758.

9. Isaac Smith, from 1757 to 1758.

10. Jeremiah Halsey, from 1757 to 1767.

11. Joseph Treat, from 1758 to 1760.

The following gentlemen were chosen Trustees during Mr. Burr's presidency:

1. James Neilson, Esq., in 1749; resigned in 1754.

2. Samuel Woodruff, Esq., in 1749; died in 1768.

3. Rev. John Frelinghuysen, in 1750; died in 1755.

4. Rev. Caleb Smith, in 1750; died in 1763. He was pastor of the church at Newark Mountains, now Orange, New Jersey.

5. Rev. Thomas Thompson, in 1751; died in 1752.

6. Rev. Samuel Finley, in 1751; resigned in 1761. In this year he was chosen President of the College.

7. Rev. Elihu Spencer, in 1752; died in 1784.

8. Rev. John Brainerd, in 1754; died in 1780.

9. Rev. Alexander Cumming, in 1756; resigned in 1761.

10. Rev. Charles McKnight, in 1757; died in 1778.

11. Richard Stockton, Esq., in 1757; died in 1781.

Of the one hundred and fourteen graduates who, from 1747 to 1757, pursued their studies under the direction of President Burr, more than half became preachers of the gospel, and about *forty* were men of more or less note in their respective callings, and of these not a few were quite eminent. To begin with *instructers in* this and in other institutions: of the class of

1752. The Rev. Jeremiah Halsey, A.M., for *ten* years a Tutor, a Professor *elect* of Mathematics, and then a Trustee.

1754. The Rev. John Ewing, S.T.D., for *two* years a Tutor in this College, Professor in the University of Pennsylvania, and also Provost of the same.

1754. William Shippen, M.D. The first Professor of Anatomy in the University of Pennsylvania.

1757. James Smith, M.D. The first Professor of Materia Medica in King's (Columbia) College, New York.

MEMBERS OF THE CONTINENTAL CONGRESS.

1748. Hon. Richard Stockton, New Jersey; *a signer of the Declaration of Independence;* a Trustee of the College.

1749. Hon. William Burnet, New Jersey; *also Surgeon-General of the United States Army.*

1751. Hon. Nathaniel Scudder, New Jersey; a Trustee of the College.

1752. Hon. Samuel Livermore, of New Hampshire; *also United States Senator, etc., etc.*

1754. Hon. William Shippen, M.D., of Pennsylvania; a Trustee of the College.

1755. Hon. Joseph Montgomery, of Pennsylvania; from 1784 to 1788.

1756. Hon. Jesse Root, LL.D., of Connecticut; also Chief Justice of Connecticut.

1757. Hon. Joseph Reed, of New Jersey and Pennsylvania; also, in 1784, President of the Pennsylvania State Convention; a Trustee of the College, etc.

OF THE UNITED STATES SENATE.

1756. Hon. Alexander Martin, LL.D., of North Carolina.

OF THE HOUSE OF REPRESENTATIVES.

1755. Hon. Isaac Smith, of New Jersey; also a Judge of the Supreme Court of New Jersey.

SECRETARY OF THE PROVINCE OF PENNSYLVANIA.

1753. Joseph Shippen, Esq.

HIGH SHERIFF OF LONDON.

1757. Stephen Sayre, Esq.

As those gentlemen whose names are about to be given are not included in any of the above lists, they will be mentioned in the order of their admission to the first degree in the Arts:

1748. Rev. Hugh Henry, Rehoboth, Maryland.

1748. Rev. Israel Reed, A.M., of Bound Brook, New Jersey; a Trustee of the College.

1749. Rev. John Brown, New Providence, Rockbridge County, Virginia.

1749. Rev. John Todd, A.M.; successor to the Rev. Samuel Davies as minister of the Providence church, Virginia.

1750. Rev. Daniel Farrand, A.M.; minister of a Congregational church in South Canaan, Connecticut.

1750. Rev. Samuel McClintock, D.D.; minister of a Congregational church in Greenland, New Hampshire.

1750. Benjamin Youngs Prime, M.D.; Tutor; an elegant classical scholar; a practitioner of medicine and surgery in the city of New York.

1750. Rev. Robert Henry, A.M.; pastor of Cub Creek church, Charlotte County, Virginia.

1752. Rev. George Duffield, D.D.; Tutor and Trustee; pastor of the Third Church, Philadelphia.

1752. Rev. Nathaniel Whitaker, D.D., of Connecticut; received his degree from St. Andrew's, Scotland.

1753. Rev. John Harris, of Delaware and South Carolina.

1753. Dr. Robert Harris, of Philadelphia; for fifty-four years a Trustee of the College.

1753. Rev. Hugh McAden, A.M., a native of Pennsylvania; pastor of the churches in Duplin and New Hanover, North Carolina.

1754. Rev. Hugh Knox, D.D.; minister at St. Croix, West Indies.

1754. David Matthews, A.M.; Mayor of New York in 1775; a Loyalist.

1754. Rev. William Ramsay, A.M.; pastor of Fairfield church, Connecticut.

1755. Thaddeus Burr, A.M.; a lawyer in Fairfield, Connecticut.

1755. Rev. Wheeler Case, A.M.; pastor of Pleasant Valley church, Dutchess County, New York; author of a volume of poems.

1756. Rev. Azel Roe, D.D., of Woodbridge, New Jersey; a Trustee of the College.

1757. Rev. William Kirkpatrick, A.M., of Amwell, New Jersey; a Trustee of the College.

1757. Rev. Alexander McWhorter, D.D., of Newark, New Jersey; a Trustee of the College.

1757. Henry Wells, A.M., M.D., of Brattleborough, Vermont.

MEMOIR OF PRESIDENT BURR.

The Rev. Aaron Burr was born in Fairfield County, Connecticut, on the 4th of January, 1716. He was the youngest son of Daniel Burr, whose father and paternal grandfather were both named John. The elder John came to Fairfield from Springfield, Massachusetts. (See Dr. Stearns's " Historical Discourses," page 151.)

In their respective sketches of the life of President Burr, Drs. Allen, Green, and Sprague agree in representing him as descended from the learned and pious Jonathan Burr, a non-conformist preacher who came from England in 1639, and settled in Dorchester, Massachusetts, where he died in 1641. John Burr, the second son of the Rev. Jonathan Burr, of Dorchester, settled in Fairfield County probably about the time that the first John came from Springfield to Fairfield, and this fact, mentioned by Dr. Allen in his " Biographical Dictionary," may have given rise to the conjecture that President Burr was descended from the Rev. Jonathan Burr. Dr. Allen expressly says that Daniel Burr, the father of President Burr, was descended from John Burr. But this cannot be unless Daniel's mother was a daughter of John Burr, of which we have no evidence or even any intimation.

The true account, therefore, of this matter is the one given by the Rev. Dr. Stearns, and for it he acknowledges himself indebted to the Rev. Dr. L. H. Atwater, then of Fairfield, but now of Princeton, who at Dr. Stearns's request ascertained the facts of the case. And here it may not be amiss to say that the fullest and the best sketch of the life of President Burr of which we have any knowledge is the one given by Dr. Stearns, in his "Historical Discourses" relative to the First Presbyterian Church of Newark.

President Burr was graduated at Yale College in the autumn of 1735, being at that time in the twentieth year of his age. At the completion of the usual College course he was a successful competitor for one of the classical scholarships founded at Yale by Berkeley, the eminent and learned Bishop of Cloyne; and having obtained this prize, he continued his studies at New Haven for another year. It was during this year that he became deeply and permanently interested in the subject of religion, and, hoping that he was called of God to engage in the work of the ministry, he resolved to devote himself to it with all his heart. And this he did. Upon being licensed as a candidate for the sacred office, he left New England and came to New Jersey. Here he labored for a short time at Hanover, in Morris County, and while there he attracted the attention of the church in Newark, which was then without a pastor. At first he was invited to preach at Newark for one year, beginning the 10th of January, 1737. At the expiration of this time he was invited to assume the pastoral office, and, accepting the invitation, he was ordained on the 25th of January, 1738, by the Presbytery of East Jersey, with which Presbytery the church of Newark was then connected.

"The settlement of Mr. Burr," says Dr. Stearns, "was a most auspicious event." This remark has special reference to the church which had just given him a unanimous call to become their pastor; but it is equally true with respect to the interests of religion and learning within the limits of the entire Presbyterian Church in this country, of which he was an eminent minister, surpassed by none in devotion to his work, or, as far as we can judge, in the greatness and successful prosecution of his various and arduous labors.

Within eighteen months after Mr. Burr's settlement at New-ark, the divine blessing manifestly rested upon his ministrations there: the people of his charge were favored with a most re-markable outpouring of the Spirit, and among all classes, young and old, there was such an awakening to their spiritual inter-ests as produced a wonderful change in the whole community. This unusual attention to religion continued for nearly two years, and during this period they had one or more visits from the pious and eloquent Whitefield, for whom Mr. Burr seems to have entertained the highest respect, which was fully recip-rocated by this famous itinerant for the gospel's sake.

Soon after his settlement at Newark, Mr. Burr became deeply interested in the matter of Christian missions among the Indian tribes of this country, and united with his friends, the Rev. Messrs. Dickinson and Pemberton, in directing the attention of the Society in Scotland for Propagating Christian Knowledge to this field of labor. The result of their correspondence was that they were chosen correspondents of the Society, and were authorized to employ two missionaries at the expense of the Society. This led to the appointment of David Brainerd and of Azariah Horton as missionaries to the American Indians.

Mr. Burr took an active part in the proceedings of the Church courts of which he was a member, and even in regard to matters in which the feelings of the members were strongly enlisted, he did not hesitate to act in accordance with his convictions; yet always exhibiting good sense and a Christian temper, he never failed in securing the respect and esteem of those from whom he differed in opinion.

His zeal in behalf of learning was conspicuous from the be-ginning of his ministry. Before a charter was obtained for the College of New Jersey, Mr. Burr established a classical school in Newark, doubtless for the special, though not for the exclu-sive, benefit of the youth of his pastoral charge. In the efforts to obtain a charter for a college he took a prominent part; and when, upon the decease of President Dickinson, he became the head of the institution, his untiring labors in its behalf ceased only with his life.

Of the success which attended these labors mention was made in speaking of his administration of the affairs of the College; but of his liberality to it, when it was without funds sufficient to meet its necessary expenses, we have not spoken. It has been said that for the first *three years* he received no salary from the College.* And it is true that in the minutes of the Trustees no mention is made of any order or vote for the payment to him of any moneys until the meeting of the Board, at Newark, on the 26th of September, 1750. In the record of this meeting there is the following minute: "Ordered, That the Clerk be allowed £5 per annum for his trouble, and that £5 be reserved for Defraying the Incidental charges of the Corporation; and that the *Residue of the Interest* in the Treasurer's hands be paid the President for his services till further orders." This was at the end of the second year of Mr. Burr's presidency under the second charter. The three years mentioned in the Obituary probably included the year that he had the charge of the College under the first charter.

The moneys in the hands of the Treasurer were those received from the lottery drawn in Philadelphia, and from *donations*, the first of which was a gift of fifty pounds *proc.* from the Hon. James Alexander, Esq., father of Major-General Lord Stirling. About this time, also, Colonel John Alford, of Boston, gave one hundred pounds to the College. The above-mentioned order seems to indicate that the Clerk's compensation and the incidental expenses were paid from the interest of moneys in the hands of the Treasurer, and doubtless the Treasurer's salary of ten pounds a year, mentioned in a previous order, was paid from the same fund. This arrangement would leave the tuition-fees to be distributed to the President and Tutors; each of the Tutors probably receiving a fixed stipend, and the President the remainder.

The first mention of a fixed compensation to the President

---

* See Dr. Stearns's "Historical Discourses," page 185, and obituary notice, from the "New York Mercury," on page 206.

is in the minutes of the Trustees for May 2, 1754, and in these words : " Voted, That the President's salary be £150 *proc.* for the year following the next Commencement." *

How much he received of *the interest* from the vested funds of the College, as ordered by the Board at their meeting in September, 1750, from this date to September, 1754, when his salary, independent of the graduation-fees, was fixed at one hundred and fifty pounds a year, we have no means of ascertaining. But it is morally certain that his entire income from the sources named was a very meagre one compared with the services rendered; and this fact shows the sacrifices made by him for the cause of religion and learning while laboring so earnestly for the upbuilding of the College ; and it also shows the generous spirit of the man, who lost sight of his own interests in efforts to serve his fellow-men. Well, therefore, might the Trustees, upon his decease and immediately before electing one to succeed him in the office of President, adopt the following resolution on the subject of the President's salary, which for the last year of Mr. Burr's life was two hundred and fifty pounds :

---

* At the same meeting it was also "Voted, That each of the two Tutors have £40 *proc.* yearly; and provided they tarry four years that they have £40 gratuity, if recommended by the President as having faithfully discharged their Trusts. The said salaries are to take place after the next Commencement." By a vote of the Board, at a meeting held September 27, 1752, two years before, each Tutor was allowed for his services twenty pounds sterling a year, reckoned to be at that time equal to thirty pounds *proc.*

The tuition-fees were fifteen shillings *proc.* a quarter, or three pounds a year. On the supposition that there were thirty students in the four classes during each of the first three years, and, judging from the number of graduates in those years, the average could hardly have been less, the entire income from the *tuition-fees* would have been two hundred and seventy pounds *proc.* For the first year there was but one Tutor, and the entire sum paid to the Tutors for these years did not exceed one hundred and fifty pounds *proc.*, which would leave one hundred and twenty pounds for the President for the three years, or an average of forty pounds *proc.* a year.

By an ordinance of the Board, passed on the day of the first College Commencement, each student " admitted to the honor of a Degree was required to pay to the President thirty shillings *proc.*" From this source he should have received, and probably did, about ten pounds more a year, making *the yearly* income from these two sources about fifty pounds proclamation money, which is only one-third of the salary voted to him by the Board for one year from September, 1754.

"The Trustees having considered that the salary which the last year was voted to the Rev. President Burr was considerably increased on account of his constant Attention, great Zeal, and indefatigable Labors for the College; and more especially for that the said President Burr, for some years in the fore Part of the Executing his said Office, had done many and great services for said College, for which he has never received any pecuniary consideration; and that any President, who now or hereafter may be chosen, cannot, for the service of this office for some Time, deserve so well of this Board: It is therefore Ordered, that the salary of the President for the time being shall be the sum of two hundred Pounds proclamation money of this Province, during the ensuing year, together with the use of the President's house,* and the improved Lands, with Liberty of getting his Firewood on the Lands belonging to the Corporation."

That Mr. Burr devoted himself to the upbuilding of the College without regard to the emolument to be derived therefrom is abundantly evident from the record just cited, and this fact shows that he was as generous as he was wise and laborious. It is no wonder that such a man should command the unlimited respect and confidence of all persons associated with him in his efforts to promote the cause of religion and learning.

For several years Mr. Burr discharged the duties both of pastor of the Newark church and of President of the College, but, in consequence of the increased number of students, and in view of the intended removal of the College, it was deemed best that Mr. Burr should devote himself exclusively to the instruction of the students and to the general interests of the College; and therefore at their meeting, September 25, 1754, the Trustees appointed a committee to wait upon the Presbytery of New York, and to ask from that body a dissolution of Mr. Burr's pastoral relation to the church of Newark. This application was accordingly made to the said Presbytery, and the petition of the Trustees was granted.

The church was very reluctant to give up their beloved and faithful pastor, whose labors among them had been signally blessed of God; but, in view of the great importance of the College, and of Mr. Burr's relations to it, they finally acquiesced in the decision of the Presbytery as right and proper.

* The mention of the President's house in this connection, and the manner of mentioning it, indicate that it had been occupied by Mr. Burr and his family. This resolution was adopted on the 27th of September, 1757, three days after the decease of President Burr.

As a scholar, a teacher, and a preacher, Mr. Burr was held in the highest esteem by his cotemporaries. His success in the discharge of his varied and responsible duties is evidence of his great intellectual vigor and of his indomitable energy; and the results seem to justify what to some may appear to be only the extravagant eulogies of warm personal friendships on the part of those who have left us memorials of Mr. Burr's life and labors as seen by themselves.

His publications were a Latin Grammar, commonly known as the Newark Grammar; a treatise entitled "The Supreme Deity of our Lord Jesus Christ, maintained in a Letter to the Editor of Mr. Emlyn's Inquiry," reprinted in Boston in 1791; "A Fast Sermon, on account of the Encroachment of the French, and their Designs against the British Colonies in America, delivered at Newark, January 1, 1755;" "The Watchman's Answer to the Question, 'What of the night?' (Isaiah xxi. 11, 12.) A Sermon before the Synod of New York, convened at Newark, September, 1750;" and a funeral sermon, at Elizabethtown, on the occasion of Governor Belcher's death, September 4, 1757. The sermon before the Synod was delivered by him at the opening of Synod's sessions, he having been the Moderator of the Synod at their meeting the year previous. The preparation and the preaching of the funeral sermon for Governor Belcher, under the exposure and the fatigue to which he had been recently subjected, brought on the extreme prostration and the accompanying fever which ended in his own death.*

It is not probable that, with the immense burden resting upon him almost perpetually after he took charge of the College, he was able to prepare for the press any other works than those enumerated above; but the writer of this article learned from Colonel Burr, the only son of President Burr, that his father's

---

* Mrs. Burr, in acknowledging the receipt of a letter addressed to President Burr by one of his friends in Scotland, thus refers to this last discourse: " I here enclose you, sir, the last attempt my dear husband made to serve God in public,— a sermon which he preached at the funeral of our late excellent Governor. You will not think it strange, if it has imperfections, when I tell you that all he wrote on the subject was done in a part of one afternoon and evening, when he had a violent fever on him, and the whole night after he was irrational." (Edwards's " Life," page 566.)

papers, and some of his own, which had been left for safe-keeping in the hands of his daughter, Mrs. Theodosia Allston, were lost with her upon her last voyage from Charleston, South Carolina, to New York, the ship having no doubt foundered at sea, as it was never heard from after leaving port.

On the 27th of June, 1752, Mr. Burr was united in marriage with Esther, the third daughter of the Rev. Jonathan Edwards, his successor in office. Mrs. Burr is spoken of as a lady remarkable for her beauty of person, her intelligence and piety, and as admirably suited to the station she was called to occupy as the wife of President Burr, whom she survived less than a year, dying on the 7th of April, 1758, a few weeks after the decease of her father, President Edwards. She left two children, a son and a daughter. The son was Colonel Aaron Burr, at one time Vice-President of the United States; the daughter, Sarah Burr, the elder of the two children, was married to the Hon. Tappan Reeve, an eminent lawyer, who was for some years Chief Justice of Connecticut, and founder of the famous Law School of Litchfield in that State.

On his death-bed, Mr. Burr gave directions that no unnecessary parade should be made at his funeral, and no expenses incurred beyond what Christian decency required; and that the sum which must be expended at a fashionable funeral above the necessary cost of a decent one should be given to the poor out of his estate.*

Upon the death of President Burr, a eulogy and a funeral sermon were prepared and published by two of his intimate friends, the eulogy by William Livingston, Esq., of New York, but subsequently the first Governor of New Jersey after the Revolution, the sermon by the Rev. Caleb Smith, of Newark Mountains. The sermon was prepared and preached at the request of the Trustees of the College, and published at their expense. A monumental stone was placed over President Burr's grave by order of the Trustees, and at their request the inscription for it was prepared by the Hon. William Smith,

---

* President Edwards, six months after, requested his own funeral might be conducted in the manner Mr. Burr's was.

Esq., a member of the Board. Obituary notices of President Burr appeared both in the " New York Mercury" and in the " Pennsylvania Gazette." It is believed, and it is by no means improbable, that the one in the " Gazette" was written by its eminent editor, Benjamin Franklin. It was as follows: " Sept. 29, 1757. Last Saturday died the Rev. Aaron Burr, President of the New Jersey College, a gentleman and a Christian, as universally beloved as known; an agreeable companion, a faithful friend, a tender and affectionate husband, and a good father; remarkable for his industry, integrity, strict honesty, and pure, undissembled piety; his benevolence as disinterested as unconfined, an excellent preacher, a great scholar, and a very great man." After citing this notice, Dr. Stearns makes the following comment: " The glowing eulogy of William Livingston, supported by the plain, unvarnished statements of Caleb Smith, and endorsed by the weighty testimony of Benjamin Franklin, seems to leave little more to be desired in attestation of the genuine merit of the subject of its commendation;" and yet the writer will venture to add the testimony of President Edwards in his letter of October 19, 1757, to the Trustees of the College: " This makes me shrink at the thought of taking upon me in the decline of life such a new and great business, attended with such a multiplicity of cares, and requiring such a degree of activity, alertness, and spirit of government, especially as succeeding one so remarkably well qualified in these respects, giving occasion to every one to remark the wide difference."

The following is the inscription on President Burr's tombstone:

M. S.
Reverendi admodum Viri,
Aaronis Burr, A.M., Collegii Neo-Cæsariensis Præsidis,
Natus apud *Fairfield Connecticutensium* IV. *Januarii*
A.D. MDCCXVI. S. V.
Honesta in eadem Colonia Familia oriundus,
Collegio *Valensi* innutritus.
Novarcæ Sacris initiatus, MDCCXXXVIII.
Annos circiter viginti pastorali munere
Fideliter functus.
Collegii N. C. Præsidium MDCCXLVIII accepit,
In Nassoviæ Aulam sub finem MDCCLVI translatus.

Defunctus in hoc Vico 24 Septembris
A.D. MDCCLVII. *S. N.*
Aetatis XLII.   Eheu quam brevis!
Huic Marmori subjicitur, quod mori potuit
Quod immortale, vendicarunt cœli:
Quæris Viator qualis quantusque fuit?
Perpaucis accipe.
Vir corpore parvo ac tenui,
Studiis, vigiliis, assiduisque Laboribus,
Macro.
Sagacitate, Perspicacitate, Agilitate,
Ac Solertia, (si fas dicere)
Plusquam humana, pene
Angelica.
Anima ferme totus,
Omnigena Literatura instructus,
Theologia præstantior:
Concionator volubilis, suavis et suadus;
Orator facundus;
Moribus facilis, candidus et jucundus;
Vita egregie liberalis ac beneficus;
Supra vero omnia emicuerunt
Pietas ac Benevolentia.
Sed ah! quanta et quota Ingenii,
Industriæ, Prudentiæ, Patientiæ,
Cæterarumque omnium Virtutum
Exemplaria,
Marmoris sepulchralis Angustia
Reticebit.
Multum desideratus, multum
Dilectus,
Humani generis Deliciæ,
O! infandum sui Desiderium,
Gemit Ecclesia, plorat
Academia:
At Cœlum plaudit, dum ille
Ingreditur
In Gaudium Domini
Dulce loquentis,
Euge bone et fidelis
Serve!
Abi Viator tuam respice finem!

CHAPTER VII.

THE Commencement of 1757 took place at Princeton, on
Wednesday, the 28th of September, just four days after the decease of President Burr. On this occasion the Trustees, with
one exception, were all present. At their request the Hon.
William Smith, a member of the Board, presided at the Commencement exercises, and conferred the usual degrees. The
two oldest ministers of their number, viz., the Rev. John Pierson and the Rev. Gilbert Tennent, were chosen to open and to
conclude the exercises with prayer. Twenty-two candidates
were admitted to the *first* degree in the Arts, and four to the
second degree.

At this meeting of the Board, the Trustees ordered that the
diploma fees for this Commencement be paid to Mrs. Burr
" for her proper use." They also ordered, " That any sum not
exceeding Twenty Pounds be laid out in erecting a monument
to the memory of the late President Burr." Mr. Robert Smith
was " desired to provide a proper marble stone for the purpose," and the Hon. William Smith was " requested to prepare
a Latin inscription for said monument."

The Rev. Caleb Smith was requested to prepare a funeral
sermon on the occasion of Mr. Burr's death, and to print the
same at the expense of the College. With this request he
complied, and his excellent discourse is the source from which
our knowledge of Mr. Burr's labors and life is mainly derived. The Hon. William Smith prepared the Latin inscription,
which being referred to the Rev. Messrs. Caleb Smith and
Jacob Green, and revised by them, was engraved on the marble
monument.

Governor Belcher having died on the 31st of August, 1757, Samuel Woodruff and Robert Ogden, Esquires, were requested by the Trustees "to see that all the Books, with the other Things given by his Excellency for the use of the College, be conveyed to this Place."

THE ELECTION OF THE REV. JONATHAN EDWARDS.

On the day following, viz., Thursday, the 29th of September, 1757, the Trustees took into consideration the propriety of appointing at once a successor to President Burr. The minute in regard to it is in these words:

" A choice of a President being proposed to the Board, it was ordered to be put to Vote whether the said President be now chosen or not; which being Voted accordingly, was carried in the affirmative.

" Whereupon after Prayers particularly on this occasion, and the number of Trustees present being twenty, the Rev. Mr. Jonathan Edwards, of Stockbridge, was chosen by a majority of seventeen; and this Board requests that Messrs. Livingston and Spencer, of their Number, would draw the draught of a Letter requesting that the said Mr. Edwards would accept of the said choice; and also of an Address to the Honorable the Commissioners for propagating the Gospel among the Heathen in America, in the province of Massachusetts, requesting the said Commissioners to liberate the said Mr. Edwards from his pastoral charge of the Indian Congregation at Stockbridge and the Mission given him by the said Commissioners; and that the said Letter and Address be signed in behalf of this Board by the Clerk of the same."

Previously to engaging in this election, the Trustees voted, " That the salary of the President should be two hundred pounds proclamation money of the Province, together with the use of the President's house and the Improved lands, with Liberty of getting his Fire-wood on the land belonging to the Corporation."

It was also voted that twenty pounds should be paid to the Rev. Mr. Edwards for the expenses of moving his family to Princeton. The committee appointed to prepare a draft of a letter to Mr. Edwards, and of an address to the Commissioners above mentioned, brought in the said drafts; which, being read, were approved, and the Clerk was ordered to transcribe the same and to send them as soon as may be to the persons for whom they were designed.

In reference to the grammar-school connected with the College, the following minute was made by order of the Board :

"Mr. President Burr in his life-time having set up and carried on a Grammar School in this College, which by his death will now fail unless proper care be taken for its support, the Trustees therefore, in Consideration of its importance in general and in particular to this Society, do agree to take the said School under their immediate Direction and Government, and do appoint Mr. Montgomerie to be the Master of the said School, and that Mr. McWhorter* serve as an Usher under him for the ensuing year; and if the School continues to consist of Twenty Scholars or upwards, said Master shall be allowed forty-five Pounds, and the Usher fifteen Pounds, provided he gives his attendance in the School three hours in the Day : but in case the School decrease to sixteen or under, then the Master shall have the Charge of said School, and be entitled to three Quarters of the Tuition Money. The Tuition Money for each student to be four Pounds per annum."

At this meeting provision was also made for the temporary oversight and inspection of the College, by the appointment of the Rev. William Tennent President *pro tem.*, and authority was given to the Clerk to call an extra meeting of the Board at any time within three months. And in case Mr. Edwards should not attend and accept the office of President of the College at the end of the vacation, the Clerk was instructed to request Mr. Isaac Smith, a graduate of the College in 1755, " to act in the Place of a Tutor until the President can attend."

During the last year of his Presidency Mr. Burr was assisted by two excellent Tutors, viz., Benjamin Youngs Prime, a graduate of the College in 1751, and John Ewing, a graduate in 1754. Mr. Prime having tendered his resignation, the Board adopted the following resolution, viz. :

"Mr. Prime, one of the Tutors, applying to this Board for a Dismission from his office, It is ordered, that at the request of the said Mr. Prime he be dismissed accordingly. Nevertheless, the Trustees being fully sensible of the abilities of the said Mr. Prime, and of his having faithfully executed his said Office during the Time of his continuance therein, do with great Reluctance part with the said Mr. Prime; and as a Testimony of their sense of his good Conduct and Merit, do present him with the sum of Ten Pounds over and above his salary, and are Sorry that the smallness of their Fund will not admit of their giving him a larger sum."

At this time the usual salary of a Tutor in this College was

---

* The Mr. McWhorter mentioned in this minute is the Rev. Dr. Alexander McWhorter, pastor of the First Presbyterian Church of Newark, who had just been admitted to his first degree in the Arts.

forty pounds a year, but at this meeting of the Board it was increased to fifty pounds a year; and in the case of Mr. Ewing it was also voted, " That this Board, in consideration of the extraordinary services which are justly expected of Mr. Ewing, a Tutor for the ensuing year, will allow the said Mr. Ewing the sum of fifty pounds over and above the aforesaid salary." The Mr. Ewing here mentioned is the well-known scholar and divine, the Rev. Dr. John Ewing, for many years the distinguished Provost of the University of Pennsylvania.

At their present session the Trustees also enacted several additional rules with respect to the conduct of the students in the College edifice, which rules had been prepared by a committee appointed at the last meeting of the Board, and of which committee Mr. Burr was the first named.

" The eleventh of these rules was as follows : ' Every student shall pay four shillings per Quarter for Study-rent, sweeping their Rooms, and making their Beds ; and such as smoke or chew Tobacco, five shillings, and one shilling for incidental charges.' "

The Rev. Caleb Smith having tendered his resignation as Clerk of the Board, in consequence of his residence being now at a distance from the College, by its removal to Princeton, Richard Stockton, Esq., a member of the Board, was unanimously chosen Clerk in the room of Mr. Smith, and generously undertook to discharge the duties of his office as Clerk without compensation.

The next meeting of the Trustees took place on the 14th of December, 1757, thirteen members being present, and the Hon. Thomas Leonard, Esq., in the chair.

The Trustees, taking into consideration a letter from Mr. Edwards in relation to his dismission from his pastoral charge at Stockbridge, voted,

" That it is highly proper that one of their members do endeavor, if possible, to attend the Ecclesiastical Council who are to convene for that purpose, and there represent in behalf of this Board the Reasons for the propriety of such Dismission."

Continuing their session through the following day, the Trustees, on the morning of the 15th, voted,

" That if the Rev. Mr. Edwards come and take upon him the Charge of the College this Winter, that he be entitled to the President's salary for the whole of this year; and that he have the liberty of receiving one-half of his salary at the end of six months from the last Commencement."

At their meeting, April 19, the Trustees ordered the Treasurer to pay to the executors of Mr. Edwards one hundred pounds, a half-year's salary.

The next record is as follows:

"The Rev. Messrs. Caleb Smith and John Brainerd are requested immediately to proceed to Stockbridge, if possible, to attend the Ecclesiastical Council to convene relative to Mr. Edwards's Dismission; and that the sum of £20 be paid them for their services."

It appears from the minutes of this meeting that the Rev. William Tennent, "for his services in inspecting the government of the College," was paid eleven pounds, and that the Rev. David Cowell, of Trenton, was chosen President until the next meeting of the Trustees, and that, accepting the appointment, he was qualified as the charter directs.

"It was voted, That the President of the College and the Clerk for the time being (viz., Rev. David Cowell and Richard Stockton, Esq.) be a Committee to transact the affairs about Mr. Edwards's Removal," with power to add to their number.

Messrs. Caleb Smith and John Brainerd attended the Ecclesiastical Council at Stockbridge, and secured the release of Mr. Edwards from his pastoral charge, and in the latter part of January he repaired to Princeton. The Council, as appears from a letter of Mr. Edwards, of the date of December 1, 1757, to his friend and former pupil, Mr. Bellamy, of Bethlehem, was called for the 21st of the same month, but for some reason not now known it did not assemble until the 4th of January following. The decision of the Council having been announced to Mr. Edwards and to the church of which he was pastor, he submitted to their judgment, and made his arrangements to go without delay to Princeton, leaving his family in Stockbridge, to remain there until the ensuing spring.

Upon his arrival at Princeton, measures were promptly taken to call a meeting of the Trustees of the College. They met accordingly on Thursday, the 16th day of February, 1758, and among the minutes of that meeting is the following:

"The Rev. Mr. Jonathan Edwards, at the repeated Requests and Invitations of this Board, and agreeably to a vote passed at a meeting of the Trustees in September last, attending, and having been pleased to accept the office of President of the College, so unanimously voted him, was qualified as the charter directs; and the said President Edwards was at the same time qualified as a Trustee of the College, and took his seat accordingly."

Several matters relating to the order and government of the College and of the grammar-school were considered by the Board at this meeting, and it was voted,

"That President Edwards have the direction, care, and government of the Grammar School, with its Masters and Ushers, and have authority to introduce the elements of Geography, History, and Chronology, if he judge proper; and that he have the profits of said school."

Mr. Robert Smith, the architect employed by the Trustees in the erection of the College buildings, was desired to make some improvements in the President's house. At this meeting it was

"Voted, That the Law obliging the students to wear peculiar Habits be repealed."

The law here referred to was enacted at a meeting of the Trustees held September 24, 1755.

Provision was made for an address to the new Governor in the name of the Trustees, should one be appointed and come into the Province before the next meeting of the Board. The performance of this duty was devolved upon the President of the College and the Clerk of the Board. A committee was appointed to settle with the Treasurer, and to report to the Board the amount of funds in his hands. The Treasurer was directed to pay the Rev. Mr. David Cowell, for his inspection of the College from the 14th of December to the time of President Edwards's arrival in Princeton, the sum of eleven pounds.

At the request of the senior Tutor, Mr. Ewing, that a provisional arrangement should be made for supplying his place in case he should decide to leave, it was voted that President Edwards have power, in that case, to employ any gentleman he thought proper upon Trial for the office of Tutor, until the next meeting.

. The Treasurer was directed to pay the bill for printing Mr. Burr's sermon at the funeral of Governor Belcher, and the Rev. Caleb Smith was requested to take charge of the sale of the copies, and to account to the Treasurer for the money arising from said sale.

Provision was made for the "drawing of a Lottery for the College, to raise a sum not exceeding £600, the price of a ticket to be two dollars."

It was also voted that there should be a meeting of the Trustees at every Commencement.

The above is a summary of the business done at the only meeting of the Trustees ever attended by Mr. Edwards, and that was a special meeting called more particularly for the purpose of inducting him into the office of President.

One week after this meeting, viz., on the 23d of February, he was inoculated for the smallpox, and on the 22d of March he died. His active service, therefore, in behalf of the College must all have taken place within four or five weeks, and yet the power of his name for good is felt by the College to this day. Probably no man ever connected with this institution has contributed so much to the reputation of the College, both at home and abroad. In the narrative of his life, published in connection with his works, it is said, "While at Princeton, before his sickness, he preached in the College hall, but did nothing as President, unless it was to give out some questions in divinity to the Senior class, to be answered before him, each one having opportunity to study and write what he thought proper upon them. When they came together to answer them, they found so much entertainment and profit by it, especially by the light and instruction Mr. Edwards communicated, in what he said upon the questions when they delivered what they had to say, that they spoke of it with the greatest satisfaction and wonder." (See Dr. S. E. Dwight's "Life of Edwards," page 577, copied from Dr. Hopkins's.)

The first sermon he preached in Princeton was on the unchangeableness of Christ, and it is to be found in the eighth volume of his works. From this we may infer what would have been the character of his religious teachings in the College had he been spared to preside for a length of time over its discipline and instruction.

During the time of his being at Princeton he was assisted

by two excellent Tutors, one already mentioned as a Tutor under President Burr, Mr. John Ewing, and the other Mr. Jeremiah Halsey, who, to the great benefit of the institution and to the equally great satisfaction of the Trustees, held his office for ten years. The respective duties of these two gentlemen will appear from the following minute adopted at the meeting of February 16:

"The Board further judge most advisable, in the present circumstances, and do accordingly vote, that Mr. Ewen [Ewing] take the Junior and the Sophomore classes under his particular tuition, and that Mr. Halsey apply himself to the instruction of the Senior and Freshman classes."

Of the College curriculum at this date we have no particular information, there being no Faculty records in existence, and the minutes of the Trustees containing no details of the duties discharged by the several officers of the College.

From Mr. Edwards's letter of the date of October 19, 1757, in reply to the one informing him of his election to the office of President, we may gather some idea of the course of study and of instruction:

Among the reasons which made him doubt the propriety of his accepting the appointment he mentions his deficiency " in some parts of learning, particularly in Algebra and the higher parts of Mathematics, and in the Greek classics; my Greek learning having been chiefly in the New Testament." Again he remarks, " If I should see light to determine me to accept the place offered me, I should be willing to take upon me the work of a president, so far as it consists in the general inspection of the whole society; and to be subservient to the school, as to their order and methods of study and instruction, assisting myself in the immediate instruction *in the Arts and Sciences* (as discretion should direct, and occasion serve, and the state of things require), especially of the Senior class; and, added to all, should be willing to do the whole work of a professor of divinity, in public and private lectures, proposing questions to be answered, and some to be discussed in writing and free conversation, in meetings of graduates and others, appointed in proper seasons, for these ends. It would now be out of my way to spend time in constant teaching of the languages, unless it be the Hebrew tongue, which I should be willing to improve myself in by instructing others."

In these extracts we doubtless have sketched an outline of what would have been the course of instruction during his administration had his life been spared. The plan embraces instruction in the Latin, Greek, and Hebrew languages, in the arts and sciences, and in the teachings of Holy Scripture. Most

of these studies, if not all, together with composition and
declamation, had been matters of attention under the administration of Mr. Burr. It is highly probable that Mr. Ewing, the
senior Tutor, instructed the classes assigned to him in Mathematics and Natural Philosophy, and Mr. Halsey his classes in
the Greek and Latin classics. After Mr. Ewing's decease, a
course of lectures on Natural Philosophy, delivered by him in
the University of Pennsylvania, were published at Philadelphia;
and it is by no means improbable that the substance of these
lectures was prepared for the instruction of his pupils at
Nassau Hall.

Mr. Isaac Smith, a graduate of the College in 1755, was
associated with Messrs. Ewing and Halsey, as a Tutor, for a
few months before Mr. Edwards's induction into office as President. Mr. Smith was subsequently a Judge of the Supreme
Court of New Jersey, and also a member of the National Congress.

From the foregoing narrative it appears that the following-
named gentlemen had charge of the instruction and government
of the students from the time of Mr. Edwards's election, September 29, 1757, until his decease, on the 22d of March, 1758:

Rev. William Tennent, from the opening of the session until
December 14, 1757.

Rev. David Cowell, from December 14, 1757, until Mr. Edwards's arrival in Princeton, in the latter part of January, 1758.

President Edwards himself, from the time of his reaching
Princeton until his decease, March 22, 1758.

The Tutors were Messrs. John Ewing, Jeremiah Halsey, and
Isaac Smith.

CHAPTER VIII.

MEMOIR OF THE REV. JONATHAN EDWARDS, THIRD PRESIDENT
OF THE COLLEGE.

THIS eminent man, the only son of the Rev. Timothy Edwards, of Windsor, Connecticut, was born at Windsor on the 5th of October, 1703. The mother of President Edwards was Esther Stoddard, a daughter of the Rev. Solomon Stoddard, of Northampton, Massachusetts. The father and maternal grandfather were both held in repute for talent, piety, and learning. Their families, which were unusually large, are connected by intermarriage with many of the prominent families in New England, and in other parts of our country.

The studies requisite for admission to college the subject of this memoir pursued under the direction of his father, and he was admitted to Yale College when but a youth of thirteen years of age. His proficiency even in childhood was such as to give hope of his becoming what he did become, a careful observer and a profound thinker. While yet a youth he evinced a great fondness for philosophical speculations. At the age of fourteen he read with delight and profit Locke's " Essay on the Human Understanding," and his college course was marked with sobriety of deportment and with improvement in the different branches of learning. He is said to have maintained the highest standing in his class, and to have been graduated with the highest honors.

The mention made by one of his biographers of "his thorough knowledge of the Latin, Greek, and Hebrew" does not accord fully with his own account of his proficiency in these languages, given in his letter of October 19, 1757, to the Trustees of the College, in which he says, "I am also deficient in some parts of learning, particularly . . . , and in the Greek classics; my Greek learning having been chiefly in the New

178

Testament." And again he says, "It would now be out of my way to spend time in constant teaching of the languages, unless it be the Hebrew tongue, which I should be willing to improve myself in by instructing others."

Although having a keen relish for all matters pertaining to natural philosophy, which he is said to have cultivated to the end of his life, yet moral philosophy and divinity were his favorite subjects of study.

He was admitted to the first degree in the Arts in the autumn of 1720, just before attaining the age of seventeen; and entering at once upon the study of theology, he remained at College for nearly two years after he had finished the usual under-graduate course. He was licensed to preach before he had completed his nineteenth year, and at the request of a small society of Presbyterians in the city of New York, he began his ministerial labors among them. He supplied their pulpit for about eight months; but finding that the congregation, which was a fragment of one still older, were unable to support a minister, he gave up his charge and returned to New England.

He was solicited to resume his labors in New York, but declined, influenced in all probability by the conviction that there was no sufficient reason for the attempt to erect another Presbyterian church in that city at that time, and that if he refused to return, the persons to whom he preached would resume their former relations with the church already established, and under the charge of an able and worthy minister of the gospel, the Rev. James Anderson, a native of Scotland.

In September, 1723, he received his degree of Master of Arts, and at the same time he was chosen a Tutor in Yale College. Upon the duties of this office, however, he did not enter until the next June. About this period several congregations were desirous to have him for their pastor; but all these invitations he declined. In the summer of 1726, the people of Northampton, Massachusetts, invited him to become the colleague of his venerable grandfather, the Rev. Solomon Stoddard, and among the reasons urged for his acceptance of this call was the one that his grandfather, by reason of his great age, stood in need of assistance. Accepting their proposal, he resigned his office of Tutor at the close of the college year, and on February 15, 1728, he was set apart to the pastoral office in the church of Northampton, being at that time in the twenty-fourth year of his age. His grandfather dying in February, 1729, Mr. Edwards became the sole pastor. He continued at Northampton about twenty-four years. From the time of his settlement until the year 1744, Mr. Edwards's ministrations were highly acceptable to his people and greatly blessed to their spiritual good. In the years 1734 and 1735 there was a powerful awakening among the people of his charge. " His preaching," says the Rev. Dr. Sprague, " during this period was eminently doctrinal, and was of the most pungent, heart-searching, and often terrific character. Among the subjects of the revival were persons of every class and character, and for a while the whole community seemed to have undergone a moral renovation. Towards the close of 1735 the work began to decline, after which there seems to have been no unusual attention until the early part of 1740, when there occurred another powerful revival." His pungent preaching, though doubtless distasteful to some of his hearers, was nevertheless acceptable to the people generally, and they felt honored in having for their minister a man of Mr. Edwards's rare ability in the pulpit, and one who was held in such high repute both at home and abroad. But in 1744 an event occurred which entirely ruptured the happy relations previously existing between the minister and the people, and which six years after resulted in their separation.

Being informed that certain young persons, members of the church, had in their possession books of an immoral and corrupting tendency, which they made use of to promote improper conversation and conduct, Mr. Edwards preached a sermon to indicate the duty of the church in reference to matters of this kind; and

" After the sermon he desired the brethren of the church to stop, told them what information he had received, and put the question to them in form, Whether the Church, on the evidence before them, thought proper to take any measures to examine into the matter? The members of the Church with one consent and with much zeal manifested it to be their opinion that it ought to be inquired into; and proceeded to choose a Committee of Inquiry to assist their pastor in examining into the affair. After this Mr. Edwards appointed the time for the Committee of the

Church to meet at his house; and then read to the Church a catalogue of the names of the young persons whom he desired to come to his house at the the same time. Some of those whose names were thus read were the persons accused, and some were witnesses; but, through mere forgetfulness or inadvertence on his part, he did not state to the church in which of these two classes any particular individual was included, or in what character he was requested to meet the Committee, whether as one of the accused or as a witness."

The above extract is taken from the 299th page of Dr. S. E. Dwight's " Life of President Edwards," and was probably taken by him from Dr. Hopkins's " Life of Edwards," which was the basis of his own account of President Edwards's life and labors. Only in this way can we reconcile what is said in this extract with what his biographer says on pages 432 and 433 :

" The manner in which Mr. Edwards invited the young people to meet the Committee, without distinguishing the witnesses from the accused, whether a matter of inadvertence on his part or not, was the very manner in which most other persons would have given the invitation; *and,* so far as I can see, was the only manner which propriety could have justified."

We incline, however, to the opinion that the biographer's ideas of justice must have been somewhat confused when he observes, as the ground of his own judgment in the matter,

" As therefore both the accused and the witnesses must be present before the Committee, justice as well as kindness demanded that they should be named without discrimination."

This may have been kindness to the accused, but surely it was neither kindness nor justice to those who were merely to give testimony in the case, and who were in no way implicated in the charges to be investigated. The best excuse that can be made for the course pursued is the one suggested in the first of the above extracts, that it was the result of forgetfulness or inadvertence. And no one at this day need be surprised at the excitement produced throughout the entire community at Northampton by the manner in which this whole business was conducted. For while, on the one hand, it furnishes a noted instance of Mr. Edwards's faithfulness and fearlessness in the discharge of duty, with the full conviction that it would be to him the occasion of many and bitter trials, and of his ability to rise above all personal considerations in all matters wherein the purity and welfare of the Church of Christ were concerned, yet, on the other hand, it as clearly shows a lack of practical wisdom in dealing with the errors and prejudices of those over whose spiritual interests he was called to watch. The alleged facts were *not* a matter of notoriety; they were evidently unknown to the community at large; and the first thing that brought them to the knowledge of the people generally was his discourse on this subject. Had he instituted a private investigation, and, having satisfied himself as to the guilty parties, dealt with them individually and tenderly, showing them their sin and their danger, there is reason to believe that his labors would not have been without a happy result. In cases in which the parties were insensible to his urgent and affectionate appeals, had he called to his aid the counsels and entreaties, and even the authority, of the parents of the erring youth, he might have reclaimed some of them; and not until all other methods had failed should he have resorted to this announcement of their offence, and to the exercise of discipline by the entire church. Again, notices might have been sent privately to each individual whose presence was desired by the pastor or the committee, without any public mention of names. If this view of the case be a correct one, it is easy to see why the whole community became so much excited, and that the people are not entitled to all the blame in regard to this unhappy affair, which had so much to do in the alienating of their affections from their minister.

The unwillingness of the people to proceed with the proposed investigation, upon the discovery made by them that large numbers of their children were more or less implicated in the alleged offence, not only aroused their feelings against their minister, but as naturally led the minister to ascribe their conduct to a want of a proper zeal for the honor of Christ and the purity of the Church. Hence doubts, which had already existed in his mind as to the propriety of receiving to the communion of the church any persons who did not give satisfactory evidence of being truly converted, ripened into a full conviction that none but regenerate persons ought to partake of the Lord's Supper. For many years, under the advice and teachings of his grandfather, a different course had been pursued, and all baptized persons, who were fully and correctly instructed as to the plan of salvation revealed in the Holy Scriptures, and who professed to receive it as such, and who were free from all scandal, were taught that it was their duty and privilege to come to the Lord's table, notwithstanding any doubts they might have in regard to themselves as regenerate persons, and even if they had reason to believe they were not regenerated. This view of the case had been discussed and defended by Mr. Stoddard, and was zealously maintained by the churches in Hampshire County. Mr. Edwards, having satisfied his own mind that this method was contrary to the teachings of Scripture, resolutely set himself to work to bring about a change in the practice of the church of which he was pastor. His effort in this direction was not successful, and he was finally dismissed from his charge by a council of ministers and delegates from the neighboring churches called by himself and the church at Northampton.

The opinion embraced by Mr. Edwards on this subject did not originate with him, but was held quite generally by the churches of New England at its first settlement; but no advocate of this opinion has exerted so much influence as President Edwards in the maintenance and propagation of it, both in Congregational and Presbyterian churches. This is not the time, nor is it the place, to discuss the correctness or the error of an opinion which had so important a bearing upon some of the leading events in the life of President Edwards, but it cannot be improper, in this connection, to say that his views on this subject were not the views held by his predecessors, Presidents Dickinson and Burr, nor are they in accord with the teachings of the "Directory for Worship" set forth by the Presbyterian Church in this country.* The Rev. John Blair, Vice-President of the College, and its first Professor of Moral Philosophy and Divinity, from 1767 to 1769, published, in 1771, "An Essay on the Nature, Uses, and Subjects of the Sacra-

---

* See "Directory for Worship," and "Christian Advocate," vol. x., edited by President Green, or Dr. Sprague's "Annals," vol. iii., article *Rev. Jacob Green.*

ments of the New Testament," in which he maintains and de-
fends views opposite to those of President Edwards.   Mr. Blair's
discussion of the matters handled by him is very calm and very
able, and well worthy of a perusal by those who are seeking
light in regard to these matters.   A careful comparison of the
views of President Edwards and of Vice-President Blair may
serve to elicit the exact truth more fully and clearly.

After the dissolution of his pastoral charge Mr. Edwards
remained for about a year at Northampton, but upon an invitation to take charge of the church at Stockbridge, Massachusetts,
and also of the Indian mission there established, he removed to
that village, and devoted himself assiduously to his studies and
his ministerial and missionary labors.   Here he rendered most
valuable services to the Indian mission, and also to the cause
of learning.   He was not free altogether from trials in this
chosen retreat; but the same firmness and fidelity which had
always characterized him were manifested by him in his efforts
in behalf of the Indians, and a greater degree than usual of
prudence marked his course towards those with whom he was
brought into collision; and, the Lord favoring his faithful efforts,
he was successful in defending the interests of the Indians
against the machinations of sundry individuals, whose aim
seemed to be their own aggrandizement at the expense of the
youths sent to the mission-schools to be educated.

At Stockbridge Mr. Edwards wrote his famous work on the
" Will," which added so much to his already great reputation,
and gave him rank among the first philosophers of his age.
He resided at Stockbridge for six years, at the end of which
time, upon the death of his son-in-law, the Rev. Aaron Burr,
President of the College of New Jersey, he was chosen his successor; and, as narrated in the account given of his short administration, he with much hesitation and misgiving accepted
this appointment, so honorable to himself and to the institution
over which he was called to preside.

His letter of October 19, 1757, in reply to the one from the
Trustees of the College apprising him of his election, shows
that his modesty was equal to his great intellectual endowments; and this letter, from which some extracts have been

given, is in every respect worthy of its author. His aim seems to be to prepare the minds of the Trustees for a refusal of their offer, although he highly appreciated the honor they had done him in choosing him to be the head of their important institution. In this letter he sets forth his reasons for thinking that he is not the person for such a station. Still, he deemed it his duty to submit the question of his acceptance to a council of his clerical brethren; and this he did, with a pretty clear intimation, however, of his doubts, if not of his preferences. Having received their judgment, which was in favor of his going to Princeton, he yielded, and reluctantly gave up his church and missionary work at Stockbridge to devote himself to the training of youth for the service of the Church in the gospel ministry, and for the welfare of the State in the different professions and employments.

As before mentioned, he reached Princeton in the latter part of January, and took the oath of office on the 16th of February, 1758. On the 23d of the same month, by the advice of physician and friends, he was inoculated for the smallpox, in consequence of the general prevalence of this disease. A young but skilful physician from Philadelphia, Dr. William Shippen, came to Princeton to inoculate him and his daughter, Mrs. Burr, and her two children; and after a most serious and deliberate consultation with certain friends they were all inoculated,* and for a time they all apparently were doing well; but, according to the statement of Dr. Shippen in his letter to Mrs. Edwards informing her of the death of President Edwards, it appears that

"Although he had the smallpox favorably, yet having a number of them in the roof of his mouth and throat, he could not possibly swallow a sufficient quantity of drink to keep off a secondary fever, which has proved too strong for his feeble frame; and this afternoon [March 22], between two and three o'clock, it pleased God to let him sleep in that dear Lord Jesus whose kingdom and interest he has been faithfully and painfully serving all his life." Dr. Shippen adds, "And never did any mortal man more fully and clearly evidence the sincerity of all his professions, by one continued, universal, calm, cheerful resignation, and patient submission to the divine will, through every stage of his disease, than he: not

---

* It is said that he was inoculated with the consent of the Trustees, but upon what authority I know not. The minutes of the Board make no reference to it.

so much as one discontented expression, nor the least appearance of murmuring through the whole. And never did any person expire with more perfect freedom from pain,—not so much as distorted hair,—but, in the most proper sense of the words, he fell asleep. Death had certainly lost his sting as to him."*

After he was sensible that he could not survive that sickness, a little before his death he called his daughter† to him, who attended in his sickness, and addressed her in a few words, which were immediately taken down in writing as nearly as could be recollected, and are as follows:

"Dear Lucy, it seems to me to be the will of God that I must shortly leave you; therefore give my kindest love to my dear wife, and tell her that the uncommon union, which has so long subsisted between us, has been of such a nature as I trust is spiritual, and will therefore continue forever; and I hope she will be supported under so great a trial, and submit cheerfully to the will of God. And as to my children, you are now like to be left fatherless; which I hope will be an induce- ment for you all to seek a Father who will never fail you. And as to my funeral, I would have it to be like Mr. Burr's;‡ and any additional sum of money that might be expected to be laid out that way, I would have it disposed of to charitable uses."

"He said very little in his sickness, but was an admirable in- stance of patience and resignation to the last. Just at the close of life, as some persons, who stood by expecting he would breathe his last in a few minutes, were lamenting his death, not only as a great frown upon the College, but as having a dark aspect upon the interest of religion in general, to their surprise, not imagining he heard or that he would ever speak another word, he said, 'Trust in God, and ye need not fear.' These were his last words." (Dwight's "Life.")

The Trustees caused a marble monument to be erected in honor of President Edwards. On this monument was the fol- lowing inscription:

M. S.
Reverendi admodum Viri,
Jonathan Edwards, A.M.,
Collegii Novæ Cæsariæ Præsidis,
Natus apud Windsor Connecticutensium V Octobris,
A.D. MDCCIII. S. V.

---

* See Dwight's "Life," page 870.
† His eldest unmarried daughter.
‡ See notice of Mr. Burr's funeral, page 166.

Patre Reverendo Timotheo Edwards oriundus,
Collegio Yalensi educatus;
Apud Northampton Sacris initiatus, XV Februarii
MDCCXXVI–VII.
Illinc dimissus XXII Junii MDCCL.,
Et Munus Barbaros instituendi accepit.
Præses Aulæ Nassovicæ creatus XVI Februarii
MDCCLVIII.
Defunctus in hoc Vico XXII Martii sequentis, S. N.
Aetatis LV, heu nimis brevis!
Hic jacet mortalis Pars.
Qualis Persona quæris, Viator?
Vir corpore procero, sed gracili,
Studiis intentissimis, Abstinentia, et Sedulitate,
Attenuato,
Ingenii Acumine, Judicio acri, et Prudentia,
Secundus Nemini Mortalium.
Artium liberalium et Scientiarum Peritia insignis,
Criticorum sacrorum optimus, Theologus eximius,
Ut vix alter æqualis: Disputator candidus;
Fidei Christianæ Propugnator validus et invictus;
Concionator gravis, serius, discriminans;
Et, Deo favente, Successu
Felicissimus.
Pietate præclarus, Moribus suis severus,
Ast aliis æquus et benignus,
Vixit dilectus, veneratus—
Sed ah! lugendus
Moriebatur,
Quantos Gemitus discedens ciebat!
Heu Sapientia tanta! heu Doctrina et Religio!
Amissum plorat Collegium, plorat Ecclesia;
At, eo recepto, gaudet
Cœlum.
Abi Viator, et pia sequere Vestigia.

Mrs. Edwards did not long survive her husband. In September she set out, in her usual health, for Philadelphia, to bring to Stockbridge the two orphan children of her daughter, Mrs. Burr. Upon the death of Mrs. Burr, which occurred a few weeks after her father's death, these children, a daughter and a son, had been taken care of by some friends, and they were in Philadelphia at the time of Mrs. Edwards's visit to that city. She arrived there on the 21st of September, and within a few days she was seized with a dysentery, from which she died on the 2d of October, 1758, in the forty-ninth year of her age, after an illness of five days. She suffered intensely, but died in perfect peace. Her remains were taken to Princeton, and were buried by those of her husband.

Mrs. Edwards was a remarkable woman, distinguished for her personal charms, her great intelligence, and her early and fervent piety, and also for her wise and economical management of her family affairs, setting her children an example worthy of their admiration and imitation, in her diligent attention to the affairs of her household, and in her unceasing efforts to train her children in the nurture and admonition of the Lord.

Mrs. Edwards was a daughter of the Rev. John Pierpont, of New Haven, and she was married to Mr. Edwards on the 28th of July, 1727. She was the mother of eleven children, three sons and eight daughters. Two of her daughters died young and unmarried; the other children all grew up and were married, and their descendants are very numerous, and some of them are among the most eminent in their respective callings.

The following is a list of the published works of President Edwards, taken from Dr. Sprague's sketch of his life.

1731. A sermon, "God glorified in Man's Dependence."

1734. A sermon, "A Divine and Supernatural Light imparted to the Soul by the Spirit of God."

1735. A sermon, "Curse ye Meroz."

1736. "A Faithful Narrative of the Surprising Work of God, in the Conversion of many Hundred Souls in Northampton," etc. (London.)

1738. Five Discourses, prefixed to the American edition of the preceding.

1741. A sermon, "Sinners in the Hands of an Angry God."

1741. A sermon, "Sorrows of the Bereaved spread before Jesus," at the funeral of the Rev. William Williams.

1741. A sermon, "Distinguishing Marks of a Work of the True Spirit," preached at New Haven.

1742. "Thoughts on the Revival in New England in 1740."

1743. A sermon, "The Watchman's Duty and Account," at the ordination of the Rev. Jonathan Judd, of Southampton, Massachusetts.

1744. A sermon, "The True Excellency of a Gospel Minister," preached at the ordination of the Rev. Robert Abercrombie, of Pelham, Massachusetts.

1746. A treatise concerning Religious Affections. (Printed at Boston.)

1746. "An Humble Attempt to promote Explicit, Agreeable, and Visible Union among God's People in Extraordinary Prayer."

1747. A sermon, "True Saints, when Absent from the Body, Present with the Lord," preached at the funeral of the Rev. David Brainerd.

1748. A sermon, "God's Awful Judgments in breaking the Strong Rods of the Community," occasioned by the death of Colonel John Stoddard.

1749. "Life and Diary of the Rev. David Brainerd."

1749. A sermon, "Christ the Example of Gospel Ministers," preached at the ordination of the Rev. Job Strong.

1749. "Qualifications for Full Communion in the Visible Church."

1750. "Farewell Sermon to the People of Northampton."

1752. "Misrepresentation Corrected and Truth Vindicated, in a Reply to Mr. Solomon Williams' Book on 'Qualifications for Communion;' to which is added a Letter from Mr. Edwards to His Late Flock at Northampton."

1752. A sermon, "True Grace distinguished from the Experience of Devils," preached before the Synod of New York, at Newark, New Jersey.

1754. "Inquiry into Freedom of the Will."

1758. "The Doctrine of Original Sin defended."

1765. Eighteen Sermons annexed to the "Life of Edwards" by Dr. Hopkins.

1777. "The History of Redemption." (Edinburgh.)

1788. "Nature of True Virtue."

1788. "God's Last End in Creation."

1788. Practical Sermons. (Edinburgh.)

1789. Twenty Sermons. (Edinburgh.)

1793. "Miscellaneous Observations on Important Theological Subjects." (Edinburgh.)

1796. "Remarks on Important Theological Controversies." (Edinburgh.)

1829. "Types of the Messiah."

1829. "Notes on the Bible."

1852. "Charity and its Fruits."

The most complete collection of his published works and correspondence is the one edited by his great-grandson, Rev. Dr. Sereno E. Dwight, in ten volumes, inclusive of the one containing his life. These volumes furnish evidence of his untiring industry and of his rarely equalled power of thought. The correctness of his opinions on various subjects may be questioned, but there can be no question as to the ability with which they are maintained and defended. And no theological writer of the last century exerted a more powerful influence in moulding the opinions of those who hold sentiments commonly designated evangelical. Such a master-spirit as Dr. Chalmers expresses in the following words his own appreciation of Edwards as a theologian:

"I have long esteemed him as the greatest of theologians, combining in a degree that is quite unexampled the profoundly intellectual with the devotedly spiritual and sacred, and realizing in his own person a most rare yet most beautiful harmony between the simplicity of the Christian pastor on the one hand, and on the other all the strength and prowess of a giant in philosophy; so as at once to minister, from Sabbath to Sabbath, and with the most blessed effect, to the hearers of his plain congregation, and yet in the high field of authorship to have traversed, in a way that none had ever done before him, the most inaccessible places, and such a mastery as never till his time had been realized over the most arduous difficulties of our science.

"There is no European divine to whom I make such frequent appeals in my class-rooms as I do to Edwards. No book of human composition which I more strenuously recommend than his ' Treatise on the Will,'—read by me forty-seven years ago, with a conviction which has never since faltered, and which has helped me, more than any other uninspired book, to find my way through all that might otherwise have proved baffling and transcendental and mysterious in the peculiarities of Calvinism." (Extract from a letter to the Rev. Dr. Stebbins, of Northampton, given in Dr. Sprague's Sketch of President Edwards, and the sentiments of which Dr. Sprague says Dr. Chalmers expressed to him in a private conversation.)

It does not, however, follow from all this that no false positions are assumed in the writings of President Edwards, or that he never gives utterance to forms of thought which if carried to their logical conclusion would lead to serious error. Nor does it follow that his exhibition of the religious affections and mental exercises connected with true conversion is in all cases to be taken, without any doubt or question, as being the actual and invariable experience of all persons truly regenerate.*

---

* President Edwards was a man of eminent piety, as well as a man well versed in the teachings of Scripture and the experiences of godly minds; still, there seems to be in some of his writings too much insisting upon a settled order and a certain degree of inward experiences as essential to true conversion, more likely in some cases to hinder than to aid the inquirer in coming to a right decision in regard to himself.

Doddridge's famous work on the " Rise and Progress of Religion in the Soul" is a work of this description, and while in many cases it has done great good, there are others in which to a tender conscience it has proved a real hindrance to its spiritual advancement and growth in grace. The type of piety produced under this procrustean treatment, while sometimes both genuine and beautiful, and by consequence lovely, and ever bowing with unfeigned submission to the sovereign will of God, often lacks that cheerfulness of spirit, and that exuberant joyfulness, which it should be the aim of every redeemed soul to have and to keep as pertaining to the privileges purchased and made over to it by its beloved Saviour, the incarnate Son of God. Such a work as Edwards's on the " Religious Affections" was perhaps better adapted to the state of things in his day than it is in ours; and yet this great work may be read and studied with the greatest profit by all who are desirous to distinguish true religious affections from those which are false, if they will bear in mind that while persons truly converted may be conscious of possessing *all* the views and feelings therein described, yet that such consciousness is not essential to vital piety. While they find in themselves those great distinguishing marks of true conversion, love to God, and love to man, with a humble trust in the righteousness and intercession of their Lord and Saviour Jesus Christ as the ground of their hope, and of their acceptance with God, they need not be concerned at the discovery that they possess not some of those experiences which are insisted upon by writers on Experimental Religion.

CHAPTER IX.

THE INTERVAL BETWEEN THE DECEASE OF PRESIDENT EDWARDS AND THE INAUGURATION OF THE REV. SAMUEL DAVIES AS PRESIDENT OF THE COLLEGE.

MR. EDWARDS died on the 22d of March, and the next meeting of the Board took place on Wednesday, the 19th of April, 1758, the instruction of the classes in this interval being conducted by the Tutors, Messrs. Ewing and Halsey.

Exclusive of the Governor of the State and the President of the College, the Board of Trustees consisted of twenty-one members; and of these, eleven were clergymen and ten laymen. On this occasion all the clerical members were present, and only three of the lay members.

The following is a copy of the minutes at this meeting:

"The Trustees met according to appointment at Nassau Hall, on Wednesday, the 19th day of April, A.D. 1758.

"Present,—William P. Smith and Samuel Woodruff, Esqrs.; the Rev. Messrs. Gilbert Tennent, William Tennent, David Cowell, Richard Treat, Timothy Johnes, Jacob Green, John Pierson, Samuel Finley, Caleb Smith, John Brainerd, Charles McKnight, and Richard Stockton. [Mr. Stockton was Clerk of the Board.] The Clerk certified that he had duly notified each member of this present meeting.

"The minutes of the last meeting were ordered to be read. It is ordered, that Messrs. Treat, Cowell, and Stockton, or any two of them, be a committee to ascertain the sum of money in the hands of the Treasurer which was given in Trust for the Benefit of poor Scholars, and make Report thereof to the next meeting.

"Messrs. Green, Brainerd, and Smith, appointed the last meeting to inspect the College Fund and settle the accounts with the Treasurer, having not finished the said affair, it is ordered, that they make report of the Business, and also the state of the Expenses for the current year, to the meeting of the Trustees at the next Commencement.

"It is ordered, that the Tuition money and Study Rent until the next Commencement be put into the hands of the Steward of the College, and that he pay the same unto the Treasurer.

"It having pleased God to remove by Death the late Rev. Mr. Edwards, President of the College, a few weeks after he had taken upon him the Charge of the College; It is ordered, that the Treasurer pay unto the Executors of the said Mr. Edwards the sum of One Hundred Pounds, being the one-half of his salary for one year, which he had a right to receive at the end of six months after the last Commencement; the said six months being unexpired notwithstanding.

" The Presidentship of the College having become vacant by the Death of the late Rev. President Edwards, the Trustees, after Prayer particularly on this account being made, and having taken deliberate consideration of the matter, do elect the Rev. Mr. James Lockwood, of Wethersfield, in the Colony of Connecticut, to be the President of the College; and the Clerk is ordered to write a Letter unto the said Mr. Lockwood informing him of the said Election and requesting his acceptance; and Mr. Spencer, one of the members of the Corporation, is desired to wait on the said Mr. Lockwood and deliver him the said Letter.

" It is ordered, that the Expenses attending the moving of Mr. Lockwood's Family to this Place be paid by the Treasurer.

" It is ordered, that Messrs. William P. Smith, Woodruff, Pierson, Johnes, Green, Caleb Smith, and Brainerd, or any four of them, be a Committee to transact the affair of Mr. Lockwood's Removal.

" The Rev. Caleb Smith is appointed President of this College until the next Trustee meeting; and the said appointment being made known to the said Mr. Smith, he was pleased to accept the same, and was qualified as the Charter directs.

" Mr. McWhorter, who was heretofore appointed an Usher in the Grammar School, not having accepted the same, and Mr. Strain having at the request of the Board for some time performed the said Business, and being willing to continue therein; It is ordered, that the said Mr. Strain be paid at the rate of £40 per annum for the Time he has acted, and shall act as Usher in the said school.

" The Board adjourned until 7 o'clock to-morrow morning.

" 2d Day, 7 o'clock. The Trustees met according to adjournment.

" Present as before.

" The Rev. Samuel Finley is appointed to take upon himself the Charge of the College and act as President thereof until the 22d day of May next, and the said Mr. Finley was qualified as the Charter directs." No reason is given for this action of the Board just at the close of their session. Only the simple fact is a matter of record.

Here we have a regularly elected President, viz., the Rev. Mr. Lockwood, and two acting Presidents, chosen at the same meeting of the Board. It is obvious why a *pro tem.* President was chosen upon the election of Mr. Lockwood, who, whatever might be his decision, would not be able at once to take upon himself the charge of the College; and the suggestion of Dr. Green in his "Notes" doubtless assigns the true reason why Mr. Finley was chosen to serve in the office of President for a short but definite period, and that, too, just after Mr. Smith had been qualified to act as President until the next meeting of the Trustees. Dr. Green's suggestion is this: that Mr. Smith finding he could not attend to the duties of the office before the

22d of May, Mr. Finley was chosen to take his place until that time. From the subsequent minutes of the Board it appears that both Mr. Finley and Mr. Smith took upon themselves the oversight of the College for the time allotted to each respectively.

" The next meeting of the Trustees took place at Nassau Hall, on Wednesday, the 16th of August, A.D. 1758. There were present His Excellency Francis Bernard, Esq., the Hon. James Hude, Esq., the Hon. Samuel Woodruff, Esq., William P. Smith, Esq., Peter V. B. Livingston, Esq., the Rev. Messrs. Caleb Smith, John Pierson, Gilbert Tennent, William Tennent, David Cowell, Richard Treat, Samuel Finley, Jacob Green, Alexander Cumming, Charles McKnight, and Richard Stockton, Esq.

" The Clerk certified that he had duly notified each member of this present meeting.

" His Excellency Francis Bernard, Esq., Governor of this Province, having been pleased to attend the present meeting of the Trustees, was qualified as the Charter directs, and took his seat as President accordingly.

" The definitive answer of the Rev. Mr. Lockwood, of Wethersfield, the President elect of this College, was read; by which it fully appears that the Rev. Mr. Lockwood had refused accepting the Presidentship agreeably to the choice of this Board; whereupon, after mature deliberation, the Board proceeded to the election of a President of the College, when the Rev. Mr. Samuel Davies, of Virginia, was duly elected. On which the Clerk is ordered as soon as possible to communicate the Notice of the said Election to the said Mr. Davies, and desire his acceptance thereof, and request his answer as soon as may be, and if it suits Conveniency, his attendance at the next Commencement. And the Treasurer is hereby ordered to pay the expenses of removing Mr. Davies's Family to this Place.

" The Rev. Mr. Smith is desired and hereby empowered to preside until the next Commencement, and then to give the Degrees to the Candidates; and in case of his absence, the Rev. Mr. Cowell or Cummings are hereby empowered to transact the said affair.

" The Board adjourned till 8 o'clock to-morrow morning.

" A Committee was appointed to manage the affair of Mr. Davies's removal to Princeton; and the same Committee was authorized to send to England for what Books they may think necessary for the use of the College and Grammar School, not exceeding £40 sterling; also to settle with Mr. Robert Smith (who built the President's house), and the Executor of President Burr, the matter relative to the surplus over and above £600 for which the said house was to have been built; and also to conclude about finishing the President's house and College."

From this and other minutes it appears that neither the College nor the President's house was completely finished at the time they were first occupied.

The Rev. Mr. George Duffield, who had served as Tutor from 1754 to 1756, was chosen senior Tutor, with the desire expressed by the Board that he might be permanently connected with the College. They offered him one hundred pounds a year, with a promise to increase this salary as they reasonably could should his circumstances require it. The offer was not accepted.

There being no regularly organized Presbyterian church in Princeton, and no building for regular religious services on the Sabbath, the President of the College for the time being preached regularly in the College Chapel; and such residents of the village and vicinity as desired so to do were permitted to attend the services in the College, and separate pews were assigned to such as were willing to pay for the use of them. Some of the occupants of these pews having neglected their pew-rents, it was

"Ordered, That the pew-rents in the Hall for the last year be immediately paid unto the Steward of the College, and on failure of compliance of any Person, that such Person forfeit his Pew."

The tuition-fees for a year were increased from three pounds to four pounds proclamation money: this additional charge, however, was not to be exacted of any already in college, but of those who should after this time enter the Freshman class.

The Rev. Mr. Finley was "authorized and desired to amend and prepare for the press the Newark Grammar with all possible expedition, and to transmit the same to the President of the College for the time being." This Newark Grammar was a Latin grammar said to have been prepared by President Burr.

An order was passed, that Mr. Finley be paid ten pounds for the time that he inspected the government of the College, and that Mr. Smith should be paid for his services forty pounds.

From a report made by a committee appointed at the last meeting, it appeared "that the fund for poor scholars in the Treasurer's hands" amounted to the sum of five hundred pounds *proc.*, the interest to be computed from October next; and for this sum the Trustees agreed to be accountable to the Synod of New York and Philadelphia,—the common expense and casualties to which their own funds are liable being excepted.

" The fund here mentioned," says President Green,* " was formed by donations obtained in England and Scotland by Messrs. Tennent and Davies for the education of poor and pious youth for the gospel ministry. It was loaned to the College, and was originally under the guardianship of the Synod of New York, but was now transferred to the Synod of New York and Philadelphia. . . . The fund here referred to was almost annihilated by the depreciation of paper money during the Revolutionary war. The interest arising on the remainder of it is now disposed of annually, for the benefit of some student in the College, by a committee of the General Assembly and a committee of the Trustees."

At a subsequent date, the selection of the beneficiary was given up to the College authorities.

This seems to be a suitable place to say a few words of the Rev. James Lockwood, who was chosen to succeed Mr. Edwards in the office of President of the College, but declined the appointment. " The reasons which induced Mr. Lockwood to refuse the Presidency," says President Green, " cannot now be known. He was a man of great worth and high reputation." The Trustees, however, were not unanimous in his election. This is not apparent from the minutes of the Board; but Mr. Davies, in writing on the subject to his friend Dr. Gibbons, of London, says, "The trustees were divided between him, another gentleman, and myself, but I happily escaped." The other gentleman referred to was most probably the Rev. Samuel Finley, who was also named as a candidate for the office at the time Mr. Davies was chosen.

Mr. Lockwood must have been a man of much more than ordinary merit. In 1766, upon the resignation of President Clap, of Yale College, Mr. Lockwood was chosen his successor. But this appointment he also declined. " The reason given," says Dr. Sprague, "for his non-acceptance in both cases was his strong attachment to the people of his charge, and his consequent unwillingness to separate himself from them. He continued their pastor, greatly respected and beloved, till the close of life. He died July 20, 1772, in the *fifty-eighth year* of his age, and the *thirty-fourth* of his ministry." He was very friendly to Mr. Whitefield, and countenanced his labors in the great revival of 1740. This circumstance probably contributed to his

---

* See his " Notes."

election as President of the College of New Jersey. His wife was a daughter of the Rev. Moses Dickinson, a brother of President Dickinson. Mr. Lockwood was a graduate of Yale College, as were the first three Presidents of this College, Messrs. Dickinson, Burr, and Edwards.

The Commencement of 1758 took place on Wednesday the 27th of September; but the record of this meeting is so defective that we have the name of only one of the Trustees present on this occasion. Eighteen candidates were admitted to the first degree in the Arts, and seven received their second degree. The record is not in the handwriting of the Clerk, nor is the entry made at the proper page.

As the Rev. Caleb Smith was the President *pro tem.*, and as he had been requested to preside at the Commencement exercises, it is most probable that the degrees were conferred by him.

At an adjourned meeting of the Board, held November 22, 1758, there were present fourteen members,—nine ministers and five laymen.

The Rev. George Duffield having declined the appointment tendered to him by the Trustees at their meeting in August, they now elect Mr. Joseph Treat a Tutor, and order that his salary shall begin from the preceding Commencement. From which order it is evident that without a formal appointment he acted as Tutor, and probably at the request of some one or more of the Trustees.

" The Committee empowered to transact the affair of Mr. Davies's removal having produced his answer, and the Trustees having considered the same, adjudge that the said answer is final in the Negative."

The Board then adjourned until eight o'clock the next morning. There were present the same persons as on the preceding day. They elected the Rev. Jacob Green, a member of the Board, Vice-President of the College, to serve until a President should be chosen; and it was ordered that his salary be at the rate of two hundred Pounds per annum, for the time he shall serve in the above character. It was also ordered that he should have care and general government of the grammar-school. Mr. Green, accepting this appointment, was qualified as the Charter directed.

It was then "ordered, that there be a meeting of the Trustees on the second Wednesday in May next, principally designed for the Election of a President of the College.

" Agreeably to this order, there was a meeting of the Board on Wednesday, the 9th day of May, 1759, thirteen members present.

" After acting upon a report from the Referees appointed to settle the dispute between the Executor of Mr. Burr and the Board about the President's House, and agreeing to pay the surplus of the £600, for which said house was to have been built, the Board adjourned till 2 o'clock P.M.

" At 2 P.M. the Trustees again met. His Excellency Governor Bernard and three other members of the Board having arrived, there were present in all *seventeen*, nine ministers and eight laymen."

The following is a copy of the minutes at this important meeting :

"The Rev. Mr. Samuel Davies was proposed as a Candidate for the Presidency of the College, and admitted, Nem. Con.; and also the Rev. Mr. Samuel Finley was admitted a Candidate in the same manner.

" Whereupon, after mature Deliberation of the Premises, the Rev. Mr. Samuel Davies was duly elected President of this College, and as this Society has been so long a time destitute of a fixed President, and by means thereof the former flourishing State so greatly affected, the Trustees desire and do hereby appoint the Rev. Messrs. Caleb Smith, John Brainerd, and Elihu Spencer, of their number (who design to meet the Synod of New York and Philadelphia on next week), and any other gentlemen of this Board who shall be there, to request the said Synod to dismiss the said Mr. Davies from his pastoral charge, that he may be thereby enabled to accept of the said Office.

" The Reverend Mr. Green having fulfilled the term of his former Election of Vice-President of the College, he is hereby appointed to continue in his said office until a fixed President can attend for the service of that Office.

" It is ordered, that hereafter whenever a Vacancy shall happen in the Presidentship of the College by Death or otherwise, that the Clerk with all convenient speed convene Six of the Trustees, and by their appointment shall give Notice (declaring such vacancy) of a meeting of the Trustees at any Time, not less than four months accounted from the date of said Notice, in Order for electing a President, and that all Notices thus given shall be regular to all Intents and Purposes.

" Mr. Caleb Smith produced a Plan of Union among the several Colleges in these Provinces, drawn up by Mr. President Clap, of Yale College, in Connecticut; which, being read, was referred for further consideration.

" It is ordered, that there be a meeting of the Trustees of the College at the next Commencement, and that the members take notice thereof accordingly."

Before the next meeting President Davies arrived at Princeton, and entered upon the duties of his office on the 26th of July, although he was not formally inducted, by the taking of the oaths required by the charter, until Wednesday, the 26th day of September, 1759.

From March 22, 1758, the day on which President Edwards died, until the 26th of July, 1759, the day on which President

Davies entered upon his duties, the space of an entire year and four months, the College was without a regular or permanent President; and although the reverend gentlemen who during this interval presided over the institution were all well qualified for their positions, yet the mere fact that the College was all this time without a permanent head was a great drawback to its prosperity, and made the Trustees the more anxious to secure without further delay the services of Mr. Davies, when it became known to them that if again elected he would accept the appointment.

As mentioned above, the minutes of the Trustees for the meeting of Wednesday, 27th of September, 1758, are very deficient, and a full and accurate account of the negotiations cannot be obtained from the minutes alone. Mr. Davies was first chosen President on the 16th of August, 1758. He referred the question, whether he ought to accept this appointment, to the Presbytery, of which he was a member, and they decided that he ought not to relinquish his pastoral charge. He therefore wrote to the Trustees declining their offer. But upon further reflection, fearing he might have erred in deciding not to accept the Presidency, he writes to the Rev. David Cowell, most probably in reply to a letter from Mr. C., and authorizes him, in case the Trustees cannot agree upon Mr. Finley, to place him again in nomination for the office of President. Mr. Cowell was a Trustee of the College, and a member of the committee appointed by the Board to make provision for Mr. Davies's removal to Princeton.

On the 27th of September, the day of the annual Commencement, the Trustees must have received notice of Mr. Davies's refusal to accept the office of President; but instead of proceeding at once to the election of another person to said office, they desire Mr. Davies to consent to act as Vice-President of the College until the meeting of the Synod in May next, and to refer the decision of the Presbytery to the Synod for its judgment. But this proposal Mr. Davies declines, and in a letter to Mr. Cowell, of the date of October 18, he revokes the permission which he had *conditionally* given Mr. Cowell to nominate him a second time for the office of President, and urges the choosing of Mr. Finley. The Trustees met again on the 22d of November, and, learning Mr. Davies's answer, after a full consideration of the subject they postponed the election of a President, and elected the Rev. Jacob Green Vice-President, to preside until a President be chosen, and then adjourned, to meet on the 9th of May next, chiefly for the purpose, as stated in their minutes, of choosing a President for the College.

In a letter of the date of December 25, 1758, Mr. Cowell informs Mr. Davies that it is impossible to unite upon Mr. Finley, that there was a bare quorum of the Trustees to receive his second denial, that the Governor (Governor Bernard) desired them not to proceed to the election of a President at this time, and that they had chosen Mr. Green Vice-President *pro tem.*

It is evident that a majority of the Trustees present on this occasion were not prepared to choose any other person than Mr. Davies, and it is probable that they still hoped that he might be induced to accept the office should it again be tendered to him.

In Mr. Cowell's correspondence with Mr. Davies, Mr. C. remarks, " The College is to be esteemed of as high importance as any institution in the land. Our beginning was small; God has carried it on until it is a marvel in our eyes."

From information received from the Rev. John Ewing, of Nottingham, Maryland, and formerly a Tutor in the College, Mr. Cowell, in his letter of December 25, was led to censure Mr. Jeremiah Halsey, then the senior Tutor, for endeavoring to prevent Mr. Davies's acceptance of the office of President. But Mr. Davies, in his reply of March 12, 1757, fully exculpates Mr. Halsey; and yet it is very probable that the information which was given him by Mr. Halsey, at Mr. Davies's own request, had considerable influence in determining him to decline the second proposal made to him.

In his correspondence with Mr. Cowell, which took place between the two meetings of the Board, November 22, 1758, and May 9, 1759, Mr. Davies, while consenting on certain conditions that he should again be nominated for the Presidency, expressly insists that the first election, viz., the one on the 16th of August preceding, should be regarded as null ; and that, if the

Trustees still desired him to accept the office, they must elect
him again, and the election be subject to the consent and approval of the Synod. To this condition the Trustees could
have no objection, as they were morally certain that the Synod
would give their consent, and as they knew that Mr. Davies
could not give up his pastoral charge in Virginia unless the
Synod permitted him to do so.

There can be no doubt that the two things which more than
anything else made Mr. Davies hesitate in regard to accepting
the offer of the Trustees, were his unwillingness to quit his field
of labor in Virginia and his knowledge of the fact that there
was a division in the Board of Trustees. A minority of the
Board held with Mr. Davies himself, that Mr. Finley was the
better qualified man for the position; but the majority believed
that Mr. Davies was the man for the place, and they determined
to get him if they could.

In a letter of the date of January 1, 1759, to Dr. Bellamy, the
Rev. David Bostwick, of New York, and subsequently a Trustee
of the College, remarks, " Mr. Davies sent an absolute refusal,
grounded upon information that there was a party against him.
The Trustees divided between him and Mr. Finley. And party
spirit, I fear, runs pretty high. The majority carried it that Mr.
Davies should be tried again. Mr. Green is Vice-President till
May." It does not appear from the minutes of the Board that
the majority formally decided that Mr. Davies should be tried
again; but their action was in accord with such a purpose. Mr.
Davies's own account of the matter is to be found in his
farewell sermon, preached at Hanover, Virginia, on the 1st of
July, 1759, and confirms the view here given, although it
abounds less in details. (See Davies's " Sermons," in three
volumes, published in New York in 1842.)

The officers and teachers of the College during this interval
were, the Rev. Caleb Smith, President *pro tem.*; Rev. Samuel
Finley, President *pro tem.*; Rev. Jacob Green, Vice-President
pro tem.; Mr. John Ewing, Tutor; Mr. Jeremiah Halsey,
Tutor; Mr. Joseph Treat, Tutor.

The Tutors were admirably qualified for their work, and
became men of note.

At the Commencement of 1758, eighteen were admitted to the first degree in the Arts, and the same number at the Commencement of 1759, at the latter of which Mr. Davies presided, although he had little or nothing to do in the instruction of the candidates.

Of the class of 1758 were Peter R. Livingston, chosen, in 1776, President of the Provincial Congress, New York; John Van Brugh Tennent, one of the founders of the first medical school of New York, and its first Professor of Obstetrics; Rev. Wm. Tennent, son of the Rev. Wm. Tennent, of Freehold, New Jersey, an eloquent preacher and an ardent patriot; Jeremiah Van Rensselaer, a Member of Congress, and a Lieutenant-Governor of New York; Rev. Wm. Whitwell, of Marblehead, Massachusetts.

Of the class of 1759 were Rev. James Caldwell, A.M., of Elizabethtown, New Jersey, a Trustee of the College; Jabez Campfield, A.M., a Surgeon in the American army; Rev. John Carmichael, A.M., of Delaware; Rev. James Hunt, for many years at the head of a flourishing classical school in Maryland; James Leslie, founder of the " Leslie Trust Fund," for the education at the College of New Jersey of pious and indigent candidates for the ministry; Samuel Spencer, of North Carolina, a Justice of the Supreme Court of that State.

Fourteen of the graduates in these two years became ministers of the gospel, the best known of whom are the five clergymen mentioned above.

CHAPTER X.

MR. DAVIES entered upon the duties of his office on the
26th of July, 1759, as appears from the following minute of the
Trustees at their meeting on Wednesday, the 26th of September, being the day of the annual Commencement for that year:
" The Rev. Mr. Samuel Davies having, pursuant to the measures taken by this Board, arrived at Nassau Hall in July last,
and entered on the office of President of the College on the
26th day of that month, was now qualified by taking the several oaths as the Charter directs. And the Board unanimously
voted that Mr. Davies's stated salary shall begin from the Thir-
teenth Day of May last, which was the Day of the Dissolution
of his Pastoral Relation from the People of his former Charge."
It was on the 17th, and not on the 13th, that this dissolution
occurred, as appears from the minutes of the Synod of New
York and Philadelphia. It is probable that Mr. Davies announced to his church on the 13th, which was the Sabbath, his
purpose to accept the offer of the Trustees of the College and
to apply for a dissolution of the pastoral relation.

There was no meeting of the Board between that which occurred on the 9th of May, 1759, at which Mr. Davies was a
second time chosen· President, and this meeting of the 26th of
September; but in pursuance of the wishes of the Trustees, expressed at the time of Mr. Davies's second election, he did not
wait for a formal induction into office to begin his work as
President. What special matters occupied his attention from
the time of his arrival until the ensuing Commencement we
have no means of ascertaining; but, from the character of the
man, there can be no doubt that he abounded in labors for

the upbuilding of the institution as a seminary of religion and learning.

Mr. Davies presided at this Commencement. Eighteen candidates, who had pursued their studies at Nassau Hall, were admitted to the first degree in the Arts; and two others, graduates of Yale College, were admitted to the same honor in this College. The second degree in the Arts was conferred upon eight candidates, seven of whom were graduates of the College.

The Treasurer was directed to " pay to Mr. Davies the sum of £60.17.3, to defray the expenses of removing his family from Hanover (Virginia) to Princetown."

By a resolution of the Board, the Steward was "allowed the sum of Twenty Shillings per annum for every Boarder in the College for the ensuing year, which is to be continued during the time of his continuance in the service." This seems to have been in lieu of a fixed salary, and constituted a part of the expenses incurred by the College in supplying the students with board, the profit or loss from which accrued to the College, and not to the Steward. It was "Ordered, That Mr. Davies's salary for the first half-year be paid at the end of six months, and half-yearly for the future, when practicable." This expression, " when practicable," shows that in these early times in the history of the College, notwithstanding all the aid they had received from abroad, as well as at home, the Trustees did not always find it easy to meet the necessary expenses of the institution.

The Treasurer was directed to "pay Mr. Green the sum of £100 for his six months' services in the College." This vote shows that Mr. Green did not perform the duties of the Vice-President for the whole term intervening between his appointment on the 22d of November, 1758, and the 26th of July, when Mr. Davies entered upon his duties as President.*

It is most probable that, upon learning the decision of the Synod in favor of Mr. Davies's release from his pastoral charge,

---

* The entire minute of the Synod in reference to the dissolution of Mr. Davies's pastoral charge may with propriety be here inserted, as showing the carefully considered judgment of the Synod in reference to his duty in this matter. The minute is as follows:

" An application to the Synod from the Board of Trustees of the College of New

Mr. Green deemed it best to retire at once from the government of the College. The six months during which he discharged the duties assigned him expired upon the 22d of May, and it was doubtless for the services rendered during these six months that he received the £100 voted to him on this occasion in accordance with the resolution adopted at the time of his appointment, that his salary should be at the rate of £200 per annum.

The next act of the Board was to " relinquish the grammar-school into the hands of President Davies, to be wholly his property, as it was formerly the property of the late President Burr."

Mr. Davies was granted the liberty of educating any of his sons in the College free from the charge of tuition-money. It is due to the Rev. Jeremiah Halsey, the senior Tutor, that the following minute should be copied into every history of the College :

" Voted, That Mr. Halsey, the Senior Tutor, be desired to accept the sum of £20, as an acknowledgment from this Board for his extraordinary Services in Favor of the College."

The following important order was made by the Board in reference to absences from College exercises :

" Ordered, That all licenses for students to absent themselves from the College, or from their stated Duties or Exercises, be granted solely by the President, or in his absence by the Tutor of such student applying for the same.

" The Board then adjourned until 8 o'clock next morning, at which hour the members again assembled, present as before."

From a resolution passed by the Board at this meeting, with respect to the College building and the President's house, it would appear that neither building had been completely finished at this time.

Jersey for the liberation of Mr. Davies from his pastoral charge, that he may accept the Presidency of said college, to which they elected him, was brought in and read.

" A supplication was also brought in from Mr. Davies's congregation, earnestly requesting his continuance with them.

" The Synod, having seriously considered the congregation's supplication, and fully heard all the reasonings for and against Mr. Davies's liberation, after solemn prayer to God for direction, do, upon the whole, judge that the arguments in favor of said liberation do preponderate, and agree that Mr. Davies's pastoral relation to his congregation be dissolved, in order to his removal to the college, and do accordingly hereby dissolve it."

In reference to the purchase of books the following resolution was adopted:

"That the order for a Committee to send to London for Books for the use of the College and the Grammar School be revoked, and that President Davies be desired to send for such Books as shall be requisite for the use of the students for the future, and that he fix the Prices of said Books, and commit them to the care of the Steward of the College for sale; and Mr. Livingston is desired to assist Mr. Davies in said Affair."

The Mr. Livingston here mentioned is Mr. P. Van Brugh Livingston, of New York, a merchant of that city, and a Trustee of the College. The importation of books by the College authorities, for the use of the students, continued, to a greater or less extent, as late as the earlier part of President S. S. Smith's administration, which extended from the spring of 1795 to the autumn of 1812.

President Davies was desired, as soon as convenient, "to take a Methodical Catalogue of the Books of the College Library, and order the same to be printed at the expense of the College." Such a catalogue was prepared, and it was published January 29, 1760. It was printed at Woodbridge, New Jersey, at the well-known press of James Parker.

A copy of this catalogue has recently fallen into the hands of the writer of this work. It is contained in a small pamphlet of thirty-six pages, the last two of which are wanting. The number of works in the library must have been about eight hundred, the number of volumes nearly twelve hundred. The volumes were numbered as they were placed upon the shelves, and the highest number in the above-mentioned copy of the catalogue is eleven hundred and seventy-five.

This printed catalogue includes the names of ten books belonging to Governor Belcher's private family and given by him to the College. The Governor's collection contained four hundred and seventy-four volumes, *sixty* of which were folios, and many of them valuable works. The other books were chiefly presents from other friends of the institution. These volumes, with all the other books then belonging to the College library, were consumed by the fire of March, 1802, which made Nassau Hall a ruin.

The following preface to the catalogue sets forth " The Design of the Publication":

" A large and well-sorted Collection of Books on the various Branches of Literature is the most ornamental and useful Furniture of a College; and the most proper and valuable Fund with which it can be endowed. It is one of the best Helps to enrich the Minds both of the Officers and Students with Knowledge; to give them an extensive Acquaintance with Authors; and to lead them beyond the narrow Limits of the Books to which they are confined in their stated Studies and Recitations, that they may expatiate at large thro' the boundless and variegated Fields of Science. If they have Books always at hand to consult upon every Subject that may occur to them, as demanding a more thoro' Discussion, in their public Disputes, in the Course of their Studies, in Conversation, or their own fortuitous Tho'ts; it will enable them to investigate Truth through its intricate Recesses; and to guard against the Stratagems and Assaults of Error. It will teach them Modesty and Self-Diffidence, when they perceive the free and different Sentiments of Men equally great and good; and give at least such Hints, as their Invention may afterwards improve upon, when they appear in public Life, in a Country where Books are so scarce, and private Libraries so poor and few, that their principal Resources must be their own Invention.

" The College of New Jersey is so evidently adapted and intended for the Advancement of Religion and useful Learning among all Denominations of Protestants, that it has been the favourite Object of public Charity, both in Great Britain and America, from its first Institution. And by that Assistance alone it has been raised from Nothing to its present State in a few Years; a Monument to Posterity of the Generosity of the Age in which it was founded; and a public Proof of the Agency of Providence in Favour of great and good Designs, however impracticable they may appear in their first Projection. Its Library in particular has been almost entirely formed of the Donations of several public-spirited Gentlemen upon both sides of the Atlantic; whose names Gratitude would not put herself to Pain in concealing, were they desirous, or even patient, of the universal Praise their disinterested Charity deserves.

" But after all this liberal Assistance, a survey of its literary Wealth, whcib is exposed to view in the following Catalogue, will soon convince the Friends of Learning and Nassau Hall how poor it still is in this important Article; to which no Additions can be made from the Treasury, which is far from being equal to other unavoidable and more indispensable Exigencies. But few modern Authors, who have unquestionably some Advantages above the immortal Ancients, adorn the Shelves. This Defect is most sensibly felt in the study of Mathematics and the Newtonian Philosophy, in which the Students have but very imperfect Helps, either from Books or Instruments.

" As some valuable Benefactions have been spontaneous Offerings of unsolicited Charity, without any other Excitement than the Knowledge of the Poverty and the public Utility of the Foundation, this Catalogue is published to give Information to such, who are watching for Opportunities of doing good; and to afford particular Benefactors the Pleasure of seeing how many others have concurred with them in their favourite Charity."

This preface was written by President Davies, and it was probably the first article penned and published by him in the interests of the College after he became its President. The remarks respecting the urgent need of a large and well-selected library for the College were as apposite in every subsequent part of its history, until very lately, as they were when first written.

The recent munificence of John C. Green, Esq., of New York, has made provision for the increase of the College library, and for its preservation, such as in all probability would more than have satisfied the enlarged views and earnest desires of President Davies. All that is now wanting, so far as the library is concerned, is a fund to pay a well-qualified librarian to devote to it his whole time.

The next record had reference to a provision for the Trustees dining together; but it was cancelled,—for what reason, or by whom, it does not appear. It is possible that the record was an error, and that the motion was not adopted. As far as it can now be deciphered, the minute was in these words:

"Voted, That in future at all meetings of the Trustees the Steward of the College be ordered to furnish a Dinner for the Corporation, with proper Liquors, that the several members may have the conveniency of being together, and that the said

"Every Person dining at such Table may deposite what gratuity he thinks proper for defraying the Expense thereof."

The custom here introduced, or proposed to be introduced, has prevailed ever since. At all their meetings the Trustees dine together; but of late years the "proper Liquors" have been dispensed with; and no gratuity is expected of any Trustee or invited guest.

Messrs. Davies, Tennent, and Cowell were appointed a committee to purchase a lot of land contiguous to the College grounds, and belonging to the estate of the late Mr. Samuel Hazard, of Philadelphia. The purchase was made.

At this meeting of the Board, the first ever attended by President Davies, several matters of much interest to the College claimed the attention of the Trustees, but the most weighty of them were embraced in these two resolutions, viz.:

" *Resolved,* That Governor Bernard, Messrs. Davies, [W.] P. T. Smith, W. Tennent, Finley, Green, Cummings, and Stockton, or any three of them, be a committee to draw up a System of Regulations concerning Admission into College, with the requisite Qualifications for Degrees, and that all the Trustees who choose to be present have liberty of voting.*

" *Resolved,* That Governor Bernard, Mr. Hude, Mr. W. P. T. Smith, Wm. Smith, Esq., Mr. Woodruff, Messrs. Cowell, Treat, Tennent, Finley, Green, Cummings, and Stockton, be a Committee, any five of whom to be a Quorum, to consider of proper measures to enlarge the Fund and to extend the usefulness of the College. All other Trustees shall have votes in the above Committee."

The last clause in each of these resolutions virtually made the two committees one. They held their first meeting at Perth Amboy, the residence of Governor Bernard, the chairman of both committees, on the 24th of October, 1759. There were present on this occasion his Excellency the Governor, President Davies, Mr. Hude, Mr. Woodruff, Mr. W. P. T. Smith, Mr. [W.] Tennent, and Mr. Cummings.

The following are the minutes of the committee:

" The Committee not being able at present to resolve upon any methods that will have a probable Tendency to increase the Funds of the College, do agree to postpone the consideration of this Affair.

" The Committee then proceeded to take into Consideration the Qualifications necessary to entitle the students to the usual Degrees. And are of the Opinion that a Residence at College for some Time, and proper Collegiate Exercises, are necessary to be enjoined on those youths who apply for said Degrees. And the Committee request the President of the College to draw up some Regulations upon this Head, to be laid before them at their next meeting, to [be held] the first Day of December next; President Davies to give notice of the meeting."

Whether the committee held another meeting is uncertain, as there is no record of their having done so. But, whether they did or did not, President Davies drew up the proposed regulations, which, with the consent no doubt of the members of the committee, either formally or informally given, were submitted to the Board at their meeting on Wednesday, the 24th of September, 1760, the day of the annual Commencement. The minute of the Board in reference to the action of the committee is in these words:

---

* These matters received due attention at the time Mr. Burr was chosen President under the second charter, November 9, 1748. But it is probable that in the judgment of the Trustees, as well as in that of President Davies, it was deemed expedient to revise the existing rules and to add to their stringency.

" The Committee appointed at the last meeting to draw up a System of Regulations concerning Admission into College, and to Degrees of Bachelor and Master
of Arts, having produced a Draught thereof, and the same being considered and
amended by the Trustees, was confirmed in the Terms following, to wit:

" The conferring of Academical Honours was intended as an Incentive to a laudable Ambition in Study, and as a Reward of literary Merit. And the different
Degrees of these honorary Distinctions conferred at different Periods suppose a
proportional Increase of literary Merit ; and consequently a sufficient Time of Residence in College, for further prosecution of Study, and a proper previous Examination, to discover the Improvement of the Candidates. And when they are
promiscuously distributed as cursory Formalities after the usual Intervals of Time,
without any previous evidence of suitable Qualifications, they sink into Contempt
as insignificant Ceremonies, and no longer answer their original Design. Therefore
the Trustees are determined to admit none to a Degree in this College but upon
the following terms, in Addition to those already established :

" Graduates from other Colleges, upon producing Diplomas or other sufficient
Testimonials, shall be admitted to the same Degree in this, without any previous
Examination. But it shall be inserted in their Diplomas and publickly declared
by the President in conferring it, that it is conferred *Honoris causa*, according to
the Manner of some Universities abroad. But if they stand Candidates for a
higher Degree than they have yet been admitted to, they shall submit to all the
Regulations contained in the following Articles.

" All Candidates for a Master's Degree shall reside in or near the College at
least one Week immediately preceding that Commencement at which they expect
to receive their Degrees. During which Time they shall submit to the Laws and
Orders of the College. And on the Tuesday morning immediately preceding
the last Wednesday of September (on which the Anniversary Commencement is
always held) they shall attend in the College in order to pass such an Examination
as the Trustees then present shall think necessary; especially in such Branches of
Literature as have a more direct Connection with that Profession of Life which
they have entered upon or have in View, whether Divinity, Law, or Physick, and
shall make such preparation for the Commencement as the Officers of the College
shall judge proper.

" As so short a Residence can be an intolerable Inconvenience to but very few,
and will render the second Degree a real Honor, the Trustees will not dispense
with it in ordinary Cases. Yet as the peculiar Circumstances of some Persons of
sufficient Accomplishments may render them incapable of Residence, they are desired to inform the President by Letter, some convenient Time before the Commencement at which they intend to offer themselves Candidates, of the Reason of
their Incapacity; that the Trustees may judge whether they are sufficient for a Dis-
pensation for the whole or any Part of the Time required, and what Exercise shall
be substituted instead of Residence.

" None shall be admitted to the Honours of the College without Testimonials of
their good moral conduct, while absent from College, signed by two or more gentlemen of Note and Veracity, in the Place where they have resided, or unless they
are recommended from personal knowledge by one of the Trustees or College
Officers."

Additional regulations respecting the terms of first admission into College :

" Every student shall be obliged to reside in College at least two years before his first graduation ; and therefore, after the Expiration of one year from the next Commencement (A.D. 1760), none shall be admitted later than the Beginning of the Junior Year. But that anybody may have Liberty to offer himself at the Public Examination as a Candidate for a Bachelor's Degree, and if approved shall be admitted thereto accordingly upon paying the sum of Eight Pounds, being the Tuition Money for Two years, exclusive of Degree Fees.

" Candidates for the Freshman Class shall be regulated by the Law already made in such case. But Candidates for any of the higher Classes shall not only be previously examined, as usual, but recite for Two Weeks upon Trial in that particular Class to which they stand Candidates, and then shall be fixed in that or a lower, as the College Officers shall judge them qualified."

How far the rules respecting the examination of candidates for the second degree in the Arts, and of their residence at the College for one week, were carried into effect, and how long they continued in force, we have no means of ascertaining. It is not probable that they were very rigidly enforced, for after the adoption of these rules the Bachelors of Arts admitted to their second degree continued to be in about the same proportion to those who did not receive it that they had previously been. Had Mr. Davies lived, it is probable that he would have enforced the observance of these rules more resolutely than his successors in office were disposed to do, as they doubtless originated with him. There is very little reason, however, for thinking that the experiment would have been a successful one even in his energetic hands, or a very useful one if carried into effect. This remark has special reference to the rule requiring of candidates for the second degree a week's residence at or near the College. At the present day the proposed examinations of the candidates, except as a mere form, would be a simple impossibility. The demands upon the time and strength of the officers during the week preceding the annual Commencement are as much as they can meet, without engaging in a general examination of the candidates for the second degree, were they but one-half, or even one-fourth, of their present numbers. The present plan is the only feasible one, viz., evidence that the candidate has been engaged in professional or other studies, and that he is a person of correct deportment.

A residence of one year is now required on the part of all candidates for the *first* degree in the Arts, instead of two years called for in this report, which was designed to be a bar to any one's admission to a higher standing than the Junior class upon his first entrance into College. It seems in strange contrast with this rule that there should be an exception to it, to the extent that anybody may have liberty to offer himself at the public examinations as a candidate for a Bachelor's degree, and if approved shall be admitted thereto accordingly upon paying *the tuition-money for two years*, exclusive of the degree-fees. The latter part of this provision is of doubtful propriety, and, so far as is known, there is no instance in the history of the College of a degree having been conferred upon the condition here mentioned.

No change was made at this time in the terms of admission into the Freshman class, with the exception that the candidates must be acquainted with "Vulgar Arithmetic," in addition to the studies previously required.

To incite to diligence in study, it was " Voted, That for the future the President and Tutors, with any other gentlemen of Education who shall choose to be present, shall examine annually," before the Commencement, " the several classes, and that such as are found unqualified shall not be allowed to rise in the usual course."

This whole action shows that there was a desire and a purpose on the part of President Davies to elevate the standard of scholarship, both before and after the conferring of the *first* degree in the Arts, among those who sought to obtain from the College literary honors.

Besides the measures mentioned above, most of which were designed to stir up the students to greater diligence, several other matters of moment to the College received the attention of the Board and led to action on the part of the Trustees. Among these were the following, viz.: provision for an annual inspection of the Steward's accounts, and also of the Treasurer's, and for a full and regular report by the Examining

Committee; the purchase of additional lots contiguous to the College; an order that in future no candidate be admitted to a Degree unless he produce a certificate that he is not in arrears to the College; a discretionary power given to the President and Tutors to substitute other punishments, short of suspension, in lieu of fines for minor offences against College order; an authority to substitute Psalmody at evening prayer, for reading a portion of Scripture,—the reading of which had been usual both morning and evening in the Chapel service.

The President and Tutors were authorized to appoint any of the students to read a portion of the sacred Scriptures out of the original language at morning prayers. This indicates that the study of the Scriptures in the original languages was an object of careful attention at this time. Measures were also taken for the preparing of a historical account of the rise and progress and present state of the College. This matter was intrusted to a committee consisting of President Davies, the Rev. William Tennent, Rev. David Cowell, and Richard Stockton. Doubtless the expectation was that President Davies would write the history. But his sudden death, in the course of a few months after, prevented his performing this service for the College. Mr. Cowell, another member of the committee, died a short time before Mr. Davies himself.

As there is no intimation in the minutes of the Board of any material change in the course of instruction during the administration of Mr. Davies, it is more than probable that it continued to be very much the same as it was previously to his accession to the Presidency; with the exception, perhaps, that more attention was given to public speaking. President Green, in his " Notes," remarks of President Davies, " A poet and an orator himself, he turned the attention of his pupils to the cultivation of English composition and eloquence with great effect. He introduced the practice, ever since continued, of delivering monthly orations by members of the Senior class."

President Green further observes, " The number of students under the administration of President Davies cannot be exactly ascertained. It probably did not at any time exceed a hundred, and at his death it must have come very little short of that number." If an estimate can be made from the number of graduates from 1759 to 1761, the entire number of students in the College at any one time during President Davies's administration must have fallen considerably short of a hundred; although there is reason to believe that there was a much larger number at the time of his decease than at the time of his accession to the Presidency.

The various matters detailed above indicate that there was at this period of its history an active mind at the head of the College, from whom great things might have been expected had it pleased God to spare him to the institution. But, in the wise and holy ordering of Divine Providence, President Davies was removed by death on the 4th of February, 1761; having served the College in his office as President a little more than eighteen months.

The officers of the College during his administration were Messrs. Samuel Davies, A.M., President; Jeremiah Halsey, A.M., Senior Tutor; Joseph Treat, Jr., A.B., Tutor; Jacob Ker, A.B., Tutor.

Mr. Halsey was a Tutor in the College from 1757 to 1767, and he was a Trustee in the College from 1770 to 1781. He was an excellent teacher, and a most valuable College officer; and as such was held in great esteem by the College authorities. At the time of his death he was minister of the Presbyterian church of Lamington, New Jersey. He died in 1781.

Mr. Treat, in October, 1762, was installed as a colleague of the Rev. David Bostwick, pastor of the Presbyterian church in the city of New York. He left the city at the beginning of the Revolutionary War, and never returned, but served the churches of Lower Bethlehem and Greenwich, in Sussex County, New Jersey, until his death in 1797.

Mr. Ker was ordained by the Presbytery of New Brunswick in 1764, and on the 29th of August in that year he was installed as pastor of the churches of Monokin and Wicomico, Maryland, where he remained until his death, July 29, 1795. In a minute adopted by the Presbytery of Lewes he is spoken of as a great and good man, whose loss was sensibly felt by the Church in general, and by that Presbytery in particular.

In the summer of 1759, Governor Bernard was transferred to Massachusetts, as Governor of that Province, and his Excellency Thomas Boone, Esq., succeeded him in the government of New Jersey.

On his first visit to Princeton, July 8, 1760, Governor Boone was attended by Mr. Chief-Justice Morris and several other gentlemen of distinction, and he was introduced into Nassau Hall by the President and Tutors, who presented the following address:

" To his Excellency Thomas Boone, Esq., His Majesty's Governor and Commander-in-Chief of the Province of New Jersey, Chancellor and Vice-Admiral of the same, etc.

" The humble Address of the President and Tutors of the College of New Jersey.

" SIR,—The President and Tutors of the College of New Jersey give your Excellency a most cordial welcome to Nassau Hall, and beg leave warmly to congratulate your Excellency upon your accession to the Government of this Province, where the minds of so many are happily prepossessed in your favor by the agreeable anticipations they have received of your Excellency's character.

" Though we form a very high estimate, Sir, of the importance of your Excellency's patronage to the prosperity of this Infant College, which has been founded by one and countenanced by another of your predecessors, yet we would use no artifice to pre-engage your Excellency's friendship and protection without the sanction of your own well-informed judgment; but we lay ourselves open to your Excellency's inspection, and invite you to enquire into its constitution, the modes of instruction and discipline, the care taken of the principles and morals of the Students, and their progress in the various branches of literature; and then we shall cheerfully leave your Excellency to follow the conduct of your own judgment and the impulse of a patriot heart, ever friendly to true learning and virtue, but ever an enemy to pedantry, bigotry, and idle pretensions, only begging your Excellency would make some candid allowances for those unavoidable imperfections that result from the present Infant State of this Institution, which has been raised from nothing in a few years, by the hand of public charity recommended only by its poverty and apparent subserviency to the general good.

" We beg leave, Sir, particularly to request your Excellency to honor the next public Examination with your presence, when you will have the best opportunity of informing yourself what are the branches of literature taught in this Seminary, and what proficiency has been made by the young Gentlemen under our tuition.

" We hope, Sir, our future conduct will verify the engagements which we now voluntarily assume to your Excellency, That we shall continue with the utmost assiduity to instil into young minds such principles as thro' the blessing of Heaven form the Scholar, the Patriot, and the Christian. And should we neglect so essential an article of our duty we should anticipate our own doom, and expect your Excellency's severest animadversions, in conjunction with the other Trustees, of whom you are now President; and who, we doubt not, will give your Excellency proper expressions of their duty and congratulation at their next convention.

"May all the happiness a Patriot can diffuse, or a free People enjoy, attend your administration! and may all the felicities which Heaven has made the rewards of such a beneficent administration ever attend your Excellency!

"SAMUEL DAVIES, President.

"To which his Excellency was pleased to return the following answer:

"GENTLEMEN,—I am exceedingly obliged to you for this polite Salutation on my arrival among you. The proper education of Youth influences so materially all Government, that this laudable Establishment has a natural claim to the patronage of his Majesty's Substitute; and with the advantage of such eminent and respectable tuition, I have not the least doubt but the Youth will be distinguished by the acquisition of every useful and valuable accomplishment.

"THOMAS BOONE.
"Prince-Town, July 8, 1760.

"His Excellency was also complimented by two young gentlemen of the Senior Class, in a Latin and an English Oration; and an air of sincere congratulation appeared on every countenance."

The same year the Governor was present at the Commencement exercises, and presided at the meetings of the Board. This was the only Commencement attended by Governor Boone, who the next year was made Governor of South Carolina, and it was the second and last Commencement at which Mr. Davies presided.

The following report of the Commencement is copied from the "Pennsylvania Gazette" of October 9, 1760:

"Prince Town, Nassau Hall, September 25, 1760. Yesterday the Anniversary Commencement of the College was held here. The Procession of the Trustees and Candidates from the President's House to Nassau Hall began at the Ringing of the Bell precisely at 10 o'clock in the forenoon. The Order was, The Candidates for the Degree of Bachelor of Arts first, two and two, uncovered; the Candidates for the Degree of Master of Arts followed next, uncovered; and the Trustees, according to their Seniority, the youngest first, and the Governor and President last, concluded. When the Candidates arrived at the steps of the Middle Entrance into the Hall they stopt, and the whole Procession divided itself equally on each side of the gravel Walk, and entered in an inverted Order. The Collegiate Exercises began with a handsome Salutatory Oration in Latin, pronounced by Mr. Jonathan Smith; then followed a Latin Syllogistick Dispute, wherein the Respondent held that 'Sermo primitus ab Inspiratione divina Originem duxit,' which was well maintained and opposed. When this was concluded, Mr. Benjamin Rush arose, and in a very sprightly and entertaining Manner delivered an ingenious English Harangue in Praise of Oratory. Then succeeded a Forensick Dispute in English, in which it was held that ' The Elegance of an Oration much consists in the Words being consonant to the Sense.' The Respondent, Mr. Samuel Blair, acquitted himself with universal Applause in the elegant Composition and Delivery of his Defence; and his Opponent answered him with Humour and Pertinency. This was succeeded by a Latin Dispute in a Socratick Way, in which the Respondent affirmed that ' Systema Ethicæ perfectum in præsenti Hominum Conditione, sine Ope divinæ Revelationis, construi nequit;' and by a well-composed Valedictory Oration in English by Mr. Enoch Green. The Singing of an Ode on Science, composed by the President of the College, concluded the Forenoon Exercises.

" The Entertainment in the Afternoon began with the Address to His Excellency the Governor [Boone] by Mr. Stockton in the Name of the Trustees. After which the Candidates for the Master's Degree disputed in Latin the following Question : ' An Rector civilis ullam, in Rebus Fidei, Potestatem habeat,' and ' Nonne absurdum est Deum immutabilem precari,' which were learnedly defended and ingeniously opposed. The President then descended from the Rostrum, and with the usual Formalities conferred the Degrees of Bachelor of Arts and of Master of Arts.

" Mr. Joseph Treat, one of the Masters of Arts and a Tutor in the College, then ascended, and delivered an elegant, pathetic Valedictory Oration in English, in the Close of which he very handsomely touched upon the present flourishing State of our Public Affairs in North America. The Singing of an Ode on Peace composed by the President concluded the whole, to the Universal Pleasure and Satisfaction of a numerous Auditory."

The Odes, one on Science and the other on Peace, composed by President Davies, and sung at the close of the morning and evening exercises, were many years later confounded with a poetic dialogue recited, with choral songs, at the Commencement of 1762.

The reader will probably observe that in the above account of this Commencement all the *substantives* are begun with a capital letter,—a mode of writing and printing formerly much in vogue, and to which Dr. Franklin gave a decided preference, as being "so useful to those who are not well acquainted with the language." This appears from a letter of his, of the date of December 26, 1789, to Noah Webster, Esq., "On Modern Innovations in the English Language and in Printing."

Among the graduates of the College during Mr. Davies's administration who rose to greater or less distinction were the following, in 1760:

Joseph Alexander, D.D. He was very active in the cause of education in both North and South Carolina, and founder of a school, which became a college, under the title of Queen's Museum.

John Archer, M.D.   He was a member of the House of Representatives of the United States from 1801 to 1807.

Samuel Blair, D.D., son of the Rev. Samuel Blair, of Fagg's Manor.   When twenty-six years of age he was chosen by the Trustees President of the College, but declined the appointment.

Enos Kelsey.   During the Revolution he held a responsible office in the Clothier-General's office.   For many years he was the Treasurer of the College.

Benjamin Rush, M.D.   A signer of the Declaration of Independence; Physician- and Surgeon-General for the Middle Military District; member of the Convention for forming the Constitution of the United States; and Professor in the Medical Department of the University of Pennsylvania.

Jonathan Bayard Smith, a member of the Continental Congress, from Pennsylvania, in 1777 and 1778.   Mr. Smith made a large donation of books to the College library.

CHAPTER XI.

PRESIDENT DAVIES was born near Summit Bridge, New Castle County, Delaware, November 3, O. S., 1723. At that time Delaware was a part of Pennsylvania. The year here mentioned is given upon the authority of a table in President Davies's handwriting. The Bible, upon a blank leaf of which this table was written, was in the possession of some of President Davies's descendants, residing in Petersburg, Virginia, as late as the year 1853, as appears from a sketch of his life in the " Presbyterian Magazine" for that year. This sketch, although very brief, is very valuable, as it contains information previously published nowhere else, except in Dr. Foote's "Sketches of Virginia." The year of his birth, as given upon his tombstone, is 1724; and this has been doubtless the occasion of a like error in several of the biographical notices of him. He was of Welsh descent, and his parents were of humble origin, but persons of good character and fervent piety. The mother is said to have been a woman of uncommon powers of mind, and also eminent for her faith and zeal. He was named Samuel, after Samuel the prophet. The mother of the prophet called him Samuel because she had asked him of the LORD; and for the same reason the mother of President Davies called her son Samuel, thereby expressing her belief that God had heard her prayer, as, ages before, he had heard the prayer of Hannah. Like Hannah, we have reason to believe, she had solemnly vowed that if the LORD would give her a man-child she would devote him to the LORD all his days; and from the birth of her son she seems to have regarded him as a child given to her to be trained for the gospel ministry.

In a letter to his friend Dr. Gibbons, of London, after speaking of these things, President Davies adds, "This early dedication to God has always been a strong inducement to me to devote myself to Him by my own personal act; and the most important blessings of my life I have looked upon as immediate answers to the prayers of a pious mother. But, alas! what a degenerate plant am I! How unworthy such a parent and such a birth!"

In his early childhood he was taught by his mother, and when ten years of age he was sent to an English school some distance from his father's residence, and remained there two years. At this school he is said to have made rapid progress in his studies. For want of the religious training which he enjoyed at home, he became somewhat careless in his attention to his religious interests; but he still made a practice of secret prayer, especially in the evening. And it is worthy of note that in his prayers at this very time he prayed more earnestly that he might be a minister of the gospel than for any other thing. In the fifteenth year of his age he made a public profession of his faith in Christ, and entered upon a course of study preparatory to the ministry. Two or three of his biographers speak of his uniting with the Church, forgetting that in virtue of his birth he was a member of the Church and that by his baptism in infancy he had been recognized as a member.

His classical studies were begun under the tuition of the Rev. Abel Morgan, a Baptist preacher of much note at that time; but he was afterwards sent to the school of the Rev. Samuel Blair, at Fagg's Manor, Chester County, Pennsylvania. Under the guidance of this learned and eloquent divine he was trained for the gospel ministry, and on the 30th of July, 1746, being in the twenty-third year of his age, he was licensed to preach by the Presbytery of New Castle. By this same Presbytery he was ordained as an evangelist, February 19, 1747, O. S., with a view to his visiting the Presbyterian churches in Virginia. On the 23d of October, 1746, he was married to Miss Sarah Kirkpatrick, who, with her infant son, died on the 16th of September, 1747. At the time of his licensure his health was quite feeble, and it continued so for some years: still, he was resolved that while life and sufficient strength remained he would devote himself earnestly to the work of preaching the gospel; and this he did with eminent success. His going to Virginia was not of his own motion, but in compliance with the advice and desire of the Presbytery.

Before visiting Hanover, which was more especially to be the field of his labor, he visited Williamsburg, the seat of the Colonial Government, and petitioned the General Court to grant him "a license to officiate in and about Hanover at four meeting-houses." The court hesitated; but the Governor, the Honorable Wm. Gooch, favoring the application, the license was granted.

At this very time there were pending in this court suits against sundry members of the Presbyterian Church, for attending religious assemblies at unlicensed houses and listening to preachers who had not obtained from the General Court permission to preach. From an early date Episcopacy was established in Virginia, and the Church in this Province had been placed under the ecclesiastical jurisdiction of the Bishop of London, whose Commissary resided at Williamsburg, and was a member of the General Court, and also Rector or President of William and Mary College. The first Commissary, the Rev. John Blair, may be regarded as the founder of the College, as he more than any other person was instrumental in obtaining for it a royal charter, and also important grants both from the King and from the Colonial Legislature. Dr. William Dawson, the Commissary when Davies applied for his license, was a liberal-minded man, *for those times*, and he is believed to have voted in favor of granting the license sought. Yet it would seem from some of his correspondence with the Bishop of London that even he was somewhat disturbed at the success of Mr. Davies, and at the numerous additions to the Dissenters from the ranks of the conformists. Mr. Davies's labors were most arduous, and no one but a man of resolute will and of great natural resources could have done what he by the grace of God was stirred up to undertake and enabled to accomplish.

Having obtained his license, Mr. Davies went to Hanover, and was received with outbursts of joy. "His coming," says

Dr. Foote, "with his license was like a visit from an angel of mercy. His ardent sermons refreshed the congregation, and his legal protection turned the enmity of his opposers to their own mortification." He continued at Hanover several months.

Of his mission Mr. Davies thus writes: "I preached frequently in Hanover and some of the adjacent counties, and though the fervor of the work was considerably abated, and my labors were not blessed with success equal to that of my brethren, yet I have reason to hope they were of service in several instances. The importunities they used with me to settle with them were invincible; and upon my departure they sent a call for me to the Presbytery."

The death of his first wife, which occurred about this time, greatly depressed him: this, together with feeble health and threatening consumption, disinclined him to settle anywhere permanently as the pastor of a church; and he continued to travel and preach wherever a favorable opportunity presented itself. Dr. Gibbons, narrating the circumstances as he received them from Mr. Davies, says, " Finding himself upon the borders of the grave, and without any hopes of a recovery, he determined to spend the little remains of an almost exhausted life in endeavoring to advance his Master's glory in the good of souls. Accordingly, he removed from the place where he was to another about an hundred miles distance, that was then in want of a minister. Here he labored in season and out of season. And, as he told me, he preached in the day and had his hectic fever by night, and that to such a degree as to be sometimes delirious and to stand in need of persons to sit up with him." (See Dr. Gibbons's "Two Discourses, occasioned by the Death of President Davies." London, 1761.)

In the spring of 1748 " he began to recover, though he looked upon it only as the intermission of a disorder that would finally prove mortal. Many earnest applications were made for his pastoral services. The one from Hanover, signed by about one hundred and fifty heads of families, came with renewed importunity, and, aided by the voice of the living messenger despatched by the people to urge their call, moved his heart."

He accepted their call, "hoping," as he himself expresses it, "I might live to prepare the way for some more useful successor, and willing to expire under the fatigues of duty rather than in voluntary negligence."

"It is scarcely possible," says Dr. Foote, "for a missionary to have gone to Virginia in circumstances better calculated to make an impression in favor of the gospel which he preached. In his domestic afflictions and bodily weakness Davies felt the sentence of death gone out and already in execution. His soul burned with the desire of usefulness, and his tongue uttered the earnest persuasions of a spirit that would reconcile man to God, and lay some trophies at the Redeemer's feet, before his lips should be locked up in the grave. He longed to carry with him to the heavens some gems for the eternal crown. The people of Hanover were ready for an elevated spirit to lead them on through common and uncommon difficulties, through trials incident to all men, and the trials peculiar to their situation from the laws of the province, complaints, ridicule, indictments, fines, and heavy costs of court, to virtue and eternal life." (Foote's "Sketches of Virginia," page 163.)

In his second visit to Virginia he was accompanied by his fellow-student and earnest friend the Rev. John Rodgers, who later in life was minister of the Presbyterian churches in New York. But, not being able to obtain a license from the General Court, Mr. Rodgers tarried only for a short time, and Mr. Davies was left alone to minister to the Dissenters in Hanover and the adjacent counties. The different congregations or assemblies to which he ministered were scattered over a large district of country, not less than sixty miles in length, and the licensed places for preaching, of which there were seven, were, the nearest, twelve or fifteen miles apart. A license for Mr. Davies to preach, at a house to be erected for the purpose in the county of New Kent, granted by the court of that county, was revoked by the General Court, which claimed exclusive jurisdiction in this matter. The vexations to which Dissenters in Virginia were subjected at this time—a hundred and twenty-five years ago—would seem incredible were it not a thing of unquestionable record. As the religious teacher of his people, and also as the advocate and defender of their civil rights and religious liberties, Mr. Davies labored with untiring diligence. He preached with a power that attracted the attention of both friends and opponents; and before the court he maintained, in opposition to the Attorney-General of the Province, and with an ability which elicited the commendation of the members of the bar, the rights of the Dissenters in Virginia to all the concessions in the English Act of Toleration. He wrote to the well-known Dr. Doddridge, of England, and solicited and obtained his aid in bringing to the notice of the Bishop of London the hardships to which the Dissenters were subjected by what he regarded as the false interpretation given to the "Toleration Act" as in force in England and Wales. Dr. Doddridge's ill health prevented his pursuing the subject beyond sending to Mr. Davies the answer of the Bishop, and copies of some extracts from letters sent to the Bishop from the friends of Episcopacy in England.

To the Bishop's letter to Dr. Doddridge Mr. Davies prepared an elaborate reply, in which he argues at great length, and with much force, against the position assumed by the Bishop, and the charges insinuated against himself in the letters sent to his Lordship. This reply Mr. Davies sent to Mr. Mauduit, of London, to be communicated to Drs. Avery and Doddridge, leaving it to their discretion whether to forward it to the Bishop or not. Dr. Doddridge died before the letter reached England, and Dr. Avery and Mr. Mauduit decided against sending it; and Dr. Avery so informed Mr. Davies. The length of the letter he regarded as a serious objection to it, and one which he thought was sure to prevent its consideration, and even the reading of it, by the prelate to whom it was addressed. Another reason assigned by Dr. Avery for coming to the decision he did was the fact, that, in replying to a statement made by the Bishop, in his letter to Dr. Doddridge, that the non-conformists of New England were strongly opposed to the appointing of two or three Bishops for the Plantations, as those Provinces were then called, although the Bishops were to have no jurisdiction except over the clergy of their own Church, Mr. Davies says that in the Synod of which he is a member he never heard of an objection to the appointment of Bishops for the purpose mentioned in his Lordship's letter, and that he was extremely surprised at the information received by his Lordship concerning the reception of this proposal by the non-conformists in New England, and that they used all their influence to obstruct it. And Mr. Davies adds, " I never had the least intimation of it before, although some of the principal ministers maintain a very unreserved correspondence with me, and I have also the other usual methods of receiving intelligence from a country so near. If it be true, I think with your Lordship that it was hardly consistent with a spirit of toleration ;" and more in a like strain.

In writing to Mr. Davies the reasons why Mr. Mauduit and himself agreed that it was not advisable to send to his Lordship Mr. Davies's letter, Dr. Avery says:

" I shall not enter into any debate with you concerning the scheme proposed for erecting a Bishoprick in North America. The less said on that head, either on your side or on our side of the water, I believe the better. But one thing in yours, addressed to his lordship, greatly surprised me. You represent your friends in North America, particularly in New York, Virginia, and Massachusetts, as far as your correspondence reaches, if not as desiring, yet as willing to acquiesce, in having such an ecclesiastical superior officer sent over to America, with power to ordain, confirm, &c. Now all my accounts from Connecticut, the Jerseys, and Massachusetts directly and strongly contradict this. They uniformly speak of it as a measure quite inconsistent with their peace and tranquillity. From both the ministry and laity in these colonies I have received thanks for doing the little I did do, or could do, to prevent so sore a calamity as that seemed likely to prove to the colonies. These I have had from many quarters; and some of them expressed in strong and irritating terms. Yours to his lordship is the first letter I have seen from those parts expressing a desire, or so much as an indifference and coolness, on that head. This must be my excuse for not forwarding your letter to his lordship; though on several other accounts, on which I cannot enlarge, I should not have thought it proper to be put into his hands."

The admirable good sense and great modesty of Davies, as well as his truly catholic spirit, are manifest in his reply to Dr. Avery's letter informing him why his letter to the Bishop of London was not forwarded to that prelate, as will appear from the following extract :

" Since I received yours I have been uneasy lest my letter to his lordship should be put into his hands without your approbation, as my sentiments therein expressed, concerning the mission of bishops to North America, were different from yours in your letter to me. When I expressed my satisfaction in the proposal, I spake in the simplicity of my heart and according to my judgment, which I have had no reason to alter since, but only your dissent, in which I put implicit confidence, as you have better opportunities to discover the consequences of such missions than I. That the settlement of bishops in the dissenting colonies would be injurious to them I can easily see; but I find by the Bishop of London's letter to Dr. Doddridge that this was not proposed. And I was not able to discern what injury the settlement of a bishop in Virginia or Maryland, where the Church of England is established, would be to the few dissenters in them, and I was not without hopes it might tend to purge out the corrupt leaven from the established church, and restrain the clergy from their extravagances, who now behave as they please, and promise themselves impunity, as there is none to censure or depose them on this side of the Atlantic. However, dear sir, if you think me mistaken, you may take what measure you think proper to prevent any ill consequences that may be occasioned by the unreserved declaration of my opinion in my letter to his lordship. And as I shall hereafter impose upon you the trouble of rescinding and reviewing the papers I may find occasion to transmit to England on the affairs of the dissenters in Virginia, I not only allow, but request you, sir, to correct or suppress them as your superior judgment may direct you. As I judge the matter is of great importance to the interests of religion in this colony, I would not willingly incur guilt by omitting any means in my power to reflect light upon it; but for want of judgment and a more thorough acquaintance with the state of affairs in England, I may sometimes fail in the right choice or prudent use of means for that purpose, and therefore, to prevent any ill consequences, I must call in the assistance of your judgment and that of the Committee."

The committee here mentioned was one which was charged with the duty of looking after the interest of the Dissenters in all matters brought to the notice of the Government or Court. Of this committee, as appears from Mr. Davies's journal while he was in England, Dr. Avery was for thirty years or more a prominent and active member.

It was at this period, and not during Mr. Davies's visit to England, as has been said in some sketches of his life, that he obtained the opinion of Sir Dudley Ryder, the Attorney-General of England, sustaining his view of the rights of the Dissenters under the Toleration Act.* This legal opinion was obtained by Dr. Avery, chairman of the above-named committee, who sent a copy of it with the letter from which the above extract was

---

* It was Sir Dudley Ryder's opinion, that under the Act of Toleration Dissenters might ask for the licensure of as many houses as they thought necessary, without fear of refusal, and also that this interpretation of the Act extended to Virginia. Whereas the Governor and Council claimed the right to determine the number of houses of worship to be allowed the Dissenters. And the Bishop of London favored this claim of the civil authorities in that Province.

taken, in order that Mr. Davies might lay it before the Governor and Council of Virginia.

"Here," says Dr. Foote, "the matter rested till Mr. Davies visited England. After his return from England he received two letters from the committee. . . . . They show the interest taken in the cause of the Dissenters in Virginia by the Dissenters in England, and that all hope of redress from civil authority lay in an appeal to the King."

The labors of Mr. Davies challenge our admiration. They were in season and out of season. Not only did he watch for the spiritual good of his hearers, residents of Hanover and of four contiguous counties, preaching statedly at the seven different licensed houses, and carry on an extensive correspondence with prominent ministers at home and abroad, but he found time to attend the meetings of Presbytery and Synod, to make missionary tours in the counties of Cumberland, Powhatan, Prince Edward, Charlotte, Campbell, Nottaway, and Amelia, and thus prepare the way for the erection of churches in these counties, and to maintain, as we have seen, the religious liberties of his people against the bigotry and tyranny of their oppressors; and all this before attaining the age of thirty years.

The following extract, taken from one of his letters to Dr. Bellamy, and copied from Dr. Green's "Notes," gives no doubt the most reliable account of his pastoral labors during the first three years of his ministry in Virginia:

"In October, 1748, besides the four meeting-houses already mentioned, the people petitioned for the licensing of three more, which, with great difficulty, was obtained. Among these seven I have divided my time. Three of them lie in Hanover County, the other four in the counties of Henrico, Caroline, Louisa, and Goochland. The nearest are twelve or fifteen miles distant from each other, and the extremes about forty. My congregation is extremely dispersed; and notwithstanding the number of meeting-houses, some live twenty, some thirty, and a few forty miles from the nearest. Were they all compactly situated in one county, they would be sufficient to form three distinct congregations. Many of the church people also attend when there is a sermon at any of these houses. This I looked upon, at first, as mere curiosity after novelty; but as it continues, and in some places seems to increase, I cannot but look upon it as a happy token of their being at length thoroughly engaged. And I have the greater reason to hope so now, as experience has confirmed my former hopes; fifty or sixty families having thus been happily entangled in the net of the gospel by their own curiosity, or some such motive. There are three hundred communicants in my congregation, of whom the greatest number are, in the judgment of rational charity, real Christians; besides some who, through excessive scrupulousness, do not seek admission to the Lord's table.

"There is a number of Negroes, sometimes I see a hundred or more, among my hearers. I have baptized about forty of them within these three years, upon such a profession of faith as I then judged credible. Some of them, I fear, have apostatized, but others, I trust, will persevere to the end. I have had as satisfying evidence of the sincere piety of several of them as I ever had from any person in my life, and their artless simplicity, their passionate aspirations after Christ, their incessant endeavors to know and do the will of God, have charmed me. But, alas! while my charge is so extensive I cannot take sufficient pains with them for their instruction, which often oppresses my heart. There have been instances of unhappy apostasy among us; but, blessed be God, not many in proportion to the number brought under concern. At present there are a few under promising impressions, but in general security prevails," etc.

· "The home of Mr. Davies," says President Green, "was in the county of Hanover, about twelve miles from Richmond; but his occasional labors were extended through a considerable part of the Colony, and he acquired an influence greater, probably, than any other preacher of the gospel in Virginia ever possessed. It was the influence of fervent piety and zeal directed by a mind of uncommon compass and force. He took pains to instruct the negroes, and a considerable number of them were seals of his ministry. Till this day [1822] many of the descendants of his negro converts manifest the happy effects of the pious instructions and example of their parents."

In the autumn of 1752 the Synod of New York held their sessions at Newark, New Jersey, the day after the College Commencement. Mr. Davies was present at the meetings of the Synod, and on this occasion he met President Edwards, who was on a visit to his son-in-law, the Rev. Aaron Burr. Writing to a gentleman in Scotland under the date of November 24 of that year, Mr. Edwards says, "When I was lately in New Jersey, in the time of the Synod there, . . . I then had the comfort of a short interview with Mr. Davies, of Virginia, and was much pleased with him and his conversation. He appears to be a man of very solid understanding, discreet in his behavior, and polished and gentlemanly in his manners, as well as fervent and zealous in religion." High praise from a high source! No doubt this interview confirmed the exalted opinion Mr. Davies had of the great talents, learning, and piety of Mr. Edwards,* and increased his desire that Mr. Edwards

---

* In his farewell sermon to his people in Hanover he speaks of Edwards "as the profoundest reasoner and the greatest divine that America has ever produced."

upon leaving Northampton should remove to Virginia, and to effect which he labored with his wonted promptness and assiduity. But Mr. Edwards removed to Stockbridge, Massachusetts, and his connection there with the Indian missions prevented his entertaining the earnest solicitation of Mr. Davies and his friends, that he should come to Virginia and settle there, where adequate provision for the support of himself and family was promised, and, we may add, was virtually secured.

In the account given of President Burr's administration, chapter vi., mention was made of the fact that, at the request of the Trustees of the College, the Rev. Messrs. Gilbert Tennent and Davies visited Great Britain and Ireland to solicit funds in aid of the College, and more especially for the erection of suitable buildings for the accommodation of the officers and the students. Mention was also made of the great success of their mission, whereby ample funds were obtained for the erection of the edifice known as "Nassau Hall," and for the building of the President's house, and the foundation of the charitable fund of the College, which by several bequests in later times was much augmented, and has done a great work in opening the way for the liberal education of poor and pious young men who were willing and even desirous to devote themselves to the gospel ministry. Of these matters we shall not here speak further; but of Mr. Davies's visit to England and Scotland, of his preaching, and of the numerous and valuable acquaintances formed by him while abroad, and of the deep impression which he made upon the minds of those with whom he came into contact, it is both proper and just that something should be said in a sketch like this.

Having agreed to accompany Mr. Tennent in this agency in behalf of the College, in case the Synod of New York should approve of his so doing, Mr. Davies left Hanover on Monday, the 3d of September, 1753, to attend the sessions of the Synod of New York, to be held in the city of Philadelphia, in the early part of October, and that he might have an opportunity to confer with the College authorities and to make the requisite preparations for his voyage to England. His memorandum under the date of September 3, 1753, is in these words:

"This morning I felt the painful rupture of the tender relative ties which bind me to Hanover. I took my leave of some thousands yesterday in public, and to-day I parted with some select friends, and my dear, dear spouse, my honored parents, and three helpless children, and left them in tears. To thee, O Lord, I then solemnly committed them, and now I renew the dedication. I know not that I shall ever see them again, but my life and theirs are in the hands of Divine Providence, and therefore shall be preserved as long as is fit," etc.

On his way to Philadelphia and Newark, Mr. Davies spent several days at the house of his friend, and his successor in the office of President of the College, the Rev. Samuel Finley, who was then residing at Nottingham, Maryland. Here he met a committee of his Presbytery, and in conjunction with Messrs. Finley, Roan, and (Robert) Smith, revised and corrected a draft drawn up by Mr. (John) Blair, of a warning or testimony of the Presbytery of New Castle (New Side) against several errors and evil practices of Mr. John Cuthbertson, a native of Scotland.*

The five members of the Presbytery here mentioned all became men of note; and it is worthy of remark that two of them, viz., Davies and Finley, were, some years after, Presidents of the College of New Jersey, that Mr. Blair was the first prominent Vice-President and Professor in the College, and that Dr. Robert Smith was the father of the Rev. Dr. S. S. Smith, the seventh President of the College. From Nottingham he went to Fagg's Manor to see Mrs. Blair, the widow of the Rev. Samuel Blair, his venerated teacher, under whose guidance he was prepared for the office of the holy ministry, and of whom he speaks in this connection as "the great Mr. Blair," and elsewhere as "the incomparable Mr. Blair." On the 15th of September he reached Philadelphia, and was kindly received by Mr. Tennent and his other friends there. Upon visiting his dear and valuable friend Captain Grant of that city, he was

---

* The errors on which the Presbytery animadvert are these: "That God has made over Christ and all his benefits to all that hear the gospel by a deed of gift (as he affects to speak), so that every sinner that hears the gospel offer ought to put in a claim of right to him as his Saviour in particular. That saving faith consists in a persuasion that Christ is *mine*, and that he died for *me* in *particular*. That redemption is universal as to purchase. That civil government, both heathen and Christian, is derived from Christ as mediator."

shown a letter received by that gentleman from Mr. De Berdt, of London, in which was the following sentence :

"That the principles inculcated in the College of New Jersey are generally looked upon as antiquated and unfashionable by the Dissenters in England." "A dismal omen," adds Mr. Davies, "to our embassy, and, I fear, to the interests of religion."

He reached Newark on the following Thursday, "and was received with much affection by the worthy President," and was honored with a visit and with free conversation with his Excellency the Governor, and on the next day he waited on Governor Belcher, at Elizabethtown, in company with President Burr and his lady. The Governor treated him with marked attention, and insisted upon his preaching for Mr. Spencer, pastor of the church in that town, which he did on Sunday, the 30th of September. On the preceding Sabbath he preached twice in Newark; and he also heard President Burr preach a farewell sermon to the candidates for a degree at the Commencement to take place on Wednesday of that week. Mr. Burr's text was, "And now, my son, the Lord be with thee and prosper thee." "And I was amazed," says Mr. Davies, "to see how readily good sense and accurate language flowed from him extempore. The sermon was affecting to me, and might have been to the students."

On Commencement-day Mr. Davies delivered a thesis (Personales Distinctiones in Trinitate sunt æternæ), and vindicated it against the opponents, and afterwards was honored with the degree of Master of Arts.

While in Newark, he spent a part of his time in drawing up a petition from the Synod of New York to the General Assembly of the Church of Scotland. Upon leaving Newark, he visited New York, and Elizabethtown, took leave of Governor Belcher, lodged at the house of the Rev. John Brainerd, who had succeeded his brother, David Brainerd, as a missionary among the Indians, at or near Cranbury, and visited the Indian town or settlement. He then proceeded to Philadelphia, to attend the Synod, which convened in that city on Wednesday, the 3d of October. On Friday evening he heard Mr.. Bostwick preach, and inserts in his journal this remark respecting him: "He has, I think, the best style extempore of any man I ever heard."*

Mr. Davies preached several times in Philadelphia, and occasionally in neighboring places, while waiting for the sailing of the vessel in which he and his associate, the Rev. Gilbert Tennent, were to take their passage. And during this period he found time to attend a meeting of his Presbytery at Fagg's Manor, and to visit his intimate friend the Rev. John Rodgers, at St. George's, Delaware. The delay in the sailing of the vessel was a severe trial to his patience, and the more so from the circumstance that it was probable that it would add much to the discomforts of the voyage, which proved to be the case. The pilot did not leave the ship until the afternoon of the 18th of November, and it was not until the 25th of December that the fellow-voyagers reached the city of London. The vessel having ascended the Thames, they landed near London bridge, and were conducted to the house of Mr. De Berdt, the gentleman named above as a correspondent of Captain Grant, of Philadelphia, and of whom Mr. Davies says in his journal that he "is a most amiable, pious gentleman, and entertained us very kindly till we could provide a lodging."

Mr. Whitefield very promptly and kindly invited them to make his house their home; but upon consultation with some other friends they deemed it expedient to decline his generous offer, and to take lodgings and board in a private boarding-house; which they did. Not only by this eminent preacher but by sundry other of the leading non-conformists were they courteously received and entertained. Prominent among these were the Rev. Mr. Stennet, of the Baptist Church, to whose kind offices they were indebted for much of their success in London; the Rev. Mr. Gibbons, minister of the Independent congregation at Haberdashers' Hall, and Mr. Davies's correspondent, and who upon the death of Mr. Davies published a volume of his sermons, with a sketch of the author's life.

---

* Mr. Bostwick was at this time minister of the Presbyterian church of Jamaica, Long Island, and in 1755 he removed to the city of New York and took charge of the Presbyterian church in that city. In 1761 he was chosen a Trustee of the College of New Jersey, and held this office till his death.

Of these two distinguished preachers Mr. Davies makes frequent mention, expressive of his high respect, and of his great indebtedness to them. In his "Diary," under the date of January 8, 1754, a fortnight after his arrival in London, he makes this entry:

"Dined at Mr. Eleazer Edwards's, . . . of the Baptist persuasion. Here we enjoyed Mr. Stennet's company, and his son's. He is a judicious, prudent, and candid gentleman, and has more influence in court than any dissenting minister in London. Mr. Tennent having visited Mr. Partridge, the Agent of Pennsylvania, was advised to apply to some of the court, particularly to the Lord Chancellor, Lord Halifax, and Mr. Pelham [the Prime Minister], and he seemed inclined to do it. But to me it appeared very doubtful; I was afraid, in case the College should be discountenanced by them, they would find some flaw in the charter, and so overset it; and that a refusal at court would have a bad influence upon those who otherwise might contribute towards it. We consulted Mr. Stennet, and he was fully of my mind."

Mr. Stennet accompanied Messrs. Tennent and Davies to the Duke of Argyle's when they went to deliver to his Grace the letter for him given to them by Governor Belcher. The Duke having advised them to call upon Lord Halifax, or Lord Duplin, both of whom were members of the Board of Trade and Plantations, Mr. Stennet went for them to Lord Duplin and consulted him in confidence, and his Lordship assured Mr. Stennet that he would do nothing to their injury.

On the day after their arrival in London they were visited, says Mr. Davies, "by a venerable old gentleman, Mr. Hall, author of some of the 'Lime Street Sermons,' who seems to be of a true puritanic spirit and full of religion;" by Mr. Gibbons, "my dear correspondent, who informed us of the general apostasy of the Dissenters from the principles of the Reformation;" and by "good Mr. Cruttenden, who sent me over ten pound sterling worth of books to be distributed among the poor in Virginia."*

---

* This last-named gentleman, Mr. Robert Cruttenden, the Rev. Richard Webster thinks (see note to page 557 of his History) was *probably* the friend who suggested to Mr. Davies, after his return from England, a plan for obtaining, if practicable, some three or four young Africans, who still retained their native language, were pious, and of good abilities, to be educated at the College of New Jersey for missionaries. Whether Mr. Davies availed himself of this suggestion is not known. But nearly twenty years after, the well-known Dr. Samuel Hopkins, a pupil of the Rev. Jonathan Edwards, and his first biographer, adopted a like scheme, and in

In the prosecution of their work they called upon all or nearly all the Dissenting ministers in London and its vicinity, and in general they were kindly received and encouraged, although not a few of these ministers had no sympathy whatever with Messrs. Tennent and Davies in their religious views and feelings, being tainted with anti-Calvinistic and latitudinarian principles. The diversity of views among the Dissenters was a source of no small embarrassment to these agents of the College; and on this head Mr. Davies makes this remark:

"There are so many parties here that it is very perplexing to us to know how to behave so as to avoid offence, and not to injure the business of our embassy. The Independents and Baptists are more generally Calvinists than the Presbyterians, though I fear some of them are tainted with Antinomianism."

By Mr. Chandler, a Presbyterian minister of much note, they were advised to represent, in their petition for the College, that it would be of use "to keep a sense of religion among the German Protestant emigrants settled in the British plantations, to instruct their children in the principles of our common Christianity, and to instruct them in the knowledge of the English language, that they may be incorporated with the rest of his Majesty's subjects." Mr. Davies adds, "Mr. T. approved of the addition, but I could not help scrupling it, because the College is not immediately intended to teach the English language; but I submitted." They finally, however, determined to "soften the terms in the clause about the German Protestants." On the day following that of their call upon Mr. Chandler, viz., on January 19, 1754, they "were sent for by a company of lords and gentlemen who have the disposal of the money lately given by the King for the support of schools among the Germans in Pennsylvania." "Mr. Chandler," adds Mr. Davies, "who is the Company's Secretary, introduced our affairs, and our petition

---

conjunction with the Rev. Dr. Ezra Stiles, afterwards President of Yale, formed the design to prepare two African youths, members of his church in Newport, Rhode Island, for preaching the gospel in Western Africa. That they might be prepared for their missionary work, it was judged expedient to send them to Princeton, New Jersey, to be for a season under the tuition of the Rev. Dr. Witherspoon. How long they continued here, and what proficiency they made in their studies, are matters respecting which we have no record. (See Dr. Alexander's "History of Colonization," pages 48–523.)

was read.   There was no time to consider it, and it was deferred
until their next meeting." It does not appear that the petition
was ever again brought before them for consideration; but Mr.
Chandler himself gave it his countenance and recommendation,
as did some sixty or more of the Dissenting ministers, including Baptists, Independents, and Presbyterians.   Among these
are some of the well-known scholars of that day,—*e.g.*, Rev.
Drs. Lardner, Jennings, Guyse, Benson, Price, and Milner.   The
Rev. Dr. Samuel Chandler, spoken of above as the Rev. Mr.
Chandler, was an eminent scholar, and he had the happiness to
number among his pupils Archbishop Secker and Bishop Butler.   His sermons were published in four volumes quarto, and
as early as 1725 he published his "Vindication of the Christian
Religion."

There was danger at one time that Mr. Chandler would dis-
countenance the efforts of Messrs. Tennent and Davies, a copy
of Mr. Tennent's famous Nottingham Sermon having been
placed in his hand, with this very end in view, through the
agency of a member of the Synod of Philadelphia.   But upon
receiving a full explanation of all the facts, Mr. Chandler signed
their petition.   Messrs. Tennent and Davies waited also upon
Mr. Penn, the Proprietor of Pennsylvania, and were kindly received by him ; but he gave them no encouragement, regarding
himself as under peculiar obligations to favor the Academy in
Philadelphia.   From a Mr. Cromwell, a great-grandson of the
Protector, Mr. Davies received three guineas for the College.
Messrs. Tennent and Davies, while yet in London, dined with
the Marquis of Lothian, and at dinner met Lord Leven, the
King's Commissioner and representative at the sessions of the
General Assembly of the Kirk of Scotland.   These noblemen
favored their mission and encouraged them in their work.

Mr. Davies was frequently invited to preach by the Dissenting
ministers of London, and he was repeatedly urged to prepare a
volume of his sermons for publication, which he tells us he had
serious thoughts of doing.   An anecdote has been very current
in the United States to the purport that on one occasion his
Majesty George the Second heard Mr. Davies preach, and
that he was so delighted with the eloquence of the speaker as

to express aloud his approval, and to call down upon himself a reproof for his interruption of .the service ; and that by invitation Mr. Davies waited upon the King and received from him a handsome donation for the College.   There is not the least foundation for this story.   His " Diary" shows beyond all doubt that Mr. Davies never saw his Majesty, and that he had no desire to see him or the members of his court, lest inquiry should be made respecting the validity of the charter given to the College by Governor Belcher, and the character of the charter essentially altered, if not totally suppressed.

Upon leaving London, Messrs. Tennent and Davies went directly to Edinburgh, where they met with a very kind reception from all classes, clergy and laity, nobles and commoners.

In their application to the General Assembly of the Church of Scotland they were successful beyond all expectation.   On Monday, the 27th of May, their petition was received by the Assembly, and it was agreed to without an objection from any one.   Their cause was ably advocated by Mr. Lumsden, Professor of Theology at Aberdeen, who, without any conference with either Mr. Tennent or Mr. Davies, urged that it was the duty of the Assembly to promote such institutions as the College of New Jersey, and especially among the Presbyterians in the Colonies.   Mr. Lumsden was seconded by Mr. McLagan, and a committee was appointed to draw up an act and a recommendation for a national collection.   Of this committee Mr. McLagan was a member.

" The approbation of the General Assembly," says Mr. Davies, in his " Diary," May 27, 1754, "will be attended with many happy consequences; particularly it will recommend our College to the world, and wipe off the odium from the Synod of New York as a parcel of schismatics."

The action of the Assembly was the more pleasing to Messrs. Tennent and Davies, from the circumstance that special pains had been taken by one or more of the members of the Synod of Philadelphia to excite a prejudice against their mission by means of a letter written for this very purpose, and by the distribution of copies of Mr. Tennent's Nottingham Sermon.   Mr. Tennent and Mr. Davies waited also upon the Society for Propagating Christian Knowledge, of which the Marquis of

Lothian was the President, and at the request of the Society gave them their advice as to the best method of conducting the mission among the Indians. The members of the Society also drew up a letter in favor of the College of New Jersey, to be annexed to the Act of the General Assembly. On the same day Messrs. Tennent and Davies dined with his Grace the Lord Commissioner.

From Mr. Davies's journal, it appears that he preached in several of the principal churches of Edinburgh, and to very crowded auditories, having among his hearers on one occasion the Lord Provost and the Magistrates of the city. He preached three times in the College Kirk, and evidently with much acceptance, and to the profit of not a few of his hearers. He had every reason to be pleased with his reception in Edinburgh, and we are not surprised at his remark,—

" I met with more Christian friendship in Edinburgh than anywhere in Great Britain. There is too general a decay of experimental and practical religion, and yet there is a considerable number of pious people in the City." (Davies's Journal, June 15, 1754.)

Under the same date with the above he adds:

" I find a great number of the clergy and laity have of late carried church power to an extravagant height, deny to individuals the right of judging for themselves, and insist upon absolute universal obedience to all the determinations of the General Assembly. I heard several speeches in the House on this head which really surprised me. The nobility and gentry, who are lay elders, are generally high-flyers, and have encroached upon the rights of the people, especially in the choice of their ministers. Violent settlements are enjoined by the authority of the General Assembly, and there is no prospect of redress. There is a Piece published, under the title of ' The Ecclesiastical Characteristics,' ascribed to one Mr. Weatherspoon [Witherspoon], a young minister. It is a burlesque upon the high-flyers, under the name of *moderate men*, and I think the humor is nothing inferior to Dean Swift."

It never occurred to Mr. Davies while penning the above sentence that this " one Mr. Weatherspoon" would ever have any connection with the College of New Jersey, much less that they would both be Presidents of it ; and yet within fifteen years from this time they both were,—Mr. Davies from 1759 to 1761, and Mr. Witherspoon from 1768 to 1794.

After spending a month or more at Edinburgh, Mr. Tennent

left for Ireland, to present the cause of the College to the Irish
Presbyterian Synod, and Mr. Davies went on a visit to Glasgow, where he was kindly received and hospitably entertained.
The freedom of the city was presented to him, and at the same
time it was conferred upon Mr. Tennent and Mr. President Burr,
although they were not there.   Mr. Davies tarried at Glasgow
about ten days, and preached there six times.   He formed firm
friendships with some of the leading ministers of that city, and
more especially with Mr. Gillies,—afterwards the Rev. Dr. Gillies,
—by whom some of his letters to his English and Scotch correspondents were preserved and published.   Upon the decease
of the Rev. Mr. McLaurin, another of his Glasgow friends, he
made in his " Diary" the following entry : " That city has lost
one of its brightest ornaments, the Church of Scotland one of
its most excellent ministers, and the College of New Jersey one
of its best friends."   The attentions which were paid to him in
Glasgow were owing, no doubt, in part to the circumstance that
Governor Dinwiddie, of Virginia, without Mr. Davies's knowledge, had kindly commended him to his brother, the Provost of
the city, and to his brother-in-law, the Rev. Mr. McCulloh, at
Cambuslang.   This gentleman, "an humble, holy minister of
Christ," as Mr. Davies calls him, had a conversation with Mr.
Davies about a donation of two hundred pounds for propa-
gating the gospel among the Indians.

Mr. Davies also visited the Rev. John Erskine, of Culross,
afterwards the Rev. Dr. Erskine, of Grey Friars' Church, Edinburgh.   This distinguished divine took a lively interest in the
welfare of the College, and revised and prepared for the press a
sermon of Mr. Davies's on 1 John ii. 2, and published it, with a
preface in favor of the College, which, says Mr. Davies, "has
already had happy effects in Braintree, and excited sundry to
double their intended benefactions."   At the place named resided
Mr. Samuel Ruggles, a gentleman of wealth and of great liberality, who first subscribed thirty pounds to the fund for the College, and who subsequently increased his subscription and made
it fifty pounds.

Upon his way from Edinburgh to London, Mr. Davies stopped
at Durham, and waited upon his Lordship the Bishop of that

diocese. This right reverend prelate, the immediate successor of the eminent scholar Bishop Butler, "gave me," says Mr. Davies, "a condescending reception. He particularly inquired whether the Church of England had any share in the management of the College, complained of the intolerant principles of the Dissenters in New England, asked me if I had waited upon the Archbishop of Canterbury, or obtained the consent of the Society for Propagating the Gospel in Foreign Parts, and told me until I had done so he could not in a public character do anything in favor of the design. But he gave me five guineas as a private person; which afforded me no small satisfaction, as it may open the door for further benefactions in the Established Church." But it did not.

Mr. Davies also visited Norwich and several of the other larger towns and cities in England. He reached London on the 1st of October, and found there a letter from Mr. Tennent, informing him that Mr. Tennent, having finished his applications in the west of England, intended to come to London as soon as possible, to prepare to embark for America.

"The prospect of so speedy a return gave me," says Mr. Davies, "no small pleasure; but the prospect of a winter passage was very shocking, especially as I had such a melancholy time in my last voyage, and in the present diffident state of my mind I am not a little intimidated at the dangers of the ocean."

Nor is his state of mind at all surprising, in view of the perils then attending a voyage across the Atlantic in midwinter. Among the reasons urged by the friends of Episcopacy in America for the consecration of one or more Bishops in this country was the loss of life on the part of the candidates who went to England to be admitted to orders by the Bishop of London. The Rev. Dr. Thomas Bradbury Chandler, in his Appeal, asserts that one-fifth of all who had gone to England for ordination, up to 1767, had died of disease or had been lost at sea.

Mr. Tennent left London on the 13th of November, in a vessel going directly to Philadelphia. Mr. Davies sailed on Friday, the 15th of the same month. The reasons for not returning home in the same vessel are briefly given by Mr. Davies in his "Diary," under the date of November 18: "The impossibility of getting the Trustees together, and of my travelling home by land from Philadelphia, determined me, with Mr. Tennent's consent, to deny myself the pleasure of his company and sail directly for Virginia, that I may the sooner see my earthly all at home." After a long and tempestuous voyage, he arrived at York, Virginia, on the 13th of February, 1755, and reached his own home on Saturday, the 15th of that month, "and found all well. What shall I render to the Lord for all his goodness ?"

The above recital gives a succinct view of Mr. Davies's labors and of his success in fulfilling the duties of his mission in behalf of the College ; but it gives no intimation of his anxieties and trials occasioned by his long and painful separation from his family, to which he often refers in expressions of earnest feeling. Nor has any mention been made of the sudden and threatening attacks, superinduced, doubtless, by his untiring and arduous labors, one of which, an apoplectic fit, as it was regarded by the physician in attendance, came very near terminating his life, during his visit to the city of Norwich, in the month of September, 1754.

The sums of money collected by Messrs. Tennent and Davies, although far exceeding the most sanguine expectations of themselves and of the Trustees, are by no means the full measure of their services to the College and to the interests of religion and learning in the American Colonies. Their mission added much to the reputation and the usefulness of the College, and turned the attention of not a few persons of influence and of wealth to the great importance of promoting Christian education among all classes in this country. Their preaching, and more especially the preaching of Mr. Davies, attracted much attention, and doubtless was productive of much good. In the course of the eleven months which Mr. Davies spent in England and Scotland he preached sixty or seventy times, and he was earnestly solicited, in conversation and by letters, to publish some of these discourses.

While he diligently and successfully prosecuted the work of collecting funds for the College, he at the same time availed himself of every opportunity to further the interests of his Dis-

senting friends in Virginia, and to secure for them all the privileges conferred by the Act of Toleration upon Dissenters in
England. The hope that he might accomplish something in
this line was a strong inducement with him to accede to the
proposal of the Trustees that he should accompany Mr. Tennent to Britain. And the last thing which he did before leaving
London was to call upon Dr. Avery, Mr. Mauduit, Dr. Stennet,
and others with the petition sent to him from Virginia, in reference to the rights of the Dissenters there under the English
Act of Toleration, and to solicit their aid in this matter which
he had so much at heart. At his earnest request these gentlemen promised their assistance; nor were they unmindful of their
engagement. They conferred with the committee of the depu-
tation of Protestant Dissenters in regard to the expediency of
presenting the petition to the King in Council, and it was
deemed imprudent to present it at that time. The committee
gave it as their advice that the Dissenters in Virginia should
apply first to the County Court; and if refused, then to the Governor and Council; and if refused by them, to use the house for
which a license had been sought, as if it had been licensed; and
if prosecuted for so doing, to let the committee know. At the
same time the committee sent them private instructions, in case
any persons should be prosecuted for using such unlicensed
houses, that they should appeal to the King in Council, and the
committee engaged to prosecute the appeal. But no appeal
was ever made. By the time Mr. Davies returned home, the
state of public affairs in Virginia was so much changed, in consequence of the incursions of the French and of the Indians
upon the western frontiers, that the Colonial Government, which
depended in no small degree upon the aid of the Dissenters to
repel these hostile aggressions, had less time and probably less
inclination to molest these loyal men, who were ready to lay
down their lives, if need be, in defence of their country. Mr.
Davies was among the foremost in urging upon his friends the
duty of taking up arms in defence of their King and of their
homes; which, under the influence of his powerful appeals, they
promptly did, and in large numbers.

In a note to a sermon preached on the 17th of August, 1755,

to the first volunteer company raised in Virginia after Braddock's defeat, occur these words :

"I may point out to the public that heroic youth, Col. Washington, whom I cannot but hope Providence has hitherto preserved in so signal a manner for some important service." Washington was then in the twenty-fourth year of his age. By his prudence and courage he had rescued from destruction the remnant of Braddock's army.

About this time, too, the Established clergy became involved in a controversy with the Legislature with respect to the payment of their stipends of sixteen thousand pounds of tobacco, "whether they should be paid in kind or at an estimated value." "While this contest waxed hotter and hotter, Dissenters of different names," says Dr. Foote, "multiplied, and the rigor of the courts relaxed. This unadvised proceeding of the clergy did more for the Dissenters than all their appeals to natural and constitutional law had been able to accomplish."   The Revolution of 1776 put an end to all the restraints to which the Dissenters had been subjected by the laws of Virginia, and gave them that perfect freedom in all matters of religion for which Mr. Davies so long and so earnestly contended. But amidst all his labors in defence of civil and religious liberty, he never forgot that his chief business was to preach the gospel; and this he continued to do most diligently to all classes, rich and poor, white and black.

In December, 1755, the Presbytery of Hanover was formed, and of this Presbytery Mr. Davies was the first Moderator.   It comprised all the Presbyterian ministers in Virginia and North Carolina, with their respective charges.   "Of the whole Dissenting interests in these two colonies, Mr. Davies," says President Green, "was the animating soul. He made his influence felt everywhere; he transfused his spirit into the bosoms of his associates, and roused them by the force of his example. His popularity in Virginia was almost unbounded; so that he was invited and urged to preach in almost all the settled portions of that colony."

Three years and a half after his return from England, Mr. Davies was chosen President of the College of New Jersey.

By the advice of his Presbytery he declined this invitation; but subsequently, with the approval of the Synod, he accepted the office upon a tender of it a second time; and he entered upon its duties on the 26th of July, 1759.

In the sketch given of his administration, it was shown that his career, though short, was brilliant, and that the highest hopes were entertained by the friends of the College that his direction of its affairs would be attended with the happiest results. But these hopes were doomed to a sudden and unexpected disappointment; and it is by no means improbable that his constant and earnest devotion to his official duties served to undermine his strength, and caused him to succumb the more readily to the fever of which he died.

"Towards the close of January, 1761," says President Green, "he was seized with a bad cold, for which he was bled. The same day he transcribed for the press his sermon on the death of George the Second.* The day following he preached twice in the College Chapel. The arm in which he had been bled—surely for a reason sufficiently obvious—became much inflamed, and his febrile disposition was much increased. On the morning of the succeeding Monday he was seized, while at breakfast, with violent chills, succeeded by an inflammatory fever, which in ten days terminated his life." "The violence of his disease deprived him of the exercise of his reason through most of his sickness, . . . and even in his delirium he manifested what were the objects which chiefly occupied his mind. His faltering tongue was continually uttering some expedient to promote the prosperity of the Church of Christ and the good of mankind."

He died on the 4th of February, 1761, in the thirty-eighth year of his age.

A sermon on the occasion of his death was preached in London on the 29th of March, by his friend and correspondent, the Rev. Dr. Thomas Gibbons; and another at Princeton on the 28th of May, by the Rev. Dr. Samuel Finley. (Sprague's "Annals.") The one by Dr. Finley was printed at the request of the Trustees; and it was republished in London by Dr. Gibbons, in connection with his own sermon. Both these discourses were prefixed to the first volume of Mr. Davies's sermons, edited by Dr. Gibbons. The Rev. David Bostwick, of New York, another intimate friend, who had been intrusted with the printing of President Davies's sermon on the death of

---

* This sermon was preached by Mr. Davies in the College Chapel, January 14.

George the Second, wrote a preface to this sermon, " in which the talents, piety, and usefulness of Mr. Davies were exhibited, and eulogized with much warmth." (President Green's Sketches.) These were the first tributes of respect to the memory of this remarkable man and most eloquent preacher ; but they are not the only ones. Memoirs of President Davies have been given to the public by the Rev. Dr. John Rice, of Virginia, in his " Literary and Evangelical Magazine ;" by the Rev. Dr. Green, in his Sketch of the College ; Rev. Dr. Allen, in his " Biographical Dictionary ;" Rev. Dr. Foote, in his " Sketches of Virginia ;" Rev. Dr. Sprague, in his "Annals of the American Pulpit ;" and Rev. Albert Barnes, in a preface to the third New York edition of Davies's sermons. Mention of him and of his writings is made in Middleton's " Biographia Evangelica," in Allibone's "Dictionary of Authors," and in other publications.

Distinguished as he was in various respects, he was pre-eminent in the pulpit, of which fact the great demand for his published sermons is sufficient evidence were there none other. Before the close of the last century not less than nine editions were printed in England. (See Dr. Green's Sketches of the College.) And the publishers of the first stereotyped edition in this country tell us that in 1842, "notwithstanding four large American editions have been published, the book is entirely out of the market." Fifty years ago—viz., in 1822— Dr. Green remarked, "Probably there are no sermons in the English language which have been more read, or for which there has been so steady and unceasing a demand for more than half a century." And to this remark he justly and wisely adds the following criticism :

" They are certainly not distinguished for minute accuracy of language, or those terse periods which many later compositions of the same kind possess. Nor can they, in all their parts, be vindicated from the charge of something that appears loose, tumid, and declamatory. The general run of the sentences, however, is harmonious ; and they everywhere contain so much just thinking, such powerful reasonings, such pungent addresses to the conscience and the heart, with such an unction of piety, and such a popularity of manner, as may well account for the favorable reception they have met with. The reader soon ceases to attend to anything but the subject discussed, and is carried delightfully along by the powerful charm of genius and piety in happy union."

The following is a list of President Davies's published works as given by Dr. Sprague in his "Annals of the American Pulpit":

"A sermon on Man's Primitive State, 1748. 'The State of Religion among the Protestant Dissenters in Virginia, in a Letter to the Rev. Joseph Bellamy,' 1751. A sermon preached before the Presbytery of New Castle, 1752. A sermon preached at the installation of the Rev. John Todd, 1752. 'Religion and Patriotism, the Constituents of a Good Soldier:' a sermon preached before a company of volunteers, 1755. 'Virginia's Danger and Remedy:' two discourses occasioned by the severe drought, and the defeat of General Braddock, 1755. Letters showing the State of Religion in Virginia, particularly among the Negroes, 1755–1757. A sermon on the Vessels of Mercy and the Vessels of Wrath, 1757. A Sermon on Little Children invited to Jesus Christ, 1757. 'The Curse of Cowardice:' a sermon before the militia of Virginia, 1758. A Valedictory Discourse to the Senior Class in the College of New Jersey, 1760. A sermon on the Death of George II., 1761. He was also the author of several important documents of a public nature, and various hymns and other pieces of poetry of no small degree of merit.

"A collection of his sermons, including most of those which had been printed in his lifetime, was published after his death, in three volumes octavo."

To the above list may be added a sermon on John ii. 2, revised and edited by the Rev. Dr. Erskine, of Scotland, from the manuscript notes of Mr. Davies, furnished by himself, 1754; his "Diary" or journal of his mission to England, from July 2, 1753, to February 13, 1755, given in Dr. Foote's "Sketches of Virginia;" also sundry letters, including those to Dr. Doddridge, the Bishop of London, and Dr. Avery, respecting the condition of the Dissenters in Virginia. The sermon before the Presbytery of New Castle, 1752, was on Isaiah lxii. 1; and when he was in England he was urged by friendly ministers and others in various parts of Great Britain to give this sermon a second edition, which in his "Diary," September 28, 1754, he expresses his purpose to do.

In his "Notes," published in 1822, President Green makes the following mention of the family of President Davies:

"Of the family left by President Davies the writer is able to give but little information. The funeral sermon preached by Dr. Finley is dedicated to Mrs. Martha Davies, the mother, and Mrs. Jean Davies, the widow, of the late President Davies. Of his widow, it is only known that she returned to her friends in Virginia, and remained there till her death. Her eldest son, Colonel William Davies, was educated at Nassau Hall, and graduated in 1765. He studied law, and settled at Norfolk, in Virginia. In the Revolutionary War he obtained the rank of a Colonel in the American Army, was an officer of distinguished merit, and possessed in an eminent degree the esteem and confidence of the commander-in-chief, the illustrious Washington. He was well known to the writer [Dr. Green], and was unquestionably a man of powerful mind, highly cultivated, and enriched by various knowledge. He died in Virginia a few years since. John Rodgers Davies was also educated at Nassau Hall, and graduated in 1769. He likewise studied the law. Samuel Davies, the third son, was settled in Petersburg, and died there several years ago.* His mother, Mrs. Martha Davies, made a part of the President's family at the time of his death. The writer [President Green] has been well informed that when the corpse of her son was laid in the coffin, she stood over it, in the presence of a number of friends, for some minutes, viewing it attentively, and then said, 'There is the son of my prayers and my hopes,—my only son,—my only earthly support. But there is the will of God, and I am satisfied.' This eminent saint was received into the family of the Rev. Dr. Rodgers, of New York, and by him was treated with the utmost kindness and veneration till the time of her death."

President Davies was buried by the side of President Edwards, and over his remains the following inscription was placed:

Sub Hoc Marmore sepulchrali,
Mortales Exuviæ
Reverendi perquam Viri,
Samuelis Davies, A.M.
Collegii Nov-Cæsariensis Præsidis,
Futurum Domini Adventum præstolantur.
Ne te, Viator, ut pauca de tanto
Tamque dilecto Viro resciscas,
Paulisper morari pigeat.
Natus est in Comitatu de Newcastle, juxta Delaware,
III Novembris, Anno Salutis reparatæ,
MDCCXXIV. S. V.
Sacris ibidem initiatus, XIX Februarii,
MDCCXLVII.
Tutelam pastoralem Ecclesiæ
In Comitatu de Hanover, Virginiensium, suscepit,
Ibi per XI plus minus Annos,
Ministri Evangelici Laboribus
Indefesse, et favente Numine, auspicato perfunctus.
Ad Munus Præsidiale Collegii Nov-Cæsariensis gerendum
Vocatus est, et inauguratus, XXVI Julii,
MDCCLIX S. N.
Sed, proh Rerum inane! intra Biennium, Febre correptus,
Candidam Animam Cœlo reddidit, IV Februarii, MDCCLXI.
Heu quam exiguum Vitæ Curriculum!
Corpore fuit eximio; Gestu liberali, placido, augusto
Ingenii Nitore,
Morum Integritate, Munificentia, Facilitate,
Inter paucos illustris,

---

* In a letter from the Rev. David Bostwick to the Rev. Dr. Bellamy, of the date of March 17, 1761, Mr. Bostwick observes: "The people of Philadelphia have collected £95 per annum for five years to support his three sons at College, and Philadelphia and New York have raised between four and five hundred pounds for the widow and two daughters, for he left very little estate."—J. M.

Rei literariæ peritus; Theologus promptus, perspicax,
In Rostris, per Eloquium blandum, mellitum
Vehemens simul, et perstringens, nulli secundus,
Scriptor ornatus, sublimis, disertus.
Præsertim vero Pietate,
Ardente in Deum Zelo et Religione Spectandus,
In tanti Viri, majora meriti,
Memoriam duraturam,
Amici hoc qualecunque Monumentum,
Honoris ergo et Gratitudinis, posuere.
Abi, Viator, ei æmulare.

The following extracts will conclude this memoir:

" Mr. Davies's death has struck us with astonishment, and spread a gloom over the whole country. The loss cannot be expressed. I believe there never was a College happier in its President, or in a more flourishing state. He far exceeded the expectation of his best friends. As you were not personally acquainted, you can hardly conceive what prodigious uncommon gifts the God of heaven had bestowed upon that man to render him useful to the world,—but he is gone! O what he might have been, what he might have done, had he lived! But methinks I hear the admonition, *Be still, and know that I am God.*"

" His sermon on the death of his late Majesty I purpose to send you with this; the first impression, tho' 1000, is gone; a second is in the press. It was the last work of a public nature he ever did."—*Rev. Mr. Bostwick's letter of March 17, 1761, to the Rev. Joseph Bellamy.*

" As to his natural genius, it was strong and masculine. His understanding was clear, his memory retentive, his invention quick, his imagination lively and florid, his thoughts sublime, and his language elegant, strong, and expressive." . . .

" His appearance in company was manly and graceful; his behavior genteel, not ceremonious; grave, yet pleasant, and solid but sprightly too. In a word, he was an open, conversable, and entertaining companion, a polite gentleman, and a devout Christian."

" In the sacred desk, zeal for God and love to men animated his addresses, and made them tender, solemn, pungent, and persuasive; while at the same time they were ingenious, accurate, and oratorical. A certain dignity of sentiment and style, a venerable presence, a commanding voice, and emphatical delivery concurred both to charm his audience and overawe them into silence and attention."

" Nor was his usefulness confined to the pulpit. His comprehensive mind could take under view the grand interests of his country and of religion at once; and these interests as well as those of his friends he was ever ready zealously to serve."

" His natural temper was remarkably sweet and dispassionate, and his heart was one of the tenderest towards the distressed."

" He was among the first and highest examples of filial piety."

" In a word, think what might rationally be expected in the present imperfect state, in a mature man, a Christian in minority, a minister of Jesus, of like passions with others, in a gentleman, companion, and cordial friend, and you conceive of President Davies."

"I never knew one who appeared to lay himself more fully open to the reception of truth, from whatever quarter it came, than he."

"The unavoidable consciousness of native power made him bold and enterprising. Yet the event proved that his boldness arose, not from a partial, groundless self-conceit, but from true self-knowledge. Upon a fair and candid trial, faithful and just to himself, he judged what he could do; and what he could, when called to it, he attempted; and what he attempted he accomplished." (From Dr. Finley's Sermon on the Death of President Davies.)

The above is the testimony of men who knew him well, and who were able to form a correct judgment of such a man as Samuel Davies.

CHAPTER XII.

THE ELECTION AND THE ADMINISTRATION OF THE REV. SAMUEL
FINLEY, THE FIFTH PRESIDENT OF THE COLLEGE OF NEW
JERSEY.

AT the time Mr. Davies was first chosen President, some of
the Trustees were in favor of electing Mr. Finley, and on the
death of Mr. Davies no other person appears to have been
thought of to supply his place. Before the meeting of the
Trustees, which had been appointed for the 28th of May, there
was, doubtless, more or less correspondence among the members of the Board in regard to this important measure, and an
understanding that Mr. Finley would be their choice. Mr.
Bostwick, a devoted friend of President Davies, in his letter to
Mr. Bellamy, of the 17th of March, 1761, speaking of the death
of Mr. Davies, adds, "Our eyes are on Mr. Finley, a very accurate scholar, and a very great and good man. Blessed be
the Lord that such an one is to be found. The internal state
of the College is good, and the management of the Tutors so
generally approved, that there will be no pro tempore President, and the time appointed for choice is the 28th of May."
At this date, however, as appears from the minutes of the Board,
a quorum did not assemble. "Express messengers were despatched to several of the absent members, and on Monday,
June 1, 1761, being called over, the following members appeared, viz.: Messrs. William Smith, Samuel Woodruff, John
Pierson, Gilbert Tennent, William Tennent, Caleb Smith, Jacob
Green, John Brainerd, Samuel Finley, Elihu Spencer, Charles
McKnight, John Light, Richard Stockton."

The following proceedings of the Board at this meeting are
copied from their minutes:

"The Rev. Mr. David Bostwick, of the city of New York, the Rev. Mr. Israel
Reed, of Bound Brook, Dr. John Redman, of Philadelphia, and Doctor Robert

Harris, of New Brunswick, were duly elected Trustees of the College in the room of the Rev. Messrs. Davies and Cowell, deceased, and of Mr. Cummings removed to Boston, and Mr. Livingston resigned. Mr. Bostwick was qualified as the Charter directs, and took his seat accordingly."

. "It having pleased a Sovereign God since our last meeting to remove by death the late reverend and ingenious Mr. Davies, President of the College, the Trustees proceeded to the election of a President, whereupon the Rev. Mr. Samuel Finley, of Nottingham, in the Province of Pennsylvania, was unanimously chosen President of the College in the room of the said Mr. Davies. And the said Mr. Finley, being informed of the above election, was pleased modestly to accept the same. Whereupon Mr. Treat, one of the members of the Board, is desired to attend the meeting of the Presbytery to which Mr. Finley belongs, to request that he may be liberated from his present pastoral charge."

"It is ordered, that Mr. Finley's salary as President of the College be the sum of £200, proclamation, per annum, with the usual privileges and perquisites. And that the expense of moving Mr. Finley's family to this place be paid by the Treasurer."

There is evidently an inaccuracy in the minute respecting the election of two of the new Trustees, in which they are said to have been duly elected in the room of Messrs. Davies and Cowell, deceased. Mr. Davies was a Trustee only in virtue of his being the President of the College; and the only person who could succeed him as a Trustee would be his successor in the office of President. Mr. Finley, by accepting this office, thereby vacated his seat at the Board as a regular and permanent member, which made one of the two vacancies among the clerical members of the Board that were filled by the election of the Rev. Messrs. Bostwick and Reed.

The next meeting of the Board took place on Wednesday, the 30th of September, 1761, the day of the annual Commencement. His Excellency Governor Boone was present on this occasion, and so were all the Trustees but three, making the number in attendance twenty.

Although Mr. Finley upon being chosen President of the College had signified his willingness to accept the office, he could not formally do so until he had obtained the consent of the Presbytery of which he was a member; and therefore his inauguration as President was deferred until this meeting of the Trustees. Having taken the prescribed oaths, he appears to have taken his seat at the Board without any other formality or ceremony.

The Trustees next attended the Commencement exercises, when fourteen young gentlemen were admitted to the first degree in the Arts, and three others to their second degree. It appears from a minute adopted at this meeting that one of the students was in considerable arrears for his tuition, and the Board directed that, " in case these arrears were not fully discharged before the end of the ensuing vacation, he should be dismissed from the College." Nothing is said of his ability to pay the tuition-fees; the only thing mentioned is that he was in arrears for his tuition. At this time no provision had been made for the payment of the tuition-fees of young men in indigent or moderate circumstances, except to a small extent in the case of those preparing for the ministry. Of late years, happily, any worthy youth unable to pay his tuition-fees has had them remitted upon an application to the President or other officer of the College having the oversight of this matter.

The decision reached in the case just mentioned led to a further consideration of the whole subject of College dues, and to the adoption of the following minute :

" The Trustees taking into consideration the damages the Institution has sustained by the Deficiency in the Payment of the Students' Quarterly Bills,* It is Ordered, That for the future every Student who enters College be obliged to give sufficient security by Bond or otherwise to the Treasurer for the punctual payment of all his Dues to the College, which Law [is] to take place at the expiration of the present year, in case no objection appears to this measure at the next meeting of the Trustees."

The rule now in force on this subject, and which was adopted many years ago, is, that all charges for College expenses shall be paid in advance at the beginning of each term.

The settlement of the Steward's accounts was generally one of the items of business which demanded the attention of the Board; and it is evident from the various resolutions on this subject that there was no little difficulty in adjusting these accounts to the satisfaction of the parties concerned.

---

* The bills for the entire year, at this period in the history of the College, amounted to about £25.6.0 *proc.* These included charges for tuition, £4; board, £15; washing, £3; fire-wood and candles, £2; room-rent, £1; and contingent charges, 6 shillings.

Happily for the College, this whole system of providing meals for the students has been given up; yet payments for board continue to be made to the Treasurer of the College, for the better security of the boarders and of the boarding-houses. The change here referred to took place in 1855.

The examination of candidates for degrees was ordered to be held in future on the third Wednesday in August. Previously to this the examination took place on the last Wednesday in July. No change was made in the time of the annual Commencement.

For his extra services while the College was without a President, the Trustees made Mr. Halsey, the senior Tutor, a present of twenty pounds in addition to his salary.

The following extracts will explain themselves, while they show the action of the Board in reference to matters of more or less interest in the history of the College :

"Voted, That the Treasurer of the College pay President Finley the sum of £22.11, it being the expense of his removal to the College."

" Voted, That President Finley's salary begin from the third Wednesday in June last, it being the time of his dismission from his people at Nottingham."

"Ordered, That Mr. Stockton, the Clerk, be desired to return the thanks of this Board to the Gentlemen in Philadelphia who have generously undertaken the management of the Lottery now on foot in favor of the College."

"Ordered, That all moneys arising from the Lottery made in Philadelphia, for the Benefit of the College, be deposited in the hands of Mr. Sergeant, the Treasurer, as soon as possible, and that the said moneys be by him immediately put out to Interest as soon as opportunities present."

"Voted, That President Finley be desired to print his Sermon preached at the funeral of Mr. Davies, at the Expense of the College, and that they be disposed of for the Benefit of the College."

A few extracts from this sermon are given at the close of our memoir of President Davies. This sermon was not preached at Mr. Davies's funeral, but at or near the beginning of the summer term of the College, Thursday, May 28, 1761. The Trustees were to have had a meeting on the previous Thursday, May 21, for the purpose of choosing a President in the room of Mr. Davies. But, a quorum not assembling on that day, they could not proceed with this business, and they only took measures to secure the attendance of a sufficient number on the 1st of June.

The next meeting of the Board was held on Wednesday, the 29th of September, 1762, the day of the annual Commencement. His Excellency Governor Hardy was present, and took his seat as President of the Board. The following address to the Governor, and his reply, are copied from the New York "Mercury" of October 18, 1762, there being no note of them in the minutes of the Board:

"To his Excellency Josiah Hardy, Esq., Captain-General, Commander-in-Chief in and over his Majesty's Province of Nova Cæsarea, or New Jersey, and territories thereon depending in America, Chancellor, and Vice-Admiral in the same.

"May it please your Excellency: We, his Majesty's most dutiful and loyal subjects, the Trustees of the College of New Jersey, with the greatest pleasure take this opportunity of publickly congratulating your Excellency upon your appointment to and acceptance of this Government. And we are particularly happy in believing, from the specimen your Excellency has already given of your good Disposition, that the loss we sustained in the speedy removal of your immediate Predecessor is made up in you; and that as the College of this Province has been favoured with the patronage of each of our Governors since its Institution, your Excellency will be pleased to take it under your Protection. We can assure you that the general Principle of preparing youth for public service in Church and State, and making them useful members of Society, without concerning ourselves about their particular religious denomination, is our grand Idea. And we [hope], when you shall be pleased to look into the Constitution of this Seminary of Learning, and, by honouring us with your personal Attendance at our Meetings, see the Manner of our Procedure, you will conceive it an object worthy of the notice of the Supreme Magistrate.

"We acknowledge the Honour your Excellency has done us by your present Attendance, and we most heartily wish you a long-continued and prosperous Administration in this Province. Signed in the name of the Trustees,

"RICHARD STOCKTON, Clerk.

"To which his Excellency was pleased to return the following answer:

"GENTLEMEN,—I hereby thank you for your Address. It will be at all times a particular satisfaction to me to give you every assistance in my power in promoting the prosperity of this useful Seminary of Learning.

"JOSIAH HARDY.
"PRINCET., Sept. 27, 1762."

The following account of the proceedings at this Commencement is given in the "Pennsylvania Gazette" of the 21st of October, in a letter dated

"Princeton, September 30, 1762. Yesterday the Trustees of the College of New Jersey, with His Excellency the Governor, attended the Commencement. After the usual Procession, and a solemn Invocation of the Divine blessing on the business of the day and the candidates for the honors of the College, the ex-ercises were introduced by

" 1. An elegant Salutatory oration in Latin, pronounced by Mr. James Manning.

" 2. The young gentlemen gave an agreeable specimen of their skill in Disputa-tion, which was carried on alternately in the syllogistic and forensic way.   The subject of the first, which was syllogistic, was the following Thesis:

"'Conservatio non est continua creatio,' which was well defended and opposed.

" 3. This was followed by a forensic dispute on this question: ' Whether a Prince endowed with the virtues of civil government, but not with military, is to be pre-ferred to one of the most shining military genius if he is destitute of the virtues necessary for governing in peace?' Which was decided in the affirmative, after being debated on both sides with much spirit and eloquence.

" 4. To relax the attention of the audience, an English oration on politeness was pronounced by Mr. Joseph Periam, which gave universal satisfaction for the justness of the sentiments, the elegance of the composition, and the propriety with which it was delivered.

" 5. The Thesis next debated was, ' Anima humana dum in corpus infunditur a Deo immediate creatur,' which afforded pleasure to the learned portion of the Auditory.

" 6. The exercises of the forenoon were concluded by a forensic dispute on this subject : ' Whether moral as well as mathematical truths are capable of demonstra-tion?' Which was judiciously maintained and determined in the affirmative to general satisfaction.

" 7. The entertainments in the afternoon were begun by a dispute, which was very ingeniously managed by the respondent, on this Thesis: ' Sensus moralis qua simplex perceptio atque moralis obligationis fundamentum non datur.'

" 8. The last question disputed by the Bachelors, being, ' Whether Noah's Flood was Universal?' gave agreeable amusement to the Auditory by the popular and pertinent manner in which it was canvassed.

" 9. A Valedictory oration in English, pronounced by Mr. Isaac Allen with graceful ease and propriety, closed the exercises of the candidates for the honor of Bachelor's degree.

" 10. The following Thesis was learnedly defended and opposed by the candi-dates for Master's degree : ' Deus hominem sine virtute non primario creavit neque creare potuit.'

" 11. After this, twenty-one young gentlemen were admitted to the honor of Bachelor of Arts, and twelve to the second degree.   In behalf of the last-men-tioned candidates was agreeably delivered an English oration by Mr. James Lyon.

" 12. Mr. Ker, who for some time past had officiated in the character of a Tutor, took his leave of the society in a short Valedictory address.

" The whole concluded with a Poetical Entertainment given by the candidates for Bachelor's degree, interspersed with choruses of Music, which, with the whole performance of the day, afforded universal satisfaction to a polite and crowded auditory."

The entertainment here referred to was entitled " The Mili-tary Glory of Great Britain." In his notes of President Davies's administration, Dr. Green speaks of it as "a poetic dialogue, the subject of which was the glorious achievements of the British arms both by sea and land," and which was supposed by him to have been written by President Davies, and to have been recited at the Commencement of 1760 (see his "Notes," page 339); but it was a part of the exercises of the class of 1762, at least eighteen months after the death of Mr. Davies, and there was in this class talent fully equal to such a production.

A copy of this dramatic exercise has been recently given to the College library. It is printed in a quarto pamphlet, and on its title-page it is spoken of as performed at the close of the Commencement of 1762. Dr. Green's account of it is given from a recollection of what he heard in his boyhood, as he himself says.

At this meeting of the Board there was a further recognition of Mr. Halsey's valuable services, and a vote to add fifteen pounds per annum to his salary.

The President's salary was also increased by adding to it fifty pounds proclamation money a year, with the profits of the grammar-school; and it was voted that he be paid his salary half-yearly; and, further, that he should have the privilege of educating his sons at the College, as in the case of President Davies, without charge for their tuition.

The following minute was adopted in regard to the tuition-fees of students entering advanced classes:

"The Trustees having considered the Law formerly made by this Board, ordering that the Students who enter in any year after the Freshman year should pay the Tuition Money of the preceding years; It is now Voted, That those who enter this year and hereafter shall enter the Sophomore Class, shall only pay the sum of thirty shillings proc.; and those who enter the Junior year, shall pay the sum of forty shillings entrance money, besides the ordinary tuition."

Among the more important measures of the Trustees at this meeting were the following:

1. The confirming of the gift of a lot of land which ten of the Trustees, not a quorum of the Board, had made to sundry inhabitants of Princeton for the erection of a church building.

2. Requesting Mr. Wm. Peartree Smith, a member of the

Board, to draw up a full account of the College from its foundation, and to print the same at the expense of the College.

3. Ordering the erection of a kitchen for the use of the College.

4. The appointment of managers of the first and only lottery ever granted to the College by the Legislature of the Province, and the returning of the thanks of the Board to the Legislature for the privilege given.

The sum authorized to be raised by this lottery was three thousand pounds *proc.*

5. The appointment of Messrs. Samuel Blair and James Thompson to be Tutors.

The next meeting was held on Wednesday, the 28th of September, 1763, the day of the annual Commencement. His Excellency William Franklin, Esq., recently appointed Governor of the Province, President Finley, and fourteen of the Trustees, were present on this occasion. The Trustees availed themselves of the opportunity now afforded by the Governor's presence to present to him an address, which, with his answer, is taken from the " New York Gazette" of October 11, 1763, there being no reference to it in the minutes of the Board:

" May it please your Excellency:

" The Trustees of the College of New Jersey deem themselves happy in this opportunity of presenting your Excellency with their respects; and beg that you will be pleased to accept their congratulations upon your appointment to this Government. They have only to wish that a more early day had been in their Power.

" Your Disposition to favor every Institution calculated to promote Learning and the general Good of Mankind is not to be doubted; and therefore with Pleasure we beg leave to recommend to your Excellency's Patronage the College under our care. We can assure you that we have endeavored to form it on such a plan, and to conduct it in such a manner, as to make it of the most general and extensive usefulness. Our Idea is to send into the World good Scholars and useful members of Society. Your Excellency's Predecessors, since the founding of this College, have severally, in their turns, been pleased to think it worthy of their regard; which, with the Benefactions of the Public Spirited at home and abroad, under the divine blessing, has brought it to its present flourishing state. We hope for and expect its increase under your Excellency's Influence.

" The Governor of this Colony, for the time being, by the Charter of Incorporation is a member and President of our Board; and we hope your Excellency will be pleased to honor this Institution by your personal attendance in these capacities. Your Excellency has our most cordial wishes for your Public and Domestic Happiness, and for your Peace, Comfort, and Usefulness in the Administration of the Government of this Province.

"RICHARD STOCKTON, Clerk.

"To which his Excellency was pleased to give the following Answer:

"GENTLEMEN,—My cordial Acknowledgments are due to you for this obliging Testimony of your Regard. I am fully sensible of the Utility of the Institution under your care, and have the highest opinion of the merits of the Gentlemen by whose good Management it has been brought, in so short a space of time, to its present flourishing condition. If my endeavors can in any way contribute to the further perfecting of this salutary work, you may depend it shall never be wanting."

Nineteen members of the Senior class were admitted to their first degree in the Arts, and eleven graduates to their second degree. Several of those admitted to these degrees at this time became distinguished in the several professions.

The Rev. Charles Beatty was chosen a Trustee, in the room of the Rev. Caleb Smith, deceased, and John Berrien, Esq., in the place of James Hude, Esq.

Among the matters which claimed the attention of the Board at this time was the grant of a lot of land which had been made to the inhabitants of Princeton for the erection of a church edifice, and in reference to this there is the following minute:

"It is ordered, That Mr. Wm. P. Smith, Mr. Woodruff, Dr. Redman, Mr. Treat, and Mr. Brainerd be a committee to settle with the Congregation of Princeton the matter respecting the lot of land which this Board heretofore has ordered to be conveyed to them, for the erection of a church and for a burying-ground, and that the said committee have full power to offer the Congregation such terms as they think proper, in consideration of their releasing their claim to the said lot of land, or to make such other agreement with the said Congregation touching the premises as the said committee shall judge proper."

"It appears from this minute," says President Green, "that the lot granted by the Trustees to the Congregation of Princeton, for the erection of a church and for a burial-ground, was expected to revert to the College. This, however, did not take place. The transactions between the Trustees of the College and the Congregation of Princeton relative to this concern were numerous and of long continuance. A particular detail of them will not be given. The result was that in 1762 and 1763 a church was built on the lot originally given by the College; that the Trustees of the College lent about £700 to the congregation to aid in building the church; that a burial-ground was obtained in another place, as a donation from Dr. Thomas Wiggins; that the money loaned to the congregation was eventually paid; that the inside of the church, as well as of the College edifice, was destroyed by the British and American armies during the Revolutionary war, and repaired at a very considerable expense; that the church was entirely consumed, except the walls, which were of brick, by a fire which took place by accident in February, 1813;

that it was rebuilt at the expense of the congregation, with the aid of $500 contributed by the College; that the College has by contract an exclusive right to the church on the day of Commencement, on the evening that precedes it, and at such other times as the faculty shall state in writing that it is needed for the public exercises of the institution; and also a claim to one-half the gallery for the use of the students on the Sabbath."

Upon what authority Dr. Green says that the burial-ground mentioned above was the gift of Dr. Wiggins the writer of this history is unable to discover; and he apprehends that it is an error, and that the error arose from the fact that Dr. Wiggins, either then or subsequently, owned some twenty acres of land, more or less, adjacent to the lot used by the College and congregation for a burial-ground, and which lot was purchased by the College of the Hon. Thomas Leonard, in 1757, several years prior to these transactions between the College and the people of the town. Of Judge Leonard's deed to the College mention is made in the first volume of the Minutes of the Board, pages 193, 340, and 361. The cemetery now in possession of the First Presbyterian Church of Princeton is an enlargement of the above-mentioned burial-ground by adding to it several acres of land, a part of Dr. Wiggins's real estate, bequeathed by him, in 1804, to the trustees of said church.

The church was burnt again in the summer of 1834, and was rebuilt at the expense of the congregation, with some aid from the College, at which time the College relinquished all claim to the use of the church for public exercises, with the exception of those connected with the annual Commencement.

At this meeting of the Board measures were taken for the purchase of a small lot of ground adjacent to the College grounds, and belonging to Mr. Robert Smith, of Philadelphia, the architect and builder of the College edifice.

The next minute of the Board is important, as indicating the time when the spring vacation began, and is as follows: " It is ordered, that a meeting of the Trustees be attended on Wednesday before the second Monday in April next, at which time the Spring vacation begins."

The annual Commencement at this time was held on the last Wednesday in September, and the autumnal vacation began at the close of the Commencement exercises. This plan of having two terms and two vacations continued for more than a hundred years, viz., from the foundation of the College until the year 1867, in which year the plan of having three terms and three vacations was introduced. But before this, viz., in 1844, a change was made in the day of holding the Commencement from the last Wednesday in September to the last Wednesday in June, and a corresponding change occurred in the College terms and vacations.

Mr. Wm. P. Smith having declined the service of drawing up an account of the College, the President of the College, Rev. Dr. Finley, was desired to do the same, and to have his draft ready to lay before the Board at their next meeting in the ensuing spring.

The salaries of the President and of the Tutors were all increased at this meeting of the Board : the President's to three hundred pounds *proc.* per annum, the Senior Tutor's to seventy-five pounds, and those of the two Junior Tutors to sixty-five pounds each ; and it was ordered that the late Tutor, Mr. Ker, should be allowed twenty-five pounds in addition to his salary.

It was also ordered, "That an English School be forthwith erected in this College, which is to be under the inspection and government of the President of the College for the time being."

A grammar-school, in connection with the College, was established in Mr. Burr's time. Respecting these schools the following remarks occur in the account of the College published by order of the Trustees, in 1764 :

"There is a grammar-school annexed to the College as a nursery for it, under the general inspection of the President, though not a part of the original constitution. This was first set up by President Burr, and has been handed down to his successors, the Trustees taking it under their patronage during the several vacancies in that office. Besides the Latin and Greek languages, into which the youth are here initiated, they have been early taught the graces of a good delivery, and spent a small portion of every day in improving their handwriting, for which purpose a proper attendant hath been hitherto provided. But this expedient being found by experience not fully to answer those purposes, it was lately judged proper that an English school should be also established, for the sole intention of teaching young lads to write well, to cipher, and to pronounce and read the English tongue with accuracy and precision."

The next meeting of the Board occurred on Wednesday, the

20th of June, 1764. At this meeting there were present his Excellency Governor Franklin, President Finley, and thirteen other Trustees. Robert Ogden, Esq., of Elizabethtown, New Jersey, was chosen Trustee of the College, in the room of the Rev. David Bostwick, deceased, and the Rev. Lambert De Ronde, of New York, in the room of the Rev. Jacob Green, resigned.

"The President informed the Board that he had erected an English school in the College, and employed a master for that purpose," of which the Board expressed their approval, and desired the President "to carry on the same in such manner as he shall think most advantageous for the College."

The following minute occurs in reference to Mr. Samuel Blair, who, two years after, was chosen President of the College, but who declined the appointment upon learning that Dr. Witherspoon was willing to accept the Presidency should he receive a second invitation so to do:

"The Trustees having received information that Mr. Samuel Blair, lately a Tutor of this College, has done extraordinary services in his office, it is ordered, That £25 be presented to the said Mr. Blair by the Treasurer in consideration thereof."

There is no intimation whatever as to the character of these extraordinary services, and, for some good reason, no doubt, nothing further is said in regard to them. At the preceding meeting of the Board, in September, 1763, the President of the College, Dr. Finley, was requested to prepare for publication an account of the College. It is probable that the declining state of his health and his various and arduous duties prevented his attending to this matter personally, and that he placed the materials for such a history in the hands of Mr. Blair to prepare the desired account; that it was written by Mr. Blair under the direction and, it may be, under the supervision of Dr. Finley, and printed by order of the Trustees, as stated in the title-page of the pamphlet containing said account, although no mention of any of these things is made in the minutes of the Board.

This account is spoken of by President Green and others as Dr. Finley's history of the College. But the writer's name is not given on the title-page, and the pamphlet itself is entitled "An Account of the College of New Jersey, in which are described the Methods of Government, Modes of Instruction, Manner and Expenses of Living in the same, &c., with a Prospect of the College neatly engraved. Published, by order of the Trustees, for the information of the public, particularly of the friends and benefactors of the institution in Europe and America. Woodbridge in New Jersey. Printed by James Parker, 1764."

From a comparison of dates, it appears that the presenting of the twenty-five pounds took place the very year in which the account of the College was published by order of the Board. The conjecture given above finds abundant corroboration in the fact that within a few years after its publication the pamphlet is mentioned as the work of Mr. Blair. Mr. Madison, the fourth President of the United States, was a student and a graduate in 1771 of the College. In a letter of his, of the date of August 16, 1769, to the Rev. Thomas Martin, who had been an inmate of his father's family and Mr. Madison's tutor, this sentence occurs : " I have been as particular to my father as I thought necessary for this time, as I send him an account of the institution wrote by Mr. Blair, the gentleman formerly elected President of this place." (See Mr. Madison's letter in Professor Cameron's " History of the American Whig Society," pages 231, 232.)

The manner in which Dr. Finley and his administration of the College are spoken of in the pamphlet makes it evident that the pamphlet was not all written by him, and the unity of the style shows it to be the work of one individual, and that individual we believe to be Mr. Blair.

Here it may not be amiss to say that in the view given of the origin of the College we differ from Mr. Blair, who speaks of the College only under the second charter, and who probably was not aware that the College was in existence under a previous charter, given by the Honorable John Hamilton, President of the Council and acting Governor of the Province.

It seems to have been a favorite aim of some of the leading friends of the College, after the granting of the second charter, to regard Governor Belcher as its founder ; and Mr. Blair not unnaturally adopted their view of the case. But, for reasons assigned in the chapter on the College charters, it is only in a very limited sense that he can be styled its founder.

The pamphlet here referred to is one of forty-eight pages, small octavo, neatly printed ; and of course the account given of the origin of the institution, and of its progress and condition for a period of sixteen years, must be a very succinct one. Still, it is a very valuable work to any one desirous to learn the state of the College at the time of its publication.

Of the meeting of the Board and of the exercises at the Commencement September 26, 1764, there is no record in the minutes of the Trustees. Two blank pages were left for the insertion of these minutes.

It appears from the minutes of September 25, 1765, that the Rev. John Rodgers, then of St. George's, Delaware, afterwards of New York City, was chosen a Trustee at the meeting of the Board in September, 1764. And in the triennial catalogue are given the names of those who were admitted to their first degree in the Arts. The programme of the Commencement exercises for the year 1764 gives the names of all who took part in these exercises, with the exception of the Salutatory and Valedictory orators. (See pages 268–272, post.)

The next Commencement of the College was held on Wednesday, the 25th of September, 1765, and it was the last one at which President Finley presided. The College was in a very flourishing condition, the number of students larger than at any previous date in the history of the institution, the attention to study and the orderly behavior of the students highly commendable. Thirty-one members of the Senior class were admitted to the first degree in the Arts, and eleven to their second degree.

Dr. William Shippen, of Philadelphia, was chosen a Trustee, in the room of the Rev. John Pierson, resigned, and Mr. Joseph Periam was chosen a Tutor. Mr. Periam was also chosen Clerk of the Board, in the room of Richard Stockton, Esq., resigned. It appears from the minutes that Mr. Periam had discharged the duties of a Tutor during the previous year without a formal appointment by the Board.

The President of the College having informed the Board that sundry inconveniences had resulted from having the English school kept in the College building, he was requested to make provision for it elsewhere, and in such manner as he thought proper.

The first order touching the planting of shade-trees on the College grounds was passed at this meeting of the Board; and it may interest the students and graduates of the College to know that the two very large sycamore-trees standing near the front gate of the President's yard at this date, December 6, 1872, and in their full vigor, are the remnants of the trees planted in the autumn of 1765.

The President's salary was increased one hundred pounds.

It was ordered, that every student and graduate, the officers of the College excepted, who makes use of the College library, should pay the sum of two shillings and sixpence every quarter of a year, to be expended for the use of the library. And it was further ordered, that no student of the College should be allowed to have the key of the library; and that every person who is admitted there should be introduced by one of the officers of the College.

The door to the cupola of the College was ordered to be kept constantly locked; it was also ordered that no person should be permitted to have the key but the President, the Tutors, the Steward, and the servant charged with the care of the belfry. The main object of this order was probably to guard against the danger from fire, the roof and belfry being wholly of wood, although the outer walls were entirely of stone and all the inner walls of brick. Every possible care was taken by the College authorities, both before and at this time, to protect the building from fire,—by digging an additional well, and providing a fire-engine, ladders and buckets, and everything that would be of use in case of a fire. These precautions were all right and proper, and may have prevented an earlier destruction of the main building than that which took place in March, 1802.

The next meeting of the Board was held at Nassau Hall, on Wednesday, the 25th of June, 1766. From the minutes of this date it appears that the Trustees received, by the hands of Dr. Redman, one of their number, an order for one hundred pounds sterling, for the use of the College, in support of a Divinity professor. This was the gift of Mr. John Williamson, of Hanover, Virginia, to whom the Board returned their thanks for his generous donation. And the gift was as seasonable as it was generous, for it enabled the Board not long after to appoint a Professor of Divinity, in the person of the Rev. John Blair. The order was upon Mr. Samuel Waterman, of London; and the obtaining of the money was intrusted to the care of Richard Stockton, Esq., a member of the Board, who had gone to New York on his way to London, on his private affairs, but who availed himself of the opportunity to render the College not only this particular service, but others of even greater moment, as will appear in the course of this history.

A committee, consisting of the Honorable William Smith and the Rev. Messrs. De Ronde and Rodgers, was appointed to prepare an address to his Majesty "for his gracious condescension to these Colonies in the repeal of the Stamp Act;" and also a petition, to be presented at the same time, for a grant of sixty thousand acres of land in the Province of New York, from the lands then recently added to New York from the Province of New Hampshire. The address and the petition were accordingly prepared, and, being signed by the Honorable Edward Shippen, the acting President of the Board at this meeting, were sent to Mr. Stockton, with the request that he should take such measures and engage such friends of this institution in London to assist him in this matter as he should be advised by the Rev. Dr. Chandler would be most expedient. A letter was written by the committee to the reverend Doctor, soliciting his aid. The Dr. Chandler here spoken of is the same gentleman who is mentioned by Mr. Davies as exercising his friendly offices in behalf of the College at the time Messrs. Tennent and Davies visited London.

Upon his return home, Mr. Stockton reported to the Board "that he had the honor of presenting to his Majesty the address of the Trustees, which was very graciously received; that the petition was lodged in the Plantation Office; and that my Lord Shelburne had promised him to lay the same before the King in Council." The Board returned their thanks to Mr. Stockton for his services to the College while in Great Britain.

Whether the petition was ever brought to the notice of the King and Council is not known; but one thing is certain, that it did not obtain for the College the grant of land asked for in the petition.

" The Rev. Mr. De Ronde" (of New York) "having laid before
the Board a plan for the introduction of a professor of divinity
to be obtained from Holland, for the service of the Dutch as well
as English Presbyterian Churches in these parts, the Trustees
having maturely considered the same, are of the opinion that
the proposal is not yet ripe for prosecution, and therefore defer
the further consideration thereof to the next meeting." At the
next meeting it was again deferred, and this was the end of it.
In 1769, Mr. De Ronde resigned his place at the Board.

" It was ordered, That no student hereafter board out of the College unless by
permission of the President, or, in his absence, of the next senior officer, to be given
only in case the student applying for such permission produce a certificate of a
physician that the state of his health renders such an indulgence necessary."

Dr. Finley was not present at this meeting of the Board.
The cause of his absence is apparent from the following
minutes :

" As Dr. Finley, the President of this College, is now in a languishing state, and
as it is highly probable that he will be removed by death before the next Commencement, or at least that he will be unable to preside at the public exercises on
that occasion, the Trustees have unanimously appointed the Rev. Mr. Spencer
to preside on that day, and to confer the degrees in the usual manner; and the said
Mr. Spencer was pleased to signify his acquiescence in this appointment. And the
Trustees do further direct, that in case of the President's death, the fees and perquisites usually paid to the President for the degrees be received by the eldest
Tutor, to be disposed of as the Trustees shall hereafter direct."

" It having pleased our holy God to visit Dr. Finley, the worthy President of
this College, with great and distressing illness, whereby he is at present entirely
unable to perform the duties of his important station; and it appearing necessary for
the welfare of this institution that some person be invested with the power and authority of the President, in order the better to manage the affairs of the Seminary; this
Board have appointed the Rev. Mr. Wm. Tennent to act in the room and stead of
President Finley during his absence, and do hereby invest him with full power and
authority to execute the said office until next Commencement, or during President
Finley's absence and disability; and Mr. Tennent was qualified accordingly."

Dr. Finley died on the 17th of July, 1766, in the city of
Philadelphia, to which city he had gone that he might have
the benefit of the best medical skill, and he was buried there
by the side of his intimate friend, the Rev. Gilbert Tennent.

The following references to his illness and death, and to
the services of Messrs. William Tennent, Spencer, and Halsey,
occur in the minutes of this meeting of the Board:

" The Trustees taking into consideration the good services of the Rev. Mr. William Tennent since the disability and *death* of the late Rev'd and worthy Dr. Finley, do unanimously agree to present the said Mr. Tennent with the sum of twenty pounds, besides defraying his necessary expenses in town during that time; and also to the Rev. Mr. Elihu Spencer, the sum of ten pounds, in consideration of his presiding and conferring the degrees at the public Commencement; both which sums Mr. Baldwin, the Steward, is directed to pay the said gentlemen."

" Whereas sundry weighty and important reasons have induced this Board to augment the late worthy President's salary, from time to time, to the sum of £400; but inasmuch as the occasion of the late necessary augmentation is removed, and the present low state of the College funds will not allow this Board to continue that salary for the future in its present circumstances; it is agreed, therefore, that the stated salary of the next President shall be £250, with the usual perquisites."

" The Trustees also considering the great and important services that have been rendered to this institution by Mr. Jeremiah Halsey, over and above the necessary duties of his office as Tutor of the College, do, in consideration of his extraordinary and faithful services, unanimously agree that the sum of sixty-one pounds, being the graduation money, by calculation, now in his hands, be presented to him, or whatever the fees may amount to, be the same more or less."

Mr. Jonathan Edwards, a son of President Edwards, was unanimously chosen a Tutor of the College, in the room of Mr. Periam, resigned.

The following extracts, from the authorized account of the College mentioned above, will show the course of instruction during the Presidency of Dr. Finley. (See pp. 23-30.)

" As to the branches of literature taught here, they are the same with those which are made parts of education in the European Colleges, save only such as may be occasioned by the infancy of this institution. The students are divided into four distinct classes, which are called the *Freshman*, the *Sophomore*, the *Junior*, and the *Senior*. In each of these they continue one year, giving and receiving in their turns those tokens of respect and subjection which belong to their standings, in order to preserve a due subordination. The Freshman year is spent in Latin and Greek languages, particularly in reading *Horace, Cicero's Orations*, the Greek Testament, Lucian's Dialogues, and *Xenophon's Cyropædia*. In the *Sophomore* year they still prosecute the study of the languages, particularly *Homer, Longinus*, &c., and enter upon the sciences, geography, rhetoric, logic, and the mathematics. They continue their mathematical studies throughout the *Junior* year, and also pass through a course of natural and moral philosophy, metaphysics, chronology, &c.; and the greater number, especially such as are educating for the service of the church, are initiated into the Hebrew. . . . The Senior year is entirely employed in reviews and composition. They now revise the most improving parts of Latin and Greek classics, part of the Hebrew Bible, and all the arts and sciences. The weekly course of disputation is continued, which was also carried on through the preceding year. They discuss two or three theses in a week; some in the syllogistic and others in the forensic manner, alternately; the forensic being always performed in the English tongue. A series of questions is also prepared on the principal subjects of natural and revealed religion. These (disputations) are delivered publicly, on Sundays, before a promiscuous congregation, as well as the College, in order to habituate them early to face an assembly, as also for other important and religious ends, to which they are found conducive. There is likewise a monthly oration-day, when harangues, or orations of their own composition, are pronounced before a mixed auditory. All these compositions before mentioned are critically examined with respect to language, orthography, pointing, capitalizing, with other minutiæ, as well as more material properties of accurate writing."

" Besides these exercises in writing and speaking, most of which are proper to the *Senior* class, on every Monday three, and on other evenings of the week, excepting Saturdays and Sundays, two out of each of the three inferior classes, in rotation, pronounce declamations of their own composing on the stage. These too are previously examined and corrected, and occasion taken from them early to form a taste for good writing. The same classes also, in rotation, three on Tuesday evenings, and two on other evenings, with the exceptions just mentioned, pronounce, in like manner, such select pieces from *Cicero, Demosthenes, Livy,* and other ancient authors, and from *Shakspeare, Milton, Addison,* and such illustrious moderns, as are best adapted to display the various passions, and exemplify the graces of utterance and gesture. A good address, and agreeable elocution, are accomplishments so ingratiating, and so necessary to render a public speaker, especially, popular, and consequently useful, that they are esteemed here as considerable parts of education, in the cultivation of which no little pains are employed.

" The classics are taught, for the three first years, in nearer the usual method of grammar-schools than in the last. The students then revise them, principally as examples of fine composition. They first give a more literal translation of a paragraph, afterwards the sense in a paraphrase of their own, and then criticise upon the beauties of the author. In which work they are assisted by the President. No authors are read more particularly with this view than *Homer, Horace,* and especially *Longinus. . . .*

" Each class recites twice a day: and have always free access to their teachers, to solve any difficulties that may occur. The bell rings for morning prayer at six o'clock, when the Senior class read off a chapter from the original into English. The president then proposes a few critical questions upon it, which, after their concise answers, he illustrates more at large. The times of relaxation from study are about an hour in the morning, two at noon, and three in the evening; and in these are included the public meals. Evening prayer is always introduced with psalmody; and care is taken to improve the youth in the art of sacred music."

" The usual method of instruction in the sciences is this. The pupils frequently and deliberately read over such a portion of the author they are studying, on a particular science, as it is judged they can be able thoroughly to impress upon their memories. When they attend their recitations, the tutor proposes questions on every particular they have been reading. After they have given, in their turns, such answers as show their general acquaintance with the subject, he explains it more at large; allows them to propose any difficulties; and takes pains to discover whether his explications be fully comprehended. Advantages which are seldom attainable in the usual method of teaching by lecture.

" In the instruction of the youth, care is taken to cherish a spirit of liberty and free enquiry; and not only to permit, but even encourage their right of private judgment, without presuming to dictate with an air of infallibility, or demanding an implicit assent to the decisions of the preceptor."

" The *Senior, Junior,* and (towards the conclusion of their year) the *Sophomore* classes are allowed the free use of the college library, . . . and especially to assist them in preparing their disputations and other compositions." . . .

" On the third Wednesday in *August* annually,* the *Senior* class are examined by the trustees, the college officers, and other gentlemen of learning then present, throughout all the branches of literature they have been here taught. And if approved as worthy of academical honors, the president assigns them the parts they are respectively to perform at the anniversary commencement; the general proceedings of which are so publicly known as to supersede all necessity of description. They are then graduated *Bachelors of Arts.* After an interval of three years they are usually admitted to the Master's degree." . . .

The rules adopted, while Mr. Davies was President, in reference to the conferring of the second degree in the Arts (see page 210), continued in force during the administration of President Finley. Although the author of the above extracts deemed the general proceedings at the annual Commencements to be so well known to the public as to do away with the necessity of any mention of them as they were at that time; still, the students and graduates of the present day will read with pleasure the following programme of the Commencement exercises of 1764, copied from Dr. Green's Sketch of the College.

Dr. Green transcribed it from a paper in the handwriting of President Finley, sent to him by Dr. James Edwards Burr Finley, of Charleston, South Carolina, a son of President Finley. This gentleman is mentioned by Dr. Green under the name of Ebenezer Finley, which was the name of an elder brother, who died several years before Dr. Green received the paper.

" THE PROCESS, ETC.

The Trustees, being at the President's house, the candidates standing at the door, two and two, upon his saying,

Progredimini Juvenes, they walk,—

1. The Bachelor candidates.
2. The Masters.
3. The Tutors and any Ministers present.
4. The Trustees.
5. The President,—the Governor at his right hand.

All seated, Prayer succeeds.
Præses (capite tecto).

' Auditores docti ac benevoli, Juvenes primam Lauream ambientes, cupiunt vos per Oratorem salutare; quod illis a vobis concessum fidunt.'

Ascendat Orator Salutatorius.

*   *   *   *   *   *   *   *   *   *   *

---

* At first the final examination took place on the last Wednesday in July.

Distribuantur Theses.

*   *   *   *   *   *   *   *   *   *   *

Quoniam, docti Auditores, accurata disputandi Ratio ad verum a falso secernendum plurimum valet, Juvenes Artibus initiati, parvula quædam eorum in ea specimina, vobis jam sunt exhibituri.

Prima Disputatio, syllogistice tractanda——

Thesis est,

Mentiri, ut vel Natio conservetur, haud fas est.

Qui hanc Thesin probare atque defendere statuit, ascendat.

Foster

Qui Thesin oppugnari judicavit, ascendat.

Primus Opponens——Lawrence.

Quanquam concederetur Sermonem ad felicitatem hominum provehendam constitutum fuisse, attamen non æque nobis constat quid semper ad eum finem conducit; sed majus credendum est Mendacium nunquam ad eum facere; dum exemplum Virtutis omnibus prodesse potest.

Secundus Opponens——Smith.

Determinatio.

Mentiri, quacunque de causa, ignobile et sua Natura pravum esse, res ipsa clamat, et ferme ab omnibus, præcipue Virtutem colentibus, conceditur. Quod si omnino fas esse possit, Deus comprobat; et si ille possit probare, non est necessario verax; sed impossibile est eum mentiri, ergo et mendacium probare.

Nec ratio Veritatis ab hominum Felicitate, sed Dei Rectitudine pendet; et quoniam sibi semper constare necesse est, non potest non esse rectus. Ergo falsum necessario improbat, ut ejus naturæ oppositum; et vetat Malum facere, ut quidvis Bonum inde sequatur, etiam ut Natio conservetur.

*   *   *   *   *   *   *   *   *   *   *

The following is an English forensick Dispute, which, for Reasons often mentioned, is introduced, viz., it entertains the English part of the Audience, tends to the cultivation of our native language, and has been agreeable on former occasions; which I presume are sufficient apologies for continuing the custom.

The Thesis is—

Somnia non sunt universaliter inania, et nihil significantia.

In English—

All dreams are not useless and insignificant.

Who undertakes the defence of this position?—Miller.

Whoever has any objections against what has been offered, let him speak.—Tredwell.

Who judges it fit to answer these objections?—McCreery.

Determination.

Although I see no necessity of accounting for all dreams from the Agency of other Spirits (any more than to interest them in the Reveries of the mind, when lost in mere imaginary scenes, while we are awake, without reflecting that they are not realities); yet that foreign Spirits have access to ours, as well when we are asleep as awake, is inconsistent with no Principle of Reason. And if some dreams cannot be otherwise accounted for, than by having recourse to foreign Spirits, we must then admit their agency; since there can be no effect without a cause. And though it must be granted that our own Spirits at the same time think, yet there is no Inconsistency in supposing that other Spirits gave Occasion to their thinking of some subjects rather than others, as is the case in conversing together when we are awake.

What has been matter of fact is certainly still possible; and we know that in some cases infinite Wisdom chose to employ Angels to communicate divine Instructions in Dreams, which establishes the general Doctrine.   And Experience assures us that Impressions made on these Occasions are very deep and lively; and, as has been observed, those very Dreams, that come from fulness of Business, or other causes mentioned, shew us the Temper of our Minds, and in that view are useful and significant.

    *   *   *   *   *   *   *   *   * .   *   *

To unbend the Mind by an agreeable Variety, as far as may consist with the Exercises of the Day, an English intermediate Oration is next to be delivered.

Ascendat Orator intermedius.

  *   *   *   *   *   *   * `   *   *   *   *

Thesis proxime discutienda, modo pene forensi, est,
Lux Rationis sola, Incitamenta ad Virtutem satis efficacia, non præbet.
Qui hanc Thesin primus defendere statuit, procedat.—Woodhull.
Qui primus opponit Thesi procedat,
Lawrence,
Leake.

Qui Objectiones refellere, et Thesin firmare suscipit, procedat.

Recte notatum fuit, quod Naturam Peccati probe scire necessarium est, ad Virtutem rite æstimandum.   Peccato enim ignoto, odisse illud nequimus; et sine Peccati odio, nulla datur Virtus.   Et quoniam clarum est, quod homines, Luce Naturæ sola freti, ignorarunt quid sit virtus, et quales ejus Consequentiæ in Seculo futuro; nesciverunt Deum, veræ Virtutis Exemplar, nec non Amorem et Satisfactionem Domini Salvatoris, quæ sola sunt Incitamenta ad Virtutem idonea; Thesis Valet.

The next Thesis is—
Nullam veram Virtutem habet, qui omnes non habet.
In English—
He has not one true virtue, who has not every one.

Who undertakes to defend this position?—Tuttle.

If any think to oppose it, let him appear.—Hazard.

Who judges he can confute these arguments, let him speak.—Clagget.

Determination.

That the Thesis is true, appears demonstrable both from the Simplicity of the Soul and the Nature of Virtue.   As the soul cannot be divided into any Parts, if one vice is prevalent it possesses the soul entirely, and the whole principle of action is vitiated.   And as Virtue is a Disposition of Mind to whatever is morally good, and Goodness must be uniform and of a piece, it can no more be dismembered than the Soul: therefore whatever mixture of vice there may be with virtue, one of them must necessarily predominate; for seeing that they are perfectly opposite to each other, it is as impossible for a Person to be under the governing power of both at once, as for Fire and Water to subsist together, without the one's being extinguished or the other evaporated.

Virtue consists in the Love of God and Man, nor can it be separated. The Pretence is not tolerable, that a Hater of his Brother should be a Lover of God. Now 'tis certain that one cannot love and hate the same thing at the same Time, and in the same Respect. There must then be such a necessary Connexion of all virtues, that one cannot possibly be without all; consequently a single virtue, where any vice prevails, is but a counterfeit.

Exercitia quæ restant ad tertiam Horam P. M. postponuntur.

The remaining exercises of the Day begin at three o'clock, afternoon.

* * * * * * * * * * *

Orator hujus Classis valedictorius ascendat.

Exercitia, quæ a Candidatis secundi Gradus præstanda sunt, jam sequuntur.

Thesis disputanda hæc est, scil:

Jephtha Filiam non immolavit.

Ascendat hujus Quæstionis Respondens.—Mr. Ker.

Ascendat primus qui hanc Thesim veram esse negat.

Determinatio.

Fatendum est, quod in hac Quæstione docti in Partes abeunt. Sed ut Theseos Veritas appareat, considerandum est quod fuit Jephthæ Votum. 'Qui—vel, quodcunque—exierit e foribus Domus meæ, in Occursum meum, erit Domini, et, vel, offeram illud in Holocaustum,' q. d., vel aptum erit at Sacrificium, vel non: si prius, erit in Holocaustum; si non, erit Domino sacrum, devotum. Hebrææ Voces non aliter necessario significant; nam *Vau* sæpe disjunctive sumitur, ut multis exemplis patet. Adde, quod Deus detestatus est humanas Victimas, et improbavit; quod cum Sacerdotes saltem norunt, non verisimile est Jephtham eos in tanta causa non consuluisse. Nec parvum habet momentum, Filiam ejus Spatium deflendi, non Mortem sed Virginitatem, petiisse; cum enim dicitur Jephtha fecisse quod voverat, sequitur, et non cognoverat Virum.

Descendant Candidati hujus Collegii ambientes.

Ad Curatores.

Juvenes, quos coram vobis, Curatores honorandi ac reverendi, jam sisto, publico Examini, secundum hujus Academiæ Leges subjecti, habiti fuerunt omnino digni qui Honoribus academicis exornarentur: Vobis igitur comprobantibus, illos ad Gradum petitum, toto Animo admittam.

Eadem Auctoritate regia, virum Davidem McGregor, Novangliæ, de Religione et Literis bene meritum, ad secundum in Artibus Gradum, Honoris causa, admitto.

Eadem Auctoritate, Reverendum Nathan Ker, Davidem Caldwell, Concionatorem Evangelii, necessario absentem; Reverendum Johannem Strain, hujus Collegii alumnos, ad secundum in Artibus Gradum admitto. Hoc Anno etiam, Jacobus Thompson, A.M.; Thomas Henderson, A.M.; Johannes Lefferty, A.M.

Forma constituendi A.B.

Auctoritate, regio Diplomate mihi collata, pro More Academiarum in Anglia, vos ad primum in Artibus Gradum admitto; vobisque hunc Librum trado, una cum Potestate in Artibus prælegendi et docendi, quotiescunque ad hoc Munus evocati fueritis; cujus, hoc Instrumentum, sigillo nostri Collegii ratum, Testimonium sit.

Forma constituendi A.M.

Auctoritate, regio Diplomate mihi collata, pro More Academiarum in Anglia, vos ad secundum in Artibus Gradum admitto; vobisque hunc Librum trado, una cum

Potestate in Artibus prælegendi, publiceque profitendi ac docendi, quotiescunque ad hoc Munus evocati fueritis : cujus hoc Instrumentum, sigillo nostri Collegii ratum, Testimonium sit.

———————

In constituendo A.M. honorarios, inseratur hæc Clausula, scil—ad secundum in Artibus Gradum, Honoris causa, admitto.

———————

Orator Magistralis valedictorius.
Rev. McGregor.
Rev. Nathan Ker.
Dialogue.
Prayer."

The rules for admission into the several classes were very much the same as in the preceding administrations; as will appear from a comparison of the following extracts, from the account of the College in 1764, with the requisites for admission in Mr. Burr's time :

" Candidates for admission into the lowest or Freshman class must be capable of composing grammatical Latin, translating *Virgil, Cicero's Orations,* and the four Evangelists in Greek; and by a late order [made in Mr. Davies's administration] must understand the principal rules of vulgar arithmetic."

" Candidates for any of the higher classes are not only previously examined, but recite a fortnight upon trial, in that particular class for which they offer themselves ; and are then fixed in that, or a lower, as they happen to be judged qualified. But, unless in very singular and extraordinary cases, none are received after the Junior year."

" Besides these examinations for admission into the respective classes, and the last examination of the Senior class, previous to their obtaining the first collegiate honors, the three inferior classes, at the end of every year, are examined in such of the classics, arts and sciences, as they have studied, in order for admission into the next. And such as are found unqualified are not allowed to rise in the usual course. These, in like manner as the last examination of the Senior class, are attended upon by the president and tutors, in conjunction with any other gentlemen of liberal education who choose to be present. Dr. Finley hath also instituted quarterly examinations of the three classes before mentioned. But these are not so universal as the former, being restricted to what they have studied during the quarter. They have been found to answer excellent purposes ; for thereby the instructors can easily observe the gradual progress each one makes, and are thence enabled to encourage or warn them, as their several cases require. Hence also it may be easily imagined, it hath not a little conduced to the assiduity and carefulness of the students in their daily preparations."

From the beginning, the government and discipline of the College were administered by the President and the Tutors;

and with eminent success. During the year in which the above-mentioned account of the College was published, viz., 1764, there were one hundred and twenty students, and there were "very few whose conduct rendered them obnoxious even to the milder methods of punishment." The laws authorized the infliction of fines, but at this period in the history of the College this mode of punishment seems to have been given up; and admonition, private and before the classes, and suspension from the privileges of the College, became the exclusive punishments for violations of the established rules of the institution. Expulsion, then as now, could be inflicted only with the consent of the Trustees.

At the conclusion of this "account of the College of New Jersey" it is spoken of as "a College originally designed for the promotion of the general interests of Christianity," as well as the "cultivation of human science." And the writer of the account adds, " To the singular favor of Heaven on the means of instruction here used, it must be gratefully ascribed that many youth who have come to *Nassau Hall* for education, without any just sense of the obligations either of natural or revealed religion, have been here effectually reformed, become men of solid and rational piety, and now appear upon the stage of public action employing their talents to the honor of the Supreme Bestower and in promoting the good of mankind."

In the year 1762 there was an unusual attention on the part of the students to the subject of religion, and at the close of the College year, viz., in September, one-half of the students were deemed to be hopefully pious.

An interesting account of this work of grace, written by the Rev. Dr. John Woodhull, is given in Dr. Green's Historical Sketch of the College.

During Dr. Finley's administration the following-named gentlemen were members of the Faculty, viz.:

The Rev. Samuel Finley, President from 1761 to 1766.

Jeremiah Halsey, A.M., pastor of the church at Lamington, New Jersey, Tutor from 1757 to 1767.

Jacob Ker, A.M., pastor of the churches at Monokin and Wicomico, 1764 to 1795, Tutor from 1760 to 1762.

Samuel Blair, A.M., pastor of Old South Church, at Boston, Tutor from 1761 to 1764.

James Thompson, A.M., Tutor from 1762 to 1770.
Joseph Periam, A.M., Tutor from 1765 to 1766.

The following were elected Trustees during this period:

1761. Rev. Israel Reed, A.M., pastor of the Presbyterian church of Bound-brook, New Jersey, of the class of 1748.

1761. David Bostwick, A.M., pastor of the Presbyterian church of New York.

1761. Dr. John Redman, Physician, of Philadelphia.

1761. Dr. Robert Harris, Physician, of New Brunswick, and afterwards of Philadelphia.

1763. Rev. Charles Beatty, A.M., successor of the Rev. William Tennent as pastor of the church of Neshaminy.

1763. Hon. John Berrian, Judge of the Supreme Court of New Jersey.

1764. Robert Ogden, Esq., of Elizabethtown, New Jersey.

1764. Rev. Lambert De Ronde, of New York City.

1765. Rev. John Rodgers, D.D., of St. George's, Delaware, and afterwards of New York.

1765. Dr. William Shippen, Professor of Anatomy, Philadelphia.

Of one hundred and thirty graduates of the College who were students during the presidency of Dr. Finley, fifty-nine became ministers of the gospel.

The following named were among the graduates of the greatest note, viz.: of the class of—

1761. Rev. David Caldwell, D.D., President of the University of North Carolina.

1761. Hon. Thomas Henderson, A.M., member of the Continental Congress, and also of the United States House of Representatives.

1761. Rev. Nathan Ker, A.M., Goshen, New York.

1761. Rev. David Rice, of Virginia and Kentucky.

1762. Hon. Ebenezer Hazard, A.M., Postmaster-General of the United States.

1762. Rev. James Manning, D.D., the first President of Rhode Island College, now Brown University, and in 1786 a member of the Continental Congress.

1762. Rev. Joseph Periam, a Tutor of the College, distinguished for his attainments in mathematics, metaphysics, etc.

1762. Jonathan Dickinson Sergeant, a grandson of President Dickinson, and a member of the Continental Congress.

1762. Rev. Hezekiah Smith, S.T.D., of Massachusetts, an eminent Baptist preacher.

1763. Rev. James Boyd, of Pennsylvania, a Trustee of the College.

1763. Rev. Robert Cooper, D.D., of Pennsylvania.

1763. David Cowell, A.M., M.D., of New Jersey, for two years the Senior Physician and Surgeon of the United States Military Hospitals.

1763. Rev. John Craighead, A.M., of Pennsylvania. He raised a company from the people of his charge, and joined the army in New Jersey under Washington.

1763. Rev. Samuel Eakin, A.M., of West Jersey.

1763. Rev. John Lathrop, D.D., of Massachusetts, a Fellow of Harvard College.

1763. Hon. William Patterson, LL.D., a member of the Continental Congress; also of the Convention to form a constitution for the United States, Attorney-General and Governor of New Jersey, and a Justice of the United States Supreme Court.

1763. Hon. Tapping Reeve, LL.D., founder of the Litchfield Law School, and Chief Justice of Connecticut.

1763. Rev. John Simpson, A.M., a native of New Jersey, but a resident of North Carolina.

1763. Rev. William M. Tennent, D.D., of Abington, Pennsylvania, a Trustee of the College.

1763. Right Rev. Thomas John Clagget, D.D., Bishop of the Diocese of Maryland.

1764. Rev. Wm. Foster, A.M., of Pennsylvania, a teacher of theology.

1764. Rev. Joseph Smith, A.M., of Western Pennsylvania.

1764. Hon. Thomas Treadwell, a member of the U. S. House of Representatives.

1765. Rev. John Bacon, A.M., a member of the U. S. House of Representatives, and President of the Senate of Massachusetts.

1765. Rev. Joel Benedict, D.D., of Connecticut, a Biblical, classical, and mathematical scholar.

1765. Colonel Wm. Davies, A.M., of Virginia, eldest son of President Davies. Colonel Davies was an officer held in high esteem by Washington.

1765. Rev. Jonathan Edwards, D.D., President of Union College, New York.

1765. Robert Halsted, A.M., of Elizabethtown, New Jersey, a prominent physician.

1765. Hon. Richard Hutson, a member of the Continental Congress, and Chancellor of South Carolina.

1765. Rev. Samuel Kirkland, A.M., a missionary to the Seneca tribe of Indians. He contributed very much to the founding of Hamilton Academy, now Hamilton College.

1765. Robert Ogden, A.M., Esq., of Elizabeth, New Jersey, a counsellor-at-law.

1765. Ebenezer Pemberton, LL.D , an eminent classical teacher.

1765. David Ramsay, M.D., of South Carolina, a member of the Continental Congress, and author of " The American Revolution," and other works.

1765. Rev. Theodore Dirck Romeyn, D.D., of New Jersey, Professor of Theology in the Dutch Reformed College.

1765. Hon. Jacob Rush, LL.D., Chief Justice of Pennsylvania.

1766. Rev. Jacob Van Artsdalen, A.M., of New Jersey, a Trustee of the College.

1766. Hon. Waightstill Avery, A.M., Attorney-General of North Carolina.

1766. Rev. Hezekiah Balch, D.D., President of Greenville College, Tennessee.

1766. Hon. Oliver Ellsworth, LL.D., Chief Justice of the United States, and a member of the Convention to form a constitution for the United States.

1766. David Howell, LL.D., a member of the Continental Congress, and Professor of Law in Brown University.

1766. Rev. David McCalla, D.D., of Pennsylvania, Virginia, and South Carolina.

1766. John McPherson, A.M., Aid-de-Camp of General Montgomery at the attack on Quebec.

1766. Hon. Luther Martin, LL.D., Attorney-General of Maryland, and a member of the Convention to form the United States Constitution.

1766. Nathaniel Niles, A.M., Judge of the Supreme Court of Vermont, and a member of Congress from that State.

1766. Rev. James Power, D.D., one of the pioneer preachers of Western Pennsylvania.

1766. Rev. Isaac Skillman, D.D., pastor of a Baptist church, first in Boston, Massachusetts, and then in Salem, New Jersey.

1766. Micah Townsend, A.M., Secretary of the State of Vermont.

1766. Rev. John Woodhull, D.D., an eminent minister and teacher of theology, and for forty-four years a Trustee of the College.

CHAPTER XIII.

DR. FINLEY was a native of Ireland. At the time of his birth, 1715, his parents resided in the county of Armagh. In 1734 they came to America, and arrived at Philadelphia on the 28th of September. The family settled in West Jersey. Before leaving Ireland he began to prepare for the gospel ministry; and with this end in view he made considerable progress in classical learning, in which he afterwards became a proficient. After his arrival in this country he devoted several years to study, giving special attention to theology. It is thought, and it has even been affirmed, that he completed his studies at the Log College. But of this there is no certain evidence. It is rather a matter of conjecture, founded upon the well-known facts that his religious views were fully in accord with the teachings of that school; that he labored assiduously and boldly in support of the measures adopted by the Tennents and their friends for the promotion of religion; and that at this time the Log College was the only preparatory school for the ministry within the bounds of the American Presbyterian Church. But these facts do not determine this question, as he may have pursued his studies privately under some approved divine.

He was licensed to preach the gospel by the Presbytery of New Brunswick on the 5th day of August, 1740, and was ordained by the same Presbytery on the 13th of October, 1742. His preaching was attended with great success, especially in Pennsylvania and in the lower counties of New Jersey. In 1743, calls for his ministerial services were made by the churches of Cohansey and Deerfield, New Jersey, and from Milford, Connecticut. The Presbytery sent him to Milford "with allowance

277

he should preach for other places thereabouts when Providence may open a door for him." Being at Milford, he went by request to preach for the Second Society in New Haven. As this Society or Church had not been recognized either by the civil authority or by the New Haven Association, it was contrary to a recently enacted law of the Province for any one to preach for said Society, although it had been organized in conformity with the usages of the Congregational churches. Whether Mr. Finley had any knowledge of this prohibitory enactment is not known. He accepted the invitation, and on his way to the place of meeting he was arrested and confined. This occurred on the 5th of September, 1743, and on the 11th of the same month he was presented by the grand jury, and was sentenced to be transported out of the Colony as a vagrant, and under this sentence he was removed from the Province. In the following month he petitioned the Colonial Assembly to review the case, but his petition was refused. This of course prevented his going again to Milford.

For six months he preached as a stated supply for a new congregation in Philadelphia, of which the Rev. Gilbert Tennent became the first pastor.

In June, 1744, Mr. Finley accepted a call to the church at Nottingham, Maryland, at which place he continued in the faithful discharge of his pastoral duties for seventeen years. Here he established an academy, which acquired a great reputation, and one well deserved. Among his pupils at Nottingham were Governor Martin, of North Carolina, Governor Henry, of Maryland, Dr. Benjamin Rush, his brother, Judge Jacob Rush, Ebenezer Hazard, Esq., Colonel John Bayard, and the Rev. Dr. William M. Tennent, of Pennsylvania, the Rev. Dr. McWhorter, of Newark, New Jersey, and the Rev. Dr. James Waddell, of Virginia.

He was, says Dr. Sprague, an accomplished teacher, and among his pupils were some of the very best scholars of the day. He boarded most of them in his own house and at his table. He often indulged in a vein of pleasantry with them.

In the summer of 1745, Mr. Finley, in company with the Rev. Gilbert Tennent, and by appointment of the conjunct

Presbyteries of New Brunswick and of New Castle, waited upon Governor Gooch, of Virginia, with the view to repel certain insinuations and charges made against the Rev. John Roan, a member of the New Castle Presbytery, who by order of his Presbytery had spent some months in Virginia in missionary labors. Mr. Rowan's zeal and success, and perhaps some unguarded expressions, stirred up the wrath of his opponents, who hesitated not to charge him and the New Lights generally " with reflecting upon and vilifying the Established Religion," and who were so far successful that they enlisted in their movement against Mr. Roan the influence of that eminently candid and liberal-minded Governor. Messrs. Tennent and Finley were kindly received by Governor Gooch, who gave them permission to preach in Hanover. They continued there a week, and " much good was done by their ministry. The people of God were refreshed, and several careless sinners were awakened." (See report of their visit by Mr. Samuel Morris, in Foote's " Sketches of Virginia.")

Upon the death of President Davies, Dr. Finley was unanimously chosen his successor. Davies's own opinion of Finley's qualifications for the office is apparent from the following extracts. Writing to the Rev. Mr. Cowell, of Trenton, a Trustee of the College, in reference to the choice of a President, he says :

" I recommend Mr. Finley, from long and intimate acquaintance with him, as the best qualified person, in the compass of my knowledge, in America,—incomparably better qualified than myself. Though the want of some superficial accomplishments for empty popularity may keep him in obscurity for some little time, his hidden worth, in a few months, or years at most, will blaze out to the satisfaction and even astonishment of all candid men. A disappointment of this kind will certainly be of service to the College."

The letter from which this extract is made was written after Mr. Davies had declined the appointment of President, and also after he had refused to act as Vice-President for six months.

On another occasion Davies speaks of Finley as " the best of men, and my favorite friend."

The College flourished greatly under his administration of its affairs, and he himself enjoyed in a very high degree the confidence and respect of the Trustees, as is evident from their resolutions and minutes, and still more from the liberal provision they made for his support when his protracted illness, which ended in death, rendered necessary an increased expenditure of funds. His reputation was not limited to the Colonies. He was well known to not a few of the prominent Presbyterian and Dissenting ministers in Great Britain, with some of whom he kept up a friendly correspondence. Such was the opinion which they entertained of him as a scholar and a divine that, without his knowledge, they procured for him from the University of Glasgow the degree of Doctor in Divinity. This is said to have been the second time that this degree was ever conferred upon an American divine by a British university, the Rev. Dr. Francis Allison, of Philadelphia, being the first to receive this honor.

The diligence and earnestness with which Dr. Finley devoted himself to the discharge of his official duties, after a few years sensibly and most seriously affected his health. As mentioned in the sketch of his administration, he went to Philadelphia for medical advice and attendance, and he died in that city on the 17th of July, 1766, in the fifty-first year of his age.

"When he first applied to the physicians in Philadelphia," observes Dr. Green, "he had no apprehension that his dissolution was so near as it afterwards appeared, for he observed to his friends, 'If my work is done, I am ready. I do not desire to live a day longer than I can work for God. But I cannot think this is the case as yet. God has much more for me to do before I depart hence.'

"About a month before his death his physicians informed him that his disease appeared incurable. Upon which he expressed his perfect resignation to the Divine will, and from that time till his death he was employed in setting his house in order. Upon being told by one of his physicians that according to present appearances he could live but a few days longer, he lifted up his eyes, and exclaimed, 'Then welcome Lord Jesus.'"

All his remarks and all his conversations with his friends indicated a tranquil and even a joyous state of mind in view of his departure. He had no doubt as to his personal interest in Christ, and he felt assured that, for him, to die would be gain. Upon seeing a member of the Second Presbyterian Church in Philadelphia he said, " I have often preached and prayed among you, my dear sir, and the doctrines I preached to you are now my support, and, blessed be God, they are without a flaw. May the Lord bless and preserve your church! He designs good for it yet, I trust." To a person from Princeton he said, " Give my love to the people at Princeton, and tell them I am going to die, and that I am not afraid to die."

On the day before his death, " with a pleasing smile and with a strong voice, he cried out, ' Oh, I shall triumph over every foe ! The Lord hath given me the victory! I exult! I triumph !'" And he did triumph over death, and, committing his spirit to his Lord, he fell asleep, in the assured hope of a happy resurrection.

Dr. Finley's remains were interred in Philadelphia by the side of his friend the Rev. Dr. Gilbert Tennent, the heat of the weather not permitting their removal to Princeton. His funeral sermon was preached by the Rev. Dr. Richard Treat, D.D., of Abington, Pennsylvania, a Trustee of the College. A large number of the College students attended the funeral, and he was carried to his burial by eight members of the Senior class. The Trustees caused a cenotaph to be erected to his memory in the graveyard at Princeton, in a line with and nigh to the tombs of his predecessors in the office of President.

Ebenezer Hazard, Esq., of Philadelphia, formerly Postmaster-General of the United States, and, as before mentioned, a pupil of Dr. Finley's at the Nottingham Academy, gives this testimony to his honored preceptor :

" He was remarkable for sweetness of temper and politeness of behavior. He was given to hospitality, charitable without ostentation, exemplary in the discharge of all relative duties, and in all things showing himself a pattern of all good works. As a divine he was a Calvinist in sentiment. His sermons were not hasty productions, but filled with good sense and well-digested sentiment, expressed in language pleasing to men of science, yet perfectly intelligible by the illiterate. They were calculated to inform the ignorant, to alarm the careless and secure, and to edify and comfort the faithful."

Another pupil, the late Rev. Dr. John Woodhull, of Monmouth, New Jersey, thus speaks of him in a communication written at the request of Dr. Green :

" Dr. Finley was a man of small stature, and of a round and ruddy countenance. In the pulpit he was always solemn and sensible, and sometimes glowing with fervor. His learning was very extensive. · Every branch of study taught in the

College appeared to be familiar to him.   Among other things he taught Latin, Greek, and Hebrew in the Senior year.   He was highly respected and greatly beloved by the students, and had very little difficulty in governing the College. He died in Philadelphia, of a complaint in the liver, and requested to be carried to the grave by some of the Senior class.   This was done accordingly, and I was one of those who were bearers of his corpse."

In early life President Finley manifested a fondness for public disputation, and sometimes an undue warmth and earnestness in maintaining his views.   But mature age and Christian experience corrected this tendency to harsh judgment and expression; and he became an acknowledged model of courteous deportment and sweetness of temper, a man greatly beloved.

Soon after he was licensed he went within the bounds of the Donegal Presbytery, in Pennsylvania, and gave his countenance to the Rev. Alexander Craighead in his disorderly opposition to the Presbytery, by taking part in reading to the people Mr. C.'s defence of himself.   January 20, 1741, he preached, at Nottingham, Maryland, a sermon on Matthew xii. 27, 28: "If I by Beelzebub cast out devils, by whom do your sons cast them out ?"   This sermon was published under the title of "Christ Triumphing and Satan Raging," and was reprinted both at Boston and at London.   He also wrote a letter in commendation of Mr. Whitefield, which was published.

Dr. Finley's other publications were :

"A Refutation of Mr. Thomson's Sermon on the Doctrine of Conviction," 1743. A sermon on 2 Thessalonians ii. 11, 12, against the Moravians, being the substance of several sermons preached in Philadelphia, showing the Strength, Nature, and Symptoms of Delusion, 1743.   "A Charitable Plea for the Speechless," 1747, and a Vindication of it, in 1748.   A sermon preached at the ordination of the Rev. John Rodgers, at St. George's, Delaware, 1749.   A sermon on the death of the Rev. Samuel Blair, 1751.   A sermon from 2 Cor. x. 4, preached at Newark, New Jersey, before the Synod of New York, 1754.   A sermon entitled "The Curse of Meroz, or the Danger of Neutrality in the Cause of God and our Country," 1757.   A sermon on the death of President Davies, 1761.   A sermon preached at the funeral of the Rev. Gilbert Tennent, D.D., 1764.

A few years before the publication of his "Charitable Plea for the Speechless," and not long after his licensure by the Presbytery of New Brunswick, Dr. Finley engaged in a public debate on the mode and subjects of baptism with the Rev. Abel Morgan, Jr., of Middletown, New Jersey, a Baptist preacher of much note in those days. The debate was begun at Cohansey, in West Jersey, and resumed at Cape May, at which latter place there was at this time "a powerful revival of religion, in which," says Dr. Sprague, "the labors of Baptist and Presbyterian ministers were to a great extent intermingled." At this time, as we learn from the Rev. Richard Webster, two elders and six members left the Presbyterian Church for the Baptist. To the Charitable Plea Mr. Morgan replied in a pamphlet entitled "Anti-Pedo-Rantism, or Mr. Samuel Finley's Charitable Plea for the Speechless examined and refuted, the Baptism of Believers maintained, and the Mode of it by Immersion vindicated." To this Dr. Finley published a rejoinder in vindication of his plea, to which Mr. Morgan published a reply, and this ended their discussion. (See Sprague's "Annals of the American Pulpit," vol. vi. page 34, *art.* Abel Morgan, Jr.)

Dr. Finley was twice married. His first wife was Miss Sarah Hall, whose mother was the second wife of the Rev. Gilbert Tennent. She is spoken of by President Green as a lady of amiable character, who was truly a helpmeet to her husband, and by Dr. Sprague as a lady of rare excellence. By her Dr. Finley had eight children. She died in 1760, previously to his leaving Nottingham. The year following he married Miss Ann Clarkson, whose father, Matthew Clarkson, had been an eminent merchant in New York, and who was a lineal descendant of David Clarkson, B.D., one of the two thousand ministers ejected for non-conformity in England in 1662. Miss Clarkson was also a lady distinguished for her piety.

Dr. Finley's son Ebenezer Finley was graduated at Nassau Hall in 1772, and resided in Charleston, South Carolina. By some persons he has been confounded with his brother James E. B. Finley, a physician of Charleston. William Perroneau Finley, LL.D., a grandson of President Finley, was also graduated at this College, in 1820, with great distinction. He studied law, and he is now (1873) engaged in the practice of his profession. For several years he was President of Charleston College. Professor Morse, so well known for his connection with the electro-magnetic telegraph, is a grandson of Dr. Finley's daughter, Mrs. Breese, wife of Samuel Breese, Esq., of New Jersey.

The cenotaph erected to the memory of President Finley by the Trustees of the College has the following inscription :

Memoriæ Sacrum
Reverendi Samuelis Finley, S.T.D.   ·
Collegii Neo-Cæsariensis
Presidis,
Armachæ in Hibernia natus, A.D. MDCCXV.
In Americam migravit, Anno MDCCXXXIV.
Sacris ordinibus initiatus est, Anno MDCCXLIII,
apud Novum Brunsvicum,
Neo-Cæsariensium.
Ecclesiæ Nottinghami, Pensylvaniensium,
Munus pastorale suscepit, XIV. o Kal. Julii, MDCCXLIV;
Ibique, Academiæ celeberrimæ
diu præfuit.
Designatus Præses Collegii Neo-Cæsariensis,
Officium inivit, Id. Julii MDCCLXI.
Tandem, dilectus, veneratus,
Omnibus flendus
Morti occubuit, Philadelphiæ,
XV. o Kal. Sextilis, A.D. MDCCLXVI.
Artibus literisque excultus.
Præ cæteris præcipue enituit.
Rerum divinarum scientia.
Studio divinæ gloriæ flagrans
summis opibus
Ad veram Religionem promovendam,
et in concionibus,
et in sermone familiari
Operam semper navabat
Patientia, modestia, mansuetudo
Miranda
animo moribusque enituerunt,
Ob charitatem, observantiam, vigilantiam,
erga juvenes fidei suæ mandatos
fuit
insignissimus
Moribus ingenuis, pietate sincera,
Vixit omnibus dilectus,
Moriens triumphavit.

CHAPTER XIV.

THE INTERVAL BETWEEN THE DEATH OF DR. FINLEY AND THE ACCESSION OF DR. WITHERSPOON, FROM JULY 18, 1766, TO AUGUST 17, 1768.

DURING Dr. Finley's last illness, his death being apprehended, the Trustees, at a meeting held on the 25th of June, made provision for the government of the College by appointing the Rev. William Tennent "to act in the room and stead of President Finley," and by investing him "with the power and authority of the President."

The Board had their next meeting on Wednesday, the 25th of September, the day of the annual Commencement, and admitted the members of the Senior class, thirty-one in number, to their first degree in the Arts, the Rev. Elihu Spencer presiding and conferring the degrees. The usual exercises on such occasions were attended to, and also the ordinary routine of business, but the Trustees thought it best to defer the election of a President, for which they appointed a special meeting to be held on Wednesday, the 19th of the ensuing November. Mr. Jonathan Edwards, son of the late President Edwards, was chosen a Tutor of the College.

In reference to the salary of the President, they adopted the following minute:

" Whereas sundry weighty and important reasons have induced this Board to augment the late worthy president's salary from time to time to the sum of £400, but inasmuch as the occasion of the late necessary augmentation is removed, and the present low state of the College funds will not allow this Board to continue that salary for the future in its present circumstances, it is agreed, therefore, that the stated salary of the next president shall be £250, with the usual perquisites."

Having met on the day appointed, they elected the Rev. Dr. John Witherspoon, of which the following is the record:

"It having pleased a holy and wise God to remove by death the late Reverend and worthy Dr. Samuel Finley from the Presidentship of the College, the Board proceeded to the choice of another to succeed him in that office; when, after mature deliberation, the Reverend Dr. Witherspoon, of Paisley, Scotland, was duly elected as the Charter directs, *nemine contradicente;* and it is ordered, that a copy of this minute be enclosed and transmitted to the said Dr. Witherspoon, in a letter, signed by the President, from this Board, praying his acceptance of the said office. And it is further ordered, that a letter, in like manner, be transmitted to Richard Stockton, Esq., one of the members of this Board, now in London, enclosing the above to his care; and requesting his personal application to Dr. Witherspoon, to solicit his acceptance, and informing him that this Board will defray his, the said Mr. Stockton's, expenses in his journey to Scotland for the said purpose; and also that another letter, to be signed in like manner, be transmitted to Mr. Dennys De Berdt, Merchant in London, enclosing a duplicate of the letter to Dr. Witherspoon, in case the said Mr. Stockton should not happen to be in London, requesting the said Mr. De Berdt to forward the same; and that he would be pleased to use his influence and interest for the same purpose.

"Ordered, That Messrs. Spencer, Redman, and Shippen do prepare draughts of said letters, to be laid before this Board to-morrow morning.

"Resolved, That in case of Dr. Witherspoon's acceptance of the Presidentship of this College, the sum of one hundred guineas be allowed to defray the expenses of his removal and voyage; and that his salary do commence on the day of his arrival in North America."

On the following day the committee charged with this duty submitted drafts of letters to Dr. Witherspoon, Richard Stockton, Esq., and Mr. De Berdt, which were read and approved.

It was then ordered, that these letters be transcribed and signed by the President of the Board (for the time being), Mr. William Peartree Smith; who was requested to despatch the same by the first vessel bound from New York to London. All which was done, as appears from a report made by Mr. Smith at the next meeting of the Board.

Mr. Jonathan Edwards, elected a Tutor at the last meeting of the Board, appeared, and was qualified in accordance with the charter.

The Rev. William Tennent, who (both before and after the decease of President Finley) had discharged the duties of President of the College *pro tempore*, greatly to the satisfaction of the Board, was again requested to take upon himself the charge and burden of this office until the services of a permanent President were secured; and he having complied with this request was qualified as directed by the charter.

At this meeting there was begun a most important negotiation in reference to the establishment of sundry professorships in the College, and the selection of the incumbents from the two parties in the Presbyterian Church which, before the reunion of the Synods of New York and of Philadelphia, had been known under the designations of *Old Side* and *New Side*. The first minute relative to this business is in these words:

"Messrs. George Bryan, John Johnson, William Allison, James Meas, and Samuel Purviance, from Philadelphia, waited upon the Board, and presented a petition signed by some gentlemen of Lewistown, in Pennsylvania; and also a letter signed by twenty-six gentlemen of Philadelphia, requesting and recommending, among other things, the establishment of several Professorships in the College.

"Ordered, That the said papers do lie on the table for further mature consideration."

The following remarks on this overture are copied from the Notes of President Green, and they give within a comparatively narrow compass a clear view of the ends sought to be attained by the respective parties. On one point, however, the writer dissents from his venerated preceptor, viz., as to the origin of the College, which was originally established, not by the Synod of New York, or under its auspices, but by the leading ministers of the Presbytery of New York:

"In order to understand fully the nature of a negotiation of which this minute gives the first intimation, but which will afterwards be found to have occupied the most serious attention of the Board, it will be necessary to recollect what has been said in regard to the rival Synods of New York and Philadelphia; and that the College was the offspring and favorite child of the former of these bodies. It has been cursorily mentioned that the schism was healed in the year 1757, and that the two Synods were again united. This, notwithstanding much of the spirit which had produced the separation still remained, and indeed was not extinct till many years after this period. The cause and peculiarities of the Synod of Philadelphia had been denominated *the old side*, and those of the New York Synod *the new side;* and these shibboleths of party remained long after the formal union of the Synods. It is hoped that none of the acrimony with which they were once used any longer exists; but they still serve as convenient designations of parties which once divided the Presbyterian Church.

"The College of New Jersey, notwithstanding the adverse circumstances which it experienced in the death of four Presidents in less than nine years, had, on the whole, been advancing in reputation ever since its establishment; and under Dr. Finley had probably risen higher than at any preceding period. At his death it was unquestionably the most reputable institution of which the Presbyterians could boast. This circumstance, it is believed, induced the old side party to seek an alliance with it;

and if a cordial alliance could have been formed, it would, without doubt, have been an event highly favorable for the College, and for the Presbyterian Church at large.   That some of the leading men in each party hoped that this might be effected, and honestly labored to bring it about, there is good reason to believe. But there was still too much of party views and feelings to admit of such an issue. The whole transaction bears marks of jealous caution and diplomatic arrangement on both sides.   The College being now without a President, and known to be in great want of funds, the opportunity was thought to be favorable for obtaining a participation, by the old side party, in the whole government and instruction of the institution, in consideration of the pecuniary aid which that party could afford to give.   But the Board of Trustees proceeded, as we have seen, to elect a President, even before they opened a negotiation; and with a design, it is believed, to fore-close all interference or propositions in regard to the choice of that officer.   On the other hand, such representations were speedily made in Scotland of the state of the College as were calculated to induce Dr. Witherspoon to refuse the Presi-dency, and which actually had that effect till his misapprehensions were removed by an agent of the Board.   The writer has in his hands the unquestionable evidence of this fact, although it does not appear in the records of the Trustees."   (See Dr. Green's " Notes.")

Of the precise character of this evidence the venerable writer gives us no intimation; but his positive declaration is conclusive as to the existence of such evidence at the time he penned this statement.*

On the next morning, November 20, the Trustees continued their sessions, and in the minutes for that day the following record occurs:

" A letter was delivered into this Board, signed by several gentlemen of Balti-more, Maryland, on the subject-matter of those presented yesterday.

" Ordered, That the said letter do lie with the others on the table for further consideration."

" Resolved, That Messrs. Woodruff, Tennent, Spencer, and Rodgers be a com-mittee forthwith to wait upon the gentlemen from Philadelphia who have signified it to be their desire to meet a committee of this Board in order to a free conference on the subject-matter of sundry letters, &c., which have been delivered by them; and that the said committee do report the result of the said conference to this Board."

" The committee appointed to wait upon the gentlemen from Philadelphia, being returned, reported, That they had a full and free conference together upon the subject-matter of the petitions and letters presented by those gentlemen.   That the said gentlemen observed that the proposals made to the Trustees being upon the footing that the President's chair was vacant, they were disconcerted in their gen-

---

* It is probable that "the unquestionable evidence" mentioned by Dr. Green was contained in a letter from the Rev. Charles Beatty to Rev. Dr. Treat, of Abington, Pennsylvania.   (See sketch of Dr. Witherspoon's Life.)

eral plan by the election of Dr. Witherspoon to the Presidentship before their proposals were presented; that the said plan being thereby altered, they were not authorized to determine absolutely what would be done hereafter by their constituents respecting the general object they had in view; that nevertheless they were truly desirous that some effectual method might be taken to complete the proposed design. That a proposal was made by the said committee, viz., that on the supposition of the nomination of two gentlemen for Professorships, to wit, the Rev. Messrs. Blair* and McDowell, on the condition that money could be raised by the friends of this Institution to support them, Whether their constituents would be satisfied, and they would undertake to promote a subscription for their support; to which the said gentlemen replied, That however desirous they were to accomplish so excellent a design, they would not at present engage for the future conduct of their constituents."

" The Board, taking in mature consideration the above Report, came to the following resolution :

" Whereas it is an object of their greatest concern that union and the strictest harmony among all the friends and patrons of religion and sound literature might be promoted by every proper method, and that this Institution may have every possible advantage of increasing its Reputation and advancing the cause of Learning ; And as there appears reason to expect great and happy consequences both to the interest of religion and of this Seminary from putting into execution the general design of the proposals made, they will gladly do everything in their power to accomplish the said end ; and accordingly declare themselves greatly desirous that a sufficiency of moneys by subscriptions or otherwise might be obtained to accomplish this noble design ; and are cheerfully willing to join in any particular method that can be devised for raising the necessary sums. For though this Board would gladly proceed to the election of Professors without delay, were there funds sufficient to support such an additional expense ; yet they judge it by no means expedient to take that step before they have a certain medium for their support."

The above extracts comprise all the action on this subject at this meeting of the Board.

The Rev. John Blair, of Fagg's Manor, Pennsylvania, was chosen a Trustee of the College, in the room of the Rev. John Light or Leydt, pastor of the Dutch Reformed Church, New Brunswick, resigned.

---

* Knowing that some of the Trustees, and probably a majority, were desirous, even at this time, to appoint Mr. Blair Professor of Divinity in the College, the Rev. James Caldwell, of Elizabethtown, the Rev. Alexander McWhorter, of Newark, neither, at that time, a Trustee of the College, and Mr. Jonathan Edwards, Jr., then a Tutor in the College, were earnestly in favor of having Dr. Hopkins appointed instead of Mr. Blair. They were of the opinion that the requisite funds to sustain Mr. Blair could not be had from the friends of the College, and this encouraged these gentlemen to make a strenuous effort to secure the appointment of Dr. Hopkins. (See letter of Mr. Caldwell, in the Bellamy Manuscripts.)

As the Grammar School connected with the College was "likely to become chargeable to the College funds," the Board resolved that the teacher (Mr. Avery) might continue the school in the College, on his own account, if he thought it expedient; but that they would no longer be responsible for its support.

"Mr. Samuel Breese, one of the Executors of the Estate of Dr. Finley, deceased, requesting an order of this Board upon the Treasurer, for the payment of the salary which became due to the said Dr. Finley at the time of his death, the Clerk is directed immediately to make out an order on Mr. Sergeant for the payment of whatever sum remained due to the said Dr. Finley as his salary at the time of his death, together with the interest of the same from the day of his decease; and that he take a discharge of the same from the Executor of the Estate."

The next meeting of the Board took place on Wednesday, the 30th of September, 1767, the day of the annual Commencement.

After the exercises usual on such occasions, eleven candidates were admitted to the first degree in the Arts.

The next day, October 1, the Board met again; sixteen Trustees being present. The Hon. Edward Shippen, of Lancaster, Pennsylvania, one of the Trustees named in the second charter of the College, tendered his resignation, for the reason that "he finds himself incapable, through growing infirmity and distant residence, of giving attendance." His resignation was accepted.

Mr. William Peartree Smith "communicated a letter to this Board from the Rev. Dr. John Witherspoon, wherein that gentleman is pleased to decline an acceptance of the Presidentship of this College, to which he was elected in November last."

"Mr. Halsey, eldest Tutor of this College, now thought fit to resign his office; and requesting testimonials in his favor from the Trustees, It is ordered, That an ample certificate be made out, to be signed by the Clerk in the name of this Board and sealed with the Corporation seal, certifying the said Mr. Halsey's faithful services and good conduct during his Tutorship in the College, with Recommendation of him as a Gentleman of Genius, Learning, and real Merit."

The Rev. William Tennent, the President *pro tem.*, submitted the draft of sundry laws for the better regulation and order of the College; which were read, considered, amended, and unanimously adopted.

The *first* one empowered the officers of the College to examine the classes at any time of the year, at their discretion.

The *second* prohibited the students from taking any part in the choice of orators for Commencement and other public exhibitions.

The *third* was a law to prevent damage to the several rooms and apartments of the College and to the furniture of the same. In accord with this last regulation, Mr. James Thompson, one of the Tutors, was appointed "Inspector of the Rooms," and was allowed five pounds per annum for this service.

The committee, Messrs. Woodruff and Ogden, to examine into the general state of the College funds, reported "that they find the sum total in the hands of the Treasurer, in Bonds, Notes, &c., to amount to the sum of £2815.3.1, of which they find only £950, or thereabouts, to be at present under actual improvement at interest."

Soon after the opening of their session this day, Mr. Stockton mentioned to the Board that there were several gentlemen from Philadelphia now in town, viz., Messrs. George Bryan, William Allison, John Chevalier, John Boyd, and John Wallace, who had informed him that they had something to offer to this Corporation, and were desirous of being heard. Mr. Stockton was accordingly requested immediately to wait upon those gentlemen and inform them that the Trustees were now ready to hear them.

" The Philadelphia gentlemen, being introduced by Mr. Stockton, begged leave to remind the Trustees that they had the last year presented sundry papers and letters containing proposals relative to the establishment of a Faculty in this College; that their constituents were still very desirous that the general plan should be carried into execution if the circumstances of the College would possibly admit of it; and prayed that the same might be reconsidered. The said gentlemen were then assured that this Board would come to some determination thereon as soon as possible."

" Ordered, That the several letters and proposals above mentioned be read and maturely considered; which were read and considered accordingly."

" Resolved, That Messrs. Stockton, Ogden, and [Dr. W.] Shippen be a committee to confer more fully with those gentlemen on the subject-matter of said proposals."

This committee had a conference with the delegates from Philadelphia, and made the following report to the Board, viz.:

" That they find those gentlemen and their constituents still heartily desirous of concurring with the Trustees of this College in the establishment and support of a Faculty, and promising to unite their utmost endeavors to raise the necessary funds to carry the same into speedy execution; that the said gentlemen being asked by the Committee whether the appointment of all or any of the particular persons to Professorships in their proposals named and recommended was intended as a Term of their acceding to and assisting in the establishment proposed, replied, That it was not the intention to make the appointment of any of the particular persons named by their constituents a term of the proposed Union; but that any other gentlemen who might be deemed qualified for their offices, and indiscriminately chosen without regard to party distinctions, would be acceptable to them."

" The Board having taken the whole into mature consideration were unanimously of the opinion that the constitution of a Faculty to consist of well-qualified Professors in the several branches of Academical Science to be chosen without regard to any little party differences would greatly subserve the interests of Religion and Learning in this Seminary, and would tend to the better and more perfect instruction and government in the same. And it was accordingly resolved, that in pursuance of said plan, the choice of a Faculty to consist of Professors in some of the most essential parts of literature be entered upon to-morrow morning."

" October 2, 9 o'clock A.M. Met according to adjournment, and present as yesterday. The Trustees having thought proper, pursuant to their resolution of yesterday, to enter upon the choice of a Faculty, to consist of Professors in the most necessary branches of education in the College, did, in the first place, proceed to the appointment of a Professor of Divinity and Moral Philosophy; when, after mature deliberation, the Rev. Mr. John Blair, of Fog's [Fagg's] Manor, in Pennsylvania, and one of the members of this Board, was chosen to that office. Adjourned to 3 o'clock P.M.

" The Trustees now proceeded to the choice of a Professor of Mathematics and Natural Philosophy, when Dr. Hugh Williamson, of Philadelphia, was duly elected to that office; and Mr. Jonathan Edwards, now a Tutor in this College, was also duly chosen to the Professorship of Languages and Logic.

" The Rev. Dr. John Witherspoon having thought fit to decline the invitation of this Board to the Presidentship of the College, the Trustees proceeded to the choice of a President to succeed the reverend and worthy Dr. Finley, deceased. After mature deliberation, the Rev. Mr. Samuel Blair, of Boston, in New England, was duly elected President of this College, and also Professor of Rhetoric and Metaphysics. Nemine contradicente.

" Mr. George Bryan, of Philadelphia [one of the delegates from that city to confer with the Board], was unanimously chosen a Trustee, in the room of Edward Shippen, Esq., resigned."

"Voted, That the sum of one hundred pounds proclamation be allowed to the Rev. Mr. William Tennent in consideration of his services to this College as Vice-President *pro tem.* from the 19th of November last to the present Commencement; and ordered, That the Treasurer pay unto the said Mr. Tennent the said sum of £100 out of the first moneys that he may have in his hands.

"Voted, That the annual salaries of the President and Professors, now chosen, to commence from the time they shall respectively enter upon their several offices, shall be as follows:

To the President and Professor of Rhetoric and Metaphysics	£200
" Professor of Divinity and Moral Philosophy	175
" Professor of Mathematics and Natural Philosophy	150
" Professor of Languages and Logic	125

"The Trustees having now, pursuant to the plan proposed, nominated and chosen several gentlemen of reputation in the literary world and undoubted skill in those branches of science to which they are designed, do find, that notwithstanding they have annexed the most moderate salaries to the respective offices, the present state of the College revenues renders it impossible for them to provide the sum total of the said salaries, and that it is therefore not in their power immediately to invite and introduce together the four Professors elect to the actual execution of their offices, as a Faculty, even should they all acquiesce in their present election, which is yet an uncertainty; and as four Instructors are immediately requisite to carry on the business of the College, it is resolved to continue the present constitution under a Vice-President and three Tutors, at least during the year ensuing,—that at the end of the year the President elect be called to the exercise of his office,—and if, in the interim, any means may be devised to enable the Trustees to support two other Professors (viz., the Professor of Mathematics and Natural Philosophy, and the Professor of Languages and Logic), in that case the gentlemen now elected to those offices shall be called to enter upon the same, and the constitution by a Faculty shall then take place.

"Pursuant to the above resolution, the Rev. Mr. John Blair, who is pleased to accept of the Professorship of Divinity and Morality, was chosen Vice-President until the next Commencement, and was accordingly qualified to [hold] those offices, as the Charter directs.

"Mr. Joseph Periam was also duly elected Senior Tutor of the College, in the room of Mr. Jeremiah Halsey resigned, and [was] qualified, as the Charter directs.

"Mr. James Thompson, Second Tutor, and Mr. Jonathan Edwards, Junior Tutor, whose services and conduct in their respective offices being much approved, were requested by Mr. Tennent, in the name of this Board, to continue in their said offices for the year ensuing, to which they were pleased to signify their compliance."

"Voted, That there be allowed the sum of one hundred pounds *proc.* to each of the Tutors, as their respective salaries for the year ensuing."

"Voted, That the expenses that may accrue to the Rev. Mr. John Blair, in the removal of himself and family to Nassau Hall, be defrayed out of the College treasury."

"Dr. Shippen is desired to inform Dr. Williamson, by letter, in the name of this

Board, of his election to the Professorship of Mathematics and Natural Philosophy, and to acquaint him with their resolution to defer calling him to the exercise of the said office for at least one year, and until they are enabled to provide the support annexed to the same.

" Mr. Spencer is desired to notify the congregation at Fog's [Fagg's] Manor of Mr. Blair's election to a Professorship in this College, and to pursue the necessary steps, in behalf of this Board, for obtaining the said Mr. Blair's discharge from his pastoral office, in order to his speedy removal."

The Rev. Wm. Kirkpatrick, of Amwell, New Jersey, was elected a Trustee, in the room of Mr. Blair, resigned.

Mr. Blair was released from his pastoral charge, and removed to Princeton. None of the other Professors accepted their appointments; and no reference to their appointments occurs in the subsequent minutes of the Board, with the exception of the following minutes, of December 10, 1767 :* "The Trustees having thought it expedient, in order to enable them to establish and support a number of Professors in this College, that subscriptions in this and the neighboring colonies should be set forward among the friends of religion and learning, and Mr. [W. P.] Smith presenting a draught of a preamble to said proposed subscription papers, the one designed to be subscribed by such persons as may choose to contribute a sum in gross, the other as an annual subscription to continue for seven years, from the 1st of August, 1768, the same were examined and approved; and Mr. Bryan is desired to order three hundred of each sort to be forthwith printed at Philadelphia, and to distribute a number of each to every member of this Board, who mutually engage to use their best endeavors to promote subscriptions in the Country. And the said Mr. Bryan is directed to draw upon the Treasurer for the expense of printing the same."

"This Board being informed that the Synod of New York and Philadelphia have lately appointed an annual contribution to be made in the several congregations throughout their bounds for the laudable purpose of promoting Christian knowledge, and conceiving a yearly appropriation of some part of said contribution for and towards the support of a Divinity Professor in this College would perfectly accord with the views of the Synod in the said appointment, as the well training up and instruction of our youth in the doctrines of Christianity would be one of the most effectual means to accomplish the excellent purposes designed by said contributions, It is therefore ordered, That the Rev. Mr. Rodgers do prepare a draught of a letter to said Synod, requesting an annual appropriation of part of those collections towards the maintenance of a Professor of Divinity in this College, to be laid before the Board this afternoon."

" Mr. Rodgers, pursuant to order, laid before the Board a draught of a letter to the Reverend the Synod of New York and Philadelphia; which being read and approved, it was ordered that the same be transcribed and signed by the Clerk, and that Mr. Rodgers do present it at the next meeting of said Synod."

This letter was laid before the Synod, at their sessions in

---

* On page 181 of the first volume of Minutes there is a reference to the plan for appointing Professors, but no reference to the particular appointments now made.

Philadelphia, in the month of May, 1768, and the following is the minute of the Synod's action in regard to it:

"A supplication was brought in from the honorable the Board of Trustees of the New Jersey College, praying assistance in supporting a Professor of Divinity, from the last year's collection, and was fully considered, and the Synod judge that they cannot give any part of the money collected last year towards the support of a Professor of Divinity in said College, but do agree, and hereby order, that a general collection be made for this purpose in all our congregations; and that the money raised by this separate collection be applied particularly by this Synod, yearly, for this purpose till expended; and in the mean time, in order to assist in supporting a Professor of Divinity in said College, the Synod do agree to give the present Professor the sum of fifty pounds out of the money now in the hands of our Treasurer, to be refunded next year.

"Ordered, That Mr. Treat, our Treasurer, pay this sum to the Trustees of the College of New Jersey."

Mr. Blair, the Professor of Divinity, was the Moderator of the Synod this year.

Under the date of the 25th of May, 1769, the following minute occurs in the records of the Synod:

"The Synod do agree to give the honorable Board of Trustees of the New Jersey College, towards supporting a Professor of Divinity in that institution, sixty pounds for the last year, and sixty pounds for the current year, out of the collections made in our congregations for this purpose, agreeable to an order of last session. The fifty pounds lent that honorable Board last year is refunded."

At the opening of the next term after his election, Mr. Blair, as Vice-President, took the oversight of the College, and, aided by the three Tutors above named, conducted its instruction and government, as previously ordered by the Board,—it being expressly said at the time of their appointment that the President elect, the Rev. Samuel Blair, and the Professors elect of Mathematics and of Languages, were not expected to enter upon the duties of their respective offices for at least one year.

"These arrangements," says President Green, "appear to have been proposed on the one side, and acceded to on the other, with a view to show a conciliatory disposition. One professor of the old side party was chosen; and at the same meeting one gentleman of that party was unanimously elected to fill a vacancy which had taken place in the Board of Trustees. While this was done, effectual care was taken to give no pledges which could produce subsequent embarrassment. These measures were, perhaps, the best which the circumstances in which the Board was placed would admit; yet it seems strange that any one should seriously expect that they would ever be carried into effect. It is believed by the writer [Dr. Green] that many members of the Board, at this very time, cherished a pretty sanguine hope that Dr. Witherspoon would yet become the President of the College. That event, whether expected or not, did at length take place; and not a word afterwards appears on the records in regard to the appointments which were now made, nor in reference to any part of this negotiation and agreement relative to a faculty. There had never, indeed, been any *open* or avowed opposition to the election of Dr. Witherspoon. And when he entered on his office, his prudence, talents, and weight of character not only put an end to party measures in the Board of Trustees, but contributed greatly to produce effect in the councils of the Church to which he belonged."

At the meeting of the Board at which the matters above mentioned took place,

" Mr. Tennent communicated a letter from Mr. Stephen Sayre, of London, merchant, wherein he is pleased to offer, if properly empowered, to exert his endeavors in England for obtaining benefactions in favor of this College. Resolved, That the thanks of this Board be transmitted to that gentleman for his polite and generous offer, and that Mr. Rodgers do write to the said Mr. Sayre in the name of this Board, expressing their grateful acknowledgments for his proffered services in England; and at the same time to enclose a general commission from the Trustees of this College, to be signed by the Clerk in their name, and sealed with the Corporation seal, empowering him to act as their agent and attorney in soliciting and receiving benefactions in Books, Philosophical Instruments, and subscriptions for the use of said College, and to employ any attorneys under him for said purpose." *

Mr. Halsey, who had been a Tutor for ten years, having resigned his office, the Trustees, in addition to the testimonial which they directed should be given, voted him forty pounds over and above his regular salary for the year.

The Treasurer was ordered to collect the outstanding debts of the last lottery with all possible despatch.

A committee was appointed to settle Mr. Stockton's account with the College while he was in Great Britain.

---

* "Stephen Sayre, the gentleman named in this minute," says Dr. Green, "was a native American, and graduated at Nassau Hall in 1757. He was at this time an eminent London merchant, and afterwards the high sheriff of that city. His kind dispositions towards his Alma Mater were certainly commendable; but there is no record of any donations which he obtained for the College. Perhaps his earnest expectations were disappointed by the ardent controversies which about this time took place in regard to the claims of the mother-country and the colonies. In those controversies Mr. Sayre participated deeply. He eventually left Britain, returned to his native country, and lived in retirement to a very advanced age. He died in Virginia about four years since, about the year 1818."

Provision was made for a new edition of the Newark (Latin) Grammar, to be revised and published by the Rev. Mr. Caldwell, and Messrs. Reeve and Pemberton, masters of the grammar-school at Elizabethtown.

December 9, 1767, a special meeting of the Trustees was called, in accordance with the charter, at the request of six members of the Board.

At this meeting Mr. Wm. P. Smith, the senior Trustee present, and who presided on this occasion,

"communicated a letter from the Rev. Samuel Blair to the Honorable William Smith, Esq., the President of the Trustees at their last meeting, wherein the said Mr. Blair declines accepting the Presidentship of this College, to which he was chosen; and the said office was accordingly declared to be vacant."

At this same meeting

"Mr. Stockton communicated to the Board sundry letters he had recently received from Scotland, informing him that the difficulties which had prevented Dr. Witherspoon's acceptance of the Presidentship to which he had been chosen were now removed, and that upon a re-election he would esteem it a duty to enter into this public service. The Board, receiving the intelligence with peculiar satisfaction, proceeded immediately to a re-election, when the said Dr. Witherspoon was again unanimously chosen to the said office;" and it was

"Resolved, That the salary to be allowed Dr. Witherspoon as President of the College be according to the propositions made to him in the letter wrote him by the President of this Board upon his former election; together with the explanation thereof mentioned to the said Dr. Witherspoon by Mr. Stockton, one of the members of this Board, in his letter from Edinburgh, dated 2d March, 1767. And that the same sum of one hundred guineas, as on his former election, be allowed him for the expenses of removing himself and his family to this place."

"Resolved, That the President of this Board be desired immediately to transmit a copy of the above vote to Dr. Witherspoon; and also to send a duplicate of the same by the first opportunity, to be accompanied with his letter, requesting the said Dr. Witherspoon to hasten his coming over as soon as he conveniently can."

The Rev. Samuel Blair mentioned above as having declined the Presidency was the son of the Rev. Samuel Blair, of Fagg's Manor, Pennsylvania, and, like his father, was distinguished for talent and learning as well as for piety. He was also a nephew of the Rev. John Blair, the Professor of Divinity and Moral Philosophy. He was a graduate of the College in 1760, and was a Tutor for three years during the administration of President Finley, and, as mentioned in the sketch of that administration, he was the author of the account of the College published

by order of the Trustees in 1764.   At the time of his election
as President of the College he was a colleague of the Rev. Dr.
Sewall, minister of South Church, Boston.   He was not thirty
years of age when he was chosen President.   Speaking of this
event, and of his declining the appointment, President Green,
in his " Notes," observes, " But at that time a youth of higher
promise was probably not to be found in the American Church."

" The writer," continues Dr. Green, " has learned from good authority that as soon
as Mr. Blair had ascertained that a re-election of Dr. Witherspoon would secure his
services and influence in favor of the College, a voluntary and prompt tender of
the resignation here recorded prevented the embarrassment in which the Trustees
might otherwise have been involved.   Dr. Witherspoon has been known to mention this act as an instance of disinterestedness and generosity highly creditable to
Mr. Blair.

" This gentleman, shortly after his resignation of the Presidency, fell into a vale-
tudinary state, which induced him to resign his pastoral charge in Boston, and
which rendered his subsequent life little else than a long disease.   He resided for
many years at Germantown, in the neighborhood of Philadelphia, and performed
such ministerial services as his health would permit.   For two years he served as
chaplain in Congress.   The writer recollects many pleasing hours spent in his
company in an acquaintance of nearly thirty years' continuance.   He died about
two years since [1820]."—(See Dr. Green's " Notes.")

After their second election of Dr. Witherspoon, the Trustees
passed a resolution designed to prevent candidates from entering any other than the Freshman class ; but this order was soon
repealed and the previous rule re-established.

The following important rule was adopted at this time :

" Voted, That the practice of sending Freshmen upon errands, or employing them
as servitors in any manner whatsoever, be from henceforth totally discontinued."

" Mr. Stockton having informed the Board that he had received when in England
the sum of one hundred pounds sterling, which was given to the Trustees of this
College in trust for and towards the support of a Divinity Professor in the same, by
Mr. Williamson, of Hanover, in Virginia ; Resolved, That Dr. Redman do transmit
the thanks of this Board, by letter, to the said Mr. Williamson for his generous
donation."

The grammar-school in connection with the College having been discontinued
after the death of President Finley, the Trustees now appointed a committee " to
consider of ways and means for setting and promoting the same, . . . and to report
at the next meeting."

During this interval the following gentlemen were chosen Trustees :
The Rev. John Blair, in the room of the Rev. John Light (Leydt), resigned.
Hon. George Bryan, in the room of Hon. Edward Shippen, resigned.

The Rev. Wm. Kirkpatrick, in the room of the Rev. John Blair, elected Professor. The following gentlemen composed the Faculty :

The Rev. William Tennent, President *pro tem.*, from July 17 to October 2, 1767.

The Rev. John Blair, Vice-President, from October 2, 1767, to August 17, 1768; Professor of Divinity and Moral Philosophy until the annual Commencement, September 27, 1769.

Mr. Jeremiah Halsey, Senior Tutor.

Mr. James Thompson.

Mr. Joseph Periam, Senior Tutor upon Mr. Halsey's resignation.

Mr. Jonathan Edwards.

At the annnual Commencement of 1767 there were *eleven* graduates, and at that of 1768 there were also eleven; total for both years, twenty-two. Of these, *eight* became ministers of the gospel. The most distinguished of these graduates in after-life were—of the class of

1767. Francis Barber, A.M., of New Jersey, a classical teacher of much repute; also Lieutenant-Colonel in the U. S. Army.

1767. Nathaniel Ramsay, A.M., of Maryland, a lawyer of eminence, a Colonel in the Revolutionary Army, and a member of the Continental Congress.

1767. Samuel Witham Stockton, A.M., Secretary of State for New Jersey; previously he was Secretary of the American Commission to the Courts of Austria and Prussia.

1768. Rev. Robert Blackwell, D.D., of Philadelphia, an Episcopal clergyman, a Chaplain and also a Surgeon in the U. S. Army.

1768. Ephraim Brevard, M.D., reputed author of the Mecklenburg Resolutions; a Surgeon in the U. S. Army.

1768. Pierpont Edwards, A.M., a son of President Edwards, Judge of the U. S. District Court for Connecticut, and a member of the Continental Congress.

1768. Wm. Churchill Houston, A.M., Professor of Mathematics in the College of New Jersey; a member of the Continental Congress.

1768. Adlai Osborne, during the Revolution a Colonel in the U. S. Army; also a Trustee of the University of North Carolina.

1768. Rev. Thomas Reese, D.D., of South Carolina, a scholar and a minister of much repute.

1768. Rev. Elias Van Bunschooten, a minister of the Reformed Dutch Church. He left a large legacy to Queen's College, New Brunswick.

CHAPTER XV.

DR. WITHERSPOON was inaugurated on the 17th of August, 1768, at a special meeting of the Board called for this purpose. The minute of the Board in reference to his inauguration is as follows: " The Rev. Dr. Witherspoon being now arrived from North Britain to preside at the head of this Institution, pursuant to his re-election at the last meeting, was duly qualified as the charter directs; and, having taken the oaths of office as one of the Trustees and President of the College, took his seat accordingly."

So far as appears from the minutes, there was no other ceremony connected with his entrance upon the duties of his office; but in a short sketch of his administration, given by the Rev. Dr. Ashbel Green before the Alumni Association in 1840, and published in the "Presbyterian Magazine" for 1854, it is expressly said that he delivered a Latin inaugural address on the union of Piety and Science. The venerable author of this statement confirmed it by adding, " I had an opportunity, when a member of the Senior class in College, of perusing the Address, in the handwriting of its author; but it has not been found among the manuscripts which were left by the Doctor at the time of his death."

Dr. Witherspoon was most cordially welcomed by the Trustees and other friends of the College, and also by the community at large. They all expected great benefits to result to the College from his accession to the Presidency; and in this they were not disappointed.

The first order passed by the Board, after his inauguration, was one directing the Treasurer of the College to pay Dr.

300

Witherspoon, "with the first moneys that may come into his hands, one hundred guineas, the same being the sum that was voted by this Board for defraying the expenses of his removal to this country." This shows the low condition of the College funds at this time.

The following resolutions were also passed:

"Voted, That the salary of the President of this College be fixed at three hundred and fifty pounds proclamation money of this Province, exclusive of house and the customary use of the College lands. Which sum of £350 is equal to £206 sterling money of Great Britain, mentioned to Dr. Witherspoon at his first election, in a letter sent him by order of this Board, and agreeable to an explanation of the same in Mr. Stockton's letter written to him from Edinburgh, 2d of March, 1767."

There is no mention in the minutes of the meeting at which Dr. Witherspoon was chosen President of the College that his salary should be three hundred and fifty pounds *proc.* At a meeting of the Trustees, held some weeks before his election, it was agreed that the President's salary should be two hundred and fifty pounds *proc.*, with the usual perquisites. It is not improbable, however, that in the letters sent to Dr. Witherspoon and to Mr. Stockton there were intimations of a willingness to make his salary three hundred and fifty pounds.

"Voted, That the President's salary do commence from the fifteenth day of May last, being the day of his discharge from his pastoral office at Paisley to enter upon this service."

"Dr. Witherspoon, President of this College, having, at the request of several friends to this Institution, taken a tour from Paisley to London, and from thence to Holland, and having thereby done eminent service to this College, It is ordered, That the thanks of this Board be given to the said Dr. Witherspoon, and that the Treasurer is ordered to pay unto him the balance of his account of expenses on that service, amounting to the sum of £42.9.0, sterling money of Great Britain."

Of the precise character of this "eminent service" no mention is made in the minutes of the Board. It no doubt consisted, in part, in a successful effort to enlist the kind feelings of sundry friends of religion and learning in behalf of the College, and to prepare the way for benefactions in books, apparatus, and gifts to the College treasury. For at the time the above minute was made we find also the following:

"The President having informed the Board that he had brought over a considerable number of Books for the use of the College, amounting to about 300 volumes, which were gifts of sundry friends abroad, and that he soon expects another considerable benefaction in Books, the Trustees do most thankfully accept the same, and request that the President will be pleased, by letter, in their name, to express to the several Benefactors their grateful acknowledgments for these useful donations."

It was next " Voted, That Dr. Witherspoon be allowed the privilege of educating his sons in this College, without payment of tuition-money or other occasional fees."

After a reference to the action of the Board in 1751 on the subject of College habits, of which action, however, no mention is made in the minutes of that year, but to which there is an allusion in the minutes of 1752, the following stringent rule was adopted, viz. :

" That from and after the next Commencement Vacation in this present year, 1768, all the officers and students of Nassau Hall shall appear uniformly habited, in a proper collegiate black gown and square cap, to be made in the manner and form of those now used in some of our neighboring colleges, and perfectly uniform, excepting proper distinctions that may be devised by the officers of the College to distinguish the habits of the President, Professors, and Tutors from those of the students.   And it is hereby strictly ordained, That no resident student or undergraduate, subject to the rules and orders of the College, shall at any time, after the next Commencement vacation, appear either at church, in the College Hall at prayer, or at any other collegiate exercises, or at any time abroad, or out of the Hall (excepting the back-yard of the College only, and that on necessary occasions), without being clothed in their proper College habits, on penalty of five shillings proc. money, to be levied upon every student who shall offend against this law."

How far this rule was ever enforced is not known.   To us it seems ill adapted to an American college, not to speak in stronger terms.   If it ever went into operation to its full extent, it happily soon ceased to be of binding force with respect to some of its provisions.   For many years, indeed, the students were required each to wear a black gown at *all* services in the College Chapel and at all public declamations; but at this day (1873) College habits are seen only at Commencements and other exhibitions, and this has been the case for nearly, if not quite, fifty years.

The law respecting College habits, passed in 1751, was repealed by the Trustees at the only meeting at which President Edwards was present, viz., of February 16, 1758.   But to this repeal no reference is made in the preamble to this order.   The

action of the Board in 1758 may have escaped the recollection
of the author of the above minute, who, *probably*, was Mr. Wm.
P. Smith, the gentleman who, in the year 1752, procured two
habits, one for the use of the President, and the other as a pattern for the habits to be worn by the students, who were left at
liberty to wear them or not, as they pleased. It is not improbable that Dr. Witherspoon, just arrived from Scotland, where
college habits were customary, was in favor of the rule now
adopted. The minutes show that Mr. Smith was present at this
meeting of the 17th of August, 1768.

The next meeting of the Board was on Wednesday, the 28th
of September, 1768. Eleven members of the Senior class were
admitted to their first degree in the Arts, among whom were
Ephraim Brevard, the author of the Mecklenburg Resolutions ;
Pierpont Edwards, a son of President Edwards, and Judge of
the United States District Court in Connecticut ; and Wm.
Churchill Houston, the first Professor of Mathematics and Natural Philosophy in the College, and afterwards a member of the
Convention that formed the Constitution of the United States.

At this meeting William Livingston, Esq., of New York, was
chosen a Trustee. This gentleman was afterwards Governor of
New Jersey, and *ex officio* President of the Board of Trustees.

Mr. Wm. P. Smith communicated a letter from Mr. Jonathan
Smith, of Philadelphia, one of the executors of Colonel Peter
Bayard, of Maryland, wherein he informed the Board that Colonel Bayard left to the College a legacy of twenty pounds, to
be paid within one year after his decease, to be applied to the
education of candidates for the ministry ; and that the executors
were prepared to pay the same. The Treasurer was ordered to
receive the same and to give the executors a full discharge.

A new arrangement was made with the Steward for the
boarding of the students, according to which the Steward en-
gages to "find and provide for the said scholars such food as
has been heretofore served up to them, and *Small Beer to drink*,
at the Price of six shillings and sixpence proclamation money
of New Jersey, by the week," or, in other words, for eighty-six
and one-third cents a week.

The attention of the Board was given very much to the augmentation of the funds of the College, and to the collecting of moneys due the Corporation. And while the Trustees, in the straitened condition of the College treasury, were liberal towards the President, they were not equally generous towards Mr. Blair, the Professor of Divinity and Moral Philosophy. To him they gave but one hundred and seventy-five pounds *proc.*; and when the congregations of Maidenhead (now Lawrence) and Kingston desired to secure his services as their preacher, on alternate Sabbaths, for the ensuing year, the Trustees consented to his acceptance of their offers on the condition that of the ninety-five pounds which he was to receive for this service he should pay to the Treasurer of the College, for the use of the institution, forty-five pounds; and this they required on the ground that it was a part of his official duty to preach to the students. Had their consenting to this arrangement involved the incurring of additional expense on the part of the Board for the supply of the pulpit, the condition would not have been unreasonable; but Dr. Witherspoon was on the ground, and was ready and willing to preach to the students. We shall find, however, that the Trustees thought better of this demand on their part, and relinquished it. Mr. Blair was a man of rare talent and learning, and an able preacher. He was chosen Professor of Divinity and Moral Philosophy, and *pro tem.* Vice-President of the College, after Dr. Witherspoon declined his first invitation from the Board to become the President, and for nearly a year before Dr. Witherspoon's arrival in this country Mr. Blair was at the head of the institution.

But notwithstanding all their efforts to obtain funds, and their success to some extent, by contributions from individuals and from the churches under the care of the Synod of New York and Philadelphia, it was found very difficult, if not impossible, to meet all the demands upon the treasury of the College. To relieve the Board from their pecuniary embarrassment, Mr. Blair, of his own motion, addressed to the Trustees a letter, of the date of April 6, 1769, offering to resign his place in the College. The paper was read and ordered to be entered on the minutes, and was made the basis of the Board's action in this matter.

"GENTLEMEN,—I do hereby gratefully acknowledge the honor you have conferred upon me in calling me to this Institution as Professor of Divinity and Moral Philosophy, and it would be very agreeable to me, in itself considered, to continue in this service. But it is a very discouraging consideration that the funds are so very inadequate to the expense as to render it very doubtful whether after the utmost efforts a sufficient capital can be raised. In the course of divine Providence, too, a state of things very different from that in view at the time of my election has taken place. If, therefore, it appears to the Board that the business they have been pleased to assign me may devolve upon the President, and thereby the expense of my salary be saved, in that case I would willingly resign. And the dismission may take place at what time this Honorable Board may judge most convenient. This matter is submitted to your consideration by, Gentlemen, your very humble servant, J. BLAIR.

"April 6, 1769.

"The Board, taking into consideration the above request of Mr. Blair, do agree to his resignation for the reasons therein mentioned, particularly on account of the insufficiency of the College Funds for the present support of a Divinity Professor. And they consider this application as a distinguished proof of his disinterestedness and public spirit; so they look upon themselves as obliged to give him the thanks of the Board for his services in the College, of which they will retain a grateful sense, and to testify their entire approbation to his whole conduct, both in the point of instruction and government, during his continuance in office. And it is Resolved, That the said Mr. Blair's salary as Professor of Divinity do continue until the next Commencement. And it is also voted, That the sum of one hundred pounds be allowed him over and above the same, to become payable at the next Commencement, together with the remission of the moneys which were to have been paid by him into the College Treasury in consideration of the relinquishment of his services as a preacher to the students for the last half-year; which the Board have considered as a reasonable compensation for the difficulties and expenses the said Mr. Blair may be put to upon so sudden a removal. And it is further Resolved, That a former vote of this Board respecting a Faculty to be established in this College be, for the reasons above, wholly vacated and annulled.

"The Board then proceeded to the election of a Divinity Professor in the room of Mr. Blair resigned, when the Rev. Dr. Witherspoon, President of the College, was unanimously chosen; and in consideration of the additional services thereby required of him they added fifty pounds a year to his salary, to begin on the last Wednesday in September next, the day of the annual Commencement."

Dr. Witherspoon acquainting the Board "that from accounts received from Boston near £1000 *proc.* hath been subscribed, and part of the same remitted, for the use of this College, the Board requested that he would be pleased, by letters in their name, to return the thanks of the Trustees of this College to the Benefactors who have so generously assisted the Institution."

Of the three gentlemen elected Professors in 1767, Mr. Blair was the only one who entered upon the duties of the chair to which he was called. At the time of his appointment he was pastor of the Presbyterian church of Fagg's Manor, Pennsylvania, and the principal of the Classical and Theological School established by his brother, the Rev. Samuel Blair, his predecessor both in the church and in the school.

Upon leaving Princeton he was settled as pastor of the church at Goodwill or Wallkill, in the State of New York. He was a man of eminent piety, and of a sound and vigorous intellect: a logician of a high order. His treatises " On the Nature, Uses, and Subjects of the Sacraments," " On Regeneration," and " On the Nature and Uses of the Means of Grace," exhibit clear, discriminating, and candid views of these important topics, and as such must commend themselves to the pious and intelligent reader, whether he can or cannot assent to all his positions.

Mr. Blair was a native of Ireland, born there in 1720, and died at Wallkill, December 8, 1771.

His letter, given above, shows him to have been a man of noble and generous impulses, and entirely free from all selfish aims and considerations.

The President moved " that an extract from a letter to him from William Phillips, Esq., of Boston, might be inserted in the minutes." The same was ordered to be inserted accordingly, and is in the words following:

" My two brothers have subscribed £100 each (Boston lawful), which, with my subscription, makes £300, or 1000 dollars; which I mention, as we are desirous it may be kept by itself, as it may be applied to some particular use hereafter, provided the funds of the College shall admit thereof, and you advise to such appropriation. In that case it may be enlarged."

" The Board, considering the Intimation in the above extract contained, desired the President of the College to write to the said Mr. Phillips, and refer the appropriation of money subscribed by himself and brothers to such uses and purposes as he or they shall think fit to direct."

This generous gift, or rather the disposing of the annual increase of the same, became the occasion for a time of a serious discussion between a committee of the Board and the President, as to the right of the latter to expend the income from this fund for the benefit of the College, at his discretion. Contrary to the judgment of the committee which made a report upon this subject, and especially of the author of the report, the Board *finally* decided that it was the intention of the donors that Dr. Witherspoon should have the disposal of the income from this fund.

" The Board being informed that the Rev. Mr. Caldwell, of Elizabethtown, had taken a journey to the eastern parts of Long Island, and had set on foot a subscription there, as well as at Elizabethown, for the use of the College," Mr. W. P. Smith (the Clerk) " was desired to give to Mr. Caldwell the thanks of the Board, and to request his endeavors to have the money collected when payable, and sent to him ; and that he remit the same, when received, to the Treasurer of the College, taking his receipt in discharge."

Hoping, from information received, that considerable bene-factions would be obtained from the friends of learning and re-ligion in South Carolina should a *personal application* be made to them by a duly-authorized agent, the Board requested the Rev. Dr. John Rodgers, of New York, a member of the Board, to undertake this service ; which he consented to do, with the understanding that provision should be made for the supply of his pulpit during his absence.

Other friends interested themselves in behalf of the College, as appears from the following minute :

" The Board being informed that several friends of the College in different parts of the country have set on foot subscriptions to increase the funds, do approve and gratefully acknowledge the measures taken by them for this purpose, and do recom-mend the further promoting and encouragement of like subscriptions."

Upon the examination of the Treasurer's accounts, it appeared that there was due to the Treasurer the sum of £183.11.6. What was the amount of the bonds held by the College at this time does not appear from the report of the committee charged with the duty of making this examination.

The next meeting of the Board was held on Wednesday, the 27th of September, 1769. This was the day of the annual Commencement ; and this Commencement is one of note, from the following circumstances :

1. That the class then graduated was the first one which had had the privilege of being under the tuition and guidance of Dr. Witherspoon.

2. That not a few of the graduates on this occasion became men of note in their day; and one of their number, Samuel Stanhope Smith, succeeded Dr. Witherspoon in the office of President of the College.

3. That at this Commencement the degree of Doctor of Laws was conferred upon two distinguished civilians of our country, viz., John Dickinson and Joseph Galloway, Esquires, of Philadelphia,—*this being the first time that this degree was conferred by the Trustees of this institution.*

Upon the resignation of Mr. Periam, Mr. Jeremiah Halsey was chosen Professor of Mathematics and Natural Philosophy, with a salary of one hundred and twenty-five pounds; but he declined the appointment. Mr. Wm. Churchill Houston, the Master of the College grammar-school, was then chosen a Tutor in the room of Mr. Periam. At the same time Mr. Tapping Reeve was appointed a Tutor in the place of Mr. Pemberton, resigned.

The Rev. James Caldwell was chosen a Trustee to fill the vacancy occasioned by the decease of the Rev. William Kirkpatrick; and the Rev. John Blair, the late Professor of Divinity and of Moral Philosophy, was elected a Trustee in the room of the Rev. Mr. De Ronde, resigned. The Rev. Mr. Caldwell was also appointed "an agent of the Board to solicit subscriptions for the benefit of the College in Maryland, Virginia, the two Carolines, and Georgia,"—the Trustees engaging to pay his expenses, and also the expense of supplying his pulpit during his absence.

Mr. Caldwell was well received at the South, and his mission was attended with happy results. The subscriptions obtained by him for the College were estimated at not less than one thousand pounds *proc.*, over and above all expenses. Some of the subscriptions were in moneys, and others in the produce of the country. The subscriptions in Georgia, for the most part, were to be paid in produce.

To the payment of their debts, as well as to the soliciting of funds, the Board now gave their attention. Preceding the record of the matters just mentioned occurs the following minute, under the date of September 28, 1769:

" Whereas an order hath heretofore been made on the Treasurer for the payment of a certain Bill of Exchange formerly drawn for the sum of £125 sterling by Mr. Field, Bookseller, of London, on Mr. Jeremiah Halsey ; and as a debate hath arisen relating to the rate of Exchange and Interest to be allowed on said Bill, it was now referred to the Board to ascertain the same, which being taken into consideration, the Exchange was fixed as supposed to be at or about the Time of presentation of said Bill at the rate of 72½ ; the sum therefore (including the Interest, also now calculated and allowed) was found to amount to £248.6. 6 proclamation money of New Jersey, which the Treasurer of this College is hereby warranted to pay in full discharge of said Bill of Exchange."

The chief interest of this extract is the evidence it furnishes that the purchasing of books in London for the use of the students, begun in Mr. Burr's administration, was still continued.

But money matters were not the only things to which the attention of the Board was given, essential as these were to the very being of the College.

" The Board taking into consideration the great want of a Philosophical Apparatus, for the use of the students in this College in Natural Philosophy, of which it has long been destitute, It was now Resolved, That Dr. Witherspoon, Mr. Bryan, Dr. Shippen, Dr. Redman, Dr. Harris, Mr. Beatty, and Mr. Caldwell, or any three of them, be a committee to consult and determine upon such and so many of the instruments belonging to an Apparatus as may be judged by them to be the most necessary and immediately wanted. And the said committee are empowered to send their orders to England for the same as they conveniently can : Provided the amount of the cost exceed not the sum of £250 sterling."

At the next Commencement, that of 1770, twenty-two were admitted to the first degree in the Arts, and five graduates of the College to the second degree. Four gentlemen received the honorary degree of A.M., and five others the degree of Doctor in Divinity. This was the first occasion on which this degree of D.D. was conferred by this College. The gentlemen upon whom it was conferred were,—

The Rev. Robert Finley, of Glasgow, in North Britain ; the Rev. John Gillies, of Glasgow, in North Britain ; the Rev. Archibald Laidly, of New York ; the Rev. George Muir, of Paisley, in North Britain ; the Rev. Ebenezer Pemberton, of Boston, New England.

Mr. Pemberton was one of the Trustees of the College under the first charter, as well as under the one given by Governor

Belcher. Having resigned his pastoral charge in New York, and having removed to Boston in 1754, he vacated his seat at the Board.

At this meeting of the Trustees provision was made for the sending of a small vessel from Philadelphia to Georgia in order to receive such of the promised benefactions as were to be made from the products of the country.   '

Some misunderstanding having arisen with respect to the import of a law passed by the Board in December, 1767, "for ascertaining the power and authority of the respective officers of the College," which officers at this time were the President and the Tutors,—there being no Professors or fully-organized Faculty,—the Trustees thought it proper to declare "that the President of the College for the time being is invested with the sole direction as to the methods of education to be pursued in this Seminary." The rule giving each particular officer "the sole authority of directing the times and manner of the recitations" of their respective classes was passed at a time when there was no regular President, and was designed for the guidance of the officers then in the charge of the College.

In their explanatory minute of their former action, the Trustees pay the following compliment to Dr. Witherspoon :

"And the Trustees are the rather induced to make the above explanation and amendment of said law, for that when it was enacted the President elect was resident in Great Britain, and it was uncertain how long a time might elapse before he should actually take the chair; but now he hath actually taken upon himself the charge of the College, and the Trustees have been so fully satisfied from experience of his great abilities in the management of the Institution committed to his care, and with high pleasure have seen his indefatigable labors and success in raising the reputation of the College, they are clearly of the opinion that all the authority above declared to be annexed by the said law to the office of President of the College, is highly proper to be put into the hands of the Rev. Dr. Witherspoon, the now President."

Further order was taken in regard to the investment of the College funds, and to the safe-keeping of all writings, records, and papers belonging to the Corporation, and with respect to the recording of the deeds in the possession of the Board; and also in reference to the management of the library and for the preservation and increase of the same; each student, and each resident graduate, being required to pay to the Steward of the College for the use of the library "eighteen pence per quarter."

For various purposes the Steward of the College appears to have discharged the duties of a deputy treasurer.

A legacy of fifty pounds, from the estate of the late Mr. Robert Walker, was paid to the Treasurer of the College by Richard Walker, Esq , of Bucks County, Pennsylvania, brother of the deceased, to be expended at the discretion of the Rev. Messrs. Treat and Beatty, two Trustees of the College, in aiding poor and pious youths pursuing their studies at this College with the design of entering the ministry.

Information being received of the decease of the Honorable Wm. Smith, of New York, the Rev. Jeremiah Halsey is chosen to supply his place at the Board.

In the summer of 1770, and again in 1772, there was manifest among the students an unusual interest in the subject of religion and of personal piety, of which further mention will be made in the memoir of Dr. Witherspoon.

The Tutors, Messrs. Thompson and Reeve, having resigned, Messrs. Richard Devens and Samuel S. Smith were chosen to fill their places.

The following minute shows that the Trustees still continued to recognize their close connection with the Presbyterian Church :

"Resolved, That Mr. Caldwell be desired, in the name of the Board, to transmit letters to the several Presbyteries belonging to the Synod of New York and Philadelphia who have set forward subscriptions in their respective bounds for the benefit of this College, praying their care and diligence to collect or take proper securities for the moneys subscribed, and that they be pleased to direct that exact accounts of the same be brought to the next meeting of the Synod, and that Dr. Witherspoon, Dr. Rodgers, Mr. Treat, and Mr. Bryan be a committee to settle with the Presbyteries."

Dr. Witherspoon was desired to return the thanks of the Board, by letter, to such gentlemen as were known to be most active and zealous in obtaining the late subscriptions. This collection of funds for the College was the result of the action by the Synod the year previous.*

A committee was appointed to consider the expediency of

---

* See Minutes of the Synod, pages 396 and 397.

applying to the Council of Proprietors at Perth Amboy for a grant of one thousand acres of land for the use of the institution, with power to make such application, if judged advisable. Upon conference, and probably after some inquiry, the committee deemed it inexpedient to pursue the matter, and so reported to the Board.

A new agreement was entered into with the Steward, according to which each student was required to pay *in advance*, for commons, the sum of £7.10 every half-year, which sum for twenty-one weeks, a half-year, exclusive of the vacation, was at the rate of 7.1 ¾ *s. proc.*, or 95 $\frac{5}{18}$ cents, a week; and it was further ordered, that *all* College charges should be paid *half-yearly, in advance*. It was afterwards ordered, that in case three students were lodged in the same room, they should pay in all only five pounds a year rent.

At the Commencement of 1771 there were but twelve graduates; but of these several attained great eminence, and one of them, James Madison, became the fourth President of the United States.

In the account of the competition of the students on the 24th of September, 1771, the day preceding the annual Commencement of the College, it is stated, in the " Pennsylvania Chronicle," that premiums were awarded in reading the English language with propriety, and in Orthography,—1. To Aaron Burr, of the Junior class; 2. To W. Linn, of the Junior class; and, 3. To Belcher P. Smith, of the Sophomore class. In extempore exercises in Latin, to H. Brockholst Livingston and David Witherspoon, both of the Freshman class, equally. In reading the Latin and Greek Languages with proper quantity,—1. To John Witherspoon, of the Sophomore class; 2. To Aaron Burr; 3. To Henry Lee, of the Sophomore class. For the translation of English into Latin, to Henry Lee.

In public speaking the competitors were numerous, and it was very difficult to decide the pre-eminence; but the majority of the votes gave the premiums,—1. To W. Bradford, of the Freshman class; 2. To W. Linn; 3. To Hugh Hodge, of the Freshman class.

The exercises on the 25th of September were as follows:

1. The Latin Salutatory, " De societate hominum," by Mr. Brackenridge.

2. The proposition, " Mendacium est semper illicitum," was defended by Mr. Williamson, and opposed in a syllogistic way by Messrs. McKnight and Taylor.

3. " Moral qualities are confessedly more excellent than natural; yet the latter are much more envied in the possessor by the generality of mankind; a sure sign of the corrupt bias of human nature," was supported by Mr. Black, and opposed by Mr. Cheeseman, and answered by Mr. Taylor.

4. An Oration on " The advantages of an active life," by Mr. Campbell.

The business of the forenoon concluded with an anthem.

5. At three o'clock.—An Oration on " The Idea of a Patriot King," by Mr. Spring.

6. An English forensic dispute on this question : " Does Ancient Poetry excel the Modern ?" Mr. Freneau, the Respondent, being necessarily absent, his arguments, in favor of the Ancients, were read. Mr. Williamson answered him, and Mr. McKnight replied.

7. A Poem on " The Rising Glory of America," by Mr. Brackenridge, was received with great applause by the audience.

8. An Oration on " The Power of Eloquence," by Mr. Ross.

The students sung an anthem, and twelve members of the Senior class were admitted to the first degree in the Arts, and six Alumni of the College *proceeded* Masters of Arts.

9. A pathetic Valedictory Oration on Benevolence was pronounced by Mr. Bedford.

Mr. James Madison was excused from taking any part in the exercises.

The most important measure adopted by the Board at this time was the establishing of the Professorship of Mathematics and Natural Philosophy, and the appointment of Mr. Houston, the senior Tutor, as the incumbent. The minute relating to this subject is as follows :

" Pursuant to a Plan heretofore concerted, for the establishment of Professorships in various branches of learning in this College, as soon as funds should be found to admit of their support, the Trustees resumed the consideration of that measure ; and conceiving it to be expedient that a Mathematical Professor, as most immediately requisite, be now chosen in the place of one of the Tutors, proceeded to the election of a Professor of Mathematics and Natural Philosophy, when William Ch. Houston, M.A., now Senior Tutor in the College, was declared to be unanimously elected to that office. It was then resolved that for the present the salary of the said Mr. Houston, as Professor of Mathematics and Natural Philosophy, be the sum of one hundred and twenty-five pounds proc., and that the Board will hereafter provide for his better support, as their funds will admit and the future situation of the said Professor shall reasonably require, as it is intended by this Board that the said Professorship shall be permanent in this College for the future."

In adopting the first part of this minute the Trustees seem to have forgotten their action at the time of the Rev. Professor Blair's resignation, when they resolved, " That a former vote of this Board respecting a Faculty to be established in this College be, for the reasons above, wholly vacated and annulled."

Mr. Houston accepted the appointment, and for twelve years discharged the duties of his office with great fidelity and success, and to the entire satisfaction of the Trustees, at the end of which time he resigned, to enter upon the practice of the law.

Professor Houston was a native of North or South Carolina, and a graduate of the College of New Jersey in 1768. While yet a student, he had charge of the grammar-school under the control of the President of the College. In 1769 he was chosen a Tutor, and in 1771, as above mentioned, he was elected Professor of Mathematics and Natural Philosophy. He was a member of the Continental Congress in 1780, and he was chosen a member of the Convention to prepare a Constitution for the United States. But ill health prevented his taking a seat in this body. He died at Frankford, Pennsylvania, in 1788, before the completion of his forty-third year; yet he had the reputation of being a scholar, a teacher, a lawyer, and a statesman of much more than ordinary ability.

A committee was appointed " to examine into the state of the College funds, to take an exact list of all bonds, notes, &c., now in the Treasurer's hands, an account of all interest due, and to inquire into the state of the securities. And the said Committee are empowered to direct the immediate prosecution of all such bonds, notes, &c., as they may judge to be in precarious circumstances. The Committee is also desired to make out as precise an account as possible of all the Donations, Benefactions, and Subscriptions made or received since the arrival of Dr. Witherspoon, in addition to the then Funds of the College, together with an account of all moneys disbursed; distinguishing on what particular accounts, and what sums in each account respectively; and make report of the whole at the next meeting."

There is no record in the minutes of the Board of any report from this committee. A special meeting of the Board was held on the 11th of March, 1772.

In consequence of representations made to the Board that there was "a fair prospect of collecting a considerable sum for the use of this College, in the West Indies, the Trustees requested Dr. Witherspoon to engage in this service, and provision was made to defray the expenses of his agency. Dr. Witherspoon consenting to undertake this labor, the Rev. Elihu Spencer, one of the Trustees, was chosen to act as Vice-President during Dr. Witherspoon's absence.

"Dr. Witherspoon informed the Board that his son, Mr. James Witherspoon, proposed going to Barbadoes, and generously offered his service for the benefit of the Institution. The Board therefore cheerfully agree to make out a commission for Mr. Witherspoon, enabling him to receive such benefactions as he may have the opportunity of obtaining either in Barbadoes, Antigua, or any other of the West India Islands."

The Board, taking into consideration the encouraging prospects of obtaining benefactions in Barbadoes and other of the Windward Islands, think proper to send an agent more expressly for said purpose, and desire the Rev. Charles Beatty to undertake the service in conjunction with Mr. Witherspoon, or otherwise, as may appear most advantageous to the general design. The summing up of this promising effort is to be found in the following minute of the Board, under the date of September 30, 1772: "Dr. Witherspoon did not undertake the tour to the West Indies, according to the appointment of the Board last Spring, for very sufficient reasons which occurred after the meeting. Mr. Beatty, according to appointment, went to Barbadoes, where he died on the 13th of August, before he made any collections for the College."

Upon learning that Mr. Edward Ireland, of Barbadoes, had shown particular kindness to Mr. Beatty, it was ordered, "That Mr. W. P. Smith, the Clerk, write to Mr. Ireland a letter of thanks in the name of the Board."

Within ten days after consenting to visit the West Indies, and doubtless to prepare the way for his solicitation of benefactions, Dr. Witherspoon penned an address to the inhabitants of Jamaica and other West India Islands in behalf of the College, in which he gave a succinct account of the origin and design of the College, and of the facilities it offered to the people of the West Indies for the education of their children.*

Upon the death of Mr. Beatty, the Board, not being prepared to appoint another agent for this mission to the West Indies, referred the further prosecution of it to the judgment of a large committee, of which the President of the College was made the chairman; and here the matter ended.

"The Board being informed that some persons in the County of Essex refused to pay their subscriptions to the College, Mr. [W. P.] Smith was desired to prosecute them in the name of the Board, if they refuse upon further application to them."

Dr. Witherspoon and Mr. Halsey were appointed a committee to arrange matters for the drawing of a Lottery at New Castle, Delaware, for the benefit of the College; and a bond was ordered to be given to George Monroe and others, "in the penalty of fifty thousand pounds proclamation money, with condition to indemnify them from all damages, costs, and charges which they may sustain by reason of their becoming managers of the Lottery."

Elias Boudinot, Esq., was chosen a Trustee, in the room of John Berrien, Esq., deceased.

It was ordered, "That fifty pounds proc. should be paid to Mr. Halsey for his services in the management of a previous lottery."

---

* This address is to be found in the fourth volume of his works, published in 1801, by W. W. Woodward, of Philadelphia.

Mr. Halsey, having been requested to collect the deeds belonging to the College, laid before the Board a number of deeds, one of which was a deed from Nathaniel Fitz Randolph for the lot on which the College stands, and another was a deed from Thomas Leonard for a *burying-ground.*

From a perusal of the minutes of the Board, it would seem that from the accession of Dr. Witherspoon to the presidency until the present time the attention of both President and Trustees had been directed almost exclusively to the property of the College, and to the increase of its resources; but this was far from being the case. We do not, indeed, find any detailed reports of the course of instruction, yet occasionally in these minutes we get a glimpse of what the President and Tutors were doing, and of the encouragement which they received from the Trustees; and we are assured from the success attending their teachings, and from the eminence attained by many of their pupils, both in the Church and in the State, that the instruction was most ably and efficiently conducted.

Among the minutes of the Board at this date, September, 1772, is the following:

" Teaching Hebrew being considered by the Board of great importance, especially to those who intend to study Divinity, Mr. Devens, one of the present Tutors in the College, is appointed to instruct those in Hebrew who offer themselves for that purpose. And although the Board do not enjoin it upon all, as a part of College study necessary for a degree, yet they direct the President earnestly to recommend the knowledge of Hebrew, and to take such methods as he judges most convenient to engage the students to learn as far as necessary."

The passage of this resolution at this time probably led Dr. Green to think that the introduction of Hebrew as a College study was due to Dr. Witherspoon.

Candidates for the first degree in the Arts were required to submit their speeches to the President for correction and approval at least four weeks before the Commencement; and it was resolved the next year that any candidate who should neglect to comply with this order should be denied his degree.

Mr. Devens, a Tutor, having resigned on account of ill health, Mr. James Grier was chosen to supply his place.

The custom, which continues to the present time, was now

introduced of appointing a committee of the Trustees to attend the final examinations of the students for their degrees.

With one exception, the Senior class of 1773 was the largest class graduated at this College during the presidency of Dr. Witherspoon. It contained twenty-nine members, three of whom became Governors of their respective States, and three others Presidents of three different colleges. The Governors were Henry Lee, of Virginia, Morgan Lewis, of New York, and Aaron Ogden, of New Jersey. The college Presidents were James Dunlap, of Jefferson College, Pennsylvania, John McKnight, of Dickinson College, Pennsylvania, and John Blair Smith, of Hampden Sidney College, Virginia, and afterwards of Union College, New York. The Commencement this year (1773) was honored by the presence of his Excellency Governor Franklin.

A committee, consisting of Dr. Witherspoon, Mr. Spencer, and Mr. Boudinot, was appointed to procure a public dinner at the next Commencement, and to give invitations to such strangers attending the exercises of that day as they may judge proper. The dinner was provided, and the expense was £11.15. The bill was ordered to be paid, but at the same time it was " ordered, that there be for the future no public dinner at the expense of the Board." The dinner here spoken of appears to have been the first and for some time the only public dinner at the expense of the Board.

Mr. S. S. Smith resigns his office of Tutor, and Mr. Richard Devens, for a time a colleague, and who had resigned on account of ill health, was now reappointed, but he continued in office only until the ensuing spring.

The Clerk was directed to collect all the by-laws and regulations which had been made from time to time and to lay them before the Board.

It appears from a minute of this date, September, 1773, that a legacy had been left to the College by Mr. James King, of Delaware; but what was the sum given, or the purpose of the bequest, does not appear from the minutes of the Board.

The tuition-fees were increased to five pounds a year.

A meeting of the Board was held on the 19th of April, 1774,

at which Governor Franklin, President Witherspoon, and twelve other Trustees were present.

Among the minutes of this meeting is the following :

> " And whereas it has been represented, and upon inquiry it hath appeared to this Board, that Samuel Leake, a member of the present Senior class, was not long since singularly active in encouraging and promoting some unwarrantable and riotous proceedings among the students, particularly in publickly burning the effigies of his Excellency Governor Hutchinson, and also insulting an honourable member of this Board for endeavouring in a very becoming manner to prevent the said riotous proceedings; and the Board being also informed that the said Samuel Leake, notwithstanding his conduct, hath been appointed by the Faculty to the honour of the Salutatory Oration at the ensuing Commencement, this Board doth highly disapprove of his designation to that honour, and do hereby vacate that choice, and direct the President of the College to appoint another Orator in his room."

This order of the Board was as severe a censure of the Faculty as of Mr. Leake, who appears to have been the first scholar in his class, and who, on the score of merit as a scholar, was entitled to the position assigned him by the Faculty; and if permitted to take any part in the Commencement exercises, there does not appear to be any sufficient reason why he should not have the place of Salutatory orator.   Although the President, Dr. Witherspoon, and the other members of the Faculty could not approve of the conduct of Mr. Leake and of his companions on the occasion here referred to, yet it is not improbable they looked with a more indulgent eye upon the offences of these young men than did a majority of the Board, and that the Faculty sympathized, to some extent at least, with their pupils in their disapproval of sundry obnoxious acts of the Governor of Massachusetts, and of the support he gave to those measures of the British Ministry which eventually drove the Colonies into rebellion and to establish a government for themselves free and altogether independent of the English Crown.   Two years later the very men who severely condemned young Leake were as rebellious against British rule as he ever was, and two more earnest rebels were not to be found than the President of the College and the Trustee to whom, it is believed, reference is made in the minute cited above, and who was a resident of Princeton.   In fact, the Trustees were all of them rebels and supporters of the Confederation.

After his graduation Mr. Leake received from Dr. Witherspoon a written certificate of his qualifications to teach Latin, Greek, and Mathematics, to which was appended the following:

" I must also add, that he gave particular attention to the English language while here, and is probably better acquainted with its structure, propriety, and force than most of his years and standing in this country."

Mr. Leake became a distinguished lawyer and an eminent Christian man, and he died at his residence in the city of Trenton in the year 1820.

His son-in-law, the Rev. Elijah Slack, LL.D., was Vice-President of the College and Professor of Mathematics and Natural Philosophy from 1812 to 1817.

In the summer following this action of the Board in reference to Mr. Leake, John Adams, the second President of the United States, visited Princeton, and of this visit President Adams has left the following account. It is taken from his Life by his grandson:

" August 27, 1774. About 12 o'clock we arrived at the tavern in Princeton which holds out the sign of Hudibras, near Nassau Hall. The College is a stone building about as large as that at New York. It stands upon rising ground, and so commands a prospect of the country. After dinner Mr. Pigeon, a student, son of Mr. Pigeon, of Watertown, to whom we brought a letter, took a walk with us, and shewed us the seat of Mr. Stockton, a lawyer of this place and one of the Trustees of the College; as we returned we met Mr. Euston [Houston], professor of Mathematics and Natural Philosophy, who kindly invited us to his chamber. We went. The College is conveniently constructed : instead of entries across the building, the entries are from end to end, and the chambers are on each side of the entries. There are such entries one above another in every story; each chamber has three windows, two studies with one window in each, and one window between the studies to enlighten the chamber.

" Mr. Euston [Houston] then shewed us the Library; it is not large, but has some good books. He then led us into the Apparatus; here we saw a most beautiful machine,* an orrery or planetarium constructed by Mr. Rittenhouse, of Philadelphia. It exhibits almost every motion in the Astronomical world : the motions of the sun and all the planets, with all their satellites, the eclipses of the moon, sun, &c. He shewed us another orrery which exhibits the true inclination of the orbit of each of the planets to the plane of the ecliptic. He then shewed us the electri-

---

* For a full description of this machine, see vol. i. of the " Transactions of the American Philosophical Society."

cal apparatus, which is the most complete and elegant I have seen. He charged a bottle and attempted an experiment, but the state of the air was not favorable. By this time the bell rang for prayers: we went into the chapel; the President soon came in, and we attended. The scholars sung as badly as the Presbyterians in New York. After prayers the President attended us to the balcony of the College, where we had a prospect of an horizon of about eighty miles in diameter. We went into the President's house and drank a glass of wine. He is as high a son of liberty as any man in America."

The following important minute in reference to the finances of the College was adopted :

" The Treasurer's accounts being called for, it appeared necessary that the state of the College funds should be more carefully examined and adjusted than could be done by the Board during the present session : they do therefore appoint Messrs. [W.] P. Smith, Mr. Livingston, Mr. McWhorter, Mr. Boudinot, and Mr. Caldwell, or any three of them, a committee to meet at Princeton, on the 15th of August next, at 5 o'clock P.M., and as often afterwards as they may judge necessary, to examine, adjust, and state the College funds, and draw up a plan for the conduct of the Treasurer, with respect to the management of the fund in his hands, and report the same to the next meeting of the Board. And for this purpose they have power to call upon the Treasurer for his accounts, and for any bond and papers belonging to the College in his hands. And the Treasurer is ordered in the mean time to collect all the bonds, notes, securities or their vouchers, the property of the Trustees, and to do all other things in his power that will enable the Committee to form a just estimate of the College funds."

The committee went to work in earnest, and made a very laborious examination of all matters connected with the finances of the College, and made their report in April, 1775, exhibiting the state of the several accounts to September, 1774. Although not chairman of the committee, Mr. Boudinot was the author of the report, as may be inferred from what is said in a like report made by him in 1793. (For further notice of these reports, see Appendix.)

The records for the year 1776 are very brief. Wednesday, the 25th of September, was the day for the annual Commencement, and as ten of the Trustees, including the Governor of the State and the President of the College, were assembled on that occasion, and as the exercises for the day had been assigned some time before, it is highly probable that these exercises were attended to in the usual manner ; but, as there was not a quorum of the Board present, the usual degrees could not be conferred at this time. The Trustees who were present agreed to recommend that the first degree in the Arts should be conferred upon the candidates for this distinction at the next meeting of the Board; and they directed their Clerk to summon the Trustees to a meeting to be held on the third Wednesday of the following November.

The following N. B. is appended to the minutes for 1776:

" The incursions of the Enemy into the State and the depredations of the armies prevented this meeting: and indeed all regular business in the College for two or three years."

This last remark shows what otherwise is apparent from an inspection of the first volume of the minutes of the Board, viz., that the minutes for this period were not entered at once in the volume, but some few years after.

The next meeting of the Board was held at Cooper's Ferry, New Jersey, on the banks of the Delaware, May 24, 1777, Governor Livingston, Dr. Witherspoon, and eleven other Trustees being present. The young gentlemen, twenty-seven in number, who in September last, 1776, were *not* admitted to their first degree in the Arts, for the want of a quorum of the Board, now received that honor; and it was resolved, " That they receive their diplomas as soon as the confusions of the war will admit of it."

The following extracts are taken from the minutes of the Board at this meeting:

" It was proposed for consideration, whether it will be expedient to collect the students of the College and endeavor to proceed with their usual instruction. After deliberation, Agreed, that if the enemy remove out of this State, Dr. Witherspoon is desired to call the students together at Princeton, and to proceed with their education in the best manner he can, considering the state of public affairs. And if more students can be collected than the Doctor can instruct himself, he is directed to obtain such assistance as may be necessary.

" Dr. Witherspoon, Mr. Stockton, and Mr. Spencer were appointed a committee to determine what repairs are necessary for the convenience of the students, and to order them to be made. But they are directed to go no further than shall appear requisite to save the building, and to accommodate those students who may be collected."

" Dr. Witherspoon was desired to move the Congress to resolve that troops shall not hereafter be quartered in the College."

The Trustees, receiving information of the decease of Jonathan Sergeant, Esq., the Treasurer of the College, appointed a committee to settle with Mr. Sergeant's executors, and to take charge of the College funds, and to put them into "the Continental loan office," unless a more advantageous investment could be made.   Mr. Sergeant had been Treasurer from September 26, 1750, and he had also been an active and efficient friend of the College.   He was a son-in-law of the Rev. Jonathan Dickinson, the first President.   At this meeting, also, intelligence was received of the decease of the Rev. William Tennent, of Monmouth County, New Jersey, a Trustee named in the charter given by Governor Belcher.   As the preceding history shows, Mr. Tennent was several times chosen President of the College *pro tempore*, and discharged his duties to the entire satisfaction of the Trustees and other friends of the institution.   He was an eminently good man, and an earnest and successful minister of the gospel.   The Rev. George Duffield was elected a Trustee in his room.

The Clerk was directed to give Mr. Brainerd an order upon Dr. Ewing, one of the executors of the late Treasurer, for the sum of thirty pounds, two years' interest of three hundred pounds lodged in the hands of the Corporation, at the disposal of the Synod of New York and Philadelphia, for the support of an Indian mission, and by that body granted to Mr. Brainerd.

There were no Commencement exercises in 1777, but the members of the Senior class, seven in number, were subsequently admitted to the first degree in the Arts, and were accounted graduates for this year.   In an address to the public through the newspapers, Dr. Witherspoon states these degrees were confirmed at the next meeting of the Board; and no doubt this was true, although the fact is not mentioned in the minutes of the meeting, which was held on the 16th of April, 1778.* At this meeting Governor Livingston, Dr. Witherspoon, and twelve other Trustees were present.   Three new Trustees were chosen.   These were the Rev. Azel Roe, of Woodbridge, New

---

* In the minutes for September 25, 1782, the following occurs: " Resolved, likewise, that John Noel, Samuel Vickers, and James Hanna, alumni of the College, who on account of the confusions of the war have not received their degree of B.A. at the regular time, be now admitted to it."   And in September 28, 1790, an order was passed for inserting in the catalogue for the year 1777 several names which had been omitted in the printed catalogue.

Jersey, John Bayard, Esq., of Philadelphia, and Dr. Nathaniel Scudder, of New Jersey.

It was unanimously " Resolved, That application be made to the Legislature of this State to confirm the Charter," to reduce the number requisite for a quorum, and to make such other alterations as the late revolution and the circumstances of the country may render necessary. And a committee was appointed to make a draft of a charter as conformable as possible to the existing one, excepting the alterations just indicated.

Mr. Joshua M. Wallace, Jr., was chosen Treasurer of the College, but he never took upon himself the duties of the office; and at the meeting of the Board, April 21, 1779, Wm. Churchill Houston, Esq., was chosen Treasurer, and for some years he discharged the duties of this office as well as those of his Professorship. Some years after Mr. Wallace was chosen a Trustee of the College.

It was "agreed to present a petition to the Council, and another to the Assembly [of the State], requesting them to enact a law to exempt the masters and students of the College from military duty; and Dr. Witherspoon was appointed to draw up and to present these petitions on behalf of the Board." These petitions were eventually granted by the Legislature.

It was also " Resolved, That an attempt shall be made to revive the College studies, so long interrupted by the war;" and Dr. Witherspoon was desired to publish in the New Jersey, Lancaster, and Fishkill papers that due attention will be given the instruction of youth in the College after the 10th of May next.

It was ordered, " That Mr. Halsey prepare a just statement of the accounts of the last College Lottery, and lay them before the Board at their next meeting."

There is in the minutes of the Board no record of any meeting of the Trustees at the regular time for the annual Commencement, but from an account of the proceedings published in the " New Jersey Gazette" of October 21, 1778, it appears that the Commencement exercises took place at Princeton, on Wednesday, the 30th of September, and that the first degree in the Arts was conferred upon *five* members of the Senior class, three of whom took part in the exercises. Orations were also

pronounced by two of the candidates for the degree of Master
of Arts.

The next meeting of the Board was held at Princeton, on
Wednesday, the 21st of April, 1779. The embarrassed condition of the finances very naturally demanded and received the
first attention of the Board, and measures were taken to secure
the moneys due to the College, and for the soliciting of pecuniary aid in Pennsylvania and in New England. It was also found
necessary to make further repairs to the College edifice, which
had been much injured during the time it was occupied by the
troops; and the resolutions adopted respecting the extent to
which the repairs should be made show both the injury which
had been done to the building and the low state of the College
funds. The Trustees had petitioned Congress for a remuneration
of their losses, and they seem to have had some hope that their
claim would be allowed and paid. The sum actually received
was very small as compared with the damage done by the
American soldiery.

William Livingston, Esq., having been chosen Governor of
the State, and thereby the President of the Board, Jonathan
Bayard Smith, Esq., of Philadelphia, was chosen a Trustee in
his room.

The following minute shows that the Trustees were desirous
to deal liberally with the officers of the College :

" Agreed, That notwithstanding the interruption of the College exercises by the
war, their salaries shall be continued to Dr. Witherspoon and Professor Houston.
They are, however, to give as much attention to the instruction of such youth as may
be sent to the College as their circumstances and those of the place will admit, till
the building shall be repaired, and the state of public affairs will afford an opportunity to conduct the education in the College in a more complete manner."

In September of this year the Commencement took place as
usual, and six of the students were admitted to their first degree in the Arts. They all became men of more or less note ;
the most distinguished of them being the Hon. Richard Stockton, LL.D., of Princeton, New Jersey.

Dr. Moses Scott, of New Brunswick, appointed an agent
to make collections for the College in the State of Pennsylvania, reported that he had collected, exclusive of his expenses,

the sum of four hundred and fifteen pounds, which he had paid to Dr. Witherspoon.

The most important measure taken by the Board at this time, September 29, 1779, was the appointment of the Rev. Samuel S. Smith Professor of Moral Philosophy. This appointment was made at the suggestion of Dr. Witherspoon; and the minute respecting it is evidence that the proposal was highly acceptable to the Trustees. The Professor elect was then at the head of an academy, subsequently chartered under the name of Hampden Sidney College, Prince Edward County, Virginia. He came to Princeton, and began his duties here on the 12th of December, 1779.

Dr. Witherspoon offered to relinquish one-half of his salary of four hundred pounds a year, provided the Board would make the proposed appointment, and would allow the tuition-money of the students for the ensuing year to himself, Professor Houston, and the Professor to be elected; this to be done with the understanding that if they required the assistance of a Tutor in the instruction of the students they were to pay him.

Before Professor Smith's arrival, notice was given in the public papers by President Witherspoon and Professor Houston that the vacation of the College would end on Monday, the 8th of November, and that of the grammar-school on the 27th of October. The latter part of the advertisement is as follows:

"As there is a universal complaint of the want of opportunities of educating youth among us at present, it is proper to inform the public, that agreeably to former advertisements, the instruction in this School and College has been regularly carried on since the enemy left the State. The Grammar School is numerous and flourishing, and the difficulties in the way of filling the College are now in a great measure removed. The repairs of the building are in great forwardness, and will go on without interruption, so that there will be comfortable accommodations for as many as may probably attend this fall. Tho' the number of under-graduates or proper College members did not exceed ten, yet one or other of the subscribers was constantly upon the spot. Now another Professor is chosen, and a tutor engaged, so that parents and guardians may depend upon the utmost care being taken of the youth. Boarding may be had at the same price as formerly, making allowance for the state of the currency.

"The French language is taught, and great attention paid to every branch of English Education.

"Signed,   JOHN WITHERSPOON,
           WM. CH. HOUSTON."

The above is taken from the "New Jersey Gazette" of the date of October 13, 1779, published at Trenton, New Jersey.

Four or five months after, viz., on the 24th of February, 1780, Dr. Witherspoon prepared an address to the public, giving some information respecting the College and the grammar-school, which were, to use his own words, "beginning to recover from the desolations they have suffered in consequence of the war, as the scholars are collected from the most distant parts of the continent, and even the West Indies." His main object, however, seems to have been to give some good advice to the teachers and parents of youth who were preparing to enter college. ("New Jersey Gazette" for March 15, 1780.)

At the Commencement held on Wednesday, the 27th of September, 1780, the Trustees had a meeting as usual on such occasions, and conferred the first degree in the Arts upon *six* candidates for this honor. At this and at the preceding Commencement premiums were awarded to the successful competitors for them in the matters of grammar, syntax, etc., of the Latin and English languages.

Dr. Witherspoon reported to the Board "that the Legislature have passed an act confirming the charter of the College, but have not thought proper to lessen the quorum."

"The Rev. Robert Smith reported that himself and others had taken some pains in Pennsylvania to make collections of money for the College; and he delivered to the Board two hundred and thirty-eight pounds ten shillings, which were collected in the Forks of the Brandywine, and paid to Dr. Witherspoon."

"Dr. Witherspoon proposed, that if the Board would continue the salary of four hundred pounds to himself and Professor Smith, with the tuition-money, they would procure a sufficient number of tutors to carry on the instruction of the College without any further expense to this Board."

"Resolved, That the Board do agree to the above proposal."

"Dr. Witherspoon was directed to state an account against the public for the rents of the College while it was used by their agents as a barracks and hospital, and to endeavor to recover the money as soon as possible."

"Mr. Halsey was desired to settle the accounts of the last College Lottery speedily; and in the first place to call in and pay out all debts due to or from the Lottery, particularly to discharge the debt due to Mr. Geddes, and then to lay the whole of the accounts before Mr. Boudinot, who was empowered to settle with him on behalf of the Board."

The Mr. Geddes here named had drawn a prize of several hundred pounds in the last lottery, the payment of which was deferred for some years, owing no doubt, in a great measure, to the failure to raise funds at this time through the lottery. The settlement of Mr. Geddes's claim gave the Board much trouble. One happy result of this was, that no further effort was made for thirty years to obtain authority to draw another lottery for the benefit of the College, and, more happily still, the only other endeavor to obtain permission to draw one was unsuccessful. This last application for a lottery was made in 1813 or 1814, and was denied; but not from any scruple of conscience on the part of the members of the Legislature, for while they refused permission to the College of New Jersey they allowed the Trustees of Queen's College, now Rutgers, to raise by lottery for the resuscitation of that institution some twenty or thirty thousand dollars.

The next meeting of the Board was held on the 30th of May, 1781, and in the mean time three of the Trustees had died. These were the Hon. Richard Stockton, the Rev. Jeremiah Halsey, and the Rev. John Brainerd; and in their room the Board elected his Excellency Joseph Reed, Esq., President of the State of Pennsylvania, the Rev. Dr. Alexander McWhorter, who had returned to Newark from the South, and the Rev. James Boyd.

The Board continued their sessions to next day. "The Rev. James Caldwell laid before the Board his account current with the corporation, containing an account of the moneys received and paid by him as one of the committee for managing the treasury since May 26, 1777." This account was referred to the committee for collecting and stating an account of the funds. It is evident that Mr. Caldwell, who had taken an active part in soliciting funds for the College, and who at this time was the Clerk of the Board, had the principal share of the labor assigned to the committee charged with the duties of the Treasurer. It is also evident, from the arrangement made with the President and the Professors of the College with respect to the tuition-fees, that the income of the College from this source was altogether inadequate to the support of the President and Professors,—their salaries amounting to six hundred pounds a year. And two-thirds of this sum, if not the whole of the six

hundred pounds, were payable in coin, and not in the currency
of that time, as appears from the following minute :

"In the agreement made with Dr. Witherspoon last September, the minutes do
not express in what kind of money he was to be paid; it is therefore now agreed,
in the presence of Dr. Witherspoon, that he is to receive his salary in gold and silver,
and not in current paper money of a depreciated value, which he has voluntarily
agreed to receive his salary in for the two years preceding."

Hence, in view of the funds requisite to pay the salaries of
the officers of the College, to meet the incidental expenses, and
to make the extensive repairs which were necessary to render
the College edifice fit for the purposes of its erection, it must
be obvious that there was need of large pecuniary assistance
from the friends of the institution to meet all the yearly expenses
and sustain the high standing and character which the College
had attained as a place for the education of youth.   Funds were
solicited and liberally given; not for a permanent endowment,
but for the meeting of pressing wants and immediate liabili-
ties; and by means of these generous gifts the Trustees were
enabled to maintain a Faculty composed of able men and of
accomplished instructors equal to any in the land.

At this time "a proposal was laid before the Board, signed by William C. Houston
and Samuel S. Smith, for conferring both the higher and the intermediate degrees
in Theology and Law, in some method similar to those practised by the Universities
in Europe, together with a draught of a plan for that purpose."

It was read, and the consideration of it deferred.   At the
next meeting of the Board it was referred to a committee consisting of Governor Livingston, Dr. Witherspoon, Mr. Boudinot,
and Mr. Spencer, to consider and report thereon.   The committee appear to have made a favorable report, but what were
its peculiar features is not known, as the plan is not given in the
minutes of the Board.*
From the beginning, one of the Trustees had been chosen
Clerk of the Board whenever a vacancy occurred in that office.

---

* At the meeting held September 25, 1787, the Board adopted the following resolution: "That no person be admitted to the degree of Doctor in Divinity or Doctor
of Laws unless with the consent of two-thirds of the members present."   But this
resolution, as inconsistent with the charter, was repealed in 1794.

But at this meeting a motion was made to choose a Clerk who should not be one of the Board; "many inconveniences having arisen from one of the members officiating in that department, the same was agreed to, and the Rev. Samuel S. Smith was unanimously chosen to that office."

The selecting of a member of the Faculty to discharge the duties of Clerk to the Board was continued until the year 1823, when the Trustees resolved to make another change, and they chose one of their own number, then a resident of Princeton, their Clerk. Since that time the Clerks of the Board have been selected from the body of the Trustees.

It was resolved to petition the Legislature again for an alteration in the charter, by which the number requisite for a quorum should be lessened, and also to ask the General Assembly "to prevent the quartering of troops in the College, which is frequently practised."

"Mr. Boudinot having offered to the Board the draft of a petition to that purpose, Ordered, That it be signed by the President of the Board, and delivered into the hands of Dr. Scudder to be presented to the Assembly."

Two years after, the following minute occurs: "The honorable Legislature of this State, in consequence of an application made to them by the Board through Dr. N. Scudder, have been pleased to pass a law enabling the Board to hold its sessions by smaller quorums than formerly." This alteration in the charter made nine members of the Board regularly convened a quorum, provided the President of the Board, the President of the College, or the eldest Trustee, were one of the nine. The act as now passed was limited to five years; but it was subsequently re-enacted and made perpetual.

At the Commencement of 1781, *six* young gentlemen were admitted to the degree of Bachelor of the Arts, five of whom had pursued their studies at Princeton and had passed the usual examinations. The sixth, who was from Virginia, had completed his studies under the care of Professor Smith. The Commencement this year took place on the 26th of September.

"The Committee of Repairs reported that they had not been able to effect much in repairing the College, through a failure of the remittances that were ordered at the last session of the Board." Whereupon the following order was passed:

"Ordered, That every pupil who shall hereafter enter the College shall pay entrance money of one guinea, which, together with the rents of the chambers, shall be appropriated by the Treasurer as a fund to discharge the expense of such repairs as shall be judged to be indispensably necessary in the College. And as these moneys will arise too slowly to answer the demands of the workmen, President Reed [of Pennsylvania] and Colonel Bayard are requested and authorized to borrow the necessary sum on the credit of the said fund."

This they were unable to do, and so reported at the next meeting of the Board. But they themselves generously advanced towards the repairs the sum of thirty-nine pounds, which was repaid to them by credits on the College bills of their sons.

"Dr. Witherspoon was requested to do his utmost to recover payment of the account against the United States, given to Congress, pursuant to an order of the Board, September 27, 1780, and was empowered to receive it in the name of the Trustees, and to carry it to their credit in the account of salary."

Two days after the Commencement, viz., on the 28th of September, 1781, Dr. Witherspoon prepared a communication addressed to the public on the condition of the College and with respect to the provision made for the teaching and boarding of the students. It was published in the "New Jersey Gazette" for October 10, 1781.

The following are the more important of the particulars mentioned:

1. That a considerable part of the College is already repaired, and that the Trustees have given directions for the completion of the repairs without delay; and that, as formerly, the under-graduates would be required to *lodge* in the College building, unless exempted by special permission from the President.

2. That board would be furnished by the Steward of the College for the moderate sum of ten shillings a week, and that no student would be permitted to *board* out of College without express license from the President, or, in his absence, from the senior Professor.

3. That every new scholar, at his first coming to College,

must pay one guinea entrance, and at the rate of six pounds per annum tuition, and two pounds per annum for chamber rent; and that the charges for tuition and board must be paid every six months in advance, and that punctuality in making these advance payments would be rigidly insisted on.

The most particular and doubtless the most accurate account of the condition of the College edifice at this time is one given by the Rev. Dr. Ashbel Green, who was President of the College from 1812 to 1822. It is contained in an address before the Alumni Association in 1840, in which he says:

" I entered this College on the 9th of May, 1782. . . . The College buildings at that time consisted only of this edifice [Nassau Hall], the President's house, and a dwelling for the Steward, originally constructed for a College kitchen, and then used as such, although the family of the Steward had their residence in it. The lower and upper stories of this edifice still remained in the ruined state in which they had been left by the British and American armies, entirely uninhabited and uninhabitable, except that on the lowest story [now the cellar], at the east end, Dr. Witherspoon had fitted up a room for his grammar-school, and opposite to it, on the south side, another room was so far repaired as to be used for a dining-room, and in the fourth story [now the third] the Cliosophic Society had repaired one of the half-rooms in the north projection of the College, in which their meetings were held. The Whig Society was not reorganized till the summer of my first session in the College, and in its reorganization I had a leading part. In the two middle entries [the present cellar being then the first or lowest story], rooms enough had been repaired to accommodate all the students, whose whole number was, I believe, little, and but a little turned of forty. Some of the rooms in these entries still lay waste, and the whole building still exhibited the effects of General Washington's artillery, who, in the battle of Princeton, caused it to be fired upon to drive out British troops who had taken refuge in it."

The annual Commencement for 1782 was held on the 25th of September of that year. Eleven candidates were admitted to the first degree in the Arts.

At a meeting of the Board at this time, Mr. Isaac Snowden, of Philadelphia, and the Rev. Jonathan Elmer, of Essex County, New Jersey, were chosen Trustees, in the room of Dr. Nathaniel Scudder and the Rev. James Caldwell, both deceased.*

---

* The deaths of these excellent men are remarkable for the manner of their oc-currence. Both were killed instantly,—Dr. Scudder by a musket-ball fired by one of a refugee party, from whom the doctor and his associates were endeavoring to rescue some of their friends, who by this party had been taken prisoners and carried

"Dr. Witherspoon represented to the Board the pains he had taken to have the accounts of the College against the United States given in to Congress, pursuant to an order of the Board of September 27, 1780. Resolved, That Dr. Witherspoon take that account into his own hands and endeavor to compound it with the States, or otherwise turn it to the best advantage in his power and carry it to the credit of the Trustees.

"Messrs. John Bayard, Elias Boudinot, and Jonathan B. Smith were appointed to settle the old account between Dr. Witherspoon and the Trustees, previous to the year 1775."

From an examination of the Treasurer's accounts, it appeared that the bonds and the certificates of stock, with the interest due on them, amounted to the sum of £3411.0.3. The balance in the hands of the Treasurer at this date was £13.18.

The following minutes are among the records of this meeting :

"Ordered, That the Treasurer do pay to Dr. Witherspoon on account six hundred pounds, including two hundred and seventeen pounds already paid to him by a bond on Mr. Elias Woodruff" (Steward of the College).

This bond was returned to the Board, with their consent.

"Resolved, That the management of the College be continued in the hands of Dr. Witherspoon, in the same manner as it has been ever since the confusions of the war."

"Ordered, That the Treasurer do immediately write to every obligor in arrear for interest on their respective bonds, that unless the interest is discharged without delay their bonds will be put into suit without further notice,—which he is to do accordingly,—the moneys arising therefrom to be applied to discharge the President's salary."

---

off from Colt's Neck, Monmouth County, New Jersey. His death occurred on the 16th of October, 1781. It was said of him, "Few men have fallen in this country that were so useful, or so generally mourned for in death." His pastor, the Rev. John Woodhull, a Trustee of the College, preached at his funeral a sermon from the words, "And all Judah and Jerusalem mourned for Josiah, and Jeremiah lamented for him."

Mr. Caldwell was killed by a sentinel at Elizabethtown Point, to which place he had gone to meet and to conduct to the town a sister of one of his parishioners, who was expected from New York in a flag-sloop. As Mr. Caldwell was about to step on board the sloop to return a small bundle which had been handed to him with the request that he would take it to the town, his murderer ordered him to stop, and upon his doing so the soldier presented his musket and shot him. He fell and expired immediately. He was an earnest and active patriot, as well as an able and devoted minister of the gospel. His wife was shot by a British soldier on the 8th of June, 1780. Both husband and wife were highly respected and greatly beloved. Mr. Caldwell's murderer was tried and executed.

These orders show the confidence reposed in Dr. Witherspoon, and also the low state of the College revenues.

"A letter from his Excellency John Dickinson, Esq., Governor of the Delaware State, to the President of the College, to be communicated to the Trustees, was read, enclosing *a promissory note for £100,* and proposing that *the interest of so much of it* as the Trustees may judge proper might annually, or as often as they approve, be applied in procuring a gold or silver medal to be bestowed upon the student who shall compose the best dissertation on some one of the following subjects, viz. :

"1. A zeal for religion clear of bigotry and enthusiasm.

"2. A liberality of sentiment untainted by licentiousness.

"3. A purity of manners free from censorial austerity.

"4. What are the most proper measures to be adopted by a government for promoting and establishing habits of piety and virtue among a people? .

"5. No one or more of the United States can ever derive so much happiness from a dissolution of the Union as from its continuance.

"The direction of the whole, together with a power of changing the subjects, to be vested in the Board.

"Resolved, That the Board do accept of the donation, and that a letter of thanks be written to Governor Dickinson, in the name of the Trustees, and signed by the President."

The following are the only other minutes in which mention is made of the Dickinson medal for thirty-four years:

September 24, 1783.—"According to the tenor of Governor Dickinson's donation last Fall, a partial meeting of the Trustees in the Spring appointed as the subject to be written upon for his medal the fourth question proposed by him, viz., ' What are the most proper measures to be adopted by a government for promoting and establishing habits of piety and virtue among a people?' One dissertation only appearing before the Board, the President was directed to republish the subject, and to invite the students to enter into this competition, and to bring in their dissertations at the next examinations for degrees, or at the utmost against the next Commencement; and the President and the Professor of Divinity and Moral Philosophy were directed to provide a medal, with proper devices, to be given on the occasion."

September 29 and 30, 1784.—"The medal given by Dr. Dickinson, President of the State of Pennsylvania, was adjudged to Mr. Joseph Clay, of the present Senior class, for the best dissertation on the subject proposed by the Board at their last stated meeting."*

"Ordered, That the subject to be proposed for the medal next year be the second mentioned in the letter accompanying Dr. Dickinson's donation, viz., 'A liberality of sentiment untainted by licentiousness.'"

---

* Mr. Clay was a native of Georgia. After leaving College he studied law, and became an eminent jurist, and U. S. District Judge for his native State. In 1801 he became a Baptist preacher. Mr. Clay's dissertation was published with a dedicatory preface to Governor Dickinson.

September 28, 1785.—" Whereas there was but one dissertation for Dr. Dickinson's medal produced, and that not in proper time to have the same examined and a judgment formed upon it at present, Resolved, That it be referred to the Faculty of the College for their decision; and that all future dissertations for medals be brought in to the Faculty at or before the last examination of the Senior class, that a judgment may be formed upon the same in proper season, and the victor be publicly announced on the day of commencement.

" Ordered, That the subject to be competed on for Dr. Dickinson's medal be the third contained in his letter to the Board, viz., 'A purity of manners free from censorial austerity.' "

September 23 and 24, 1788.—" Ordered, That the subject to be competed on for Dr. Dickinson's medal be the following: ' No one or more of the United States can ever derive so much happiness from a dissolution of the Union as from its continuance.' "

September 29 and 30, 1789.—" On the subject of Dr. Dickinson's and Dr. Minto's medals, Resolved, That the Faculty of the College be empowered to examine the essays that have been produced, and decree the said medals according to their judgment."

Dr. Minto's medal, of the value of five pounds, was for the best essay or dissertation on either of the following topics :

1. The unlawfulness and impolicy of capital punishments, and the best method of reforming criminals and making them useful to society.

2. The unlawfulness and impolicy of African slavery, and the best means of abolishing it in the United States, and of promoting the happiness of free negroes.

The form of expression used in the last minute, viz., that of September 30, 1789, indicates that there were some competitors for the medals named, but how many is not said or known.

One thing is certain in regard to competitions for these medals, that they ceased to take place, and most probably from an unwillingness on the part of the students to engage in them, and that the Trustees, finding this to be the case, ceased to propose any more topics for handling and for competition. These competitions, it is evident, were not favorites with the students, and it is by no means improbable that they came to an end with the tacit if not with a formal consent of Governor Dickinson, whose death did not take place until February, 1808, and the last that we hear of any competitions for his medal was in September, 1789, more than eighteen years before his death.

According to the terms of Governor Dickinson's letter, it was left to the discretion of the Trustees *how much* of the interest of his promissory note for one hundred pounds should be expended for a medal, and *how often*, his proposition being this: "that the interest of so much of it as the Trustees may judge proper might *annually*, or *as often as they approve*, be applied in procuring a *gold* or *silver* medal," etc. After a fair and full trial for several years, the matter was dropped; and there is no evidence that Governor Dickinson ever expressed any dissatisfaction with the action or non-action of the Board in regard to it.

At the Commencement of 1783, fourteen candidates were admitted to their first degree in the Arts.

This was a memorable occasion in the history of the College, rendered so by the presence of General Washington, of the National Congress, and of two foreign Ministers. Driven from Philadelphia by a turbulent corps of soldiers, Congress had assembled at Princeton, and they held their sessions in the library-room of the College, which was in the front projection, and on what is now the second or middle story of the building. This room has been divided into two by the passage-way leading from the front door of the edifice to the large room in the rear. This alteration was made upon the rebuilding of Nassau Hall after the fire of March, 1855.

During the time that Congress held its sessions at Princeton, Dr. Boudinot, a Trustee of the College, was the President of that body. "As a compliment to the College, to their own President, as well as to the President of the College, who had recently been one of their own members, Congress determined to adjourn and to attend the Commencement."

The Valedictory orator on this occasion was Ashbel Green, the same who for many years was a Trustee of the College, and for *ten* years its President. The exercises were held in the First Presbyterian Church, then the only one in Princeton. At the close of his Valedictory, Mr. Green made an address of some length to General Washington. Speaking of this occurrence, in his account of Dr. Witherspoon's administration, Dr. Green observes that his address to the General "was received with manifest feeling; and next day he met me in the entry of the College as he was going to a committee-room of Congress, took me by the hand, walked with me a short time, flattered me a little, and desired me to present his best respects to my classmates, and his best wishes for their success in life. There had never been such an audience at a Commencement before, and perhaps there never will be again. Dr. Witherspoon was of course highly gratified."

The only business transacted by the Board on that day, after the Commencement exercises, was the adoption of the following minute :

"The Board being desirous to give some testimony of their high respect for the character of his Excellency General Washington, who has so auspiciously conducted the armies of America,

"Resolved, That the Rev. Drs. Witherspoon, Rodgers, and Johnes be a committee to wait upon his Excellency to request him to sit for his picture, to be taken by Mr. Charles Wilson Peale, of Philadelphia. And that his portrait when finished be placed in the Hall of the College, in the room of the picture of the late King of Great Britain [George the Second], which was torn away by a ball from the American artillery in the battle of Princeton."

On the following day " Dr. Witherspoon reported to the Board that his Excellency General Washington had delivered to him fifty guineas, which he begged the Trustees to accept as a testimony of his respect for the College." The following resolution was then passed :

"Resolved, That the Board accept it, and that the same committee who were appointed to solicit his Excellency's picture do at the same time present to him the thanks of the Board for this instance of his politeness and generosity."

As provided for in the above resolution, General Washington's portrait, in full length, was painted by Mr. Peale, and in the background of the painting there is a representation of the battle of Princeton, and a portrait of General Mercer, who fell mortally wounded at this battle. General Mercer is represented as lying upon the ground, supported by an officer supposed to be a surgeon, and standing by this officer there is another bearing the American flag. It is said that General Mercer had a brother who strongly resembled him in appearance, and that Mr. Peale availed himself of this resemblance in painting his picture of the general. The portrait was placed in the old College Chapel.

From the position of the American army, of the College

building, and of the portrait of the King in the College Chapel, it may readily have been that the portrait was destroyed by a cannon-ball; and from the above minute it appears that this was the received tradition in regard to it. It is known that the building was struck in different places by cannon-balls during the affair at Princeton; and one may have entered the chapel, where the portrait of his Majesty was hanging, and destroyed it. But, be this as it may, the portrait was destroyed, and the frame, regilded, now contains a full-length portrait of General Washington. The portrait of his Majesty was presented to the College by Governor Belcher, to whom the College was indebted for its second charter and for his liberality and earnest devotion to its interests.

Professor Houston, having engaged in the practice of the law, resigned his offices of Treasurer and of Professor of Mathematics and Natural Philosophy. The thanks of the Board were presented to him for his past services. Professor Smith was chosen Treasurer in the room of Professor Houston.

" Dr. Witherspoon proposed to the Trustees that they ought now to take the provision of teachers upon themselves; the minute of September 29, 1779, should be revised, and that it should be entered upon record that his proposal in the first part of the minute was intended to be permanent; and that during the whole time that Professor Smith shall continue in his office, one-half of his salary shall be paid to said Professor; and that in the event of death or resignation, or in any other way his ceasing to be in that office, the President's salary shall return to its former channel.

" Resolved, That the Board do approve of this proposal and interpretation, which they consider as an act of generosity towards this corporation; and that Dr. Smith do hereafter draw for that part of his salary according to the established mode.

" The Board taking into their attention the provision necessary to be made for Dr. Smith, and considering his situation as the immediate representative of the College, and in the President's house exposed to more expense than usual in his office, Resolved, That two hundred pounds per annum be allowed him additional to the sum which he already draws out of the former salary of the President."

Dr. Witherspoon had removed from the President's house to his own private residence, known under the name of Tusculum, about a mile and a half from the College, and on a road running northward from the main street of the town, and directly opposite the College.

Mr. James Riddle, who had been Tutor in the College since the war, resigned his office; and, the Trustees deeming it best to employ two Tutors rather than one, Messrs. Ashbel Green and Samuel Beach were elected to that office.

For reasons assigned in the minute on the subject, the students were, by a resolution of the Board, prohibited from attending any dancing-school.

Dr. Witherspoon gave in his account with the Trustees, which was examined and approved, and from which it appeared that the College was indebted to him in the sum of £881.13.3.

The committee to examine the account were Messrs. William Peartree Smith and John Bayard.

An extra meeting of the Board was held on the 22d of October, 1783. The principal object of the meeting was "to consider and adopt measures *for repairing the funds* of the College, which have been so greatly injured during the late war."

> "It appearing that the necessities of the institution could not admit of any further delay, and that the favorable dispositions of the people of Europe towards America afforded a promising prospect of supplying them, by applying to their generosity, Resolved, That a mission be sent thither as soon as possible for the purpose of soliciting benefactions for the College."

Dr. Witherspoon and General Reed were requested to undertake the mission, to which they were pleased to consent.

The following minute shows the low condition of the College treasury at this time:

> "It being necessary that the debt due from the corporation to Dr. Witherspoon should be discharged, in order to enable him to undertake the voyage, and the treasury not being in a condition to answer this demand immediately, Messrs. Snowden and Bayard offered to advance to him, on the credit of the Board, any moneys that might be necessary to equip him for his voyage.
>
> "Resolved, That these gentlemen have the thanks of the Board, and their offer be accepted, and that they be empowered to draw upon the commissioners in Europe for the sum which they may advance; and that, in all events, the treasury of the College be answerable for that sum.
>
> "Resolved, That all other expenses which may be incurred by the commissioners in the execution of their mission be allowed to them out of the College treasury.
>
> "General Reed was pleased to offer to the Board to serve them in England without any expense to the corporation. Ordered, That the thanks of the Board be presented to General Reed for this generous proposal."

The mission accomplished nothing. Dr. Witherspoon visited

Scotland, and obtained in all not more than what was just sufficient to meet his expenses. It does not appear that General Reed obtained anything for the College. The matter of surprise is, that they and the other Trustees ever imagined that there was ground for a reasonable hope that any funds could be collected in Great Britain at that time for an American College, and that College the one most distinguished for the rebel character of its President and guardians.

The following extract from the commission given by the Board to Dr. Witherspoon and General Reed shows in strong language the depressed condition of the College finances :

"Whereas the College of New Jersey was founded by private liberality for the promotion of religion and learning, and had by the blessing of Heaven arisen to an eminent degree of reputation and usefulness before the late unhappy war; but being occupied as barracks by the contending armies, its library and philosophical apparatus destroyed, the funds of the College for the support of professors and masters, in consequence of the ravages and events of war, sunk and almost annihilated, the very existence of this benevolent and useful institution is become doubtful unless some certain and effectual relief can be obtained from the friends of virtue and literature who have not been exposed to such dreadful calamities."

It was resolved to present a congratulatory address to his Excellency —— Van Berkel, Ambassador from the States of the United Netherlands to the United States of America; and by request Dr. Witherspoon prepared an address, which was agreed to by the Board. His Excellency was present at the recent Commencement. In the address reference was made to the name of the principal edifice as derived from Holland.

In view of Dr. Smith's state of health, they deemed it imprudent for him to take charge of the College pulpit during the absence of Dr. Witherspoon, and they therefore resolved to ask supplies for the pulpit from the Presbyteries of New Brunswick and of New York.

The following minute in regard to Governor Belcher's portrait was adopted at this meeting of the Board :

" The Trustees, being extremely sorry that the picture of his Excellency Governor Belcher, which hung in the College Hall, has been destroyed during the late war, appointed Mr. William P. Smith to endeavor to procure an original painting from some of the remaining friends or relations of the family in New England, or if that should be impracticable, then to procure the best copy that shall be in his power,

that it may be placed where his picture formerly hung, as a testimony of the gratitude of the Board for the eminent services formerly rendered by his Excellency to
this institution."

Mr. Smith's efforts to obtain another portrait were not attended with the desired success. At this time there is a portrait of the Governor, a copy of one in the picture-gallery of
the Athenæum in Boston. The copy was made at the expense
of the late Professor George M. Giger, and by him presented
to the College.

The next Commencement of the College occurred on the 29th
of September, 1784. On this occasion the Trustees, as usual,
held a meeting. Twenty-seven candidates were admitted to the
first degree in the Arts.

" The Rev. Ezra Stiles, President of Yale College, and Doctor of Divinity in the
University of Edinburgh, was admitted *ad eundem* in this College, and the degree
of Doctor of Civil and Canon Laws [LL.D.] was conferred on the Rev. Doctor
Stiles, and on the Honorable Samuel Spencer, Esq., Chief Justice of the State of
North Carolina.

" Messrs. Wm. P. Smith and Robert Ogden, Esqrs., the Committee appointed to
examine and make report on Dr. Witherspoon's account of receipts and disburse-
ments in his mission to Europe on behalf of the College, reported that such was the
disposition of the people in Europe in general, and in Great Britain particularly,
that, notwithstanding the most faithful and prudent exertions, it was impossible to
effect anything of importance in that country for the benefit of the College; and
that, after an examination of the credits and debits of his account, they found a
balance, in favor of the College, of only five pounds fourteen shillings."

These credits included the money advanced by Messrs. Snowden and Bayard to enable Dr. Witherspoon to go to Europe.

Dr. Witherspoon reported, " That when he left Europe, he and
General Reed devolved their trust on a number of gentlemen
in Britain, who engaged themselves, as far as should be in their
power, to accomplish the object of their mission, and to make
what collections they should be able on behalf of the College,
and to remit it to the order of the Board." Whereupon it was
resolved, " That Dr. Witherspoon be appointed to correspond
with those gentlemen relative to the subject of the trust devolved upon them, and to make report thereon, from time to
time, to this Board." It does not appear from the minutes that
any report was ever made.

The European mission proving to be a failure, the Trustees next sought the aid of the Presbyteries composing the Synod of New York and Philadelphia. The minute of this action is as follows:

"The Board, observing with extreme affliction the unsuccessful result of the European mission, determined to make one more application to the charity and generosity of the people in America, for whose general use the institution was founded, and to which it is still faithfully dedicated; and in the first place to apply to the several Presbyteries that compose the Synod of New York and Philadelphia, entreating them to exert themselves with industry and zeal for the support of an institution so serviceable to the general interests of religion, which they have devoted themselves to promote. And resolved, That a memorial on this head be addressed to the Moderators of the several Presbyteries in the name of the Board, in the terms following:

"The memorial of the Trustees of the College of New Jersey to the several Presbyteries composing the Synod of New York and Philadelphia sheweth, That among the ruinous consequences of the late war, in the depreciation of the continental money and destruction of the College buildings, the funds and revenues under the care of your memorialists have been almost annihilated. That in order to re-establish these, and to repair their buildings, and to carry on the designs of the institution, application hath been lately made to obtain assistance from the friends of literature in Europe; but, unhappily, your memorialists have, from sundry unexpected causes, failed in their foreign solicitations, and have not obtained even so much as to defray the expenses of the undertaking. It is therefore become absolutely necessary to make a general application to the friends of religion and learning in this country who wish success to an institution of so much importance to our civil and religious interests. Your memorialists have in consequence deemed it a proper measure to apply themselves to the respective Presbyteries belonging to the Synod of New York and Philadelphia, wishing to impress them with a lively persuasion of the necessity of a general exertion *throughout all our churches* for the support of this College under its present state of depression. Your memorialists must refer to your wisdom the methods most proper and prudent to pursue in soliciting the aid of the people under your respective charges, and in making such personal or public applications throughout your several churches and districts as shall be judged best and likely to be most effectual.

"By order of the Board of Trustees. JOHN WITHERSPOON, President."

The writer has given this memorial in full, and has underscored the expression "throughout all our churches," that the reader may see that the Trustees of 1784, as well as their predecessors, recognized their close and intimate relations to the Presbyterian Church of this country. May their successors in office never forget it or disregard it!

On the 2d of August there was a special meeting of the

Board. "The principal object of the meeting was to consider of and adopt measures for the augmentation of the funds of the institution; and for the reimbursement of those gentlemen who advanced the necessary moneys to Dr. Witherspoon for his arrears of salary, and for defraying the expenses of his mission to Europe on behalf of the College."

Several committees were appointed to solicit funds in New Jersey and in Pennsylvania, and the Trustees residing in the city of Philadelphia were empowered to vest such proportion of the unfunded securities *subscribed* as they may think proper in lands lying in Pennsylvania. Two contingent bequests of one hundred pounds each, for the support of poor scholars at the College, by Mr. William McConkey, of Monmouth, New Jersey, were reported at this meeting.

Dr. Witherspoon was requested to prepare and present to the Board at their next meeting a statement of the accounts of the College from the time that his ledger was discontinued to the time then present. He was also authorized to settle with the executors of the late Rev. Mr. Caldwell, and to give them a final discharge upon the receipt of the balance due to the College.

A committee was appointed to direct and assist the Treasurer in calling in all the outstanding debts of the Corporation, and to vest them in public securities, funded on the excise or other certain revenues in Pennsylvania. In case the money due upon any of the bonds could not be recovered in time for such investment, the committee were required to get a renewal of such bonds, with sufficient securities.

The next Commencement was held on the 28th of September, 1785. Ten candidates were admitted to their first degree in the Arts. The Rev. John Mason having tendered his resignation, and the Honorable Joseph Reed and the Rev. Dr. Elihu Spencer having departed this life since the last meeting of the Board, John Beatty, Esq., the Rev. William Mackay Tennent, and the Rev. Alexander Miller were chosen Trustees of the College.

" Dr. Witherspoon delivered to the Board ninety-two dollars in liquidated final settlement securities, a subscription to the

funds of the College, received of Dr. Benjamin Rush, of Philadelphia."

Mr. Stephen Cook, of the island of Bermuda, was requested
to take one or more of the subscription papers prepared by
order of the Board, and to make application to the inhabitants
of that island for aid in behalf of the College.

In their pecuniary embarrassment the Trustees availed themselves of every possible chance of obtaining funds for the support of the College. Many of their efforts resulted in very
little or nothing; but the result of the whole was that they
were enabled to carry on the instruction of the College without any further interruption, although often in great straits for
funds. It was in view of existing difficulties that they adopted
the following minute :

"The Trustees pressed with the difficulties of supporting the necessary officers
of the College, and considering that the tuition and the rent of the institution have
not been raised in any proportion to the increased prices of other articles since the
war, Resolved, That two pounds per annum shall be levied upon each student in
addition to the present rates, under the title of rent."

Mr. Ashbel Green, at this time the senior Tutor in the
College, was chosen Professor of Mathematics and Natural
Philosophy, with a salary of one hundred and fifty pounds
per annum.

The following order was made:

"Ordered, That if any collections can be made by the friends of the College in
the Board, or elsewhere, for the education of poor and pious youths for the gospel
ministry, it shall be sacredly appropriated to that purpose alone; the Board taking
from every young person so educated an obligation, that if he shall afterwards
enter into any other lucrative profession, he will refund to this corporation the
moneys expended in his instruction and provision."

This the writer regards as an unwise measure. If we can
suppose a young man disingenuous enough to avail himself of
aid from such a fund to enable him to obtain a liberal education, he having no intention to enter the ministry, he will
readily devise ways and means to escape from any obligation,
written or oral, to repay the money so obtained. But if a poor
youth enter upon his studies with the intention of entering the

ministry, and, on account of failure of health, or from a conviction that he was not called of God to the work of the ministry, should give himself to some other calling, he ought not to be required to refund the money given to him. He acted in good faith in receiving the proffered aid, and in giving up his studies for the ministry he continues to act honestly, and no such impediment should be put in the way of his following the dictates of a good conscience by laying upon him, while yet a poor youth, an obligation to refund the moneys thus far advanced for his education. Should he engage in another profession, or in some profitable employment, he would, without any such written obligation, refund, if in his power to do so, with a due regard to higher obligations, what he received in the way of help, as some educated at this College have done, or expend in the assisting of others as much as they ever received, and even more.

As a matter of fact, it is not known that any one who gave a written obligation to refund ever did so. The practice of requiring such an obligation was long since discontinued in this College.

The following resolutions were adopted at a meeting of the Board held on the 19th of April, 1786:

"This College having suffered greatly by the public during the late war; and there being some probability that in the distribution of lands in the new States to the westward Congress might be induced to make a liberal grant of lands to the institution,—

"Resolved, That the President, Dr. Rodgers, and Dr. Beatty be a committee to present to Congress a petition to this effect, when they may think it most prudent and convenient."

But no lands were given.

"Resolved, That the practice of wearing College habits, agreeably to the order of the Board in the year 1768, be revived as soon as the Faculty of the College shall judge it convenient, and at farthest after the next fall vacation.

"Ordered, That a complete catalogue of the graduates of this College be prepared and published at the expense of the present Senior class; and in collecting and preparing the catalogue for the Press, Mr. Green was desired to render his assistance to the class."

The next Commencement took place on the 27th of September, 1786, and there was a large attendance on the part of the Trustees.

Twenty-five members of the Senior class were admitted to the first degree in the Arts.

"A letter was received from the Rev. Mr. Woodhull enclosing three hundred and sixty-six dollars and ten cents, . . . which sum was the subscription of General Forman, John Burrows, and Tunis Vanderveer, Esqrs."

"Dr. Smith, the Treasurer of the College, requested leave to resign that office. The Board accepted the resignation, and elected to the office Dr. Thomas Wiggins, of Princeton."

"Mr. Gilbert T. Snowden [one of the Tutors] was appointed Librarian, and overseer of College repairs, with a salary of five pounds per annum; and [it was] *ordered*, That each student pay five shillings at the beginning of each session for the use of the Library.

"That a blank book should be provided, in which all donations to the Library should be entered.

"And, That all moneys belonging to the institution shall be paid in the first instance to the Treasurer, and that the Treasurer pay the salaries of the officers of the College; and that in all other cases he pay no moneys except to the express order of the Board."

The most important action of the Board at this meeting was the last, and it is embodied in the following minute:

"The Board of Trustees considering the situation of Dr. Smith with regard to the institution, and the duties he is necessarily called to discharge, appointed him to the office of *Vice*-President of the College."

The next meeting of the Board was held April 18, 1787.

"The Rev. John Woodhull, one of the Trustees, presented to the Board two hundred and fourteen dollars and seventeen cents, in Pierce's final settlement notes, received of Kenneth Hankinson, Esq., and the balance of one formerly received in part from Tunis Vanderveer, Esq. Mr. Woodhull also reported that he had obtained of Mr. Dirck Sutphin a bond of £100, on account of Mr. Wm. McConkey, for the education of poor youth in the College.

"The thanks of the Board were presented to Mr. Woodhull for his diligence in this matter."

From a report of the committee on the late Treasurer's account, it appeared that there was due to him the sum of £301.14.7. They reported also that the Treasurer elect, Dr. Thomas Wiggins, declined the appointment on the terms prescribed by the Board. Upon which the Board resolved to proceed to another election. Richard Stockton, Esq., was chosen: neither did he accept the office.

Professor Ashbel Green, the Professor of Mathematics and Natural Philosophy, and Mr. Gilbert T. Snowden, a Tutor of the College, having resigned their offices, it was resolved to appoint two Tutors in their room. Mr. James McCoy was chosen in the place of Mr. Green, and Mr. Samuel Finley Snowden in the room of Mr. Gilbert Tennent Snowden. But neither of these gentlemen accepted the appointment, and in their room Messrs. John W. Vancleve and James Henderson Imlay were chosen Tutors by the Faculty, agreeably to an authority given to them by the Board.

The Hon. William Patterson was chosen a Trustee, in the place of Robert Ogden, Esq., deceased.

A committee of finance was appointed, and its duties prescribed.

It was ordered, that the Faculty prepare and present to the Board at their next meeting a system of laws for the internal government of the institution.

The next Commencement of the College took place on Wednesday, the 26th of September, 1787. The Board met on the day preceding, and continued in session on Wednesday and Thursday.

Dr. Rodgers, Dr. McWhorter, Mr. Smith, and Mr. Tennent were appointed a committee to prepare some regulations by which the Board may be directed in conferring the higher degrees in Theology and Law. Although the proposal of Professors Houston and Smith on this subject had met with favor from the committee to whom it was referred, and in general was acceptable to the Board, it appears from this and other minutes that it did not fully meet the views of the Trustees.

The Rev. Dr. Johnes, a Trustee of the College, presented to the Board in public securities the sum of $107.10 collected by him for the education of poor and pious youth at the College. The thanks of the Board were presented to Dr. Johnes for his zeal in promoting the interests of the College.

"The Committee to prepare rules for the conferring the highest degrees reported the following, which were adopted by the Board:

" 1. No person shall be admitted to the degree of Doctor in Divinity or Doctor of Laws unless with the consent of two-thirds of the members present of the Board.

" 2. That no person shall be admitted to either of these degrees unless his name have been proposed to the Board at least one day before conferring the degree.

" 3. It is recommended, in all cases where gentlemen are to be proposed for either of these degrees, their names be reported to the Faculty of the College at least ten days before the deliberations [of the Board], whose duty it shall be to make all necessary enquiries concerning the merits of the candidates, and report thereon to the Board."

The first of these rules was afterwards repealed, as inconsistent with the charter of the College.

The committee appointed at a previous meeting to petition the Legislature to exempt the property of the College from taxation, reported that the Legislature had not complied with the request.

Walter Minto, LL.D., a distinguished mathematical scholar and astronomer, was appointed Professor of Mathematics and Natural Philosophy, and held this office until his decease, in 1796.* He was a native of Scotland, educated at Edinburgh, and before his coming to America had made himself known to the scientific world by his mathematical and astronomical publications.

The Rev. Manasseh Cutler, LL.D., of Connecticut, a man of much note in his day, gives the following account of the College at this time (1787): " I then called upon Dr. Smith, Vice-President of the College, to whom I also had letters. He is a young gentleman, lives in an elegant style, and is the first literary character in this State. He waited on me to the College, introduced me to all the Tutors, and showed me the apartments of the College. The building is of three stories, has three cross entries, and a long one in the first story. The chambers open into these entries and render the communication more convenient. The library is small. . . . The cabinet and the philosophical apparatus are very indifferent. The only article worthy of notice was the orrery made by Mr. Rittenhouse. This is an elegant machine, and much exceeds any that has been made in Europe. . . . I was much pleased with the Hall and the stage erected for the exhibition. It is well formed for plays, which are permitted here, and the dialogue speaking principally cultivated. The Hall is ornamented with several paintings, particularly the famous battle in the town," etc. The remark concerning the permitting of plays on the College stage

* An interesting sketch of Dr. Minto is given in the " Princeton Magazine" for 1850, from the pen of the editor.

is only in so far correct as dialogues may be classed under this head. To a communication to the New Jersey Historical Society, by President Tuttle, of Wabash College, we are indebted for the above extract from Dr. Cutler's "Journal." The same gentleman communicated to the "Newark Daily Advertiser," in a letter of the date of August 23, 1873, a description of some pamphlets recently found by him in the course of his antiquarian researches, and among these pamphlets is one with the following title-page: "The Military Glory of Great Britain, an Entertainment given by the late candidates for *Bachelor's degrees*, at the close of the Anniversary Commencement, in Nassau Hall, *New Jersey*, September 29, 1762. Philadelphia: printed by Wm. Bradford, MDCCLXII." Dr. Tuttle quaintly remarks that "the careful reader of this poetical drama will be convinced that Shakspeare and Ben Jonson are in no danger from this competitor." But our object in referring to it in connection with Dr. Cutler's remark respecting the College stage is to show the wide range given to College exhibitions in the earlier periods of the College history.

The Commencement for the year 1788 was held on Wednesday, the 24th of September. Dr. Timothy Johnes, a Trustee named in Governor Belcher's charter of the College, resigned his seat at the Board, and the Rev. Andrew Hunter, of Woodbury, New Jersey, was chosen in his place. The thanks of the Board were tendered to Dr. Johnes "for his long and faithful services."

There having been some relaxation permitted during and since the war in the law requiring a residence of two years in the College previous to receiving the first degree in the Arts, it was "Ordered, That after the next session of the College the law be strictly enforced."

Mr. Isaac Snowden, Jr., was chosen Treasurer of the College, and took the oaths of office.

Mr. Imlay having resigned his position of Tutor, Mr. Vancleve and Mr. Samuel Harris were chosen Tutors by the Board, and were qualified as required by the charter.

The following resolution was adopted in regard to the Faculty:

" Whereas regular Professorships are now established in this institution, it is therefore resolved and ordered, That the president and professors form the faculty, and that the government of the College be vested in the said faculty, whose authority shall extend to every part of the discipline, except the final expulsion of a student, which shall not take place unless by the order of this board, or unless six trustees shall have been convened for the purpose, and their consent obtained."

The Commencement for 1790 took place on Wednesday, the 28th of September. Fourteen candidates were admitted to their first degree in the Arts.

" It was ordered, That the names of Mr. James Bayard, Thomas H. McCalla, James Crawford, and James Brownfield, omitted to be inserted in the catalogue for the year 1777, be now inserted in their proper place."

The Rev. Ashbel Green was chosen a Trustee, in the room of the Rev. Dr. Duffield, deceased, and the Rev. James Armstrong, in the room of the Rev. Alexander Miller, resigned.

Dr. McWhorter, from the committee appointed to settle with Elisha Boudinot, Esq., executor of Mrs. Esther Richards, reported that they had made a partial settlement of the legacy left by that lady to the College, and that they had received from Mr. Boudinot, in loan-office certificates, of the date of 1778, three thousand dollars, and of the date of 1779, three hundred dollars, which he is directed to pay to the Treasurer.

The thanks of the Board were presented to Mr. Boudinot for his care and attention to the interests of the College in ascertaining and securing the legacy left by Mrs. Richards to this institution. Mr. Silas Wood was chosen a Tutor in the place of Mr. Samuel Harris, deceased.

" It was ordered, That the Treasurer provide a folio book, in which shall be recorded the benefactions which have been, and may be, at different times, made to this College, with the names of the benefactors."

Most of the philosophical apparatus belonging to the College having been destroyed or carried off during the late war, the Board " resolved to use their utmost endeavors to procure such a sum of money as shall be adequate to supply the deficiency."

The Commencement for 1791 took place on the 27th of September, and the Board met, according to adjournment, on the preceding day, Governor Patterson, President Witherspoon, and eighteen other Trustees being present. Twenty-five candidates were admitted to their first degree in the Arts. The degree of LL.D. was conferred upon the Hon. Thomas Jefferson, Secretary of State, and also upon the Hon. Alexander Hamilton, Secretary of the Treasury.

A committee from the General Assembly of the Presbyterian Church waited upon the Board to inquire into the state of the fund for the education of pious youth, which was deposited in the treasury of the College, the interest of this fund having been placed at the disposal of the Synod of New York and Philadelphia, *now* the General Assembly. The Board, not being prepared at once to give a definite answer to the committee from the General Assembly, appointed a committee of five members to inquire into the condition of the fund, and to report to the Rev. Nathaniel Irwin, the Chairman of the Assembly's committee. The College committee consisted of Dr. Harris, Dr. Boudinot, Jonathan B. Smith, Esq., Isaac Snowden, Esq., and Dr. Green, all of the city of Philadelphia. Richard Stockton, Esq., was chosen a Trustee, in the room of Governor Patterson, who, in virtue of his office as Governor of the State, was the President of the Board.

Mr. Isaac Snowden, Jr., having resigned the office of Treasurer, Mr. John Harrison, of Princeton, was chosen Treasurer of the College. The Board resolved to renew their application to Congress for a reimbursement of damages sustained by the College during the war, and for rent while it was used for the service of the United States; and Dr. Boudinot, Dr. Green, and Mr. Jonathan Bayard Smith were the committee to make the application.

A committee was also appointed to make another revision of the laws of the College.

The next meeting of the Board was held on Tuesday, the 25th of September, 1792, and on the following day the usual Commencement exercises took place, and the first degree in the Arts was conferred upon *thirty-seven* graduates. This is the largest number ever graduated at this College up to this date, and for several years after.

"The committee appointed at the meeting of the Board, in September last, to examine into the whole stock of the College, and bring forward the accounts to April, 1792," made a report through their chairman, Dr. Boudinot. "The report was approved, and the same committee continued, and directed to endeavor to make a final report at the next meeting of the Board."

"A copy of the Will of *Mr. James Leslie*, of New York, leaving a certain legacy to the Direction of the Trustees of New Jersey College, for the education of poor and pious youth with a view to the ministry of the gospel in the Presbyterian Church, was produced to the Board. Ordered, That the same be recorded at large in the book to be appropriated to record all Donations to this College."

On the 20th of August, 1793, there was a special meeting of the Board to consider a proposal, or suggestion, from the Trustees of Queen's College, New Brunswick, in reference to a union of the two colleges. The minutes relative to this matter are the following:

"A letter was laid before the Board from Archibald Mercer, Esq., in the following terms: 'In the Board of Trustees of Queen's College in New Jersey, *Resolved*, That a committee be appointed to confer with the trustees of the College of New Jersey, or a committee of said trustees, on the subject of a federal union between the Colleges.

"'Ordered, That the committee consist of General Frelinghuysen, Dr. Linn, A. Mercer, A. Kirkpatrick, and James Schureman, Esqrs.

"'JAMES SCHUREMAN, Clerk.

"'SIR,—I take the earliest opportunity to convey to you the above resolution of Queen's College, being, with respect,

"'Your obedient, humble servant,

"'ARCHIBALD MERCER, President P. T.

"'To the Rev. Dr. WITHERSPOON, President of the Board of Trustees of the College of New Jersey.'

"Resolved, That a committee of this Board be appointed to meet with the committee above appointed on the part of the trustees of Queen's College, or with the Board of said Trustees, and confer with them on the subject of an union of the two colleges, who shall lay the result of their conference before this Board at their next meeting; and

"Resolved, That the committee consist of the following gentlemen: Dr. Witherspoon, Dr. Rodgers, Dr. Boudinot, Dr. Beatty, Colonel Bayard, and Mr. Woodhull.

"Ordered, That the President transmit a copy of the above resolution to the President of the Board of Trustees of Queen's College."

At the next meeting of the Board, which occurred on Wednesday, the 25th of September, the day of the annual Commencement, the committee made their report, which was as follows:

"NEW BRUNSWICK, September 10, 1793.

"The committees of the Trustees of the College of New Jersey and Queen's College, appointed to confer upon the subject of a union between the two colleges, met here this day, in pursuance of notice previously given for that purpose, viz.: ˙

"From the College of New Jersey.—The Rev. John Witherspoon, D.D., the Rev. John Woodhull, Elias Boudinot, John Bayard, Esqrs.

"From Queen's College.—Archibald Mercer, Frederick Frelinghuysen, James Schureman, Andrew Kirkpatrick, Esqrs.

"The committees appointed Elias Boudinot, Esq., Chairman, Andrew Kirkpatrick, Esq., Clerk, and then went into a free conference on the subject of the proposed union: whereupon,

"Resolved, unanimously, That a perfect incorporating and consolidating union between the two colleges will be the most proper and beneficial union, and will tend to the promotion of learning.

"Resolved, unanimously, That in order to effect this union application be made by both colleges to the legislature for a new charter; that the trustees to be named in the new charter consist of twenty-eight in number. That is to say, the Governor of the State for the time being, the President of the college for the time being, and thirteen of the trustees of each of the said colleges, being inhabitants of New Jersey, to be chosen and named by their respective boards.

"Resolved, unanimously, That no person not an inhabitant of the State of New Jersey shall at any time be a trustee of the college so to be constituted.

"Resolved, unanimously, That an institution at New Brunswick be established and supported by the bye-laws of the trustees of the said college, in which shall be taught the learning preparatory to entering the first class in the college, and that no other institution at Princeton shall be supported at the expense of the said trustees in which the same things shall be taught.

"Resolved, unanimously, That the present officers of New Jersey College be the officers of the college to be established on the foregoing principles.

"Resolved, That the foregoing resolutions be submitted to the boards of trustees of the said two colleges, by their respective committees, for their consideration.

"ELIAS BOUDINOT, Chairman."

The consideration of this report was postponed until the next meeting of the Board. As there was a bare quorum present, it was deemed inexpedient to decide so important a measure as that presented in the report of the two committees, and for this reason the consideration of it was deferred, and the President was authorized to call a meeting of the Board when in his judgment circumstances would justify it. The small number in attendance at this meeting was due to the general panic in the community occasioned by the prevalence of the yellow fever in Philadelphia.

Twenty-one members of the Senior class were admitted to their first degree in the Arts.

Mr. John Abeel, one of the Tutors, having resigned his office, the Faculty were authorized to appoint another in his room, if they find it necessary.

The next meeting of the Board was held at Princeton, on the 13th of December, 1793. The first business, after reading the minutes of the previous meeting, was the reading of the following letter from Archibald Mercer, Esq.:

" MILLSTONE, November 20, 1793.

" SIR,—The trustees of Queen's College met yesterday, and, I am sorry to inform you, wholly rejected the report of the committees respecting the proposed union of the Colleges.

" I have the honor to be, Sir, with the utmost respect,

" Your obliged humble servant,

"ARCHIBALD MERCER, P. P. T.

" To the Rev. Dr. JOHN WITHERSPOON, President of the Board of Trustees of the College of New Jersey."

Thus ended this negotiation, and no further action was taken in regard to it by the Trustees of the College of New Jersey. The writer thinks it doubtful whether the Trustees of the College of New Jersey would have given their consent to the proposed union had they discussed the measure and taken a vote on the proposed plan,—one most extraordinary feature of this plan being that which compels every trustee of the united colleges to be an inhabitant of the State of New Jersey, inasmuch as some of the most valuable trustees of these institutions were residents of New York and Philadelphia, and had been so from the beginning.

It is known that Dr. Witherspoon, after accepting the office of President of this College but before coming to this country, made a visit to Holland in the interests of the College, but what special objects he had in view are not clearly known. But while in Holland he visited Utrecht, where the Rev. Dr. John Livingston, then a student of theology, was pursuing his professional studies, and they had an interview and a conversation in reference to the proper policy to be pursued in America by the friends of true religion and sound learning, and came to an understanding that they would favor the adoption of a scheme according to which the Reformed Dutch Church should establish a theological professorship of their own, but that for the academical education of their youth they should avail themselves of the facilities afforded by the College at Princeton. But this measure did not meet the views of the larger party in the Reformed Dutch Church, which at the time of Dr. Witherspoon's arrival in this country had taken measures for obtaining a charter for a college to be under the control of members of their own Church, and in 1770 they succeeded in obtaining from Governor Franklin and his Council such a charter. (See Judge Bradley's Centennial Discourse at Rutgers College in 1870.)

The friends of both institutions at this day can probably see that it was better for the interests of religion and learning that the negotiations for a union of the two colleges were unsuccessful. Each college has done a great and good work for the best interests of both the Church and the State, and it is hoped they will continue to be generous rivals in this good work, and be able to increase in usefulness as they advance in age, wealth, and members.

Mr. William P. Smith having tendered his resignation as a Trustee, it was accepted, and the thanks of the Board were tendered to him for his long and faithful services. Mr. Smith was a Trustee for forty-five years.

The Hon. William Patterson was chosen a Trustee in the room of Mr. Smith, resigned, and the Rev. Jacob Van Arsdalen and Joseph Bloomfield, Esq., were chosen in the place of the Rev. Dr. Robert Smith and the Rev. Israel Read, deceased.

At the next meeting of the Board the Committee on Accounts presented a brief account, and the Committee was continued.

"A question having arisen, whether this corporation have a right to appropriate the charity of Mr. Leslie to defray the expense of the maintenance and clothing as well as of the instruction of poor and pious youth for the gospel ministry, it was determined by the corporation that they have this right." *

---

* A report was made to the Board, at this meeting, of *the certificates* deposited in the office of James Ewing, Esq., Commissioner for New Jersey. The amounts of these certificates were as follows :

Mr. Silas Wood having resigned the office of Tutor, Mr. David English was elected a Tutor in his room.

The next meeting of the Board was held on the 23d and 24th of September, 1794, and it was the last meeting ever attended by Dr. Witherspoon, who died a few weeks after.

The Commencement exercises took place on the 24th. The number of candidates admitted to the first degree in the Arts was twenty-seven.

Dr. Rodgers made a report of the moneys in the hands of Mr. Leslie's executors in New York, from which it appeared that they had in their possession bank shares and bonds, and cash to the value of £711.15.1 New York currency.* There were also two houses in the city of New York, value uncertain.

The Committee on Accounts was continued.

The Faculty of the College, finding their salaries insufficient for the support of their families, in consequence of the great increase in the prices of all the necessaries of life, which are from twenty-five to ten per cent. higher than they were two or three years ago, request the Board to devise some means of augmenting their salaries in proportion to the augmentation that has taken place in the price of grain.

MR. JAMES LESLIE'S LEGACY.

One certificate, six per cents.		$4,364.32
" " three per cents.		2,273.41
" " deferred stock		4,039.76
		$10,677.49

MRS. RICHARDS'S LEGACY.

One certificate, six per cents.		$1,119.15
" " three per cents.		1,291.60
" " deferred stock		559.57
		$2,970.32

COLLEGE FUNDS.

One certificate, six per cents.		$3,404.63
" " three per cents.		1,643.47
" " deferred stock		402.31
		$5,450.41

* "Resolved, That the Rev. Dr. Rodgers be empowered to receive whatever sums are in the hands of Mr. Leslie's executors in the city of New York."

This the Faculty conceived might be done "without encroaching on the College funds destined for other purposes, by increasing the tuition, etc., of the students. This it is hoped will appear neither unreasonable nor improper to the Trustees, as they have found it both reasonable and necessary to raise the price of board with the Steward fifty per cent. within a few years."

The Trustees postponed the final decision of this subject to the next meeting.

Dr. Rodgers was desired to request the executors of Mr. Leslie, in New York, to invest the whole property coming to the College in stock of the Bank of New York, and to transfer the same to the Trustees of the College.

The Treasurer reported that he had received from seventy-nine students, for tuition-fees and room-rent, one thousand one hundred and seventy-five dollars; from which it appears that the annual charge for tuition and rent of room to each student was a little less than thirty dollars, being eleven pounds New Jersey currency.

The Committee on Accounts made a report, and was continued, in order to bring up the accounts to the present date.

The foregoing detail shows the great difficulties with which the College had to contend throughout the administration of Dr. Witherspoon, and the strenuous efforts made to meet and overcome them. These difficulties might all have been summed up in a few words,—a want of funds and a want of students; both of these wants being occasioned chiefly by the impoverished condition of the country consequent upon the war of the Revolution. At the time Dr. Witherspoon took charge of the College it was much embarrassed for want of funds, and the energetic measures adopted to supply this want gave good ground to hope that this hindrance to the success and usefulness of the institution would soon be removed. But shortly after began the political troubles which ended in a change of government, and which finally gave freedom and independence to the country, laying the foundation of its subsequent prosperity, but, as their immediate result, producing for several years great financial embarrassment.

It is believed that no general statement of the affairs of the institution can make so deep an impression, respecting the trials and struggles to which the President, Trustees, and other officers and friends of the College were subjected during this period of its history, as a recital of their constant and untiring efforts in its behalf; and this is our apology, if one be needed, for dwelling so long upon these things.

But there is a brighter side to this picture of College affairs. For notwithstanding all the impediments in the way, occasioned by the dispersion of the students, the occupation and dilapidation of the College building by both British and American soldiery, the destruction of property and of funds, and the injury done to the apparatus and the library, in as short a time as possible the College was again opened for the reception of students, and more ample provision than ever before was made for the thorough instruction of the pupils in all those branches which in that day claimed the attention of college youth.

Although the College exercises were for a time suspended, yet every year there were some candidates for the first degree in the Arts,—whose names are given in the Triennial Catalogue of the College; the smallest number being *five*, in 1778, and the largest *thirty-seven*, in 1792. And although the average number of graduates did not exceed *nineteen* a year, there is probably no period in the history of the institution during which so large a proportion of the students, in after-life, rose to distinction. This may be accounted for in part by the circumstances of the country, which called forth all the energies of which these men were possessed, but still not a little may be claimed for the training which they here received under their able and patriotic teachers.

Of the four hundred and sixty-nine graduates of the College from 1769 to 1794, one hundred and fourteen became ministers of the gospel, of whom seventy-five were graduated from 1769 to 1776. After the war began, the candidates for the ministry were much fewer in number in proportion to the whole than they were before that event. Many of these ministers, who were trained under Dr. Witherspoon and his associates in the Faculty, became prominent and influential men in the Church and in the community at large. Among them were the following-named Presidents and Professors of Colleges in the Middle and Southern States. The names are given in the order of their graduation. Of the class of

1769. Samuel Stanhope Smith,—Dr. Witherspoon's successor in the Presidency of the College of New Jersey.

1772. Andrew Hunter, Professor of Mathematics and Astronomy in the same College.

1772. Samuel Eusebius McCorkle, Professor of Moral and Political Philosophy in the University of North Carolina.

1772. John McMillan, Vice-President of Jefferson College, Pennsylvania, and Professor of Theology in the same College.

1773. Thaddeus Dod, the Founder and President of Washington Academy, afterwards Washington College, Pennsylvania.

1773. James Dunlap, President of Jefferson College, Pennsylvania.

1773. William Graham, Founder and President of Liberty Hall, afterwards Washington College, Virginia.

1773. John McKnight, President of Dickinson College, Pennsylvania.

1773. John Blair Smith, President of Hampden Sidney College, Virginia, and also of Union College, Schenectady, New York.

1774. Thomas Harris Maccaulle, President of Mount Sion College, South Carolina.

1775. Samuel Doak, President of Washington College, Tennessee.

1783. Ashbel Green, President of the College of New Jersey.

1784. Ira Condit, Vice-President of Queen's College, now Rutgers, New Jersey, and Professor of Moral Philosophy in the same.

1787. Robert Finley, President of the University of Georgia.

1787. Elijah D. Rattoone, President of Charleston College, South Carolina, and a Presbyter of the Protestant Episcopal Church.

1789. Robert Helt Chapman, President of the University of North Carolina.

1791. Joseph Caldwell, President of the same University before Dr. Chapman.

1793. John Henry Hobart, Bishop of the Protestant Episcopal Church, New York, and Professor of Pastoral Theology and Pulpit Eloquence in the Theological Seminary of the Episcopal Church.

1794. Henry Kollock, Professor of Theology in the College of New Jersey.

Some of those here named were eminent as preachers of the gospel as well as teachers in the higher seminaries of learning.

To this list may be added the names of not a few others who were men of note as able and successful pastors of churches, *e.g.* :

1769. Samuel Niles, at Abington, Massachusetts.

1769. Elihu Thayer, at Kingston, New Hampshire.

1770. Nathaniel Irwin, at Neshaminy, Pennsylvania.

1770. Nathan Perkins, at West Hartford, Connecticut.

1771. John Black, at Upper Mars Creek, York County, Pennsylvania.

1771. Samuel Spring, at Newburyport, Massachusetts.

1772. Joseph Eckley, at Boston, Massachusetts.

1772. James Grier, at Deep Run, Pennsylvania.

1772. William Linn, at New York City, Reformed Dutch Church.

1773. John Francis Armstrong, at Trenton, New Jersey ; a Trustee of the College.

1773. Ebenezer Bradford, at Rowley, Massachusetts.

1773. Lewis Feuilleteau Wilson, at Concord, North Carolina.
1774. Stephen Bloomer Balch, at Georgetown, District of Columbia.
1774. James Hall, at Fourth Creek, Concord, and Bethany, North Carolina.
1775. John Durburrow Blair, at Richmond, Virginia.
1775. Isaac Stockton Keith, at Charleston, South Carolina.
1775. James McCrie, at Steel Creek, North Carolina.
1775. John Springer, at Washington, Georgia.
1778. William Boyd, at Lamington, New Jersey; a Trustee of the College.
1781. Joseph Clark, at New Brunswick, New Jersey; a Trustee of the College.
1783. Gilbert Tennent Snowden, at Cranbury, New Jersey.
1784. Joseph Clay, at Savannah, Georgia; Baptist Church.
1787. John Nelson Abeel, at New York; Reformed Dutch Church.
1788. Aaron Condict, at Hanover, New Jersey.
1789. Thomas Pitt Irving, at Hagerstown, Maryland; Principal of the Academy there, and Rector of the Episcopal Church.
1790. George Spafford Woodhull, at Princeton, and a Trustee of the College.
1793. Isaac Van Dorem, at Hopewell, New York; Reformed Dutch Church, and afterwards Principal of the Newark Academy.

Of the graduates from 1769 to 1794 inclusive, six were members of the Continental Congress, twenty became Senators of the United States, and twenty-three members of the House of Representatives. Of the class of

1769. John Beatty, Delegate to the Continental Congress, from New Jersey.
1769. John Henry, Delegate to the Continental Congress, from Maryland.
1771. Gunning Bedford, Delegate to the Continental Congress, from Delaware.
1771. James Madison, Delegate to the Continental Congress, from Virginia.
1773. Morgan Lewis, Delegate to the Continental Congress, from New York.
1773. Henry Lee, Delegate to the Continental Congress, from Virginia.

UNITED STATES SENATORS.

1770. Frederick Frelinghuysen, from New Jersey.
1772. Aaron Burr, from New York.
1773. Aaron Ogden, from New Jersey.
1774. John Ewing Calhoun, from South Carolina.
1774. Jonathan Mason, from Massachusetts.
1775. Isaac Tichenor, from Vermont.
1776. Jonathan Dayton, from New Jersey.
1776. John Rutherford, from New York.
1779. Richard Stockton, from New Jersey.
1780. Abraham R. Venable, from Virginia.
1781. William Branch Giles, from Virginia.
1781. Edward Livingston, from Louisiana.
1784. James Ashton Bayard, from Delaware.
1785. Robert Goodloe Harper, from Maryland.
1788. David Stone, from North Carolina.
1789. Mahlon Dickerson, from New Jersey.
1790. John Taylor, from South Carolina.

1791. Jacob Burnet, from Ohio.
1792. George M. Bibb, from Kentucky.
1794. George Washington Campbell, from Tennessee.

MEMBERS OF THE UNITED STATES HOUSE OF REPRESENTATIVES.

1769. James Linn, from New Jersey.
1772. David Bard, from Pennsylvania.
1774. Wm. Stevens Smith, from New York.
1775. John Andrew Scudder, from New Jersey.
1776. Nathaniel Alexander, from North Carolina.
1776. John W. Kittera, from Pennsylvania.
1781. William Crawford, from Pennsylvania.
1782. Conrad Elmendorf, from New York.
1782. John A. Hanna, from Pennsylvania.
1784. Peter R. Livingston, from New York.
1785. James Wilken, from New York.
1786. John Henderson Imlay, from New Jersey.
1787. Evan Alexander, from North Carolina.
1788. Nathaniel W. Howell, from New York.
1788. Wm. Kirkpatrick, from New York.
1788. Nicholas Van Dyke, from Delaware.
1789. Isaac Pierson, from New Jersey.
1789. Ephraim King Wilson, from Maryland.
1789. Silas Wood, from New York.
1792. Wm. Chatwood, from New Jersey.
1792. Peter Early, from Georgia.
1792. George C. Maxwell, from New Jersey.
1794. Thomas M. Bayly, from Virginia.
1794. James M. Broome, from Delaware.

Of the above-named members of Congress,
James Madison was the fourth President of the United States.
Aaron Burr was the third Vice-President.
John Henry was Governor of Maryland.
Gunning Bedford was Governor of Delaware.
Henry Lee was Governor of Virginia.
Morgan Lewis was Governor of New York.
Aaron Ogden was Governor of New Jersey.
Isaac Tichenor was Governor of Vermont.
Nathaniel Alexander was Governor of North Carolina.
Wm. Branch Giles was Governor of Virginia.
David Stone was Governor of North Carolina.
Mahlon Dickerson was Governor of New Jersey.
John Taylor was Governor of South Carolina.
Peter Early was Governor of Georgia.
And to this list of Governors of several of the States may be added William
Richardson Davie, Governor of North Carolina, also Envoy, with Ellsworth, an
older graduate, to France.

Of the graduates of this period, three became Judges of the Supreme Court of the United States, viz. : of the class of—

1774. Brockholst Livingston, of New York.
1788. Smith Thompson, of New York.
1790. William Johnson, of South Carolina.

Not a few others became distinguished,—some for their culture of letters, some for their medical skill and knowledge, others for their legal attainments and as judges, some as army officers, and others still as active and useful citizens. Of these, without undertaking to mention all, the following include the best-known :

1770. James Witherspoon, of New Jersey, son of President Witherspoon, killed at the battle of Germantown.

1771. Hugh Henry Brackenridge, of Pennsylvania, Judge of the Supreme Court.

1771. Charles McKnight, of New York, Surgeon-General of the United States Army.

1771. Donald Campbell, of New York, Colonel in the United States Army.

1771. Philip Freneau, of New Jersey, Poet, and Writer on Politics.

1772. Wm. Bradford, of Pennsylvania, Attorney-General of the United States.

1773. Hugh Hodge, of Pennsylvania, Physician, Surgeon in the United States Army.

1774. John Noble Cumming, of New Jersey, General in the Army.

1775. Andrew Kirkpatrick, of New Jersey, Chief Justice.

1775. Charles Lee, of Virginia, Attorney-General of the United States.

1775. Spruce Macay, of North Carolina, Judge of the Superior Court.

1775. John R. B. Rodgers, M.D., of New York, Physician, and Professor in Columbia College.

1776. John Pintard, of New York, chief founder of the New York Historical Society.

1777. John Young Noel, of Georgia, Lawyer of much eminence.

1778. Jacob Morton, of New York, Justice of the City Court, etc.

1779. Andrew Bayard, of Pennsylvania, Trustee of the College.

1779. Matthew McCallister, of Georgia, Judge of the Superior Court.

1779. James Riddle, of Pennsylvania, Judge of the Supreme Court.

1779. Aaron Dickinson Woodruff, of New Jersey, Attorney-General.

1780. Ebenezer Stockton, of New Jersey, Physician, Assistant-Surgeon in the United States Army.

1783. Nathaniel Lawrence, of New York, Attorney-General.

1783. Jacob Radcliff, of New York, Judge of the Supreme Court.

1783. George Whitefield Woodruff, of Georgia, Attorney-General.

1784. Gabriel Ford, of New Jersey, Judge of the Supreme Court.

1784. Samuel Bayard, of New Jersey, Trustee and Treasurer of the College.

1785. John Vernon Henry, of New York, Lawyer, Doctor of Laws.

1786. Charles Smith, of New Jersey, Physician, Trustee of Queen's College.

1788. John Wells, of New York, Lawyer, Doctor of Laws.

1789. David Hosack, of New York, Professor in the College of Physicians and Surgeons, Doctor of Laws.

1791. Elias Van Artsdale, of New Jersey, Lawyer, Doctor of Laws.

1792. Charles Wilson Harris, of North Carolina, Professor in the University of North Carolina, and afterwards an eminent lawyer.

1792. John C. Otto, of Pennsylvania, Vice-President of the College of Physicians.

1793. John Neilson, of New York, Physician.

1794. John N. Simpson, of New Jersey, an efficient friend of popular education and internal improvements.

Of the graduates named above as admitted to their first degree, from 1769 to 1780 inclusive, more than twenty were officers in the United States Army during the War for Independence, and all of them young men.

Of the course of instruction in the year 1772, and of the government of the College, Dr. Witherspoon, in an address to the inhabitants of Jamaica and other West India islands, gives the following account: "The regular course of instruction is in four classes, exactly after the manner and bearing the names of the classes in the English Universities,—Freshman, Sophomore, Junior, and Senior. In the first year they read Latin and Greek, with Roman and Grecian antiquities, and Rhetoric. In the second, continuing the study of the languages, they learn a complete system of geography, with the use of the globes, the first principles of philosophy, and the elements of mathematical knowledge. The third, though the languages are not wholly omitted, is chiefly employed in mathematics and natural philosophy. And the senior year is employed in reading the higher classics, proceeding in the mathematics and natural philosophy, and going through a course of moral philosophy. In addition to these, the President gives lectures to the juniors and seniors, which, consequently, every student hears twice over in his course,—first upon chronology and history, and afterwards upon composition and criticism. He also taught the French language last winter, and it will continue to be taught to those who desire to learn it.

"During the whole course of their studies, the three younger classes, two every evening formerly, and now three, because of their increased number, pronounce an oration, on the stage erected for that purpose in the hall, immediately after prayers; that they may learn, by early habit, presence of mind, and proper pronunciation and gesture in public speaking. This excellent practice, which has been kept up almost from the first foundation of the College, has had the most admirable effects. The senior scholars, every five or six weeks, pronounce orations of their own composition, to which all persons of any note in the neighborhood are invited or admitted.

"The College is now furnished with all the most important helps to instruction. The library contains a very large collection of valuable books. The lessons of astronomy are given upon the orrery lately invented by David Rittenhouse, Esq., which is reckoned by the best judges the most excellent in its kind of any ever yet produced; and when what is commissioned and now upon its way is added to what the College already possesses, the apparatus for mathematics and natural philosophy will be equal if not superior to any on the continent.

. . . "There is a fixed annual commencement on the last Wednesday of September, when, after a variety of public exercises, always attended by a vast concourse of the politest company from different parts of this province and the cities of New York and Philadelphia, the students whose senior year is expiring are admitted to the degree of Bachelor of Arts; the Bachelors of three years' standing to the degrees of Masters; and such other higher degrees granted as are either regularly claimed or the Trustees think proper to bestow upon those who have distinguished themselves by their literary productions or their appearances in public life.

"On the day preceding the commencement *last* year [1771] there was (and it will be continued hereafter) a public exhibition and voluntary competition for prizes, open for every member of the College. These were first, second, and third prizes on each of the following subjects: 1. Reading the English language with propriety and grace, and being able to answer all questions on its orthography and grammar. 2. Reading the Latin and Greek languages in the same manner, with particular attention to true quantity. 3. Speaking Latin. 4. Latin versions. 5. Pronouncing English orations. The preference was determined by ballot, and all present permitted to vote who were graduates of this or any other College.

"*As to the government* of the College, no correction by stripes is permitted. Such as cannot be governed by reason and the principles of honor and shame are reckoned unfit for a residence in a college. The collegiate censures are, 1. Private admonition by the president, professor, or tutor. 2. Before the Faculty. 3. Before the whole class to which the offender belongs. 4. The last and highest, before all the members of the College assembled in the hall. And, to preserve the weight and dignity of these censures, it has been an established practice that the last or highest censure, viz., public admonition, shall never be repeated upon the same person. If it has been thought necessary to inflict it upon any one, and if this does not preserve him from falling into such gross irregularities a second time, it is understood that expulsion is immediately to follow.

"Through the narrowness of the funds the government and instruction has hitherto been carried on by a president and three tutors. At the last commencement the trustees chose a professor of mathematics; and intend, as their funds are raised, to have a greater number of professorships, and carry their plan to as great perfection as possible."

These extracts give a clear view of the course of instruction in 1772, and of the provision made for conducting it. It also exhibits the opinions then held as to the principles upon which the government of youth in a college should proceed. Before the close of Dr. Witherspoon's administration the Faculty was enlarged, and consisted of the President, the Vice-President, who was also Professor of Divinity and Moral Philosophy, the Professor of Mathematics and Natural Philosophy, and two Tutors.

In the address from which the above extracts are taken, Dr. Witherspoon does *not* mention to what extent *religious instruction* was given in the College; but apparently assuming that this matter was fully and properly attended to, he disavows for himself and his associates any intention or desire to proselyte the youth of denominations other than their own to the peculiar and distinctive views of the Presbyterian Church; and in conclusion on this head he adds, "It has been and shall be our care to use every means in our power to make them good men and good scholars; and if this be the case, I shall hear of their future character and usefulness with unfeigned satisfaction, under every name by which a real Protestant can be distinguished."

THE AMERICAN WHIG AND CLIOSOPHIC SOCIETIES.

A few years before Dr. Witherspoon's accession to the Presidency, and certainly as early as the years 1765 and 1766, two literary societies were organized in the College, under the names of the "Well-Meaning" and "Plain-Dealing" Clubs. In consequence of some difficulties arising between these two associations, they were both required to suspend their meetings and to disband their organizations. In the summer, however, of 1769, and doubtless with the consent of the College authorities, the adherents of the Plain-Dealing Club revived their association, under the name of the "American Whig Society;" and in June, 1770, the members of the Well-Meaning Club reorganized their association, and took the name of the "Cliosophic Society." Tracing its origin back to the Well-Meaning, the Cliosophic Society held its hundredth anniversary in June, 1865. Whereas the American Whig Society, not regarding itself as strictly a continuation of the Plain-Dealing, celebrated its centennial anniversary in June, 1869.

As the histories of these Societies have been given to the public by Professors Giger and Cameron, with that fulness and general accuracy which preclude all occasion for saying anything further in regard to them, the writer of this work deems it unnecessary to add anything to what they have so well said respecting the Societies of which they were the chosen historians.

The following-named gentlemen were members of the Faculty during Dr. Witherspoon's administration, from 1768 to 1794.

John Witherspoon, D.D., LL.D., President, and, from 1769 to 1783, Professor of Divinity.

John Blair, A.M., Professor of Divinity and Moral Philosophy from 1767 to 1769.

William Churchill Houston, A.M., Professor of Mathematics and Natural Philosophy from 1771 to 1783.

Samuel Stanhope Smith, D.D., Professor of Moral Philosophy from 1779 to 1795; Professor of Divinity and Moral Philosophy from 1783 to 1795; Vice-President from 1786 to 1795.

Ashbel Green, A.M., Professor of Mathematics and Natural Philosophy from 1785 to 1787.

Walter Minto, LL.D., Professor of Mathematics and Natural Philosophy from 1787 to 1796.

James Thompson, A.M., Tutor from 1762 to 1770.

Joseph Periam, A.M., Tutor from 1765 to 1766, and from 1767 to 1769.

Jonathan Edwards, A.M., Tutor from 1766 to 1769.

Ebenezer Pemberton, A.M., Tutor from 1769 to 1769.

William Churchill Houston, A.M., Tutor from 1769 to 1771.

Tapping Reeve, A.M., Tutor from 1769 to 1770.

Richard Devens, A.M., Tutor from 1770 to April, 1773; and again from September, 1773, to 1774.

Samuel Stanhope Smith, A.M., Tutor from 1770 to 1773.

James Grier, A.M., Tutor from 1773 to 1774.

John Duffield, A.M., Tutor from 1773 to 1775.

Lewis Feuilleteau Wilson, A.M., Tutor from 1774 to 1775.

James Dunlap, A.M., Tutor from 1775 to 1777.

John Springer, A.M., Tutor from 1775 to 1777.

George Faitoute, A.M., Tutor from 1777 to 1777.

From 1777 to 1781 there were no Tutors. The few students in College during this period were instructed solely by the President and Professors.

James Riddle, A.M., Tutor from 1781 to 1783.

Ashbel Green, A.B., Tutor from 1783 to 1785.

Samuel Beach, A.B., Tutor from 1783 to 1785.

Gilbert Tennent Snowden, A.M., Tutor from 1785 to 1787.

John W. Vancleve, A.M., Tutor from 1787 to 1791.

John Henderson Imlay, A.B., Tutor from 1787 to 1788.

Samuel Harris, A.B., Tutor from 1788 to 1789.

Silas Wood, A.M., Tutor from 1789 to 1794.

John Nelson Abeel, A.M., Tutor from 1791 to 1793.

Robert Finley, A.M., Tutor from 1793 to 1795.

Charles Snowden, A.M., Tutor from 1793 to 1793.

David English, A.M., Tutor from 1794 to 1796.

Most of the gentlemen named here as Tutors of the College became men of much note in the Church or State; and not a few of them attained to great distinction in their several professions. For further information respecting them the reader is referred to the Triennial Catalogue of the College, and to the Rev. Dr. Samuel Alexander's "Princeton College."

Of those gentlemen who were Trustees of the College at the time Dr. Witherspoon was inaugurated as President, only two were members of the Board at the time of his death. These were Rev. Dr. John Rodgers, of New York City, pastor of the First Presbyterian Church there, and Dr. William Shippen, founder of the first medical school in Philadelphia.

The following were chosen Trustees after Dr. Witherspoon's accession to the Presidency: viz., in

1768. William Livingston, Esq.; from 1776, *ex officio* President of the Board, being Governor of the State.

1769. Rev. John Blair, late Vice-President of the College.

1769. Rev. James Caldwell.

1770. Rev. Jeremiah Halsey.

1772. Rev. Dr. Robert Smith.

1772. Rev. Dr. Alexander McWhorter.

1772. Elias Boudinot, Esq.

1777. Rev. Dr. George Duffield.

1778. Rev. Azel Roe.

1778. Colonel John Bayard.

1778. Dr. Nathaniel Scudder.

1779. Rev. Dr. John Mason.

1779. Jonathan Bayard Smith, Esq.

1780. Rev. Dr. John Woodhull.

1781. Hon. Joseph Reed.

1781. Rev. James Boyd.

1782. Isaac Snowden.

1782. Rev. Jonathan Elmer.

1785. Dr. John Beatty.

1785. Rev. Wm. Mackay Tennent.

1785. Rev. Alexander Miller.

1787. William Paterson, Esq., to 1790, when he became *ex officio* President of the Board, being the Governor of the State.

1788. Rev. Andrew Hunter.

1790. Rev. Ashbel Green.

1790. Rev. James Francis Armstrong.

1791. Richard Stockton, Esq.

1793. Hon. William Paterson, *re-elected.*

1793. Rev. Jacob Van Artsdale.

1793. Joseph Bloomfield, Esq.

Treasurers of the College during Dr. Witherspoon's administration:

Jonathan Sergeant, Esq., Treasurer until 1777.

Upon his decease a committee was appointed to settle with Mr. Sergeant's executors and to take charge of the funds.

Wm. Churchill Houston, Esq., Treasurer from 1779 to 1783.

Rev. Samuel Stanhope Smith, Treasurer from 1783 to 1786.

Upon Dr. Smith's resignation, two gentlemen were chosen, one after the other, but both declined to act. It is therefore probable that Dr. Smith continued to discharge the duties of the Treasurer until the appointment of

Mr. Isaac Snowden, Jr., Treasurer from 1788 to 1791.

Mr. John Harrison, Treasurer from 1791 to 1794.

The following statements respecting the course of study and the College charges are copied from the advertisements annexed to the charter and the laws, in a pamphlet published in 1794, the *last* year of Dr. Witherspoon's presidency.

" The studies of the different classes are the following :

" *Freshman*, Greek Testament, Sallust, Lucian, Cicero, and Mair's Introduction [to Latin Syntax].

" *Sophomore*, Xenophon, Cicero, Homer, Horace, Roman Antiquities, Geography, Arithmetick, English Grammar and Composition.

" *Junior*, Algebra, Geometry, Trigonometry, Practical Geometry, Conic Sections, Natural Philosophy, English Grammar and Composition.

" *Senior*, Natural and Moral Philosophy, Criticism, Chronology, Logick, and the Classicks.*

" The ordinary expenses for each student are :

Entrance money	4 dollars and 67 cents.			
Tuition do.	8 "	— "		per session.
Library do. . . .		67 "		"
Damage do. . . .		67 "		"
Room Rent	5 "	" 33 "		"
Board with the Steward . .	1 "	" 67 "		per week."

At this time—1794—the Faculty was composed of the following-named persons : John Witherspoon, D.D., President.

Samuel Stanhope Smith, D.D., Vice-President and Professor of Moral Philosophy.

Walter Minto, LL.D., Professor of Mathematics and Natural Philosophy.

Robert Finley, A.M., Tutor.

Silas Wood, A.M., Tutor.

All were, or became, eminent men.

-----

* " Besides the authors above mentioned, the following are at present taught in the College:—Wettenhall's Greek Grammar; Ovid's Metamorphoses; Kennet's Roman Antiquities; Guthrie's Geography; Lowth's English Grammar; Simpson's Algebra; Bossut's Elements of Geometry, *manuscript;* Minto's Trigonometry, Practical Geometry, and Conic Sections, *manuscript;* Sherwin's Logarithms; Moore's Navigation; Helsham's Natural Philosophy; Nicholson's Natural Philosophy; Witherspoon's Moral Philosophy, Criticism, and Chronology, *manuscript;* and Duncan's Logic."

APPENDIX

THE most perplexing matter in the report made in April, 1775, respecting the condition of the College funds, was the discrepancy between the statements of the committee and certain claims of the President.

Dr. Witherspoon had received sundry moneys for the College, and had also incurred sundry expenses, for which he claimed a credit. Some of these the committee thought ought not to be allowed, as they had been incurred without authority from the Board, and, in the judgment of the committee, unnecessarily. The President and committee also differed as to the right of the President to expend, at his discretion, for the benefit of the College, the income from the fund given by Wm. Phillips, Esq., and his brothers, of Boston; and in settling the account the committee refused to allow the President the credits claimed by him for payments made from the interest of this fund. But upon the President's producing the following letter from Mr. Phillips, the Board yielded this point, and the President continued to dispose of the avails of this trust for College purposes. (The letter is taken from page 313 of the first volume of the Minutes of the Board):

"NORWICH, March 9, 1776.

"DEAR SIR,—Your esteemed favor of the 19th ult. I have before me, and I thank you for your affectionate expressions of regard for me in my ejected state. I have great cause for thankfulness that I am not imprisoned in Boston.

"I do not recollect the particular directions I gave as to the disposal of the interest arising on the donation of my mother's [brothers'] and mine. You were the cause of obtaining it, from the confidence we had in you, as well as the affection for that Seminary.

"It is my desire, and doubt not of my mother's [brothers'] that you personally bestow the interest of the above donation till you hear further from us, as you have the best opportunity of knowing the most proper objects; at the same time desire, when anything offers, either to lay out the capital in any article, or dispose of the interest in any other way that may appear to you more for the general good of the College, you would advise me thereof."

The use of the word *mother's* for *brothers'* is, no doubt, a clerical error in copying the letter into the College records.

The minutes of the April meeting of 1775, at which this report of the committee was made in detail, are not on record, but it appears from a statement of the report of 1793, mentioned above, that the report of 1775 was approved by the Board, but that at a subsequent meeting of the Trustees, in 1778, they passed the account of Dr. Witherspoon upon the examination and report of another committee, who, it is alleged by Dr. Boudinot, had none of the former proceedings before them. But this special committee had before them what the first committee had not, viz., Mr. Phillips's letter, given above, and also some of the papers referred to in Dr. Boudinot's report of 1794, upon the strength of which the Doctor and the committee could and did say, and that, too, after including all accounts between the College and Dr. Witherspoon, as far back as 1775, disregarding the settlement of 1778:

" Your committee, moreover, feel it to be a duty not to close this report without declaring that, whereas it appears to have been apprehended that some inquiries heretofore made by this committee were intended to implicate the character of Dr. Witherspoon, no such design was ever in the contemplation of the committee. And they do now most cheerfully report, that these inquiries are answered to their entire satisfaction, from papers furnished by the President himself, and in such a manner as must convince every person who understands the subject that there is no foundation whatever for any impeachment or suspicion of the President's integrity."

A happy conclusion, and happily arrived at before the decease of Dr. Witherspoon, who died within less than two months after *this* report was made.

The first report disallowing Dr. Witherspoon's sundry claims, and making him largely a debtor to the College, was made nineteen years before his decease, and was appended to a report made seventeen years after the first one. More than a year after Dr. Witherspoon's death, Dr. Boudinot presents yet another report on the funds of the College, in which he takes occasion to say:

" Another sum is a donation from three brothers, the Messrs. Phillips, of Boston, amounting to about £535. Seven per cent. interest has constantly been credited to himself by the late Dr. Witherspoon for twenty years past, amounting to £738.16, without regard to the interest received by this Board on this sum, or any losses of the general fund during the war, by depreciation or otherwise, and without any responsibility, as to the appropriation, to this Board. This sum was refused to be allowed by the committee of 1774, which refusal was confirmed by the Board, but afterwards rescinded and allowed to the Doctor, on his producing a letter from the Donors, dated two years after the disallowance by said committee. This fund has suffered so materially by this transaction, that some attention is due to it from the Board."

At the time the Board received the money they recognized in express terms the right of the donors to dispose of the interest of this fund, and even the fund itself, at their pleasure for the good of the College; and the right to dispose of the income from the funds, the Messrs. Phillips transferred to Dr. Witherspoon until they should order otherwise.

The only further action of the Board in this matter was the adoption of the following resolution: "Resolved, That *the interest* arising from the donation of the Messrs. Phillips, of Boston, which has hitherto been submitted to the *personal appropriation* of Dr. Witherspoon, the late President, *agreeably to the instruction of the donors;* and the principal of the donation now falls into the general stock, subject to the appropriation of the Board." The appropriation was not *to* the Doctor personally, but made *by* him personally without instructions from the Board. (On page 160 of the Minutes an extract from the letter of the Messrs. Phillips was inserted at the request of the President.)

Whether Dr. Witherspoon was indebted to the College or the College to him at the settlement of September, 1774, reported in April, 1775, turns very much upon the question whether his assuming to pay £243.1.4 of Mr. Baldwin's indebtedness to the College, and also £115.6 for Mr. Woodruff (Stewards of the College), are to be viewed as debts due by Dr. Witherspoon to the College or to the persons named. In the latter case the College was indebted to him.

The following passages from a notice to the public, of the date of September 28, 1781, published in the "New Jersey Gazette" of October 10, 1782, will serve to throw some light on these assumptions of debt on the part of Dr. Witherspoon: "The entrance money and the chamber rent must be paid to the Treasurer, the tuition to the President, and the board to the Steward, in advance for six months. This last circumstance of paying in advance every six months will not be in any instance dispensed with, as the Trustees have *renewed or ratified the former law*, that if complaint is made by the Treasurer or Steward that any student has not made his advance for the current half-year, the President must either dismiss him from College or *be himself answerable for the debt.*

"With regard to enforcing punctuality in the payments, the reader will easily perceive that the burden must be wholly on *the subscriber, who has already suffered so much by arrearages and pledging himself for persons at a distance,* that nobody need expect a repetition of the same expensive and dangerous complaisance."

Signed by   DR. WITHERSPOON.

In money matters, as well as in all others, Dr. Witherspoon's course was not only perfectly correct, as finally acknowledged by the Committee on Accounts, but truly generous, especially during the period when the currency of the country was greatly depreciated. When, according to the understanding between the Trustees and himself, he was entitled to receive his salary in gold and silver, he, of his own accord, took it for two years in the depreciated currency; and in reference to his liberal and generous conduct in consenting to relinquish a large part of his salary that better provision might be made for the instruction of the students, the Trustees expressed their views by the adoption of the following resolution: "Resolved, That this Board do approve of this proposal and interpretation [of a previous agreement], which they consider as *an act of generosity* towards this corporation."

At this very time the Board was indebted to Dr. Witherspoon in the sum of £881.13.3, as appears from the report of Messrs. W. P. Smith and John Bayard, the committee appointed to examine the Doctor's accounts.

Upon the return of Messrs. Tennent and Davies from Great

Britain, they deposited with the Trustees of the College the sum of £357.4.6 sterling, given to them while they were yet abroad, for the education of poor and pious youth at the College of New Jersey,—the beneficiaries, candidates for the ministry, to be designated by the Synod of New Jersey, and also the allowances to them respectively.

After his return home, the Rev. Gilbert Tennent received from a gentleman in Scotland two hundred pounds sterling, regarded as equal to three hundred pounds *proc.* of New Jersey, which sum the donor requested should be given to the Trustees of the College, " in trust for one or other of the following purposes, viz.: to the support of a pious and well-qualified missionary in preaching the gospel among the Indians in North America; or the supporting a pious and well-qualified schoolmaster in teaching the Indians the English language, and the principles of natural and revealed religion; or for maintaining a pious and well-qualified Indian youth at the College of New Jersey while prosecuting his studies there, in order to instructing his countrymen in the English language and the Christian religion, or preaching the gospel to them; or for maintaining a pious and well-qualified youth of English or Scotch extract, at that College, during his preparatory studies for teaching; or preaching the gospel among the Indians, in case an Indian youth of suitable qualifications cannot at some particular time be obtained; with the express limitation, that the Synod of New York (by whatever name that body in time coming be called) shall *direct* and *determine* to which of the uses before mentioned the yearly interest of the aforesaid principal sum shall be, from time to time, applied; and which of the candidates for that particular use shall be preferred; and how the overplus above what may answer the particular use at any time pitched on (if any such overplus be) shall be employed, as in providing Bibles or other good books conducive to promote the general design."

The Board accepted these trusts on the conditions prescribed. Twenty years after, we find the following minutes, of the date of September 27, 1775 :

"The committee appointed at the last meeting to give their

opinion upon the appropriation of the interest of the £300 lodged in our treasury by the Synod are not prepared to deliver a report.

"The Board, however, agreed that Mr. Brainerd should enjoy that interest for the present year, according to the request of the Synod, and the Clerk was directed to give Mr. Brainerd an order to receive it.

"The Board, considering that they paid 6 per cent. interest and ran all the risk of the principal for the £500 lodged with them by [for] the Synod of New York, that they might apply the interest of it to the education of pious youth, according to the direction of the committee of the Synod appointed for that purpose, Resolved, That they would not hereafter allow more than 5 per cent. for that sum, and appointed Dr. Witherspoon, Dr. Rodgers, Mr. Treat, Mr. Spencer, Mr. McWhorter, or a majority of them, to be a committee to report this resolve to the Synod of New York and Philadelphia. If the Synod should not agree to the allowance of 5 per cent., the committee were instructed to deliver the money to that body, and were empowered to draw upon the Treasurer for the sum."

The Synod did agree to the proposed reduction in the rate of interest, and the money remained in the College treasury. During the Revolutionary War the funds of the College suffered a depreciation in their value to the extent of *sixty-six per cent.* of the entire capital; and these trust funds were made to bear their share of the loss.

It is somewhat remarkable that there should have arisen in the mind of any one a doubt as to the right of the Synod to direct to whom and for what purposes the interest accruing from these particular funds should be paid, when the persons who deposited these funds in the College treasury did provide in express terms for the Synod's control of the interest, and so informed the Synod and the Board; and for twenty years both Synod and Board had acted upon this understanding, without any doubt or scruple as to its correctness.

In the minute cited above, the fund for the education of poor and pious youth is spoken of as "lodged *by* the Synod of New York." It is not improbable that the word *by* was inadvertently used for the word *for*, the substitution of which would make the statement both precise and exact. With respect to the other fund, it was stipulated by the giver himself that the interest should be devoted to one or other of several purposes as directed by the Synod, by whatever name that body might be known in time to come; and yet we find the Committee on Accounts in 1775 (the committee named above), in their general report, questioning the extent of the Synod's powers as to these funds, and holding that, in regard to the fund for the education of poor and pious youth, the power of the Synod extended no further than to the mere nominating of the individuals to whom the income of this fund should be appropriated, and that this appropriation should be for their *education* exclusively,—that is, for the payment of their tuition-fees only,—and not at all for maintenance while engaged in pursuing their studies, and that the allowance made to each one should be determined by the Trustees and not by the Synod. It is rather extraordinary that the writer of the report, Dr. Boudinot, should consider himself better qualified to judge of the design of the donors than Messrs. Tennent and Davies, who received these funds, who deposited them with the Trustees, and who, in a letter to the Synod, from London, of the date of October 25, 1754, say, "We do by virtue of said trust [the intrusting the funds to their care for the purpose specified] put the said sum into the hands of the Trustees of the College of New Jersey, in trust, to be applied to the education of such youth of the character above mentioned as shall be examined and approved of by the Synod of New York, or by whatever name that body of men may be hereafter called, and by them recommended to the Trustees of said College, to be divided among such youth *in such proportion as the Synod shall think fit.*" (See Minutes of the Synod of New York, for October, 1755.) The only tenable position taken by the writer of the report is that the money ought to be drawn from the College treasury by order of the Trustees, and not upon an order given by the Committee of the Synod. A record of the depositing of this fund is not to be found in the minutes of the Board; yet in the subsequent minutes there are repeated references to it.

Of the other charitable fund of two hundred pounds sterling, three hundred pounds *proc.*, the College Committee on
Accounts say, "With respect to the £300 given with the design of educating scholars for Indian missionaries, the annual
interest of this money has been usually applied to the use of
the Rev. Mr. Brainerd, but upon what principle your committee
are unable to comprehend, as it appears to them to be acting
quite beyond the powers granted by the charter, and which, for
weighty reasons, the committee beg leave to recommend to the
full consideration of this corporation as a matter that greatly
concerns its Being as well as its Interests. Upon the whole, the
committee are clearly of the opinion that the income of these
moneys ought to be solely appropriated to the purpose of educating such young men as shall be directed by the Synod, or
other persons pointed out by the donor, and a particular account
be kept of such dispositions, so that it may at all times appear
that the trust has been duly performed."

This is a most extraordinary report, involving both the Board
and the Synod in the charge of violating the trust confided
to them conjointly, and that for twenty years ; and furnishing
upon the face of it complete evidence that the writer did not
understand or disregarded the terms of the trust as laid down
in the letter written by the donor himself, at the very time he
gave the money, and which was recorded in the minutes of the
Board for September, 1756; the *very first purpose* mentioned for
which the interest of the trust might be expended being "the
support of a pious and well-qualified *missionary*, in preaching
the gospel among the Indians of North America." Was not
Mr. Brainerd just such a missionary? The report does not
state correctly the design of the trust when it omits all mention
of the fact just stated, and simply speaks of the educating of
scholars for Indian missionaries as the design of it. If the
design is to be inferred from the language of the donor, there
can be no question as to the propriety of paying the interest of
this fund to Mr. Brainerd while engaged in preaching to the
Indians and in maintaining a school among them. These are
the two objects first mentioned to which the income may,
at the discretion of the Synod, be given. The educating of

youths for teachers of the Indians was a secondary object of the trust; at least it was mentioned after the other two; and the provision that they should be educated at the College of New Jersey would seem at least to justify the Trustees in accepting the trust, even if they were not clearly authorized by their charter to hold funds for other than educational purposes under their own direction. The report assumes and asserts that under the charter the Board had no right to receive this fund for any other than educational purposes, and that they should hold it for the education of youths of a certain character to be designated by the Synod, and for nothing else. If in accepting the trust the Trustees went beyond their just powers, it is certain that they did not misconceive their duty under this special trust, but had most faithfully fulfilled it.

Twenty-one years after this report on the finances of the College was presented, the writer of it, in another report, made April, 1796, makes use of the following language: "The charitable funds require the particular attention of the Board. The first sum carried to this account consists of moneys collected by Messrs. Tennent and Davies, in England, on a mission from and at the expense of this Board. Yet these gentlemen have thought proper of their own motion, without the consent of the Board, and, as your committee conceives, any act of the donors, by an instrument executed by them, to put the sum of £500 under the direction of another body no ways legally connected with this corporation, and so inattentive has this Board been to the circumstances of this case that in their minutes they have deliberately recognized this sum as lodged with them by that body of men, and agreed to allow them 5 per cent. interest for it, without there being even a color of right for such a transaction in the opinion of a majority of your committee. Since then another body of men [the General Assembly], equally unconnected in law with the corporation, have claimed the right to dispose of this money, as representing those who first laid claim to it, who now call upon this Board to account for the net proceeds thereof."

"The next is that of the £200 sterling given by an unknown person in Scotland, through Messrs. Tennent and Burr, for divers particular uses, two only of which can be executed by this Board, viz., that of educating an English or Scotch youth, or an Indian youth, for the purpose of preaching the gospel to the Indians, with the condition that the Synod of New York and Philadelphia shall determine to which of the purposes it shall be applied, and which candidate shall be preferred, the last of which only can be allowed to that Reverend Body. Your committee cannot but observe that the interest of this sum has been repeatedly paid to a purpose wholly foreign to the duties of their trust limited in their charter, and which cannot be justified by any of the powers contained therein."

If Governor Belcher, who gave the charter in the name of the King, and who had it drawn up under his own eye, and dictated its terms, and who presided at the meeting of the Board at which this special trust was thankfully received by the Board and cheerfully accepted, saw no objection to its terms; if such an eminent lawyer as the Honorable William Smith, of New York, who was also present when the trust was accepted, had no scruples and intimated no doubt as to the right of the Board to accept the trust with the conditions thereto annexed; if Presidents Burr, Davies, Finley, and Witherspoon, in succession, and for a period of forty years, did not discover that the Trustees, by giving effect to the wishes of the donor, were endangering the being as well as the interests of the College, it cannot be regarded as a matter of surprise that the Rev. Dr. Ashbel Green, a member of the committee, and President of the College at a later period, entered his dissent from this part of the report, which was evidently written in a captious and faultfinding spirit. The imputation cast upon Messrs. Tennent and Davies was wholly gratuitous, and as uncalled-for as gratuitous. They informed the Synod, and, no doubt, informed the Board, in their report of the results of their mission, that the moneys here in question had been intrusted to themselves personally to aid a certain class of youth in obtaining an education, and that they, in virtue of that trust, had put the moneys into the hands of the Trustees of the College for the aid of such young men as might be recommended by the Synod. Those who forty years before employed Messrs. Tennent and Davies in their laborious but eminently successful agency for the College were well satisfied with their course, took no exception to their conduct, and expressed their gratitude for their valuable and unrequited services.

What was to hinder the Board from taking the school at Brotherton, New Jersey, under their care, and employing Mr. Brainerd to superintend it for them, if in no other way they could accomplish the main object of the trust? The charter authorized the Board to establish a school anywhere in New Jersey, as appears from the section relating to property.

If it were so, that under the charter the Trustees could not fulfil all the terms of the trust, in the case of the two hundred pounds received from Scotland, why did not the committee recommend that the trust itself be surrendered to the Synod, or to other parties, who could legally administer it, instead of insisting that the Board should in future restrict the expenditure of the income therefrom to the education of a Scotch, English, or Indian youth, or propose that application be made to the Legislature for authority to administer this special trust in the manner specified by the donor?

Influenced by the statements and reasoning of the report of April, 1793, the Trustees decided that the Board, by the intention of the donors, was under no obligation to take any direction or advice from the Synod of New York, or their successors, in the disposal of the money obtained by Messrs. Tennent and Davies in the Island of Great Britain; and it was ordered, "That a copy of the minute on this subject should be sent to the Committee of the General Assembly appointed to designate the beneficiaries, and to apportion to them their respective allowances from the fund in question."

The General Assembly appointed a committee to confer with the Trustees in regard to this decision, and the result was, that the Board rescinded their resolution and restored matters to their former footing.

Yielding to the representations of the Committee on Accounts, made April, 1796, that the charter did not warrant their holding any funds, in trust or otherwise, except for the purposes of edu-

cation, the Board resolved, that the interest arising from the
fund for the support of an Indian mission, etc., should be appropriated by the Board to the education of a youth to be designated by the General Assembly. And it does not appear that
the General Assembly, although informed of this resolution of
the Board, made any objection to it; influenced, probably, by
these two considerations: 1, that the Indian mission at Brotherton, Burlington County, New Jersey, to the support of which
the interest of this fund had often been voted, had been given
up ; and, 2, that the original fund of two hundred pounds sterling had been reduced to sixty-eight pounds sterling, or one
hundred and two pounds *proc.* of New Jersey. The fund for
the education of poor and pious youth, collected in Britain by
Messrs. Tennent and Davies, was reduced to *one hundred and
fifty-two pounds six shillings and five pence proc.*, or £101.10.11 ⅓
sterling.

These funds being so much diminished, the General Assembly
finally gave up all control of the interest, and permitted the
Trustees to dispense it at their discretion.

As it may be as well to present at one view all matters relating to the finances of the College during Dr. Witherspoon's
administration, brief mention will here be made of the other
funds, with some comments on the report of the Committee of
Accounts respecting them.

In their report of April, 1775, this committee gave a statement
of the receipts from May, 1769, to September, 1774, and of this
account of particulars they observe, " Hence it will be seen
that since May, 1769, the Treasurer has received in donations
and subscriptions divers sums to the amount of £7468.1.1, and
that he had received, prior to the present account, before May,
1769, £311.13.6.

" Without these seasonable and providential aids your committee are of the opinion that this corporation must ere this
time have become totally bankrupt. For in 1769, before any
of these donations were received, the clear stock was (including
the charitable appropriations) about £3000, of which about
£1800 only was upon interest; and now the whole stock but
little exceeds £6000. Hence it appears that since that time

there hath been expended of what ought, or at least might, have been capital, a sum not much short of £5000."

Here there is an unqualified censure, which is not warranted by the facts of the case. The minutes of the Board furnish evidence that the College was in pressing need of funds that could be expended as soon as received, and that funds were solicited and obtained with the expectation that a considerable portion of them would be expended in paying the debts and some of the current expenses of the institution, and in making the best possible provision for the instruction of the students.

From the committee's own showing it appears that the entire sum received during these *five years* from interest of moneys loaned, tuition-fees, rent of rooms, proceeds of lotteries, and other sources, exclusive of bonds and donations, amounted to only £4617.2.2, while the expenditures for salaries, for philosophical and astronomical apparatus, for ordinary and extra expenses (including those of agencies to solicit funds, for lottery agencies, repairs of buildings, improvement of the grounds, paying of debts contracted before September, 1769), and appropriations from the trust funds, amounted to £8058.2.5, showing that the expenses exceeded the ordinary income by £3441.0.3,* which excess of the expenses was paid from the donations given not so much for the endowment of the College

---

* As given by the committee, the expenditures and the receipts from September, 1769, to September, 1774, five years, are as follows:

EXPENDITURES.

1774, September 28.
To old debts discharged, including those due to Mr. Field (bookseller of London) and Mr. Sergeant (the Treasurer) . . £649. 5.8
" Philosophical apparatus 416.13.4
" Orrery 284. 4.0
" Officers' salaries for four years 3461. 4.1
" Omitted in the above 730
" Extra and ordinary expenses, five years . . . 2210. 2.0
" Charitable appropriations (from the trust funds) . . 306.13.4

£8058. 2.5

as for placing the institution in a condition in which it should be fully able to accomplish the end for which it was established. This was done; and had not the War of the Revolution come on soon after, there is abundant reason to believe that the number of the students would have greatly increased, and that the resources of the institution would have been largely augmented. If to this sum of £3441.0.3 be added the £302.9.7 refused Dr. Witherspoon by the committee, but finally allowed him by the Board, the excess of the expenses above the ordinary receipts would be £3743.9.10, which could be paid only from the donations, which, according to the committee's report, amounted to the sum of £7468.1.1. But, taking the case as it is presented by the committee, the difference between the *donations* from May, 1769, to September, 1774, £7468.1.1, and the excess of the expenditures above the receipts, £3441.0.3, is the sum of £4027.0.10, which added to the £3000, the stock in 1769, would make the whole fund, in September, 1774, £7027.0.10. This sum, diminished by the moneys reported to be in the hands of the President and of the Treasurer respectively, and amounting to £1230.5.7, leaves £5796.15.3, which, according to the committee's own statement, is very nearly the sum actually invested in bonds and notes deemed to be good, and which, as estimated by the committee, "but little exceeds £6000." The difference between £6000 and £5796.15.3, viz., £203.4.9, is very much short of the £5000 which the committee intimated had been improperly expended. Had the Trustees undertaken to conduct the College upon the basis laid down in the report of the

---

RECEIPTS.

1774, September 28.

By interest, from September, 1769, accrued	£1829.15. 5	
" Tuition, Chamber Rent, &c., from September, 1769, to this day	2449.11. 5	
" Lottery, old account received	108. 7.10	
" Lottery account, cash received from Virginia, being amount of Samuel Morris's bond	170.13. 0	
" Cash received of Samuel Horner	27. 7.10	
" do. received of Wm. P. Smith, Esq., November, 1770	31. 6. 8	
		£4617.2.2
		£3441.0.3

committee, they would *never* have had £7468.1.1 of donations either to invest or to expend. In the report of April, 1796, it is said that the donations since the year 1768, the time of Dr. Witherspoon's accession, amounted "to the enormous sum of £22,061.19.5, *a part of which was Continental money.*" But how much was Continental money the committee do not say in their report, nor have we the accompanying statement of the various donations which make up this large sum. What proportion was paid in Continental money must be a matter of conjecture: if one-third, then its value, £17 for £1, would give as the value of this portion of the donations £433; if one-sixth, then their value would have been £216.10; and if but one-twelfth, their value would have been £108.5, according to the value of the Continental money as given in their report on Mr. Leslie's funds. Take it at one-sixth of the whole donations, then the value of the donations when made would have been, in the ordinary currency, £18,384, and this sum includes the £4529 received from the estate of Mr. Leslie and £1127 from the estate of Mrs. Richards, making together £5006, leaving to be accounted for £13,378 of donations. Of these not less than £3000 were invested, as has been made to appear from the report made in April, 1775, and which from 1777 to 1779 depreciated in value to £1000,—being a loss of £2000,—leaving but £11,378. The College stock, in 1791, was estimated at £958.6, irrespective of the trust funds, and which may be fairly regarded as donations invested, and worth, before the depreciation in the currency, £2874.18, which, deducted from the £11,378, will leave of the donations £9503.2 for excess of expenditures above the regular College receipts from 1775 to 1796, —the darkest financial period in the history of our nation,—or less than £500 a year from donations, to assist in supporting a corps of teachers and meeting all the ordinary expenses of the College, and the extra expenses incurred from injury to the College buildings, from loss of library and apparatus, from loss of funds from depreciation of stocks, from diminution in the number of students, and from a partial or total failure of persons indebted to the College. The College building was rendered unfit for use by the soldiery of Britain and America, and the demands to meet the current expenses were great; and had not the friends of the College generously come forward and contributed funds, not for investment, but to meet pressing demands, the College would have failed, or its Faculty would have been reduced below what its own interests and those of the community required.

That no mistakes were made by the College authorities of that day in regard to financial matters, it is not the design of these remarks to maintain, but it is their object to show that there was more cause for approval than for censure, and that it would have been ruinous to act upon the rule laid down by the committee in regard to the expenditure of funds, in the circumstances in which, during the whole of Dr. Witherspoon's administration, the College was placed.

No words can express so strongly the hold which Dr. Witherspoon and his associates had upon the confidence and good will of the community at large, and more especially upon the friends of religion and learning, as the fact that in their depressed condition, after a long and arduous civil war, they should have come forward with such great liberality to sustain an institution requiring help to the extent that the College of New Jersey did.

The living gave cheerfully, and the dying, with confidence, made bequests to the trust funds of the College, to secure what the friends of the College themselves had so much at heart, the preparation of pious youth for the gospel ministry.

Not to speak now of smaller bequests, it was during the administration of Dr. Witherspoon that Mrs. Esther Richards made her bequest to the College—for the purpose named—of nearly £1127, or $3000, and Mr. Leslie his of more than £4500, or $12,000,—gifts still sacredly devoted to the purpose for which they were given, and which have been of unspeakable service to the College and to the Church, in the yearly training of a number of pious youth at the College for the Church.

CHAPTER XVI.

A MEMOIR OF THE REV. JOHN WITHERSPOON, D.D., LL.D., THE
SIXTH PRESIDENT OF THE COLLEGE OF NEW JERSEY.

DR. WITHERSPOON was born in the parish of Yester, Scotland, on the 5th of February, 1722. His father, the Rev. James
Witherspoon, was the minister of the parish church, and he is
said to have been an uncommonly able and faithful preacher.
His mother, a devoted Christian woman, was a lineal descendant of the great Scottish Reformer, John Knox ; and also of
his son-in-law, the famous John Welsh, minister of Ayr, whose
wife, Elizabeth, was the youngest daughter of John Knox, a
woman in every respect worthy of such relationships. Elizabeth's mother, Margaret Stewart, was a daughter of Lord
Ochiltree ; and "the family of Ochiltree was of the blood royal."

At the age of fourteen Dr. Witherspoon entered the University of Edinburgh, where he pursued his studies for seven
years. Upon being licensed to preach, he was invited to be an
assistant minister with his father, with the right of succession ;
but receiving from the Earl of Eglinton, with the hearty consent
of the people, a presentation to the parish church of Beith, in
the west of Scotland, he decided to settle at Beith, and there
he was ordained to the work of the ministry. After a few years
he was translated to Paisley, a large and flourishing town celebrated for its various manufactures ; and here he remained until,
at the earnest request of the Trustees of the College of New
Jersey, he left Scotland to take charge of this institution, which
he did in the summer of 1768.

Dr. Witherspoon was the *sixth* President of the College.

During his residence at Paisley he was invited to Dublin,
Ireland, to take the charge of a large congregation in that city.
He was also called to the city of Rotterdam, in Holland, and to

Dundee, Scotland. All these calls he declined, being unwilling to give up his important charge at Paisley, and to enter anew upon the work of a parish minister and the formation of personal and family friendships. And when first invited to become the head of the College of New Jersey, he thought it his duty to decline the offer, especially in view of the fact that his family were unwilling to leave their native land for the trials and hardships of a new country. But, in the providence of God, he was led to review his decision, and both he and his family came to the conclusion that it would be their duty to go to America, should the offer above mentioned be renewed.*

---

* After this sketch was begun and nearly finished, the writer received from his friend the Rev. Dr. C. C. Beatty, of Steubenville, Ohio, copies of two or three letters written by his grandfather, the Rev. Charles Beatty, during a visit to Scotland in 1767. As these letters have a special value in connection with the subject of this memoir, the following extracts are here subjoined. The letters are addressed to the Rev. R. Treat, of Abington, Pennsylvania. Both Mr. Beatty and Mr. Treat were at this time Trustees of the College of New Jersey.

In his letter of the date of October 15, 1767, Mr. Beatty says, " On Saturday I went to Paisley, sent for Dr. Witherspoon to my Inn, who in a very friendly manner invited me to lodge at his house. At first I was reluctant, imagining that I could not be agreeable to Mrs. Witherspoon no more than she would be to me, according to the idea I had formed of her. However, upon his insisting upon it, I consented; and I must confess I was very agreeably disappointed, for instead of finding a poor, peevish, reserved, discontented, &c., I found a well-looking, genteel, open, friendly woman,—which perhaps you will be surprised at. I preached for the Dr. both parts of the day, and he lectured only; he appears to me, as I before observed to you, to be a good speaker and preacher, tho' not a fine speaker. I cannot think he is so old as you have heard,—tho' I did not ask his age. I see him make no use of spectacles, neither in public nor private. Mrs. Witherspoon, on Monday before I came away, having an opportunity, made some modest apology to me for her conduct when Mr. Stockton was there: she seemed to be much concerned for it. She told me to this effect: that at that time, and for some time before, she was in a weak state of health, and that in that situation things appeared very gloomy to her,—crossing the sea, and that her husband might soon die, and she be left in a strange land, &c. I need say nothing to you now about choosing a President for Jersey College,—for before now you will be fixed either by a choice in America or here. Dr. Witherspoon has had a call to a congregation in Dublin this last summer, but he declined it. In short, he told me that the call to the College had been much on his mind, and that nothing had ever given him"—The words immediately following have become illegible, but the form of expression indicates the great difficulty he had had in coming to a decision whether to accept or decline the invitation to the College.

Upon Dr. Witherspoon's refusal to accept the proffered appointment, the Trustees chose the Rev. Samuel Blair, a graduate of the College, but at this time pastor of the South Church, Boston, President, with the expectation that he would enter upon the duties of the office in the autumn of 1768. Learning that Dr. Witherspoon would probably accept the presidency of the College should it again be tendered to him, with a promptness that did him the highest honor Mr. Blair at once resigned his claim to the office, that the Trustees might have it in their power to elect Dr. Witherspoon a second time. This they did on the 9th of December, 1767, and they did it unanimously.

Released by the Presbytery from his pastoral charge, he took his final leave of the church at Paisley in the month of May, 1768, preaching a farewell discourse from the words in Acts xx. 26, 27: "Wherefore I take you to record this day, that I am pure from the blood of all men. For I have not shunned to declare unto you all the counsel of God." It appears from the minutes of the Trustees, of the date of August 17, 1768, in an order respecting the time when Dr. Witherspoon's salary should begin, that his connection with the church at Paisley ended the 15th of May preceding. And as this was a Sabbath-day, it was probably the day on which his farewell discourse was delivered. The month, but not the day of the month, is prefixed to this discourse in the posthumous edition of his works, printed and published by W. W. Woodward, Philadelphia, in the year of our Lord 1800.

It is said that a wealthy relative promised to make the Doctor his heir if he would not go to America.

Under the date of October 29, 1767, Mr. Beatty adds, "I had the other day letters from some of my friends in Edinburgh. One writes that there was a subtle letter wrote over from Princeton, under a pretence to encourage Dr. Witherspoon to accept the call of N. Jersey College; but it was quite the reverse. Complaint is also made that the Synod wants to take what was collected in Scotland out of the hands of the corporation; and that the widows' fund will, &c.,—but I shall be able to set that matter in another light."

Mr. Beatty had undertaken an agency, by the appointment of the Synod of New York and Philadelphia, to collect moneys for the establishment of a fund for the aid of ministers, their widows and families.

Dr. Witherspoon and his family sailed from Glasgow, and, after a tedious voyage, arrived at Philadelphia on Saturday, the 6th of August, 1768. In that city they were hospitably entertained at the house of Mr. Andrew Hodge; and when in a measure recovered from the fatigues of their passage, they left Philadelphia for Princeton. Here they were received with every demonstration of respect and kindness, and became for a time the guests of Richard Stockton, Esq., the gentleman through whom Dr. Witherspoon received the intelligence of his first election to the presidency of the College, and who, being in London at that time, went to Scotland to confer with Dr. Witherspoon on the subject of his removal to America. On the evening of the Doctor's arrival in Princeton the College edifice was illuminated; "and not only the whole village, but the adjacent country, and even the Province at large, shared in the joy of the occasion."*

The reception given him was very grateful to his feelings, and he is said to have alluded to it in modest and becoming terms in his first public discourse after his accession to the presidency.

His inauguration took place on the 17th of August, 1768, and on this occasion, or at the ensuing Commencement, on the 28th of the next month, he delivered an address in Latin on "The Union of Piety and Science." Although the College was in much repute at home, and was favorably known in Great Britain and Ireland, Dr. Witherspoon's administration of its affairs added much to its reputation and usefulness.

It is said by President Green that "the method of instruction by lecture had never been practised in this institution till it was introduced by Dr. Witherspoon," and that "he delivered lectures on four different subjects, namely, on Composition, Taste, and Criticism, on Moral Philosophy, on Chronology and History, and on Divinity."

His lectures on these several subjects, with the exception of those on Chronology and History, or the outlines of them, are published in Woodward's edition of his works.

---

* Dr. Green's Address before the Alumni Association in 1840.

We are inclined to doubt the accuracy of the statement that Dr. Witherspoon was the first at this College to use the method of teaching by lecture, as something very like it must have been employed by President Edwards on the few occasions on which he met the students.* And in his letter of October 19, 1757, to the Trustees, he expresses his willingness, in case he should accept their offer, "to do the whole work of a Professor of Divinity in public and private *lectures.*" It may have been, generally, and in some parts of the curriculum was the case, that the topics or theses included in the recitation were discussed by the teacher at the close of that exercise rather than apart from it.

In an account of the College published by order of the Trustees in 1764, four years before Dr. Witherspoon's arrival in this country, the author of the account, after mentioning the methods of instruction pursued in the College, speaks of them as offering "advantages which are seldom attainable in the *usual* method of teaching by lecture." (See account of President Finley's administration, page 266.)

Dr. Green also attributes to Dr. Witherspoon the introduction of the study of the Hebrew and French languages into the College course of instruction. This, so far as the Hebrew is concerned, is unquestionably an error. In the account of the College just referred to, it is expressly said that "the greater number [of the students], especially such as are educating for the service of the Church, are initiated into the Hebrew." And in his letter mentioned above, President Edwards says, "It would be out of my way to spend time in constant teaching of the languages, unless it be the Hebrew tongue, which I should be willing to improve myself in by instructing others;" the implication from which is that even in Mr. Burr's time the Hebrew language was made a College study. And in the accounts of the College published in 1764, it is said, "They now

---

* Since the above was written, the writer has learned that Mr. Lewis Evans, of Philadelphia, was employed by President Burr in the summer of 1751 to deliver twelve lectures on Natural Philosophy, and that these lectures were accompanied with experiments in electricity.

revise the most improving parts of the Latin and Greek classics, *part of the Hebrew Bible*, and all the arts," etc.*

Of Dr. Witherspoon's labors as an officer of the College, and *as an instructor of youth*, and *also of his efforts to increase the funds and the usefulness of the institution, full* mention was made in *the account of his administration of its affairs from the summer of* 1768 *to the autumn of* 1794.

In addition to his duties as President of the College, Dr. Witherspoon discharged those of minister to the Princeton church and congregation. Not that he was formally installed as pastor of this church, but that, in conformity to the course pursued by his predecessors, he preached regularly on the Sabbath to the students of the College and to the inhabitants of the village, who in these days were wont to worship together.

In the year 1770 there was manifest among the students of the College an unusual interest on the subject of religion, and a like state of things occurred also in the winter and spring of 1772. The fruits of these religious awakenings were most happy, as they gave to the Church not a few of her ablest ministers and elders, and to the State some of her best and most influential citizens. As usual in such times, some were very earnest friends to these religious revivals, and others were zealous opponents, deeming them evidence of the fanaticism of those who favored them. That the friends were always discreet, or that the opponents were always sincere and honest, is more than could reasonably be looked for in youth under this condition of things. Hence it should occasion no surprise that the more ardent of the youth, on whichever side arrayed, should regard the cautions given them by their wise and faithful President as evidence that he was not fully in sympathy with those who viewed these religious excitements as the work of the Holy Spirit, and as evidence that God had heard their prayers and had crowned with success their efforts for the conversion of not a few of their fellow-students. And this was actually the case

---

* Recently the writer has learned from a letter of Mr. Joseph Shippen, a graduate of 1753, that the Hebrew grammar was a study of the Freshman class in 1750.

in the present instance, as appears from a letter of the date of April 18, 1772, addressed to the Rev. Dr. Bellamy by one of the students, Mr. E. Bradford, afterwards pastor of the Congregational church of Rowley, Massachusetts, and from a statement made by Colonel Aaron Burr, who was also a student at that time, and published by his executor and biographer. Messrs. Bradford and Burr were fair representatives, one of the decided friends, and the other of the equally decided opponents, of the revival.

The exact truth on this head may doubtless be gathered from the following remarks by Dr. Ashbel Green, who was intimately acquainted with Dr. Witherspoon's opinions on this and other subjects; no man more so. These remarks are copied from an address before the Alumni Association of Nassau Hall, delivered in September, 1840, at the time of the annual Commencement.

"It was, if I rightly remember, in the fourth year of Dr. Witherspoon's presidency that a general revival of religion took place in the College. Several ministers of the gospel, and several men in secular life, received in this revival those impressions of religion which they carried with them through the remainder of their lives. With several of these I had in early life an acquaintance. With one I formed a most endeared friendship, and from him I received a number of particulars, which of themselves would enable me to contradict what I have heard (for I have not personally received),—a statement made in the ' Life of Colonel Burr,'— that Dr. Witherspoon thought and spoke light of this revival, and that he was, in fact, opposed to it. But in truth such a statement is so contrary to the known and avowed sentiments of Dr. Witherspoon, and even to what he declared in his ' Lectures on Theology' were his chief motives in coming to this country, that it cannot be correct, and I feel bound to make this declaration on the present occasion. He might, and I know he did, endeavor to correct some irregularities and imprudences, which usually take place when youth are under the excitement of strong religious feeling; but that he rejoiced in the revival itself, instead of opposing it, there is every reason to believe."

From the very beginning of the controversies which led to the War of Independence and to the severance of the thirteen united Colonies from their allegiance to the British Crown, Dr. Witherspoon openly and boldly took the part of his adopted country. And on the 17th of May, 1776, the day selected by the National Congress to be observed as a day of fasting and of prayer, he preached a sermon, the subject of which, "the dominion of Providence over the passions of men," was founded upon the words of the 10th verse of the lxxvi. Psalm : " Surely the wrath of man shall praise thee : the remainder of wrath shalt thou restrain." This discourse was subsequently published with a dedication to the Hon. John Hancock, Esq., President of the Congress of the United States of America, and with an appendix containing " an address to the natives of Scotland residing in America."

In handling his subject he went fully into a consideration of the state of affairs in the American Colonies, and gave some wholesome advice, in view of the arduous contest and the civil strife which were already begun, and pointed out the result which, in the ever overruling providence of God, might be hoped for in this struggle for civil and religious liberty; and he took occasion to warn his hearers and readers of the importance of being prepared for death, which could be only by repentance towards God and by faith in the Lord Jesus Christ; such faith and repentance being intimately connected with a belief in the natural depravity of man, from which sinful condition they could be rescued only by the grace and power of God.

Several things in this discourse are in full accord with the advice given in a pastoral letter written by Dr. Witherspoon and issued by the Synod of New York and Philadelphia the year before, viz., in May, 1775. This letter recommends to all under the care of the Synod *to avow their allegiance to the British Crown;* and this was assented to by the entire Synod, with the exception of the Rev. Jeremiah Halsey, who was a year in advance of his brethren in refusing allegiance. During this year a great change took place in the views and feelings of the whole community. This change is clearly pointed out in the following passage from Dr. Witherspoon's speech in Congress on the conference proposed by Lord Howe :

" We were contending for the restoration of certain privileges under the government of Great Britain, and we were praying for a reunion with her. But in the beginning of July, with the universal approbation of *all* the States now united, we renounced this connection, and declared ourselves free and independent."

The following short extracts will show why it was that Dr. Witherspoon took such a deep interest in the contest between the Colonies and the mother-country :

" You are all my witnesses that this is the first time of my introducing any political subject into the pulpit. At this season, however, it is not only lawful but necessary : and I am willing to embrace the opportunity of declaring my opinion without any hesitation, that the cause in which America is in arms is the cause of justice, of liberty, and of human nature.   So far as we have hitherto proceeded, I am satisfied that the confederacy of the colonies has not been the effect of pride, resentment, or sedition, but of a deep and general conviction that our civil and religious liberties, and consequently, in a great measure, the temporal and eternal happiness of us and our posterity, depend on the issue. . . . There is not a single instance in history in which civil liberty was lost and religious liberty preserved entire.   If, therefore, we yield up our temporal property, we at the same time deliver the conscience into bondage.

"You shall not, my brethren, hear from me in the pulpit what you have never heard from me in conversation; I mean railing at the King personally, or even his ministers, and the parliament and people of Britain. . . . I do not refuse submission to their unjust claims, because they are corrupt or profligate. . . . I call this claim unjust of making laws to bind us in all cases whatsoever, because they are separate from us, independent of us, and have an interest in opposing us. . . . This is the true and proper hinge of the controversy between Great Britain and America.   This, however, is to be added, that such is their distance from us, that a wise and prudential administration is as impossible as the claim of authority is unjust.   Such is and must be their ignorance of the state of things here, so much time must elapse before an error can be seen and remedied, and so much injustice and partiality must be expected from the acts and misrepresentations of interested persons, that for these colonies to depend wholly upon the legislation of Great Britain would be, like many other oppressive connections, injury to the master and ruin to the slave."

The views of Dr. Witherspoon, given in the above extracts, met the hearty approval of the friends of civil and religious liberty in this country; and they doubtless present, distinctly and fairly, the grounds of opposition to the absolute supremacy of the British Government in all matters pertaining to the Colonies.   The colonists, for the most part, were especially jealous of their religious freedom, and, for good reasons, were apprehensive that if their secular affairs were once under the absolute control of the British Government their religious liberty would soon be lost, by the renewed efforts which would be made to subject the people of this country to the jurisdiction of the English hierarchy in all matters connected with the education and religious instruction of the people.

This apprehension, perhaps more than any one thing else, induced the friends of religion generally to act in concert with those whose aim was simply a political one, — the separation and the independence of the Colonies.

It seems to have been assumed, both by the Government and the Church 'of England, that wherever the Crown went it of course carried Episcopacy with it. Upon no other principle can we account for their persevering efforts to establish diocesan Episcopacy in the Colonies generally. Of the attempts made to establish the Episcopal Church as a branch of the English Government in America, and the influence which these attempts had in bringing on the War of the Revolution, a detailed and very interesting account is given in Dr. Hodge's " Constitutional History of the Presbyterian Church," vol. ii. pages 448–497.

The sermon of which we speak was republished at Glasgow, and it was accompanied with notes by an unfriendly hand. In these notes Dr. Witherspoon was spoken of as " *a traitor and a rebel;*" and no doubt this Glasgow edition of the sermon had much to do in defeating the Doctor's efforts to collect funds for the College when, after the termination of the war, he went to Scotland to solicit aid to repair the wastes which the institution had suffered from the protracted conflict.

It is rather surprising that a man of Dr. Witherspoon's repute for wisdom and sound judgment should ever have consented to engage in such an undertaking, especially at such a time.

The failure of his mission to England and Scotland was, however, attended with one happy result, viz., that the Trustees were thereby made to know that, if the College was to be restored to its former prosperity and usefulness, it must, under God, be due to the efforts and liberality of its friends at home, and more especially to the countenance and aid of the members and judicatories of the Presbyterian Church ; and to them they again made an earnest and successful appeal.

In May, 1776, Dr. Witherspoon was chosen a member of the Convention which gave to New Jersey her republican Constitution.

" It has always been understood," says Judge Elmer, in his valuable " History of the First Constitution of New Jersey," " that the Rev. Dr. Witherspoon, President of Princeton College, took an active part in preparing it ;" and he adds, " This instrument bears quite as prominent marks of a clerical as of a legal origin, although two eminent lawyers, Jonathan Dickinson Sergeant and John Cleves Symmes, were members of the Committee. The Rev. Jacob Green, of Morris County, was the Chairman."

On the 22d of June, Dr. Witherspoon was chosen by the Convention, or Provincial Congress, a representative of New Jersey in the Continental or General Congress.

On the 4th of July, 1776, he voted for the Declaration of Independence, and his signature is affixed to the document containing that declaration. The Articles of Confederation between the States he signed in November, 1778, and in 1780 he left Congress, but was induced to return to it the next year.

At the close of 1782, the exigencies of the country no longer demanding of him a sacrifice of his own interests and those of the College, he retired from all service in the National Councils, . and gave himself up to the work of restoring the College to its condition before the war. Of the character of the sacrifices here referred to we may form some idea from the following extract from a letter written by Dr. Witherspoon to a friend in Scotland. The letter is of the date of March 20, 1780, and it was penned at the Doctor's farm, near Princeton.

" . . . I have now left Congress, not being able to support the expense of attending it, with the frequent journeys to Princeton, and being determined to give particular attention to the revival of the College. Professor Houston, however, our Professor of Mathematics, is a delegate this year; but he tells me he will certainly have to leave it next November. I mention this circumstance to confirm what I believe I wrote you formerly, that the members of Congress in general not only receive no profit from that office, but I believe five out of six of them, if not more, are great losers in their private affairs. This cannot be otherwise, for none of the delegates are allowed to have any lucrative office whatever either in their own States or in the United States; though their expenses should be fully borne, their time is taken up and their private estates are neglected. . . . You know that I was always fond of being a scientific farmer. . . . I got a dreadful stroke from the English when they were here, they having seized and mostly destroyed my whole stock, and committed such ravages that we are not yet fully recovered from it.

" As to public affairs, it seems to be yet undetermined whether we shall have peace soon. Greatly do I and many others desire it; and yet were our condition ten times worse than it is, nothing short of the clear independence of this country would be accepted."

It is by no means improbable that had he fallen into the hands of the English army in the early part of the war he would have received the ordinary treatment of " a traitor and rebel," if the following account of an attempt to burn him in effigy be correct. It is taken from Frank Moore's " Diary,"

of the date of July 30, 1776, and it is said to be given on the
authority of a soldier in Howe's army.

"Just before the thunder-storm last week the troops on Staten Island were preparing figures of Generals Washington, Lee, and Putnam, and Dr. Witherspoon, for
burning in the night. The figures had all been erected on a pile of fagots, the
generals facing the doctor, and he represented as reading to them an address. All of
them, excepting General Washington, had been tarred and prepared for the feathers,
when the storm came on, and obliged the troops to find shelter. In the evening,
when the storm was over, a large body of the troops gathered around the figures,
which, being prepared, were set on fire amid the most terrible imprecations against
the rebels. One of the party seeing that Generals Putnam and Lee and Dr. Witherspoon burnt furiously and were almost consumed, while General Washington was
still standing, with the tar burning off, ran away frightened, and was soon followed
by most of his companions. Next morning the figure was found as good as it ever
was; a fact which caused a good deal of fear among the Hessian troops, most of
whom were superstitious, and it was not until some of the officers told them the
cause of its not burning that they appeared contented. The reason was that; having
no tar on it before the rain commenced, it became saturated with water, and the tar
only would burn."

This story, *true* or *false*, serves to show that in the opinion of
both friends and foes Dr. Witherspoon was one of the most
prominent in advocating the Revolution ; or, to use an expression of John Adams, the second President of the United States,
respecting him, he was "as high a son of liberty as any man in
America."

While yet a member of the Provincial Congress, Dr. Witherspoon came to be regarded "as profound a civilian as he was
known to be a philosopher and divine." He had clear and
decided views concerning all matters of public interest, and in
regard to several important measures his opinions were in
advance of those of the majority in the National Congress.
Particularly was this the case with respect to the emission of
unfunded paper, and the purchase of supplies for the army by
allowing a commission on the moneys expended, to both of
which measures he was much opposed. Some who in Congress dissented from his views on these subjects afterwards
adopted them, and at their suggestion he published the speeches
in which he had given utterance to them. At this day, few
persons *acquainted with such matters* will venture to question
the soundness of his positions. Demagogues who know better

may, for party or personal considerations, advocate a different course.

The Doctor was a leading member of different committees, and occasionally he took part in the discussions that arose in Congress; but before speaking upon any important question he was wont to commit his thoughts to writing; and then, watching for a favorable opportunity, he introduced what he had to say by first alluding to something said by a preceding speaker, and thus he gave to his speeches the air of extemporaneous remarks, while they had all the advantage of a logical and compact arrangement. He knew that he was master of his subject, and those who heard him knew that what he was about to say was worth hearing. And yet, perhaps, there were but few men in such an assembly as well qualified as he to take part in an extemporaneous discussion.

He was a man of heroic spirit and of resolute purpose, and in the darkest aspect of public affairs he never despaired of the final triumph of the cause in which he had engaged, and which he regarded as the cause of religion as well as that of civil liberty.

His wisdom and foresight as a statesman are shown in a clear and strong light by the ground he took in reference to the original confederation of the States.

"He complained of the jealousy and ambition of the individual States, which were not willing to entrust the general government with adequate power for the common interest. He then pronounced inefficacy upon it. But he complained and remonstrated in vain. He particularly remonstrated against the tardy, inefficient, and faithless manner of providing for public exigencies and debts by requisition on the several States. He insisted on the propriety and necessity of the government of the Union holding in its own hands the entire regulation of commerce, and the revenues that might be derived from that source. These, he contended, would be adequate to all the wants of the United States." (See sketch of his life in Dr. Rodgers's Funeral Sermon.)

The evils against which he protested so earnestly in the plan of confederation between the States were happily corrected in the Constitution of 1789, and he was permitted to see his views on these points fully sustained by the adoption of this Federal Constitution, established for the very purpose of effecting a more perfect union of the States.

Although he became a statesman, he ceased not to be a minister of the gospel, but continued to preach as opportunity offered, and to discharge all other duties which pertained to the sacred office. But, great as were the services which he rendered the country by his wise counsels in the National Congress, and in the sessions of Presbytery and Synod, with respect to national affairs, it admits of question whether his example on the whole would not have been more salutary had he confined himself to matters which properly belong to a minister of the gospel at the head of a college.

The question, whether a minister of the gospel should take part in the administration of civil affairs, and should be allowed to hold offices of trust and power in the Commonwealth, is to be determined by the minister himself, without hindrance from any source, unless it be from the Church to whose service he professes to devote himself. As a member of the civil community, in a republic at least, he is entitled to all the privileges of a citizen; and we heartily sympathize with Dr. Witherspoon in the rebuke which he administered to the Convention that framed the Constitution of the State of Georgia,—which body proposed to deprive every minister of the gospel of the right to have a seat in the Legislature. The Doctor's strictures are contained in a letter to the publisher of a paper which had given in its columns the new Constitution: they are a comment upon the resolution, "No clergyman, of any denomination, shall be a member of the General Assembly;" and he suggests the following alterations:

"No clergyman, of any denomination, shall be capable of being elected a member of the Senate or House of Representatives, because [here insert the grounds of offensive disqualifications, which I have not been able to discover.] Provided always, and it is the true intent and meaning of this part of the Constitution, that if at any time he shall be completely deprived of the clerical character by those by whom he was invested with it, as by deposition for cursing and swearing, drunkenness or uncleanness, he shall then be fully restored to all the privileges of a free citizen; his offence shall no more be remembered against him: but he may be chosen either to the Senate or House of Representatives, and shall be treated with all the respect due to his brethren, the other members of the Assembly."

Lest the reader may infer that Dr. Witherspoon was of the opinion that in an ordinary state of public affairs it was expe-

dient or desirable that ministers should be members of the
Legislature or take part in the affairs of state, it may be well
to cite, in addition to the above, another passage from the same
article :

"Perhaps it may be thought that they are excluded from civil authority that they
may be more fully and constantly employed in their spiritual functions.   If this had
been the ground of it, how much more properly would it have appeared as an order
of an ecclesiastical body with respect to its own members.   *In that case I should not
only have forgiven, but approved and justified it ;* but in the way in which it now
stands it is evidently a punishment, by loss of privilege, inflicted on those who go
into the office of the ministry, for which, perhaps, the gentlemen of Georgia may
have good reasons, though I have not been able to discover them."

It is by no means improbable that Dr. Witherspoon found,
from his own experience, that constant attention to civil affairs
for a term of years had no tendency to promote a minister's
usefulness, but, on the contrary, that it required increased watch-
fulness on his part to prevent a decline in personal piety and
in devotion to the work of his holy calling.

Before he was chosen President of the College he had attained, both at home and abroad, a well-earned reputation as a
man of great talent, learning, and piety, and he was regarded
as the head of the orthodox party of the Church of Scotland,
and as their leader in the General Assembly of the Established
Kirk.   His opponent at the head of the Moderates, as the
dominant party was styled, was the well-known historian, Dr.
William Robertson, Principal of the University of Edinburgh.
Although usually in a minority, Dr. Witherspoon on one occasion carried, in the Assembly, an important measure against
his rival's opposition, upon which Dr. Robertson said to him,
in a pleasant manner, "You have your men better disciplined
than formerly."   "Yes," replied Witherspoon; "by urging your
politics too far you have compelled us to beat you with your
own weapons."   (See Dr. Rodgers's Funeral Sermon.)

His translation from Beith to Paisley was earnestly opposed
by the Presbytery of Paisley, on account of his being the reputed author of the "Ecclesiastical Characteristics," a keen and
severe satire upon the Moderates in the Church of Scotland.
From the Presbytery the question of the transfer came to the
Synod of Glasgow and Ayr, and by the Synod the Presbytery

was instructed to receive the Doctor as a member of their body and to instal him as pastor of the church at Paisley. His removal from Beith to Paisley took place in January, 1757, and in that or the next year he was chosen Moderator of the Synod. In 1768 he left Paisley for America. Here he soon became the leading man in the different Church courts of which he was a member, and to the close of his life he was held in the highest esteem by his brethren in the ministry. He was chairman of the large committee appointed by the Synod of New Jersey and Philadelphia, in 1785,

"to take into consideration the constitution of the Church of Scotland, and other Protestant Churches, and, agreeably to the general principles of Presbyterian government, compile a system of general rules for the government of the Synod and the several Presbyteries under their inspection, and the people in their communion, and to make report of their proceedings herein at the next meeting of Synod."

He was also the chairman of another committee, appointed at this same meeting, to confer with like committees from the "Dutch Reformed Synod, and from the Associate Reformed Synod, with respect to the measures that should be taken to promote a friendly intercourse between the three Synods; and to devise a plan of some kind of union among them, whereby they might be enabled to unite their interests and combine their efforts for promoting the great cause of truth and vital religion."

This action arose from a report made by a committee appointed, the year before, to meet one which it was expected would be appointed by the Dutch Reformed Synod, to adjust matters of difference existing between them, and to enter upon an amicable correspondence on subjects of general utility and friendship between the Churches.

The committees from the three Synods met, and they conferred at large upon the matters intrusted to them, and made an interesting report, which is given in the printed Minutes of the Synod of New York and Philadelphia, pages 518–522.

At this same meeting of the Synod, in May, 1785, measures were first taken for the division of the Synod into four separate Synods, and for the establishing of a General Synod, or Assembly; and at a meeting held in May, 1788, all the requisite steps having been taken, the proposed division of the Synod was consummated, and Dr. Witherspoon was appointed to open the sessions of the first General Assembly with a sermon, on the first Thursday in May, 1789, and to preside until a Moderator be chosen. At the same time he was appointed chairman of a committee to revise the chapter in the Directory respecting the mode of inflicting Church censures, with instructions to lay the revision before the General Assembly at their first meeting, to be considered and finally enacted. The same committee was also charged with

"the duty of revising that part of the draught for a directory for worship which respects public prayer and prayers to be used on other occasions, and to prepare it for printing with the Constitution."

These things show the active part he took in the organization of the General Assembly of the Presbyterian Church in this country. He was a member of the Assembly in the years 1787, 1791, 1792, and again, but for the last time, in 1794, in November of which year he departed this life.

Dr. Witherspoon was distinguished for the variety and accuracy of his knowledge: religion, ethics, politics, literature, science, and matters pertaining to common life had all received from him more or less attention; and his published works afford evidence of his familiarity with most of the subjects here named.

Simplicity and plainness of style, strength and purity of language, perspicuity of statement, and vigor of thought are characteristics of *all* his writings.

His discourses from the pulpit are worthy of special notice, on account of their numerous and most happy quotations from Scripture, both for proof and for illustration. In the respect just mentioned, Dr. Witherspoon's sermons are particularly deserving the attention of young ministers, who cannot fail to add to the impressiveness of their discourses by following so admirable an example. No language is better understood by most hearers in Christian congregations than the language of the Bible; and an apposite citation of Scripture texts enforces with wonderful power the lessons to be inculcated.

Dr. Witherspoon, as we learn from Dr. Green,

"was wont to deliver his discourses from memory, and yet he never repeated from memory any considerable portion of Scripture, however perfectly recollected, but opened the Bible, and read it from the sacred text. His action in speaking never exceeded a graceful motion of his right hand, and the inclination of his body forward, when much in earnest. His greatest defect in public speaking was the lowness of his voice when he began. For, although his voice was remarkably articulate, the distant part of a large audience could not hear it distinctly for a few sentences at first; afterwards, if profound silence was observed, all that he said was easily audible by every attentive hearer. He affirmed that the nature of his voice required this gradual increase of its volume to prevent its failing altogether. Yet, take his pulpit addresses as a whole, there was in them not only the recommendation of good sense and powerful reasoning, but a gracefulness and earnestness, a warmth of affection and solemnity of manner, especially toward and at their close, such as were calculated to produce the best effects of sacred oratory. Accordingly, his popularity as a preacher was great. The knowledge that he was to conduct a public service usually filled the largest churches in our cities and populous towns, and he never failed to command the attention of his audience. . . . His public prayers were admirable, plain in language, correct, methodical, abounding in a choice selection of Scriptural phrases, and uttered with the appearance of deep devotional feeling. When offered on special occasions their appropriateness was singularly excellent. His manner of introducing and administering the Lord's Supper surpassed any other performance of that sacred service which the writer [Dr. Green] ever witnessed." (See "Sprague's Annals," vol. iii.)

There can be no better authority in regard to the matters mentioned in this extract than that of its author, a favorite pupil and, in later life, an intimate friend of Dr. Witherspoon; and there can be no room for doubt that we have here the deliberate judgment of the community in general with respect to Dr. Witherspoon's preaching; and yet it occasions us no surprise that, at the time of the religious excitements which occurred in the earlier part of his presidency, he should have been regarded by some of his pupils as "a dull preacher,"—this being the expression used by one of them, in a letter to the Rev. Dr. Bellamy, to convey an idea of the opinion entertained of Dr. Witherspoon's preaching by the writer of the letter and by some of his fellow-students. It is not improbable, however, that as their warmth of feeling subsided, and they were able to look at matters more calmly, they formed a juster estimate of their President as a preacher,—instructive, earnest, and faithful.

DR. WITHERSPOON AS A TEACHER.

There can be no doubt as to Dr. Witherspoon's great ability

as a *teacher*, in awakening the attention of his pupils to the
subjects handled by him, and in impressing upon their minds
the truths he sought to inculcate. The influence he exerted in
moulding the views and opinions of a large number of youth
who in after-life became leading men both in Church and in
State, without any direct or explicit testimony on this head,
would suffice to show that his reputation as a teacher rested
upon a firm basis.

Of the four hundred and sixty-nine graduates of the College
during Dr. Witherspoon's presidency, one hundred and fourteen
became ministers of the gospel; and of these ministers *nineteen*
became Presidents or Professors in different institutions in the
States of New York, New Jersey, Pennsylvania, Virginia, North
Carolina, South Carolina, Georgia, and Tennessee; thirteen of
the nineteen being Presidents of the colleges with which they
were severally connected. Not less than twenty-seven others
became men of note and able and successful pastors of churches
in Massachusetts, New Hampshire, Connecticut, New York, New
Jersey, Pennsylvania, Maryland, Virginia, North Carolina, South
Carolina, Georgia, and District of Columbia.

Of the three hundred and fifty-five graduates not ministers of
the gospel, a very large number became distinguished civilians,
and not a few efficient officers in the United States Army.

One was for eight years President of the United States.

One was for four years Vice-President.

Six were members of the Continental Congress.

Twenty were Senators of the United States.

Twenty-three were members of the United States House of
Representatives.

Thirteen were Governors of individual States, viz., the States
of Vermont, New York, New Jersey, Delaware, Virginia, North
Carolina, South Carolina, and Georgia.

Three were Judges of the Supreme Court of the United
States.

Twenty or *more* were United States officers in the army of the
Revolution.

Thirty others, at least, became distinguished, some for their
culture of letters, some for their medical skill and knowledge,

others for their legal attainments and as judges and attorneys-general, and others as active and useful citizens.

The names of the persons here referred to are given in our history of Dr. Witherspoon's administration.

At the time Dr. Witherspoon entered upon the duties of his office as President of the College, the speculations of Berkeley were attracting the attention of the riper scholars among the students, who were fascinated by the acuteness of their author and by the novelty and boldness of his positions. But this did not long continue, and the common-sense view of things which was beginning to prevail in Scotland soon gained the ascendency here, under the guidance of the new President, and on the part of the students the doctrine of the idealists became a matter for jest rather than for serious debate. As an instance, "He has only swallowed a red-hot idea," was the sportive remark of one of them respecting a fellow-student who had been too eager to partake of some hasty-pudding.

In this connection should be stated what Dr. Ashbel Green, in his "Life of Dr. Witherspoon," says respecting his mode of treating the Ideal system of Berkeley, and of the origin of the common-sense system of Metaphysics. " He first reasoned against the [Berkeleyan] system, and then ridiculed it till he drove it out of the College. The writer [Dr. Green] has heard him say that, before Reid or any other author of their views had published any theory on the Ideal system, he wrote against it, and suggested the same trains of thought which they adopted, and that he published this essay in a Scotch magazine." *

It will readily be conceded, by those familiar with the history of our country and also with that of our College, that of the statesmen graduated here during the administration of President Witherspoon, James Madison, the fourth President of the United States, was the ablest and most eminent; and few will question the propriety of placing at the head of the teachers

---

* This passage is copied from President McCosh's admirable " History of the Scottish Philosophy," and not directly from President Green's " Life of Witherspoon."

and divines trained here during the same period Samuel Stanhope Smith, the immediate successor of Dr. Witherspoon in
the presidency of the College.   This eloquent preacher and
elegant scholar, without a rival among his class-mates, was
one of those students who were carried away with the subtleties
of the Bishop of Cloyne.   But under the more practical view
of things presented by Dr. Witherspoon in his lectures on
Moral Philosophy, he embraced the opinions of his new preceptor, and maintained them ever after.

Bishop Berkeley's great abilities no one can question, and he
was a man to be loved and honored for his noble qualities of
head and heart.

To point out the influence exercised by Dr. Witherspoon in
moulding the views and character of Mr. Madison, I shall employ the language of Mr. Madison's biographer, William C.
Rives, himself a statesman and a scholar:

"We have seen," says Mr. Rives, "how liberal and expansive a field of inquiry
was opened to the students by the additions which Witherspoon made to the previous curriculum of the College.   The increased attention paid to the study of the
nature and constitution of the human mind, and the improvements which had been
lately introduced into this fundamental part of knowledge by the philosophical
inquiries of his own countrymen, constituted a marked and a most important feature
of Dr. Witherspoon's reforms.   Mr. Madison formed a taste for these inquiries
which entered deeply, as we shall hereafter have occasion to remark, into the character and habits of his mind, and gave to his political writings in after-life a profound and philosophical cast, which distinguished them eminently and favorably
from the productions of the ablest of his cotemporaries.

*   *   *   *   *   *   *   *   *

"It is a matter of natural and interesting inquiry to learn what were the personal
relations formed between that eminent man, who was at the head of this seat of
learning and patriotism, and the pupil, upon whom more than upon any other one
he seems to have impressed the distinctive characteristics of his own mind, for no
intelligent reader acquainted with their works can fail to remark how much the
same clearness of analytical reasoning, the same lucid order, the same precision
and comprehensiveness combined, the same persuasive majesty of truth and felici-
tous diction, shine forth in the productions, whether written or spoken, of both.
Such intellectual affinities, joined to moral worth, could not but form a strong
bond of friendship, and of mutual confidence, attachment, and respect, between
them.   These sentiments are warmly manifested by the pupil in a letter written
from Princeton to his father the 9th of October, 1771: 'I should be glad if your
health and other circumstances should enable you to visit Dr. Witherspoon during
his stay in Virginia.   I am persuaded you would be much pleased with him, and
that he would be very glad to see you.'"

Mr. Rives adds, " Dr. Witherspoon continued to feel a lively interest in the studies and pursuits of his pupil after the formal connection of the latter with the College was terminated. Young Madison, appreciating at its just value the aid of so enlightened a guide and counsellor, and desiring to avail himself of the riches of the College Library, determined after his graduation to pass one year more at Princeton as a private student. The preceptor and pupil were destined to meet again, after the lapse of nine years, in the supreme councils of the country, as co-workers in the great cause of national independence and national union."

Mr. Bancroft also refers to Dr. Witherspoon's influence in impressing upon Mr. Madison's mind the only true views on the subject of religious liberty. Speaking of the declaration of rights submitted to the Convention of Virginia in May, 1776, he remarks :

" Only one clause received a material amendment. Mason had written that all should enjoy the fullest toleration in the exercise of religion. . . . A young man, then unknown to fame, of a bright hazel eye, inclined to gray, small in stature, light in person, delicate in appearance, looking like a pallid, sickly scholar among the robust men with whom he was associated, proposed a change. He was James Madison, the son of an Orange County planter, *bred in the school of the Presbyterian dissenters under Witherspoon at Princeton,* * trained by his own studies, by medita- tive rural life in the Old Dominion, and by an ingenuous indignation at the perse- cution of the Baptists, by innate principles of right, to uphold the sanctity of religious freedom. He objected to the word toleration, because it implied an estab- lished religion, which endured dissent only as a condescension ; and as the earnest- ness of his convictions overcame his modesty, he went on to demonstrate that ' all men are equally entitled to the free exercise of religion according to the dictates of conscience.' His motion, which did but state with better dialectics the very pur- pose which Mason wished to accomplish, obtained the suffrages of his colleagues. This," adds Mr. Bancroft, " was the first achievement of the wisest civilian of Virginia."

DR. WITHERSPOON'S WRITINGS.

Dr. Witherspoon's first publication appeared in the year 1753, under the title of " Ecclesiastical Characteristics, or The Arena of Church Polity," a keen satire, aimed at certain principles and practices then prevailing in the Church of Scotland. So great was the popularity of this work that no less than *five* editions of it were issued within ten years from the time of its first appearance. The name of the author was not given on the title-page, but it was generally and correctly ascribed to

* The italics by the copyist.

him ; and the manner in which it was received, by both friends and foes, was an earnest of the position he was soon to occupy in the councils of the Scottish Kirk.   The work was favorably spoken of by the Bishops of London and of Oxford, and it is mentioned in President Davies's " Diary," during his visit to England and Scotland in 1753–4, as " a burlesque, the humor of which is nothing inferior to Dean Swift's."   At the close of the introduction to this essay occurs the following :

"N. B.—I shall make very little use of Scripture, because that is contrary to some of the maxims themselves; as will be seen in the sequel."

This performance was defended in a later one under the title of " A Serious Apology" for the Characteristics.

In 1756 he published his " Essay on Justification," which has been repeatedly reprinted; and in the next year appeared his " Serious Inquiry into the Nature and Effects of the Stage," being an attempt to show that the contributing to the support of a public theatre is inconsistent with the character of a Christian.   What gave rise to the writing and the publication of this treatise was the representation in the theatre at Edinburgh of a tragedy written by a minister of the Church of Scotland.   In 1784, Dr. Witherspoon published his " Practical Treatise on Regeneration," and at the same time he republished several of his other works.   These were all issued from the London press, in three volumes.

A sermon entitled " Seasonable Advice to Young Persons" was preached by Dr. Witherspoon, on Sabbath, the 21st of February, 1762, at the Laigh Church, Paisley, from the 1st verse of the 1st Psalm : " Blessed is the man that walketh not in the counsel of the ungodly, nor standeth in the way of sinners, nor sitteth in the seat of the scornful."   The sermon was soon after published, and to it was prefixed " an authentic narrative of a disorderly and riotous meeting, on the night before the celebration of the Lord's Supper in that place, which gave occasion to the discourse."

In this " authentic narrative" he makes mention of mock preaching and praying, and use of the words employed in administering the Eucharist, and he gives the names of sundry young men engaged in these wicked and disgraceful acts. The righteous indignation of the author of the sermon and of "the authentic narrative" against the conduct of the persons concerned is more to be commended than the judgment exhibited by him in publishing their names, especially if it were the aim of the author of the narrative to bring the guilty parties to a sense of the sinfulness of their conduct, and to repentance for it. At the close of the narrative, the Doctor suggested that one of the party who considered himself aggrieved by the charge made against him, and who was a young lawyer,—a Writer to the Signet,—should prosecute one of his associates who had given the information respecting his impious allusion to the Lord's Supper, and get him punished in the manner he justly deserved if the charge were false. Acting perhaps upon this suggestion, the party chiefly implicated, or some other one of the company, brought suit against the Doctor himself for defamation of character. And although it is more than probable that the charges against the whole company were substantially true, yet, the evidence adduced failing, in the opinion of the judges, to establish their guilt undeniably, the Doctor was subjected to a fine and costs, which greatly embarrassed him, and laid his friends under pecuniary obligations from which they were not relieved at the time hè left Scotland for America. The gentleman who communicated some of these facts in a letter to Dr. Green—the letter in "Sprague's Annals," vol. iii.—gave it as his impression "that had it not been for the friendly interference of those particularly interested in his welfare, he would have been prevented at the time from leaving the country." And had he been so prevented, who can conceive the loss which would thereby have been sustained by the College and by the country at large?

The circumstances here detailed remind us of a like indiscretion on the part of President Edwards while pastor of the church at Northampton, Massachusetts (of which mention was made in our sketch of his life). And it is not a little remarkable that the two most eminent men ever at the head of our College should have involved themselves in great and apparently needless troubles from a lack of discretion in dealing

with sundry wayward young persons under their pastoral oversight by giving publicity to their faults and their names. But
these were isolated cases. On the part of neither was there
ever a repetition of the mistake; and throughout Dr. Witherspoon's administration of twenty-six years he was eminently
happy in directing the government and the discipline of the
College.

The edition of his works published in Philadelphia, in 1800,
by W. W. Woodward, printer, under the supervision of the
Rev. Dr. Ashbel Green, contains all of his writings ever given to
the public. Some of the pieces were not prepared for the press
by the author, and several of them are in an unfinished state.
His speeches and articles relative to the war and to various
political measures contain much valuable information respecting the country at that period of its history, and the circumstances contributing to the first success of the Colonies in their
struggle for independence. One of these was the ignorance
of the British Government in regard to the opinions of the
people and their determination to maintain their liberty at all
hazards. In his article on " The Controversy about Independence" the following passage occurs :

"The conduct of the British Ministry during the whole of the contest, as hath
been often observed, has been such as to irritate the whole of this continent to the
highest degree and unite them together by the firm bond of necessity and common
interest. In this respect they have served us in the most essential manner. I am
firmly persuaded, that had the wisest heads in America met together to contrive
what measures the ministry should follow to strengthen the American opposition
and to defeat their own designs, they could not have fallen upon a plan so effectual
as that which has been steadily pursued. One instance I cannot help mentioning,
because it was both of more importance and less to be expected than any other.
When a majority of the New York Assembly, to their eternal infamy, attempted to
break the union of the colonies, by refusing to approve the proceedings of Congress
and applying to Parliament by separate petition, because they presumed to make
mention of the principal 'grievance of taxation, it was treated with ineffable contempt. I desire that it may be observed that all those who are called the friends
of America in Parliament pleaded strongly for receiving the New York petition :
which plainly showed that neither one nor the other understood the state of affairs
in America. Had the ministry been prudent, or the opposition successful, we
had been ruined; but with transport did every friend to American liberty hear
that these traitors to the common cause had met with the reception which they
deserved."

" Nothing is more manifest than that the people of Great Britain, and even the king and the ministry, have been hitherto exceedingly ignorant of the state of things in America. For this reason, their measures have been ridiculous in the highest degree, and the issue disgraceful."

No one reading the above passage will question the Doctor's ardent devotion to the cause of American liberty.

Of the four octavo volumes issued by Woodward, the *first two* contain the funeral discourse, with a short sketch of Dr. Witherspoon's life, by the Rev. Dr. John Rodgers, of New York, preached at the request of the College, his essay on Justification, his treatise on Regeneration, and forty-seven sermons on various subjects. The *third* contains " An Inquiry into the Scripture Meaning of Charity," " A Letter respecting Play-Actors," " Ecclesiastical Characteristics," " A Serious Apology for the Ecclesiastical Characteristics," " The History of a Corporation of Servants," a satire, " Lectures on Moral Philosophy," " Lectures on Eloquence," " Letters on Education," " Essay on Money," " Letters on Marriage," " Pastoral Letter," prepared for the Synod of New York and Philadelphia at their sessions in May, 1775, and a burlesque " Recantation of Benjamin Towne, Printer and Publisher of the Pennsylvania Evening Post, of Philadelphia."

The *fourth* volume is of a more miscellaneous character than any of the others, and comprises his lectures on Divinity, his defence before the Synod of Glasgow, a number of essays under the title of " The Druid,"—a name, as he tells us in the first number, suggested by the place of his residence; the last three *numbers* being devoted to the notice and correction of Americanisms, cant phrases, etc.,—" Reflections on Public Affairs," " On the Controversy about Independence," " Thoughts on American Liberty," " Memorial and Manifesto of the United States," addressed to the mediating powers in the conferences for peace, " The Georgia Constitution," " The Federal City," " Sundry Speeches in Congress," " A Description of the State of New Jersey," " An Address to the Inhabitants of Jamaica and other West India Islands in Behalf of the College of New Jersey," and a few other papers of more or less importance.

Of all his writings, the two most likely to be reprinted from time to time are his " Essay on Justification" and his " Practical Treatise on Regeneration," but his entire works are a valuable addition to any library, private or public. His theology was that of the Westminster divines, as set forth in the Confession of Faith and in the Catechisms of the Presbyterian Churches of Scotland and of the United States. We are informed by the editor of this edition of his works that Dr. Witherspoon did not intend his lectures on Moral Philosophy for publication, and that he viewed them as nothing more than a syllabus or compend upon which he might enlarge before a class. In this manner they were used by Dr. Green himself during the *ten years* that he was President of the College. The lectures, as published, undoubtedly contain much valuable information respecting the various opinions entertained by preceding writers on the subjects which he handles, and also just comments on the views taken by them, rather than a precise and sharply-defined exposition of his own views.

From a letter of his, of the date of March 20, 1780, to a Glasgow friend and correspondent, it appears that his health after his removal to America had been good, with the exception of a succession of fits, thought by his physician to be of an apoplectic kind. From these, however, he recovered, and at the date of his letter he had much improved in health since these comparatively recent attacks. It has been supposed that these fits may in a measure be traced to a shock given to his nervous system while he was yet a young minister residing at Beith, in consequence of having been taken a prisoner by the High-landers in the service of the Pretender after the battle of Falkirk, January 17, 1746, and kept in close confinement by them for a fortnight: he being at that time in a feeble state of health from over-much study. Not apprehending any danger, he had gone to be merely a spectator of the expected conflict.

A short time before writing the letter above mentioned, he gave up his house at the College to his son-in-law, the Rev. Dr. Smith, the Professor of Moral Philosophy, and retired to his house and farm, about a mile, or a little more, from the College. At this rural retreat, named by him *Tusculum*, he resided fifteen years, devoting his leisure hours to the improvement of his health and his farm.

His duties at the College, however, continued to demand much of his time and attention ; nor did he remit in his devotion to the affairs of the College even after he lost his sight, which happened a few years before his decease. He employed generally one of the students to read to him and to act the part of an amanuensis in conducting his correspondence. He also continued to preach, having a sermon read to him, which without any further aid he was able to pronounce on any given occasion,—the psalms and hymns and passages being repeated from memory.

It is probable that his farming was not a success, and added but little, if anything, to his income. And it is said that certain speculations into which he was induced to enter for the purchase of lands in the newly-formed State of Vermont involved him in pecuniary embarrassments, which became a source of trouble and anxiety. He was drawn into this adventure, as appears from one of his letters, chiefly from a hope that he would have it in his power to render a service to such of his fellow-Scotchmen as might emigrate to America, by securing for them an opportunity to buy good land, contiguous to the best markets, upon the most favorable terms. For his share in this undertaking he was sharply attacked in an article published in a Scotch paper, and was charged with a want of proper regard to the interests of his native country. Although he successfully repelled the charge brought against him, it would have been better had no occasion been furnished for the bringing of it. Ministers had better remain *poor* than engage in money-making schemes, *failure* in which is sure to bring more or less reproach, and *success* no honor.

Dr. Witherspoon was noted for his social qualities. And although he never forgot what was becoming a gentleman, and especially a minister of the gospel, he made himself agreeable to the young as well as to those of mature age, and his company was eagerly sought by them, whether their object was instruction or pleasure. He possessed a vein of abundant humor, and his wit was of a special kind, of which some of his published works furnish ample proof, without any reference to the traditions respecting it still prevalent. His sermons, it is believed, show no trace of it.

Many other matters, which with great propriety might have been introduced in the foregoing sketch, were given in the account of Dr. Witherspoon's administration. These, if not wholly passed without notice, have been but little dwelt upon in this sketch of the Doctor's life.

The following remarks are copied from Dr. Rodgers's funeral discourse :

" Accustomed to order and regularity in business from his youth, he persevered in his attention to them through his whole life.   And, I may add, there was nothing in which his punctuality and exactness were more sacredly observed than in the devotional exercises of the Christian life.   Besides the daily devotions of the closet and the family, it was his stated practice to observe the last day of every year, with his family, as a day of fasting, humiliation, and prayer ; and it was also his practice to set apart days for secret fasting and prayer, as occasion suggested.   Bodily infirmities began at length to come upon him.   For more than two years before his death he was afflicted with loss of sight, which contributed to hasten the progress of his other disorders.   These he bore with a patience and even with a cheerfulness rarely to be met with in the most eminent for wisdom and piety.   Nor would his active mind, and his desire of usefulness to the end, permit him, even in this situation, to desist from the exercise of his ministry and his duties in the College, as far as his health and strength would admit.   He was frequently led into the pulpit, both at home and abroad, during his blindness, and always acquitted himself with more than his usual solemnity and animation.   And we all recollect the propriety and dignity with which he presided at the last Commencement.   He was blest with his reasoning powers to the very last.

" At length he sunk under the accumulated pressure of his infirmities, and on the 15th day of November, 1794, in the seventy-third year of his age, he retired to his eternal rest, full of honor and full of days."

The more immediate cause of his death was the dropsy.

From the University of Aberdeen he received the degree of Doctor in Divinity, and from Yale College the degree of Doctor of Laws.

DR. WITHERSPOON'S FAMILY.

When Dr. Witherspoon came to this country, his family consisted of himself, his wife, and five children, three sons and two daughters.   His wife was Elizabeth Montgomery, daughter of Robert Montgomery, of Craighouse, Ayrshire, Scotland. His three sons entered the College of New Jersey, and became graduates of this institution. James, the eldest son, was an aide to General Nash in the War of the Revolution, and was killed at the battle of Germantown, Pennsylvania. John, the second son, was a physician, and settled in the parish of St. Stephen, South Carolina. He died in 1795. The third and youngest son, David, settled in New-Berne, North Carolina, where he practised law. He married the widow of General Nash, and he was the father of the Rev. Dr. John R. Witherspoon, the Moderator of the General Assembly of the Presbyterian Church in 1836.

The eldest daughter, Ann, became the wife of the Rev. Dr. S. S. Smith, Dr. Witherspoon's successor in the office of President of the College; and her sister, Frances, was married to Dr. David Ramsay, a physician and a historian of much note, whose residence was in Charleston, South Carolina. Dr. Ramsay was a member of the National Congress, and for one year he was the President of that body.

Mrs. Witherspoon died in 1789, and about a year and a half after her death Dr. Witherspoon married Mrs. Dill, the widow of Dr. Dill, a physician of Philadelphia, and a step-daughter of the Rev. William Marshall, a minister of the Associate Church. By this marriage he had two daughters, of whom one died in infancy; the other, Mary Ann, was married to the Rev. Dr. James S. Woods, who for many years was the faithful and honored pastor of the Presbyterian church at Lewistown, Pennsylvania.

EPITAPH.

By order of the Trustees of the College, a slab of marble, with the following inscription, was placed on Dr. Witherspoon's grave:

Reliquiæ Mortales
Johannis Witherspoon, D.D., LL.D.
Collegii Neo-Cæsariensis Præsidis, plurimum venerandi,
sub hoc marmore
inhumantur.
Natus parochio Yesternensi Scotorum,
Nonis Februarii, MDCCXXII. V. S.
Literis humanioribus in Universitate Edinburgensi
imbutus.
Sacris ordinibus initiatus, Anno MDCCXLIII.

Munus pastorale
per viginti quinque annos perfunctus est,
primo apud Beith, deinde apud Paisley.
Præses designatus Aulæ Nassovicæ, Anno MDCCLXVII.
in Americam migravit, Anno MDCCLXVIII.
Idibus Sextilis.
Maxima expectatione Omnium,
Munus præsidiale suscepit.
Vir eximia pietate ac virtute
Omnibus dotibus animi præellens
doctrina, atque optimarum artium studiis,
penitus eruditus,
Concionator gravis, solemnis.
Orationes ejus sacræ
præceptis et institutis vitæ
præstantissimis,
necnon expositionibus sacrosanctæ scripturæ
dilucidis
sunt repletæ.
In sermone familiari comis, lepidus, blandus,
rerum ecclesiæ forensium
peritissimus.
Summa prudentia,
et in regenda, et instituenda juventute,
præditus.
Existimationem collegii apud peregrinos
auxit :
bonasque literas in eo multum provexit.
Inter lumina clarissima, et doctrinæ et ecclesiæ,
diu luxit.
Tandem, veneratus, dilectus, lugendus omnibus,
animam efflavit, XVI. Kal. Decem.
Anno Salutis Mundi, MDCCXCIV.
ætatis suæ LXXIII.

END OF VOL. I.

www.ingramcontent.com/pod-product-compliance
Lightning Source LLC
Chambersburg PA
CBHW032313280326
41932CB00009B/800

* 9 7 8 3 3 3 7 3 3 8 7 9 4 *